Life of Vita ... Book ... ...mes, Spectator, Independent a ~~~ *Observer*. His most recent book is *Over the Hills and Far Away: The Life of Beatrix Potter*. He is a contributor to *Country Life* and *Telegraph*.

Praise for *The First Iron Lady*:

'Matthew Dennison's sparkling new biography should do much to bring Caroline out of the shadows to which she has for so long been consigned ... Energetic and ambitious, brilliant and divisive, Queen Caroline would have been a remarkable figure in any age. It is fortunate that, in Dennison, she has found a writer able to do justice to her formidable talents'   *Country Life*

'Queen Caroline has been fortunate in attracting a seasoned and perceptive biographer of powerful women ... Matthew Dennison's judgements are always nuanced and well contextualized, particularly on the timing and type of her cultural patronage ... Dennison undoubtedly succeeds thoroughly in rescuing Caroline from historical limbo'

CLARISSA CAMPBELL ORR, *TLS*

'[A] compelling and deftly narrated study of Caroline of Ansbach ... Dennison is a talented biographer who can bring alive even the densely populated genealogies of which German princelings were inordinately proud'   *Daily Telegraph*

'One of the most intriguing imponderables about Caroline ... as Dennison skilfully explores in this finely judged and entertaining biography, is that invisible line which always seems to divide spontane~~~ ... ...viour'

Spectator

ALSO BY MATTHEW DENNISON

MATTHEW DENNISON

The First Iron Lady

A Life of Caroline of Ansbach

**WILLIAM
COLLINS**

William Collins
An imprint of HarperCollins*Publishers*
1 London Bridge Street
London SE1 9GF

www.WilliamCollinsBooks.com

First published in Great Britain by William Collins in 2017
This William Collins paperback edition published in 2018

1

A catalogue record for this book is
available from the British Library

ISBN 978-0-00-812202-7

Printed and bound by in Great Britain by
CPI Group (UK) Ltd, Croydon

For Gráinne, with love

'Behold, thou art fair, my love; behold, thou art fair ...
Thou art all fair, my love; there is no spot in thee.'
Song of Solomon

Contents

Illustrations

George Augustus, Electoral Prince of Hanover, afterwards King George II of Great Britain. (*Metropolitan Museum of Art. Gift of Irwin Untermyer, 1964*)

St James's Palace and Pall Mall. (*English School (18th century)/ National Trust, Regional Office, 20 Grosvenor Gardens, London, UK/National Trust Photographic Library/Bridgeman Images*)

Leicester House, in Leicester Square. (*Engraving after Nicholls, Sutton (18th century)/Private Collection/Bridgeman Images*)

Caroline's woman of the bedchamber Charlotte Clayton. (*Chronicle/Alamy Stock Photo*)

Caroline's maid of honour Molly Lepell. (*Coloured chalks on paper, Knapton, George (1698–1778)/Ickworth House, Suffolk, UK/National Trust Photographic Library/Christopher Hurst/ Bridgeman Images*)

Henrietta Howard, George II's mistress and Caroline's woman of the bedchamber. (*Gibson, Thomas (c.1680–1751)/Blickling Hall, Norfolk, UK/National Trust Photographic Library/ Bridgeman Images*)

Elisabeth Charlotte, Duchess of Orléans. (*Oil on canvas, after Rigaud, Hyacinthe (1659–1743)/Château de Versailles, France/ Bridgeman Images*)

Sir Robert Walpole. (*Heritage Image Partnership Ltd/Alamy Stock Photo*)

James Thornhill's huge painting of the family of George I in Greenwich Naval Hospital. (*Graham Mulrooney/Alamy Stock Photo*)

Caroline in her coronation robes, by Charles Jervas. (*Guildhall Art Gallery, City of London/Bridgeman Images*)

Caroline in 1735, by Jacopo Amigoni. (*Peter Horree/Alamy Stock Photo*)

Martin Maingaud's 1721 portrait of Caroline's three eldest daughters, Anne, Amelia and Caroline. (*Royal Collection Trust © Her Majesty Queen Elizabeth II 2017/Bridgeman Images*)

Caroline and the son she loved best, William Augustus, Duke of Cumberland. (*Aikman, William (1682–1731)/Hardwick Hall, Derbyshire, UK/National Trust Photographic Library/Bridgeman Images*)

The son Caroline grew to hate, Frederick, Prince of Wales. (*Royal Collection Trust/© Her Majesty Queen Elizabeth II 2017*)

John, Lord Hervey. (*The National Trust Photolibrary/Alamy Stock Photo*)

Caroline as queen by Enoch Seeman. (*Royal Collection Trust/© Her Majesty Queen Elizabeth II 2017*)

The Hermitage in Caroline's garden at Richmond Lodge. (*British Library, London, UK/© British Library Board. All Rights Reserved/Bridgeman Images*)

The seven surviving children of Caroline and George II by William Aikman, 1730. (*Collection of the Duke of Devonshire, Chatsworth House, UK/© Devonshire Collection, Chatsworth/ Reproduced by permission of Chatsworth Settlement Trustees/ Bridgeman Images*)

William Hogarth's oil sketch of the family of George II. (*Royal Collection Trust/© Her Majesty Queen Elizabeth II 2017*)

Caroline painted from memory in 1735 by Joseph Highmore. (*Royal Collection Trust/© Her Majesty Queen Elizabeth II 2017*)

Caroline the year before her death, by John Vanderbank the Younger. (*The Trustees of the Goodwood Collection/Bridgeman Images*)

Caroline on her deathbed, by Dorothy, Countess of Burlington. (*Collection of the Duke of Devonshire, Chatsworth House, UK/© Devonshire Collection, Chatsworth/Reproduced by permission of Chatsworth Settlement Trustees/Bridgeman Images*)

Rysbrack's marble bust of Caroline, completed after her death. (*Royal Collection Trust/© Her Majesty Queen Elizabeth II 2017*)

The Protestant Succession and the House of Hanover

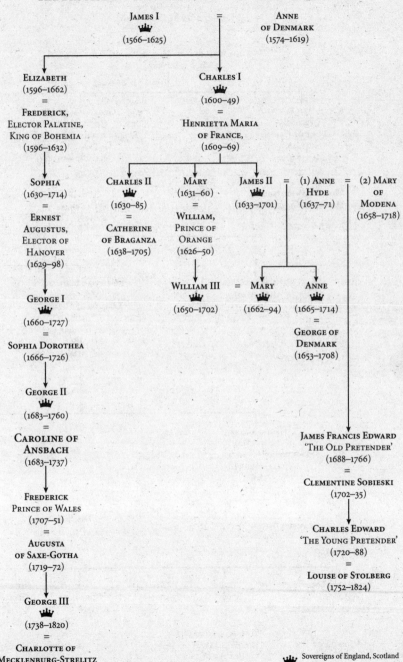

JAMES I ♛ (1566–1625) = ANNE OF DENMARK (1574–1619)

ELIZABETH (1596–1662) = FREDERICK, ELECTOR PALATINE, KING OF BOHEMIA (1596–1632)

CHARLES I ♛ (1600–49) = HENRIETTA MARIA OF FRANCE, (1609–69)

SOPHIA (1630–1714) = ERNEST AUGUSTUS, ELECTOR OF HANOVER (1629–98)

CHARLES II ♛ (1630–85) = CATHERINE OF BRAGANZA (1638–1705)

MARY (1631–60) = WILLIAM, PRINCE OF ORANGE (1626–50)

JAMES II ♛ (1633–1701) = (1) ANNE HYDE (1637–71) = (2) MARY OF MODENA (1658–1718)

GEORGE I ♛ (1660–1727) = SOPHIA DOROTHEA (1666–1726)

WILLIAM III ♛ (1650–1702) = MARY ♛ (1662–94)

ANNE ♛ (1665–1714) = GEORGE OF DENMARK (1653–1708)

GEORGE II ♛ (1683–1760) = CAROLINE OF ANSBACH (1683–1737)

JAMES FRANCIS EDWARD 'THE OLD PRETENDER' (1688–1766) = CLEMENTINE SOBIESKI (1702–35)

FREDERICK PRINCE OF WALES (1707–51) = AUGUSTA OF SAXE-GOTHA (1719–72)

CHARLES EDWARD 'THE YOUNG PRETENDER' (1720–88) = LOUISE OF STOLBERG (1752–1824)

GEORGE III ♛ (1738–1820) = CHARLOTTE OF MECKLENBURG-STRELITZ (1744–1818)

♛ Sovereigns of England, Scotland and Ireland

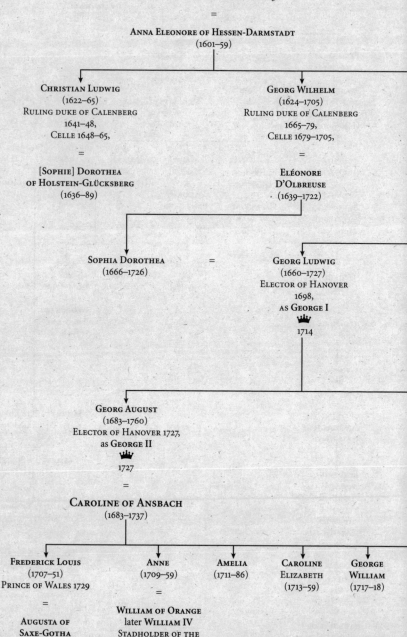

GEORG
(1582–1641)
RULING DUKE OF CALENBERG 1636

=

ANNA ELEONORE OF HESSEN-DARMSTADT
(1601–59)

CHRISTIAN LUDWIG
(1622–65)
RULING DUKE OF CALENBERG
1641–48,
CELLE 1648–65,

=

[SOPHIE] DOROTHEA
OF HOLSTEIN-GLÜCKSBERG
(1636–89)

GEORG WILHELM
(1624–1705)
RULING DUKE OF CALENBERG
1665–79,
CELLE 1679–1705,

=

ELÉONORE
D'OLBREUSE
(1639–1722)

SOPHIA DOROTHEA
(1666–1726)

=

GEORG LUDWIG
(1660–1727)
ELECTOR OF HANOVER
1698,
AS GEORGE I
👑
1714

GEORG AUGUST
(1683–1760)
ELECTOR OF HANOVER 1727,
as GEORGE II
👑
1727

=

CAROLINE OF ANSBACH
(1683–1737)

FREDERICK LOUIS
(1707–51)
PRINCE OF WALES 1729

=

AUGUSTA OF
SAXE-GOTHA

ANNE
(1709–59)

=

WILLIAM OF ORANGE
later **WILLIAM IV**
STADHOLDER OF THE
UNITED PROVINCES

AMELIA
(1711–86)

CAROLINE
ELIZABETH
(1713–59)

GEORGE
WILLIAM
(1717–18)

Genealogical Table
of the Early Hanoverians

This table only shows the principal individuals mentioned in the text and does not include all children.

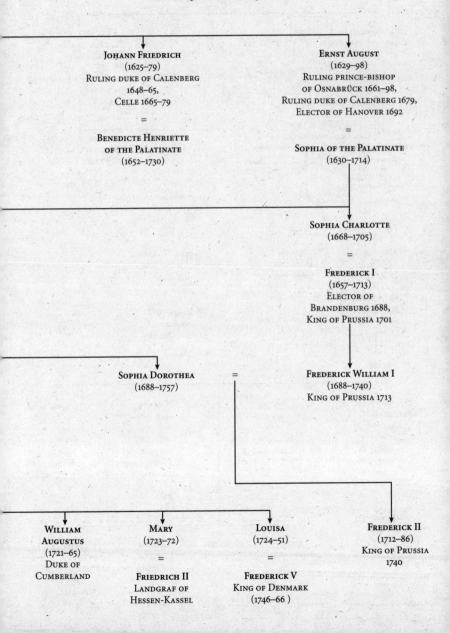

👑 Sovereigns of the United Kingdom

Johann Friedrich
(1625–79)
Ruling duke of Calenberg
1648–65,
Celle 1665–79

=

**Benedicte Henriette
of the Palatinate**
(1652–1730)

Ernst August
(1629–98)
Ruling prince-bishop
of Osnabrück 1661–98,
Ruling duke of Calenberg 1679,
Elector of Hanover 1692

=

Sophia of the Palatinate
(1630–1714)

Sophia Charlotte
(1668–1705)

=

Frederick I
(1657–1713)
Elector of
Brandenburg 1688,
King of Prussia 1701

Sophia Dorothea
(1688–1757)

=

Frederick William I
(1688–1740)
King of Prussia 1713

**William
Augustus**
(1721–65)
Duke of
Cumberland

Mary
(1723–72)

=

Friedrich II
Landgraf of
Hessen-Kassel

Louisa
(1724–51)

=

Frederick V
King of Denmark
(1746–66)

Frederick II
(1712–86)
King of Prussia
1740

THE HOUSE OF HANOVER

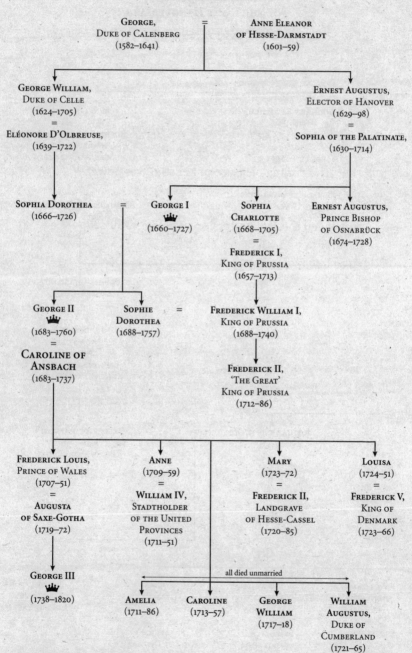

GEORGE,
DUKE OF CALENBERG
(1582–1641)
=
ANNE ELEANOR
OF HESSE-DARMSTADT
(1601–59)

GEORGE WILLIAM,
DUKE OF CELLE
(1624–1705)
=
ELÉONORE D'OLBREUSE,
(1639–1722)

ERNEST AUGUSTUS,
ELECTOR OF HANOVER
(1629–98)
=
SOPHIA OF THE PALATINATE,
(1630–1714)

SOPHIA DOROTHEA
(1666–1726)
=
GEORGE I
(1660–1727)

SOPHIA
CHARLOTTE
(1668–1705)
=
FREDERICK I,
KING OF PRUSSIA
(1657–1713)

ERNEST AUGUSTUS,
PRINCE BISHOP
OF OSNABRÜCK
(1674–1728)

GEORGE II
(1683–1760)
=
CAROLINE OF
ANSBACH
(1683–1737)

SOPHIE
DOROTHEA
(1688–1757)
=
FREDERICK WILLIAM I,
KING OF PRUSSIA
(1688–1740)

FREDERICK II,
'THE GREAT'
KING OF PRUSSIA
(1712–86)

FREDERICK LOUIS,
PRINCE OF WALES
(1707–51)
=
AUGUSTA
OF SAXE-GOTHA
(1719–72)

ANNE
(1709–59)
=
WILLIAM IV,
STADTHOLDER
OF THE UNITED
PROVINCES
(1711–51)

MARY
(1723–72)
=
FREDERICK II,
LANDGRAVE
OF HESSE-CASSEL
(1720–85)

LOUISA
(1724–51)
=
FREDERICK V,
KING OF
DENMARK
(1723–66)

GEORGE III
(1738–1820)

all died unmarried

AMELIA
(1711–86)

CAROLINE
(1713–57)

GEORGE
WILLIAM
(1717–18)

WILLIAM
AUGUSTUS,
DUKE OF
CUMBERLAND
(1721–65)

Sovereigns of the United Kingdom

'The darling pleasure of her soul was power.'
Lord Hervey, *Memoirs*

'She loved the real possession of power rather than the
show of it, and whatever she did herself that was either
wise or popular, she always desired that the King should
have the full credit as well as the advantage of the
measure, conscious that, by adding to his respectability,
she was most likely to maintain her own.'
Walter Scott on Caroline of Ansbach,
The Heart of Midlothian, 1818

Introduction

History has forgotten Caroline of Ansbach. The astuteness of her political manoeuvrings; her patronage of poets, philosophers and clerics; her careful management of her peppery husband George II; the toxic breakdown of her relationship with her eldest son, Frederick; her reputation as Protestant heroine; even the legendary renown of her magnificent bosom – 'her breasts they make such a wonder at' – have all escaped posterity's radar.[1]

Her contemporaries understood her as the power behind George II's throne. One lampoon taunted, 'You may strutt, dapper George, but 'twill all be in vain;/We know 'tis Caroline, not you, that reign.'[2] She was the first Hanoverian queen consort. On her arrival in London from Germany in October 1714, following the accession of her father-in-law as George I, she became the first Princess of Wales since 1502, when Catherine of Aragon married Prince Arthur, short-lived elder brother of the future Henry VIII.

Blonde, buxom, with a rippling laugh and a raft of intellectual hobbyhorses, in 1714 she was also the mother of four healthy children. Her fertility was in stark contrast to the record of later Stuarts: barren Catherine of Braganza, Portuguese wife of Charles II; childless Mary II and Queen Anne, whose seventeen pregnancies fatally undermined her health but failed to produce a single healthy heir. Early praise of Caroline celebrated her fecundity. Poet Thomas Tickell's *Royal Progress* of 1714 invites the reader to marvel at 'the opening wonders' of George I's reign: 'Bright Carolina's heavenly beauties trace,/Her valiant consort and his blooming race./A train of kings their fruitful love supplies.' Those magnificent breasts, so remarked upon by onlookers and commemorated in a formidable posthumous portrait bust by sculptor John Michael Rysbrack, were an obvious metaphor, key assets for the mother of a new dynasty.[3]

With conventional hyperbole, the future Frederick the Great addressed her as 'a Queen whose merit and virtues are the theme of universal admiration'.[4] Voltaire acclaimed her as 'a delightful philosopher on the throne'.[5] Her niece, the Margravine of Bayreuth, praised her 'powerful understanding and great knowledge', and an Irish clergyman noted in her 'such a quickness of apprehension, seconded by a great judiciousness of observation'.[6] In his *Marwnad y Frenhines Carolina* ('Elegy to Queen Caroline'), London-based Welsh poet Richard Morris called her *'ail Elisa'*, a second Eliza or Elizabeth.[7] Jane Brereton's *The Royal Heritage: A Poem*, of 1733, made another Tudor connection, linking the intelligent Caroline with Henry VIII: 'O Queen! More learn'd than e'er Britannia saw,/Since our fam'd Tudor to the Realm gave Law.'[8] More simply, her girlhood mentor described her company as 'reviving'.[9] Meanwhile Alexander Pope, a sceptical observer, was responsible for several critical poetic imaginings of Caroline. These include the personification of cynical adroitness he offered in *Of the Characters of Women* – 'She, who ne'er answers till a Husband cools,/Or, if she rules him, never shows she rules;/Charms by accepting, by submitting sways' – a view in line with Lord Hervey's statement that she 'governed [George Augustus] by dissimulation, by affected tenderness and deference'.[10] Caroline's dissatisfaction with the conventional limits of a consort's role – her reluctance to be defined by gynaecological prowess or her appearance – inspired conflicting responses among her contemporaries, but lies at the heart of her remarkable story.

Caroline is the heroine of sparkling memoirs by her vice chamberlain, John, Lord Hervey, written shortly after the events they describe; she is at the heart of published memoirs and diaries by two of her closest female attendants, Mary, Lady Cowper, and Charlotte Clayton, afterwards Lady Sundon. Like the majority of primary sources, none is wholly reliable. In 1900, Caroline's first full-length biography, *Caroline the Illustrious*, by W.H. Wilkins, lauded its subject as central to the successful transfer of the electors of Hanover to Britain's throne. Unlike the author, reviewers glimpsed Caroline and her world through a prism of Victorian disapproval, firmly thrusting her back into a disreputable past. 'She died as she lived, a strange mixture of cynicism and clairvoyance,' commented the *Spectator* opaquely. 'Herself the model of virtue, she spent her life in an atmosphere of vulgar vice.'[11] In 1939, a biography by Rachel Arkell again acclaimed Caroline's intellect and acuity. Both authors drew on source material in German archives subsequently damaged by wartime bombing. Published in the same year as Arkell's account, Peter Quennell's *Caroline of England* is lighter stuff, in part a portrait of robust Augustan London dandled in the face of Nazi aggression.

And then a curtain descended. Like her husband George II, in 1973 the only British monarch not to merit a volume in Weidenfeld & Nicolson's popular 'Life and Times' series, Caroline again fell out of view. Her reputation suffered eclipse by a better-known Queen Caroline, George IV's despised wife Caroline of Brunswick. The latter's rackety story invests her husband's history with tabloid sensationalism. Caroline of Ansbach's impact on her demanding spouse came closer to that of Albert of Saxe-Coburg and Gotha on Queen Victoria or Lady Elizabeth

Bowes-Lyon on George VI, an admonitory, popularising presence, albeit exercised more covertly than Albert's earnest
pedagogy.

Such wholesale neglect is the more surprising given that, in
her lifetime, Caroline inspired reverence, adulation, sneering
and hatred. A poem written to celebrate her coronation in 1727
pictured her unconvincingly as the embodiment of 'Innocence
and Mildness .../The sure Foundation of domestic Love'; a
decade later, Richard West's *A Monody on the Death of Queen
Caroline* wrongly predicted 'thy name, great Queen, shall ... live
in every age'.[12] By contrast her father-in-law described her as a
'she-devil' or 'fury'. She was burnt in effigy on the streets of
London. A rancorous elderly courtier recoiled even from her
appearance, her 'face frightfull, her eyes very small & green like
a Cat & her shape yet worse'.[13]

To others she was a poster girl for Protestant piety and, in at
least one case, no less than the earthly mediator of a Protestant
God: 'Th'Almighty seeing so much Christian Grace,/And how,
on Earth, she ran the heavenly Race;/Has constituted ROYAL
CAROLINE/His Agent here, to make his Glory shine.'[14] A panegyric stated, 'it appears to the admiration even of those who saw
her at all times and seasons, and in every hour when the Mind
is most unguarded, that her Majesty was always in a very
eminent manner the same great and good Person'.[15] A politician's wife referred to Caroline's 'ears ... always open to the
cries of the distressed'.[16]

The truth is seldom one-sided, and flattery distorts. Caroline
was villain and victim, sinner as well as saint, fond and loving
but a good hater too. Keenly interested in politics, in the decade
until her death she played a part in George II's government,
while never revealing to that prickly and self-important prince
the full extent of her interference when his back was turned.
She had no truck with political impartiality. Whig politics – a
Protestant, pro-parliamentary outlook – had placed her

husband's family on the throne, and in her relationship with pre-eminent politician of the period, Robert Walpole, satirised on her account as 'the Queen's Minister', Caroline was as fully a Whig partisan as her husband or her father-in-law George I. 'We are as much blinded in England by politicks and views of interest, as we are by mists and fogs, and 'tis necessary to have a very uncommon constitution not to be tainted with the distempers of our climate,' wrote Caroline's contemporary Lady Mary Wortley Montagu.[17] Caroline shared the blindness of her adopted countrymen. 'I am a woman and I delude myself,' she once claimed with careful disingenuousness; she was concerned with status as well as power.

During George's absences in Hanover she acted as regent on four occasions. With regal élan, she exercised patronage, commissioning architects and garden designers, providing financial assistance for poets, overseeing loose coteries of philosophers, scientists and divines; building for herself a splendid royal library adjoining St James's Palace. She championed inoculation. The report she commissioned on a Parisian orphanage shaped Thomas Coram's Foundling Hospital, opened after her death. She identified grounds for prison reform during the regency of 1732, but failed to persuade Robert Walpole to action. And from early in her marriage, aware that her husband's destiny lay in Britain, she worked consistently at self-anglicisation, this German princess determined to succeed in the role of British queen. In scale her anglophile initiatives were large and small – from cultivating the good opinion of politicians and militarists to drinking tea and subscribing £100 to Pope's translation of The Iliad. None of these acts was either wholly accidental or disjointed.

Caroline had inherited a Continental model of queenship. In German states, female consorts balanced the political and military governance of their husbands with spiritual and cultural direction. In Caroline's case, innate ambition encouraged her to look beyond prescribed bounds: with variable success she took pains to dissimulate her aspirations. She blended affability with dignity but understood the importance, on occasion, of adopting what she called '*grand ton de la reine*', full regal fig. As her unwavering support for her exacting spouse and her long association with Walpole show, she could be enthusiastic in partnership in order to achieve her ends. Others, like the letter-writing Lord Chesterfield and her husband's mistress Henrietta Howard, would experience the vigour of her disapprobation.

That visible reminders of Caroline are scant in twenty-first-century Britain ought not to blind us to her achievements – or the scale of the obstacles she mostly overcame. Hers was a world in which the political was still personal, an elision she manipulated skilfully. Her overriding aim was that of every dynast: to ensure the survival of the precarious organisation she and her husband represented. In the early days, her personal popularity played its part in countering the threat to the Hanoverians of lingering Stuart support, a movement known as Jacobitism. More charismatic than her husband, more genuinely in thrall to her adopted country, she found admirers even among disaffected Catholics and Scots. There is a spin-doctor quality to aspects of her exploitation of soft power.

The present account seeks to offer some redress to Caroline of Ansbach's historical vanishing act. Recent scholarship has re-examined George II's conduct of monarchy to reveal a statesman more perceptive and engaged than earlier versions have suggested.[18] Nor can Caroline be defined exclusively as the spirited, all-controlling heroine of Lord Hervey's *Memoirs*, the 'Goddess of Dulness' satirised in Pope's *Dunciad*, the scheming cynic who emerges from the letters of Lady Mary Wortley Montagu and Sarah, Duchess of Marlborough, or the monstrous harridan imagined by the niece by marriage who never met her: 'She was imperious, false, and ambitious. She has frequently been compared to Agrippina; like that empress, she might have exclaimed, *let all perish, so I do but rule.*'[19] As the spectacular failure of her relationship with her eldest son indicates, Caroline had her share of flaws. She also inspired powerful affection, not least in her husband, whose devotion to her survived his long-term infidelity and the corrosive sycophancy of kingship.

Caroline worked hard at queenship. She was inspired by the examples of her guardian, Sophia Charlotte of Prussia, and her husband's grandmother, Sophia of Hanover; eagerly she examined precedents established in Britain by recent queens-regnant Mary II and Queen Anne. Measured against the yardstick of her own devising, she enjoyed notable success at a time when the court still retained – in part, thanks to her – social, cultural and political significance. Although she was not single-handedly responsible for the successful establishment of the Hanoverians in Britain – or even in British affections – her understanding that she had a role to play in this process raises her above the average early-eighteenth-century princess. 'Nothing will pass for what is great or illustrious, but what has true merit in it,' wrote the unctuous Alured Clarke in *An Essay Towards the Character of Her late Majesty Caroline, Queen-Consort of Great Britain, &c*, published the year after Caroline's death.[20] We will see that Caroline's life included its measure of merit.

Prologue

'Halliballoo!'

Above the hubbub rose a single voice. On that dark December evening, the sound of a young woman singing soared above disarray. Above the noise of rain in nearby St James's Park it lifted, above the dripping branches of lime trees planted in hundreds a decade ago by royal gardener Henry Wise.

Idlers heard it above the 'racket of coxes! such a noise and halliballoo!' in gaming dens and coffee houses.[1] They heard it above the 'Modern Midnight Conversation' of boozy taverns shortly to be depicted by scourge of the age William Hogarth, above the 'violent Fit[s] of Laughter' in fashionable drawing rooms that novelist Sarah Fielding likened to 'the Cackling of Geese, or the Gobbling of Turkeys'.[2] Astringent as the sluice of ordure on wet cobbles, revoltingly inventoried by Jonathan Swift as 'sweepings from butchers' stalls, dung, guts, and blood,/ Drowned puppies, stinking sprats, all drenched in mud,/Dead cats and turnip-tops', her song trilled its defiant strain.[3] Brightly, 'despising doleful dumps', it eclipsed the stamping hooves of horses, servants' shuffling feet, hourly chimes from unlit churches.[4] It rang clear above the clatter of packing cases, including the royal close stool entrusted to woman of the bedchamber Charlotte Clayton, above orders and counter orders and – unmistakeable in the broad London street – the sound of sobbing: 'Over the Hills and Far Away'.

The Honourable Mary Bellenden was singing. Mary was a maid of honour, one of a group of high-spirited and decorative unmarried young women in attendance on Caroline, Princess of Wales. 'The most perfect creature', 'smiling Mary, soft and fair as down', 'incontestably the most agreeable, the most insinuating, and the most likable woman of her time', she was in flushed good looks tonight, singing in the shadows that skirted St James's Palace.[5] The same could not be said of her royal mistress. Two years previously, in one of his last excrescences as Poet Laureate, Nahum Tate had acclaimed flaxen-haired, inquisitive, plain-speaking Caroline as 'adorned with every grace of person and of mind'.[6] As the rank, wet December darkness enfolded princess and attendants in its clammy grip, she appeared anything but.

Loyal Mary sang for Caroline, an angry song of protest. 'Over the Hills and Far Away' was a rallying cry for Jacobites, those pro-Stuart opponents of Britain's new Hanoverian monarchy; later, Mary Bellenden would be painted by portraitist Charles Jervas in the character of Mary, Queen of Scots. Caroline, of course, was herself a key player in the usurping dynasty. On 2 December 1717 she too played her part as victim.

Her father-in-law – for three years George I, elector of Hanover since 1698 and a man accustomed to obedience – had expelled her husband George Augustus from his rickety, brick-built palace following a footling argument about the choice of a royal godparent. In a satirical age, such septic dysfunctionalism was a boon to the writers of ballads and broadsheets. To the king's chagrin, Caroline had chosen to accompany her husband into ignominy. 'You may not only hope to live but Thrive, If with united hearts and hands you live,' promised an engraving called 'The Happy Marriage', published in 1690, and throughout her marriage Caroline had done her best to present a united front.[7] Surprised and displeased, the king shrugged his shoulders, comfortable in the apartments of his bald and red-faced German mistress overlooking the palace gardens. In the words of a ballad called 'An Elegy upon the Young Prince', 'Both the Son and's Spouse,/He left 'em no/Where else to go,/But turn'd 'em out on's House'.[8]

No royal guards attended prince and princess in their hasty flit. The doors of the palace were closed against them, the Chapel Royal too, their attendance at court forbidden and every special act of deference suspended. Still the choleric and implacable monarch protested at his inability under British law to halt their payments from the civil list. Even Caroline's children, a baby of three weeks and three daughters ranging in age from four to eight, were prevented from accompanying her in this hour of disgrace. They remained abed within the palace. The king had '[taken] his grey goose quill/And dip't it o'er in gall', a balladeer wrote. His sentence was comprehensive:

Take hence yourself, and eke your spouse,
Your maidens and your men,
Your trunks, and all your trumpery,
Except your children.[9]

Where the royal couple took their unhappy caravanserai was the house of Henry d'Auverquerque, Earl of Grantham. Since February, this slow-witted loyalist, his character dominated by 'gluttony and idleness, … a good stomach and a bad head, … stupidity and ennui', had served as Caroline's lord chamberlain, the highest-ranking officer of her household.[10]

Up St James's Street the convoy jolted. Across Piccadilly to Grantham House in Dover Street it wound its way. Servants followed separately, in the glimmering illumination of the new round glass street lamps, lit only on moonless nights, that marvelling visitors to the city likened to 'little *Suns* of the

Night.[11] The Duke of Portland described the party on arrival as 'in the utmost grief and disorder, the Prince cried for two hours, and the Princess swooned several times'.[12] Caroline had given birth only weeks earlier, an event, in the words of one phlegmatic diarist, 'which occasioned great joy for the present, but proved of short duration'.[13] Following months of escalating tension, the baby's christening was the battleground on which king and prince collided. By 2 December neither Caroline's strength nor her nerves had recovered from birth or baptism. Besides the daughters she entrusted to governesses on that darkest evening, she left behind her in the care of his wetnurse her baby son.

Caroline's friend, the Countess of Bückeburg, recalled the anguish of their parting: 'The poor Princess went into one faint after another when her weeping little Princesses said goodbye.'[14] Caroline had told the king that she valued her children 'not as a grain of sand compared to [her husband]', but there was more of bravado than truth in the statement.[15] None of the family would recover from the fissure wrought that winter night. Before the spring was out, the baby Caroline left behind her 'kick'd up his heels and died'.[16] He was killed by 'convulsions', water on the brain, a cyst on his tiny heart; each internal organ was swollen, distended, angrily inflamed. The miracle was that he had survived so long.[17] That this looked bad for the king was cold comfort for a grief-stricken Caroline. 'That which, in our more liberal age, would be considered as bare invective and scurrility, was the popular language of those times,' wrote Lord Hailes, looking back in 1788.[18] In this instance scurrility rose up in Caroline's defence. Doggerel commended her suffering; it condemned the king's heartlessness: 'Let Baby cry/Or Lit [sic] it die/Own Mother's Milk deny'd,/He no more car'd/How poor thing far'd.'[19]

'Over the Hills and Far Away' sang beautiful Mary Bellenden, and rain and darkness engulfed her song. The king she meant

to upbraid was not listening, and the royal gaggle's short journey, undertaken pell-mell on foot in view of a hastily convened
sympathetic crowd, soon carried them out of earshot. In Lord
Grantham's house, smaller than their apartments in St James's
Palace, prince and princess were forced to share a bedroom.
Such intimacy, and confines of space, prevented any ceremonial
in their rising or retiring to bed, the complex rigmarole of
bedchamber staff, of basins and ewers proffered on bended
knee, shifts, chemises, gloves, fans and shoes presented or with-
drawn by attendants greedy for the privilege: the ritualised
posturing of baroque monarchy. Instead 'Higgledy-piggledy
they lay/And all went rantam scantam.'[20]

To his father, the prince dispatched the tersest of notes. 'I
have just obeyed your Majesty's orders, having left St James's.
The Princess goes along with me, and our Servants shall follow
with all imaginable Expedition.'[21] No response was requested or
forthcoming.

'I am so sorry for our dear Princess of Wales that I shed tears
for her yesterday,' her closest correspondent wrote.[22] As a measure of his distress, George Augustus succumbed to a feverish
'inflammatory distemper, with bumps in his face somewhat like
a rash'. Doctors treated Caroline for fainting fits and violent
throat pains.[23] For all its brevity, her journey from familiar
certainties, beginning with a walk in the dark, was a big one.
Her life encompasses its share of new beginnings and abrupt
severances.

PART ONE

Germany

I

Princess of Ansbach

'Bred up in the softness of a Court'

In Wenceslaus Hollar, the old palace of Ansbach – towered, turreted and architecturally uninspiring – found its ideal chronographer. An etcher from Bohemia, born in 1607 and destined, surely unfairly, to die in poverty, Hollar worked in black and white for a fixed rate of fourpence an hour, creating topographical views as intricately wrought as Flemish lace.

First printed in the 1630s, Hollar's view of the south German town of Ansbach has a congested spikiness. He delighted in inky shadows, details sharp as pinpricks, the awkward geometry of serried roofs. The tiny figures he scattered across his panorama – riding in a coach, chasing a stag across an empty field – are fragile as house spiders and likewise insignificant. Like spiders they thread the crooked streets. Their meagre limbs are gossamer alongside the solider outlines of steeples and town walls and the criss-cross fronts of timber-framed merchants' houses. Hidden from view are Ansbach's metalworkers and cloth-makers, whose workshops oozed woodsmoke and sweat. Out of earshot the ring of hammers and wooden tools, expletives, invective, laughter.

Instead, it is the old Renaissance palace that draws the eye in Hollar's etching. Built in the third quarter of the sixteenth century by an architect from Swabia called Blasius Berwart, it is a tall building of four storeys, and its walls form the sides of a square. Hollar depicts it as a cat's cradle of uprights and mullioned windows. From its corners, narrow towers rise, topped by spires. Gables frame shuttered dormers. A pennant – or possibly a weathervane – flutters stiffly from the spire of the largest, central, hexagonal tower. Above the steep-pitched roof, a chimneystack supports a bird's nest complete with resident stork. Hollar's scale is all wrong, and the stork, brought to life, would have been enormous, like an airborne dodo. At the start of our chronicle the bird is appropriate, associated with new beginnings, harbinger of new life.

In one version of Hollar's etching the building is labelled 'Furstlich Residents', 'princely seat', in letters as big as the palace windows.[1] The same print offers the viewer a key: the princely seat is sight 'A'. Hollar's contemporaries would have agreed with him that any viewer's primary interest must be the home of Ansbach's first family – not the taller Gothic churches of St Gumbertus and St John to the east, nor the palace's formal garden within crenelated walls to the west, each flowerbed a filigree square. Buildings close to the palace are nondescript by comparison: regular as boxes, like the plastic houses on a Monopoly board, much as they remain.

In Berwart's palace, in a room quite different from that later mocked up for tourists as 'Queen Caroline's apartment', complete with rococo boiseries and Chinese porcelain, Caroline of Ansbach was born on 1 March 1683. Otherwise, save in Hollar's etching, the old palace of Ansbach has been forgotten. It was remodelled and extended at the turn of the eighteenth century, after Caroline had already left it.

Today's Residenz Ansbach – now the administrative seat of the government of Middle Franconia – is an exercise in baroque symmetry begun in 1705: routinely grand. Last whiffs of absolutism confer a bland sort of glamour. Externally, pilasters divide ribbons of tall windows; from the pediment statues gesture sturdily. Vanished is the dark, mysterious poetry invoked by Hollar, gone the mighty stork on its twiggy nest, long dead those spidery figures chasing a stag, jolting in their carriage, working iron or bronze in hidden forges. Nothing remains to recall the older palace at the heart of this cluster of timber-built houses and soaring churches and small-scale provincial aspirations set amid green meadows and distant wooded hills above the Rezat river.

Several of Berwart's interiors survived the remodelling. There is little today save a handful of portraits that would be recognisable to the blonde-haired princess baptised into the Lutheran faith in the spring of 1683 as Wilhelmine Karoline. In the event, circumstances throughout her life would discourage her from looking back. First family tragedy, later political expediency, forced her to fix her gaze on the present and the future. Her contemporaries discounted her early years. British printmakers even confused her baptismal names: Edward Cooper called her 'Wilhelmina Charlotta', Thomas Bowles 'Wilhelmina Charlotte'.[2] It seems likely that she was known first as 'Wilhelmine'. The switch to 'Caroline' coincided with the prospect of a life in Britain, following her marriage into the reigning house of Hanover. 'Caroline' was easier for the British to pronounce.

Begun in the year of Caroline's marriage, Ansbach's new palace is an exercise in regal conformity: a cumbrous assertion of majesty inspired, like so much German palace-building, by Louis XIV's Versailles. Her own later life would share this concern with successfully projecting authority. Like the building she never knew, her future career encompassed baroque bombast and a focus on order, reason and measure more typical of the Enlightenment. All that lay ahead.

In March 1683, her birth was of no importance. No poets hymned her tiny limbs, no kerfuffle ruffled diplomats' dispatches. Only love could justify John Frederick, Margrave of Brandenburg-Ansbach, beginning a second family after the death of his wife Joanna Elizabeth of Baden-Durlach. The three surviving children of his first marriage, Christian Albert, Dorothea Frederica and George Frederick – seven, six and four respectively – already filled his turreted palace with noise and the surety of another generation. By 1683, Ansbach required from its ruling prince no more sons or daughters. Caroline was a baby without purpose or promise. Save in a mother's heart, few aspirations can have been nurtured for her. Yet there is no reason to doubt her parents' happiness at her birth. Given the existence already of two male heirs to the Ansbach patrimony, even her sex cannot have disappointed.

John Frederick was a man of imagination and culture. He wrote fiction, in the manner of contemporary French authors, published under the pseudonym Isidorus Fidelis ('Faithful Isidore'), and expanded and reorganised the court library; he loved music, especially opera. He employed the composer Johann Wolfgang Franck as director of court music at the outset of his career; he was a patron of composer and well-known castrato singer Antonio Pistocchi. Franck wrote two new operas during his six years in Ansbach, including a version of the story of Perseus and Andromeda: chivalry overcoming tyranny.[3] Pistocchi meanwhile would first teach Caroline to sing.[4] And John Frederick commissioned for his palace a double portrait of himself and his new wife. She was Eleonore Erdmuthe Louise, elder of the two daughters of John George I, Duke of Saxe-Eisenach. The home she left behind her lay 150 miles to the north, on the north-west edge of the Thuringian forest, an enclave every bit as insignificant as tiny Ansbach.

An uxorious image, John Frederick's marriage portrait suggests a man happy with his spouse. The sturdy German margrave leans towards his charming consort, seven years his junior, and proudly clasps her hand. Like many another princess, she was acclaimed by poets as the loveliest alive; a shrewder observer noted her mildness of temper, compliance, good sense.[5]

Her double chin, plump forearms and breasts as deliciously rounded as the peaches in the basket she cradles, indicate her conformity to prevailing notions of beauty. Visual metaphors of fecundity are easily unravelled. Less so her auburn hair, possibly a wig, a tottering confection of marshmallow curls. Corkscrew ringlets foam about her pale shoulders. She wears a necklace of pearls and bulky, square-cut jewels glimmer on her bodice. John Frederick wears a brown wig of a style that had changed little since the middle of the century.

The couple's pale eyebrows suggest that their colouring was naturally fair – as it appears in Samuel Blesendorff's engraving of the painting, as well as mezzotints of an earlier portrait of John Frederick attributed to Willem Wissing, in breastplate and chivalric orders.[6] A contemporary engraving of John Frederick by Mark Anton Gufer shows that Caroline inherited from her father her distinctively rounded face, with pointed chin and long, straight, pointed nose; her brother William Frederick resembled her closely.[7] From her mother Caroline would inherit her quantities of pale blonde hair and, as time would show, considerable strength of character. Her father bequeathed her in addition bibliophilia, a relish for poetry and music, his manipulation of cultural patronage as a medium for communicating power. Although she lacked Eleonore's uncontested beauty, Caroline would share her 'expressive countenance'.[8] Inviting curves and a splendid embonpoint – a plenitude of milk-white fleshiness and snowy bosom – were also gifts of Eleonore's. A possibly apocryphal story has a youthful Caroline being followed through Ansbach's narrow streets by a crowd of gawping admirers. Like Eleonore, she would inspire devotion in her future spouse. Like both her parents, she would make an essentially arranged marriage successful and rewarding.

At the outset she was born to high-ranking obscurity, cut off from the common herd in Berwart's palace with its garden concealed between high walls, her destiny at best marriage into a court like her father's. Seventeenth-century Ansbach was part of the Holy Roman Empire. This confederation of around three hundred more-or-less autonomous territories extended across modern-day Germany, Austria, the Czech Republic and beyond; its Habsburg overlord was chosen by a handful of the Empire's leading princes, whose role in the process earned them the title 'elector' along with covetable sinecures.[9] Situated between Nuremberg to the north-east and Munich further south, Ansbach lies in present-day Bavaria; its outlook focused on its German neighbours. Since the fifteenth century its governing family had been kinsmen of the Hohenzollerns, rulers of the much larger north German territory of Brandenburg, in one eighteenth-century estimate 'one of the most ancient and illustrious families in Europe'.[10] As their title suggests, the margraves of Brandenburg-Ansbach had connections. They had money too, from silver mines in the Harz Mountains, close to the Brandenburg border. John Frederick matched imagination with initiative, promoting traditional local manufactures, including weaving and metal-smithing. But his power was finite, confined like his sphere of influence to an area smaller than an English county, and his family history was middling. Caroline would be the first of Ansbach's princesses to marry a crown.

If Caroline remembered anything of her early childhood, a period entrusted to the care of nurses and waiting women, her memories of her mother would have been of Eleonore's near-continuous pregnancies. In January 1685 she gave birth to a son, christened Frederick Augustus, who died three weeks later. Within a year, a second son, William Frederick, was born. Then darkness fell. Two months after William Frederick's birth, John Frederick died of smallpox. He was thirty-one years old. His remains were interred in the margraves' vault in nearby St Gumbertus church. Caroline grew up with no memories of the father who died when she was three years old.

Eleonore became a widow at the age of twenty-three; she had been married four years. Six months later her father died in a hunting accident. For the grieving mother of two the darkness of Hollar's townscape became a reality. John Frederick was succeeded by the elder surviving son of his first marriage, ten-year-old Christian Albert, who felt little warmth for the stepmother who could almost have been his sister, or for the stepsister whom he regarded as a baby. His minority left no role for Eleonore. Instead Elector Frederick III of Brandenburg acted as guardian to Ansbach's underage margrave. He also provided a temporary home in Berlin for Caroline and William Frederick, in company with his gangly daughter Louise Dorothea and, from 1688, an ungovernable son, Frederick William. Alone, Eleonore retreated the short distance to a dower house in Crailsheim, south-west of Ansbach, a small medieval town of no distinction. Forced upon her by the terms of her marriage settlement and Christian Albert's indifference, her withdrawal was a species of defeat. The uncertainty that was to be the keynote of Caroline's peripatetic childhood began early.

At Crailsheim, Eleonore struggled for money. Unhappy and distracted, in the intervals when mother and daughter were reunited she neglected Caroline's education. Penury made her fretful, threatened to overwhelm her. 'She is a princess of great virtue and piety,' noted the English diplomatist George Stepney, discussing Eleonore's Lutheranism: her circumstances demanded the full resources of her faith. Stepney described her as 'one who passes for a bigot in that persuasion'.[11] Exigency is a hard taskmaster. Driven by anxiety, Eleonore was rumoured to have overcome her Lutheran bigotry to the extent of considering conversion to Catholicism in order to marry Maximilian II, elector of Bavaria, whose capital at Munich 'excel[led] and out-dazzled[d] [all] for her elegant cleanliness'.[12] Since the elector was married already, albeit to the fragile Habsburg archduchess Maria Antonia, who shortly died, this rumour – if it has any basis in truth – indicates the pitch of desperation Eleonore had reached. Understandably, her thoughts during the Crailsheim years were of escape by any means.

Through precocity, boredom or curiosity, Caroline took matters into her own hands and set about teaching herself to write.[13] For the rest of her life, her sprawling, forward-tilting handwriting with its bold loops and lopsided incontinence betrayed the struggle it had cost her. She wrote 'like a cat', her husband protested, and could never spell in any language: 'Choresbury' for Shrewsbury, 'Hamthuncour' for Hampton Court, 'Lady Bomffrit' for Lady Pomfret – even the name of her closest lady-in-waiting was variously rendered as 'Clayton', 'Claiton' and 'Klethen'.[14] Her punctuation was erratic or non-existent, an oversight in the cat-like torrents. From the inky tangle emerges a vigorous quality to her character as well as the sharpness of her intelligence. It would not be reasonable, a Church of England bishop would comment later, 'to measure the extent of her Royal Highnesses abilities by the common standard'.[15] If handwriting is a guide, Caroline was determined, quick-witted, vehement, expressive.

Happily for Caroline's future choices, Eleonore did not change her religion. When it happened, the remarriage of the widowed margravine served only to jeopardise her family's wellbeing.

In November 1691, five years after John Frederick's death, Eleonore travelled to Berlin at the invitation of Frederick III. On the eve of her thirtieth birthday she retained her good looks – '[a] beautiful person, the admiration of all who saw her';[16] unmistakeably she bore the imprint of grief, money worries and separation from her children. 'She is handsome, well shaped but too lean,' Stepney recorded.[17] Weight loss won few plaudits at the end of the seventeenth century. Nevertheless, Stepney's admiration can be inferred from the poem written in French that, despite their differences of rank, he subsequently addressed to Eleonore, and his assiduity in undertaking errands on her behalf.[18] Eleonore appears poised and strikingly attractive in a portrait of the early 1690s, sumptuously swathed in ermine and heavy silks, every inch the baroque consort. But the outline of her face is less rounded than in John Frederick's marriage portrait; ditto the fullness of that lovely décolletage.

Frederick III's purpose in summoning his widowed kinswoman was Eleonore's remarriage. His motive was neither altruistic nor prompted by affection. Improved relations between the mutually mistrustful electorates of Brandenburg and Saxony had recently been sealed symbolically by the inauguration by their rulers of a shared chivalric order, the Order of Sincerity. Frederick intended to consolidate diplomatic amity with a marriage between Eleonore and his Saxon counterpart, Elector John George IV. Her friendship with Frederick and his wife Sophie Charlotte of Brunswick-Lüneburg, and distant relationship, through her father, to the Saxon electoral family, ideally positioned Eleonore for the role of bridal pawn. In practice it proved a marriage of emotional barrenness and unusual acrimony, and spectacularly failed to benefit any of its key players.

The man who became the nine-year-old Caroline's stepfather, in a service conducted with unceremonious haste at Leipzig on 17 April 1692, following a formal exchange of treaties on 10 February, was 'round shouldered, of a sullen look, which ... does not belie his humour ... [and] of a saturnine temper'. He spoke little, 'offer[ed] no jest himself and [was] not pleased when others [did] it'; his killjoy obstinacy was marked.[19] So, too, his variable health, though he was six years younger than the bride who, by April, had seen enough to disabuse her of every romantic illusion. George Stepney described him as incapacitated by the smallest debauchery, but unable to resist the heavy drinking endemic in German courts; his kidney problems were well known. 'I look upon him as a man that will not be long-lived,' Stepney noted. Had Eleonore but known of it, this last observation would have constituted her single slender thread of hope in the nightmarish years to come. In the meantime, in Leipzig, ahead of the couple's formal entry into the city of Torgau, their marriage was 'consummated with such an air of debauchery' that courtiers muttered their misgivings. Having 'bedded his bride in her own apartments', the sated but loveless John George abandoned her rooms for his own, returning to complete his night's rest alone at five o'clock in the morning.[20]

The emotions of Eleonore's second husband could not have been more different from those of her first. John Frederick had delighted in his comely bride; John George's affections were already engaged elsewhere and, in Stepney's assessment, 'his humour … quite contrary'.[21] Stepney drew attention to the family's poor record of marital fidelity, stretching back 'two generations at least'.[22] In John George's case, he embarked on marriage under duress. Courtier and captious memoirist Baron von Pöllnitz described Eleonore in Saxony as 'a Princess, whose excellent accomplishments gain'd a great veneration'.[23] Not on the part of her new husband. John George's intentions towards Eleonore extended no further than fulfilment of his conjugal duties. Stepney described her position unenviably as 'not unlike Penelope or good queen Catherine [of Braganza] in the reign of Charles II', a combination of abandonment and clutching after crumbs of affection.[24]

How much the elector was master of his limited faculties his contemporaries were willing to debate. There were those in Saxony – including members of his closest camarilla – who considered their master a victim of witchcraft.

The source of the rot was the mistress of John George's father, Ursula von Neitschütz, the wife of a compliant army officer. *Die Generalin*, as the obliging colonel's wife was known, possessed boundless rapacity and the valuable asset of a beautiful but unintelligent daughter, Magdalena Sibylla, called 'Billa'.

Deprived of princely handouts at her lover's death in 1691, Ursula von Neitschütz conceived a plan to prolong the good times by promoting her daughter to the role she herself had previously occupied. The possibility that the late elector was Billa's father, making her John George's half-sister, did not apparently trouble her mother. 'Stories of filters [philtres] and incantations', shortly circulating in the Saxon court, suggested she had resorted to spells and magic potions to sway John George's emotions.[25] Given the latter's lack of imagination, and other instances in German courts of a single family providing royal mistresses over several generations, the real explanation is possibly less sensational. Nevertheless, in October 1695 *Die Generalin* would find herself on trial for her life, accused of being a witch. That her jurors were drawn from the law faculty of the University of Leipzig indicates the seriousness of both charge and proceedings.[26]

Eleonore was fully apprised of her new husband's entanglement before the marriage contracts were signed. Under pressure from Frederick III, realistic in her measure of the precariousness of her position, brought up to understand that royal women's purpose lay in dynastic diplomacy and with an eye to her own and her children's security, she hesitated to muster objections. For appearance's sake, Billa had been temporarily removed from John George's entourage. On 25 April 1692, when, as part of their formal entry to the electoral capital, John George and Eleonore travelled by gondola along the River Elbe, the night sky illuminated with fireworks marking out the letters of their linked monograms, Billa was included among guests at the elector's table for the banquet that followed. Eleonore's feelings are easily imagined. In Stepney's eyes she was sufficiently sensible 'to dissemble her grievance'.[27] Characteristically, John George did not stoop to dissimulation. On Eleonore's side, the marriage was an exercise in good behaviour from the outset. She paid a high price for financial stability and the outward lustre of the electress title. Her powerlessness – how well she knew it – was simply in the nature of things.

With Frederick III's departure from Torgau on 29 April, and Caroline and William Frederick still in Berlin, Eleonore found herself, less than a fortnight into her marriage, as much alone as she had been at Crailsheim. At least the splendour of Dresden, called 'the Florence on the Elbe', and the magnificent royal palace – contemporary with the old palace in Ansbach – put paid to recent memories of poverty. Behind iron shutters beyond a single door in the elector's apartments lay the Secret Repository, known as the Green Vault, built in the previous century by the elector Maurice as a treasure chamber. Its glittering collections – priceless trinkets of gold, silver, bronze, ivory, amber and precious stones – dazzled even Peter the Great, visiting six years later. Artefacts prized for the technical virtuosity of their crafts-manship inspired admiration for the electors' connoisseurship; rarefied materials suggested the wonder of the natural world.[28] In the short term Eleonore could derive some satisfaction from the discovery that she was pregnant. While John George flaunted his infatuation for Billa von Neitschütz to the extent of lobbying the Holy Roman Emperor, Leopold I, to grant her an imperial title, appearances were seemingly maintained by such obvious evidence of married relations.

Eleonore's pleasure proved short-lived. In August she miscar-ried. A second miscarriage followed in February 1693. In late October she was described as 'far gone with child', and prayers for her safe delivery were said in churches across Saxony.[29] Perhaps indicative of her state of mind, it proved a phantom pregnancy – as sympathetic bystanders were quick to discern, a victory for her enemies.[30] Laconically, Stepney commented, 'it seems a little wind could not find passage, and all the while we have mistook a fart for an heir to the Electorate'.[31]

In despair, Eleonore took to her sickbed. That she neverthe-less granted audiences to visiting diplomats suggests her determination not to be sidelined.[32] Unlike the wife of John George's successor, she did not resort to the thermal springs in the Saxon town of Teplitz to encourage conception; probably her heart was no longer in it.[33] Meanwhile, in a letter signed on 20 February 1693 by the imperial vice chancellor, Leopold von Königsegg und Rothenfels, the emperor had bestowed on Billa the title Countess of Rochlitz.[34] Four months later, on 20 June, at the midpoint of Eleonore's phantom pregnancy, the new countess had succeeded where Eleonore was to fail, and gave birth to John George's child. The bastard girl was baptised Wilhelmina Maria Frederica.

Secretly, John George offered his mistress a written pledge: surviving documents include the marriage contract he presented to her.[35] Publicly he extolled the pragmatism of bigamy. Stepney quoted claims that, among German princes, bigamy was more widespread than ever before, and that John George '*va épouser formellement la comtesse de Rochlitz*' (will formally marry the Countess of Rochlitz). Already the Saxons were referring to the 'young' electress (Billa) 'in opposition to the Old' (Eleonore).[36] Late in 1693, Stepney recorded 'a report that apartments for the countess are being prepared at the court'.[37] For Eleonore these were alarming developments: with good reason she mistrusted her husband's intentions. Bigamy or divorce aside – and political considerations meant that John George dare not attempt the latter – Eleonore understood that her death alone could make good his promise to the countess. In an argument between husband and wife over John George's gift to Billa of the valuable Pillnitz estate, only the presence of bystanders prevented the elector from stabbing Eleonore with the sword he drew on her.[38]

How much of her mother's anxiety Caroline knew about or understood at this point is unclear. Aspects of adult life remain concealed from the most precocious and observant child. Even after Caroline and William Frederick's return from Berlin, the requirements and formalities of court life separated Eleonore from her children for much of the time. It is possible that Caroline overheard gossip about John George's behaviour, and probable that she noticed her stepfather's frequent absences from the palace; she understood the extent of John George's lack of interest in herself and her brother, and was surely aware of a febrile quality in the atmosphere at court, and her mother's growing nervousness. At intervals Eleonore appears to have retreated to the safety of a house in Bayreuth with her lady-in-waiting, Madame du Mornay. When it suited him, and contrary to her intentions, John George followed her there.[39]

That she feared for her life, genuinely concerned that the Neitschütz faction intended to poison her, is not something Eleonore is likely to have shared with her nine-year-old daughter. To others she branded *Die Generalin* 'a person guilty of black practices'.[40] In explaining her decision finally to abandon the royal palace in favour of the estate, remote from Dresden, at Pretzsch on the banks of the Elbe, that had been settled on her at the time of her marriage, she doubtless happed upon a useful fiction. To the English authorities, Stepney explained that she intended to 'spend the rest of her life [there] rather than be continually exposed to hard usage'.[41] He had previously expressed concern that, in her own best interests, Eleonore should withdraw from court to the country.[42] Even if he was unaware of the full extent of the threats to her, he clearly considered that, in Dresden, no good could come to Eleonore.

Once, smallpox had deprived Eleonore of a doting husband. Now the disease struck again. '*Die Favoritin*', Billa von Neitschütz, succumbed first. 'For fear her face should suffer', her mother dispensed with doctors (such as they were) and concocted remedies of her own. The result was 'agonyes speechless'. As death approached, 'locked jaws prevent[ed] [Billa] from taking the sacrament'.[43] A grief-stricken John George ordered deep mourning for the entire court.[44] Weeks later, on 27 April 1694, smallpox claimed John George's life too, the price this head-strong and intemperate prince paid for nursing his mistress himself.[45] In the medieval church of St Sophia, the corpse of *die Favoritin* was placed on public view, her face alarmingly discoloured. An eyewitness account survives from 30 April, more than two weeks after Billa's death.[46] So, too, a scurrilous epitaph on John George's foolish mistress and her scheming and ambitious mother.[47]

In 1692, George Stepney, then agent to the Brandenburg court, had correctly forecast a short life for the elector John George IV. His appointment the following year to the post of commissary and deputy to the court of Saxony offered Stepney ample opportunity for further observation. In the aftermath of John George's death, he wrote an elegy to Eleonore, *Pour la mort de SAE de Saxe à SAE Madame l'Electrice Eleonore*. In it, he described the elector's passion for Billa von Neitschütz as 'unworthy', their love *'un indigne amour'*.[48] Finally free from the toxicity of mingled terror and humiliation, Eleonore's only response was relief. In the witchcraft trial of Ursula von Neitschütz the follow-ing year she played no part.

Eleonore had endured the death of her first son. Sincerely she had mourned her first husband. With no option but to leave the palace in Ansbach, yet insufficiently provided for, she had spent almost six years lonely, unhappy and all but penniless in provin-cial retirement in Crailsheim. Velvet-gloved but iron-fisted cajolery on the part of her 'friends' had compelled her to marry again, this time a boor and a drunkard with a pronounced streak of mental cruelty. Either her second husband, or associates of her husband's mistress, had threatened to poison her. John George himself had drawn his sword on her.

In Saxony, she was more fortunate than in Ansbach in her husband's successor. John George's heir, his brother Frederick Augustus, afterwards known as 'Augustus the Strong' on account of feats that included rolling up silver plates with his bare hands, 'revel[led] and dance[d]' at news of his death, then gave himself up to 'frolicks and debauches'.[49] In John George's beautiful widow and her children he took a passing interest, as he would continue to do, and Eleonore's life regained a semblance of normality. Among her surviving papers, for example, is the letter of recommendation – the equivalent of a reference – that she wrote in the summer of 1694 for a former page at Crailsheim.[50] George Stepney reported in August that he had twice visited Eleonore since her widowhood, and that she permitted him to call on her frequently. On both occasions she had told him 'old stories and some particulars of the disorders of the late reign which I should never have learn'd from anybody else'.[51] The following summer, in company with Caroline, she revisited Dresden on her way to spas near Koblenz, and had supper with Stepney's colleague Philip Plantamour.[52] Her journey proved unhappy: 'her wagons [were] plundered by snap-hawks [freebooters]' and she was robbed of valuable plate and goods.[53]

Whatever the anticipated benefits of Eleonore's Koblenz trip, the damage, it seemed, had been done. In the interval since John Frederick's death, her health had deteriorated irreparably. On 9 September 1696, two years after her second husband, Eleonore died. She was thirty-four years old. Her daughter Caroline, just thirteen, found herself an orphan.

A letter changed Caroline's life. It took the form of an invitation, and offered her a home – her fifth so far – and the security of guardianship. Its author was the Elector of Brandenburg, Frederick III – to date, as the tone of his letter implicitly acknowledged, an equivocal player in the life of Caroline's family. With some warmth, Frederick wrote to her in the autumn of 1696, 'I will never fail as your guardian, to espouse your interests, and to care for you as a loving father, and pray your Highness to have in me the same confidence as your mother always had, which I shall properly endeavour to deserve.'[54] Events would prove his sincerity. Caroline had made her home in Berlin before, at Frederick's glittering court, in the unsettled months preceding Eleonore's disastrous remarriage. Now, insofar as the young Caroline could ever feel she dare anticipate stability, the shadow of unsettlement temporarily dispersed. Only her parting from her brother William Frederick increased her sorrow. He had returned to Ansbach as heir presumptive, following Christian Albert's death in 1692 and the accession as margrave of the latter's unmarried younger brother George Frederick.

Yet it was not the well-intentioned Frederick but his wife, Sophia Charlotte, a Hanoverian princess known to her family as 'Figuelotte', who would provide the guardianship that had the greatest impact on an impressionable young girl only fifteen years her junior. The elector was self-important, a little pompous, excessively absorbed by minutiae of etiquette and ceremony, a zealot for elaborate dress despite a spinal deformity and gout; in his own words one who possessed 'all the attributes of kingliness and in greater measure than other kings', alternatively one who '[went] out of his way to find more and more occasions for ceremony'.[55] By contrast the electress disdained 'the grandeurs and crowns of which people make so much here';[56] she described herself as well acquainted with 'the infinitely little'.[57] While Frederick was at pains to surround himself with a court as rigidly formal as Versailles, his wife – motivated 'by the ardour that she had for the knowledge of the truth' – preferred music, reading and 'the charm of ... philosophical conversations'.[58] Court life, Figuelotte saw, threatened the truest friendships, the strongest bonds of love, however impassioned Frederick's professed opposition to 'Cabals and private Intrigues ... [and] intermeddling in other People's Business'.[59] It offered, as the philosopher Leibniz noted, 'everything that might dissipate the intellect'.[60] She was impatient of Frederick's hankering after royal *gloire*. And, until 1697, she had a powerful enemy in his close adviser and former tutor, Eberhard von Danckelmann. Studiedly detached from court politics, she occupied herself with less contentious pursuits.

To Agostino Steffani, her father's director of court music in Hanover, Figuelotte described music as 'a loyal friend that never leaves one and never deceives one, it never betrays one and has never been cruel. On the contrary all the charm and delight of heaven is there.'[61] Within months of Caroline's arrival, Figuelotte had enticed to Berlin as court composer the Italian organist and former composer to the Duke of Mantua, Attilio Ariosti. From 1702 she employed the composer Giovanni Bononcini. Both would later feature in the operatic life of London after Caroline's marriage. Among Figuelotte's costliest purchases was a harpsichord, commissioned from the court instrument-maker Michael Mietke, sumptuously decorated with panels simulating white Chinese lacquer; she also commissioned a folding harpsichord to take with her on journeys. Frederick meanwhile devoted his energies to worldly aggrandisement. In 1701, in exchange for military support for Habsburg ambitions in Spain, he won the emperor's acquiescence in his elevation from Elector of Brandenburg and Duke of Prussia to 'King in Prussia'. The previous year, in anticipation, he had given orders for a new suite of crown jewels. Like other mythomanes, at his coronation at Königsberg on 18 January, he placed the crown on his own head.

The interests of husband and wife were at variance. On closer observation the young Caroline recognised the astuteness of Figuelotte's management of her pernickety and egotistical husband and the extent of Frederick's admiration for his unconventional electress, a feeling unfettered by the acrid presence of his ambitious mistress, Katharina von Wartenburg. Over time

Caroline understood that Figuelotte's absorption in music and philosophy offered more than respite from the labyrinthine formalities of Brandenburg court etiquette and the falsity of ambitious courtiers. It was an antidote to worldliness and self-interest. It also represented one aspect of the role of consort, the soft power of cultural patronage, a division of royal influence typical of German courts in this period.

The scale of Figuelotte's sway over the teenage Caroline was quickly apparent. In physical and verbal mannerisms, Caroline became her guardian's mirror, Galatea to the electress's inadvertent Pygmalion. Figuelotte was intelligent, uncompromising and beautiful. She was irreverent – a woman who took snuff in the middle of her coronation; and she was unconventional, accompanying the court orchestra in concert performances on her harpsichord. 'She has big, gentle eyes, wonderfully thick black hair, eyebrows looking as if they had been drawn, a well-proportioned nose, incarnadine lips, very good teeth, and a lively complexion,' runs one account.[62] She also inclined to heaviness, the reason her mother had forbidden her to wear velvet prior to her marriage. A sequence of undistinguished portraits by the court painter Friedrich Wilhelm Weidemann indicates florid good looks and lugubrious stateliness. Caroline's admiration, albeit she continued to mourn Eleonore, was wholehearted. Unreservedly she acclaimed her guardian's wife as 'incomparable'.[63] But Figuelotte could not be fully satisfied with the decorative or reproductive roles typically assigned to royal spouses. The silliness of courtiers had killed her first two sons: a crown crammed on to the head of the elder at his christening, a gun salute fired too near the cradle of the second. After the birth of her third son, Frederick William, Figuelotte appeared unconcerned to provide her husband with additional heirs. By the time of Caroline's arrival in Berlin, without any outward suggestion of a breach, husband and wife lived parallel lives. Figuelotte doted on Frederick William, an unappealing child given to violent tantrums, hair-pulling and kicking valets; she was ripe to form new attachments.

The palace of Lietzenburg, or Lützenburg, in open country less than five miles from the centre of Berlin, provided the setting for her independence. Building work had begun in 1695, to a workaday baroque design by architect Johann Arnold Nering. Four years later its first phase was complete, including Figuelotte's own suite of rooms, hung with damask beneath ceilings of gilded plasterwork. Following her coronation as queen, she commissioned from court architect Eosander von Göthe a second, grander apartment aping the latest developments in French decoration. She added a sumptuously theatrical chapel and a glittering Porcelain Cabinet decorated with mirror glass and thousands of pieces of Chinese porcelain arranged on gilded brackets. Formal gardens were also French in taste, the work of Siméon Godeau, a pupil of Louis XIV's garden designer André Le Nôtre: clipped box hedges, pristine lawns with gilded statues and, in emulation of her father's summer palace, a man-made pond bobbing with real Venetian gondolas – 'a paradise only without apples'.[64] At Lützenburg, Caroline watched unfold a vision that was at the same time personal and political. Figuelotte's palace expressed her own rarefied connoisseurship; it impressed visitors with a vision of Prussian wealth, refinement and cosmopolitanism. For Caroline it encapsulated all that was most remarkable and delightful in her guardian.

In this rural escape, a private domain of her own making, Figuelotte surrounded herself with a youthful court. Here etiquette gave way to spirited misrule, like the lively amateur theatricals in which Caroline played her part alongside courtiers and visiting royals, and the birthday festivities for Frederick in 1699, when the electoral couple and their guests leaped over tables and benches.[65] Contradicting the statement of her cousin Liselotte, Duchess of Orléans, that 'it is not at all suitable for people of great quality to be very learned', at Lützenburg Figuelotte pursued interests that were explicitly cerebral.[66] From across Europe she welcomed men of intellect, regardless of the orthodoxy of their views; even visiting diplomats were subjected to 'metaphysical discourses'.[67] 'She loves to see Strangers,' wrote the English rationalist philosopher John Toland, who counted himself among their number, 'and to inform herself of all that's worthy or remarkable in their several Countries.'[68] A letter from the summer of 1698 draws attention to evidence of Figuelotte's anglophilia, too – Caroline's first introduction to pro-British views.[69]

Chief among Figuelotte's 'Strangers' was polymath philosopher, mathematician and historian Gottfried Wilhelm Leibniz, the inventor of the forerunner of modern computing, infinitesimal calculus. Her father's librarian and court adviser since 1676, engaged in writing the history of Hanover's ruling family, the Guelphs, and a trusted confidant to her mother, Leibniz became Figuelotte's correspondent late in 1697. Their letters were mostly philosophical in bent, and on 1 September 1699 Figuelotte declared herself Leibniz's disciple and avowed admirer, 'one of those who esteems you and respects your merit'.[70] For his part, Leibniz wooed her with treacle. 'The charms of an admirable princess have in all matters more power than the strictest orders of the greatest prince in the world,' he oozed.[71] He sent her a fossilised mammoth tooth unearthed near Brunswick; his accompanying commentary attempted to whet her appetite for science. Then, in 1702, in response to Figuelotte's questioning, he wrote a short essay, 'On What is Independent of Sense and Matter'.[72] In time a self-appointed unofficial go-between for the courts of Hanover and Berlin, journeying whenever possible to Lützenburg in his coffee-coloured carriage painted with roses, Leibniz took his place at the centre of Figuelotte's coterie of rationalists, free-thinkers and metaphysicians. With familiarity his admiration deepened.

'There may never have been a queen so accomplished and so philosophical at the same time,' he wrote to Queen Anne's favourite, Abigail Masham.[73] A painted fan of the 1680s depicting a French scientific salon, with men and women engaged in eager dispute over globes, telescopes, maps and books, points to the existence of other like-minded patronesses across the Continent. None eclipsed Figuelotte's sincerity.[74] At her side, winningly eager to share all her interests, Leibniz also encountered Caroline.

Contemporaries characterised Figuelotte as interested in 'the why of the why', omnivorous in her curiosity. She had inherited from her mother Sophia, from 1698 dowager electress of Hanover, a taste for disputatiousness, and her philosophical deliberations were conducted in person and by letter. Unsurprisingly she amassed an extensive music library. With Frederick she increased the collections of the library in Berlin's old City Palace.[75] She assembled an important picture collection.[76] She owned two theatres, one in Berlin, the other close to Lützenburg.[77] And in 1700 she facilitated the founding of a Brandenburg Academy of Sciences, with Leibniz as president. Frederick encouraged his wife's hobbyhorses while pursuing his own extensive building programme, aware that cultural pre-eminence among the courts of the Empire served his political aspirations well.

This symbiosis of divergent but sympathetic instincts on the parts of husband and wife was one Caroline would later have reason to remember. She too learned to relish 'the why of the why' and to value Leibniz's guidance; in time she laid out fashionable gardens, collected books and treatises, commissioned the building of a new library. Like her guardians, she would exploit visual iconography for dynastic ends. In Ansbach and Dresden, as well as in Berlin, artistic riches had been features of the shifting stage sets of her childhood. Real awareness began under Figuelotte's tutelage.

To date, Caroline's education had been patchy. Her immersion in Berlin's dynamic court life, with its combination of baroque spectacle and intellectual speculation, proved a watershed, reinforcing the cultural exposure she had been too young to absorb fully at John George's court. At Lützenburg, Figuelotte – and also her mother Sophia, a regular correspondent and occasional visitor – exemplified for the teenage princess the possibilities of life as princely spouse. Her experience of her Brandenburg guardians challenged Caroline's memories of Eleonore's suffering at the hands of John George, her helplessness and loneliness during the lean years at Crailsheim. In this surprising but benign environment, by turns extrovert, urbane and precious, the orphan princess was able to dispel misgivings about past, present and, especially, the future. For Caroline, Lützenburg provided stability, inspiration and a catalyst; it exposed her to female companionship at its most rewarding. When the time came, she would prove herself a consort in Figuelotte's mould. Like her mentor, she even took snuff.

On 7 June 1696, Duke Frederick II of Saxe-Gotha married Magdalena Augusta of Anhalt-Zerbst. The couple were first cousins and, in a markedly successful marriage, went on to have nineteen children, including Caroline's future daughter-in-law, Augusta.

A century after the event, Horace Walpole reported an over-familiar Duke of Grafton teasing Caroline that, as a young woman, she had fallen in love with Duke Frederick.[78] That Frederick's marriage took place when Caroline was thirteen and living with her mother in out-of-the-way Pretzsch seems grounds enough to query Walpole's claim. Instead the marriage of Frederick and his duchess illustrates the kind of union Caroline could reasonably have anticipated for herself.

Frederick was seven years older than Caroline. He had inherited his small duchy at the age of fifteen, and would devote a

long reign to territorial and financial advancement. His stepmother, Christine of Baden-Durlach, had previously married, as
his third wife, Caroline's Ansbach grandfather, Albert II. Among
Frederick's forebears was John Frederick of Saxony, a
Reformation hero who rebelled against the Catholicism of the
Holy Roman Emperor and for his pains forfeited his elector's
title.[79] In its ties of consanguinity, focus on localised concerns
and commitment to Protestantism, the marriage was typical of
those contracted among lesser German royalties throughout the
period. (The marriage of Caroline's half-sister Dorothea
Frederica to the heir to the tiny territory of Hanau-Lichtenberg
was another such, ditto her brother's marriage to Christiane
Charlotte of Württemberg-Winnental.) That Caroline's life
pursued a different trajectory was thanks to the sponsorship of
Frederick and Figuelotte.

She can never have doubted that a single choice – to marry
or not to marry – governed her future, a paucity of opportunity
not restricted to princesses. Furthermore, that her 'choice' in
the matter was circumscribed to an extreme degree. Too well
she understood the hazards of the world into which she had
been born. Spinsterhood was a fruitless existence for royal
women. Royal marriage was contractual, an arrangement based
on policy, unmarried princesses commodities in a calculation of
barter and exchange. Husbands took into account strategic
considerations; they expected generous dowries. Caroline knew
the modesty of her inheritance. Her only trump card – save
good looks, which other princesses shared – was the prestige of
her Brandenburg guardians, bound to her by honour but few
obligations.

Time would show, however, that Caroline was not her
mother. In 1692, destitute and miserable, Eleonore had allowed
herself to be coerced into marrying a man who offended her on
every level. She had exposed herself to humiliation, bullying
and even threats of murder in a court dominated by the septic

divisiveness of a possibly incestuous affair. When Caroline's turn came, she would prove less compliant.

Happily for us, circumstances propelled her beyond the reach of the Duke of Saxe-Gotha and his ilk. Frederick III's father, Frederick William, known as the Great Elector, had transformed the status of the Brandenburg electorate. A standing army, military victories, trading posts on Africa's Gold Coast, coffers swollen with revenues from new excise duties and a princely building programme had magnified Brandenburg's prestige and the newsworthiness of its court. Long before Frederick dreamt of his crown, his father had made claims that were altogether more swaggering for the north German state: an Alabastersaal in the palace in Berlin, furnished with twelve full-length statues of Hohenzollern electors confronting the likenesses, in ghostly marble, of a clutch of Roman emperors; a Porcelain Cabinet in the palace of Oranienburg, nodding to Dutch influences and aligning Brandenburg within an international trading network.[80] Figuelotte's peripatetic cadre of thinkers and musicians further broadcast the charms and achievements of Lützenburg; Frederick's stimulus to the manufacture of home-grown luxury goods including tapestry, lace and mirrors – much of it the work of Huguenot exiles – suggested affluence and sophistication. Brandenburg's lustre inevitably enhanced Caroline's marriageability. In addition, her presence in Berlin brought her to the attention of Figuelotte's redoubtable mother Sophia. It would prove a critical connection.

The septuagenarian Sophia was strong-willed, a gossip, ambitious for the fortunes of her princely house. As a child in Leiden in the 1630s, she had benefited from a rigorous educational programme devised by her father, the Elector Palatine. This training had reaped dividends. In 1670 the English writer and diplomat Edward Chamberlyne described Sophia as 'one of the most *accomplisht* Ladies in *Europe*', while thirty years later John Toland claimed 'she has long been admir'd by all the Learned

World, as a Woman of Incomparable Knowledge in Divinity, Philosophy, History, and the Subjects of all Sorts of Books, of which she has read a prodigious quantity. She speaks five Languages so well that by her Accent it might be a Dispute which of 'em was her first.'[81] Admittedly, the philosopher was a partisan commentator inclined to exaggerate his subject's prowess; but the sincerity of Sophia's engagement with the life of the mind, which in turn had shaped Figuelotte's upbringing, is beyond question. In those closest to her she esteemed strength of character and like-mindedness. Figuelotte's reports of her orphan protégée, made flesh during Sophia's visit to Berlin in 1704, piqued the older woman's curiosity and sowed the germ of an idea.

In the event, concerning rumours of a possible marriage for Caroline, Sophia met her match as gossip in Leibniz. Philosophical genius aside, Liebniz was a man of worldly inclinations. Liselotte described him as one of the rare 'learned men who are clean, do not stink and have a sense of humour'; it is hard to exonerate him from accusations of snobbery.[82] Silkily he ingratiated himself in high places, as one of his less philosophical letters – to Augustus the Strong's mistress, about a preventative for dysentery while travelling – testifies.[83] In surviving sources, it is Leibniz who first broke the news of a splendid match for Caroline, in a letter written in 1698 to Figuelotte's cousin Benedicta, Duchess of Brunswick-Lüneburg. The proposed alliance concerned Duchess Benedicta's nephew, Archduke Charles of Austria, the thirteen-year-old second son of the Holy Roman Emperor.[84]

Despite the incendiary quality of such a rumour, Caroline herself remained unaware of the scheme for five years. Her eventual enlightenment had a cloak-and-dagger quality. In the autumn of 1703 she received a breathless letter. By way of introduction, its clergyman-author claimed former acquaintance with her mother. The letter instructed Caroline to travel with all speed to Eleonore's younger sister, Fredericka Elisabeth, Duchess of Saxe-Weissenfels, in Duchess Fredericka's tinpot capital. 'Immediately after receiving this letter, go without the very slightest delay to the Duchess at Weissenfels, because of extremely important matters concerning your Serene Highness's greatest happiness, about which the Duchess will inform your Serene Highness.'[85] In 1703, in the life of an unmarried princess, a single eventuality merited the description 'greatest happiness': an offer of marriage. The letter was directed from Vienna. A second letter, arriving at the same time, informed her that waiting at Weissenfels would be a 'distinguished gentleman' anxious to meet her.

Caroline's reaction to these clandestine strategies included a measure of astonishment. Whether she chose to confide in Figuelotte or her brother William Frederick, who had recently succeeded his second stepbrother as margrave in Ansbach, is unclear. So is the extent, if any, to which Vienna's imperial court had communicated its intentions to Frederick as Caroline's guardian. That Caroline reached her own conclusion about events afoot appears inevitable. The Austrian emperor, Leopold I, had two sons, of whom the elder, Joseph, King of Hungary, was married already. On 24 February 1699 he had married Duchess Benedicta's daughter, Amalia Wilhelmine.

In Weissenfels, as if to emphasise to Caroline the honour of an imperial visit, Fredericka Elisabeth's spendthrift husband provided for the young Archduke Charles a 'generous and magnificent reception' costing 'tons of gold'. In September 1703, in accordance with an agreement brokered in 1699 by Louis XIV and England's William III as a contingency plan following the death of Spain's feeble-minded and childless Carlos II, Charles had been proclaimed King of Spain.[86] Although the War of the Spanish Succession would deny him his Spanish pretensions, his behaviour in the meantime indicated in full measure consciousness of his eminence. A later observer commended Charles's 'art of seeming well pleased with everything without so much as smiling once all the while'.[87] Leibniz labelled him 'an amiable prince', but he can scarcely have been an easy guest.[88] It says much for the charms of the twenty-year-old Caroline that Charles's aide-de-camp was able to assure her by letter that, after five hours in her company, their 'most happy and delightful meeting had filled [the Archduke] with the liveliest admiration'.[89] On 1 October, anticipating Caroline's return from her brother's court at Ansbach, Figuelotte described recent improvements in her looks as likely to attract a suitor.[90]

In the language of the time, this sort of lively admiration amounted to a decided expression of interest, albeit not a formal proposal. By a circuitous route, Charles set off from Weissenfels to claim his crown in Spain. His aide-de-camp informed Caroline of his progress and the golden opinions he won along the way, including at Queen Anne's court at Windsor and in Lisbon, where, in honour of a new alliance, the Portuguese king, Pedro II, outdid himself in the splendour of his ceremonial welcome; Anne commissioned his portrait from Godfrey Kneller.[91] For six months, these long-distance tweets proved Caroline's only update on the 'extremely important matters concerning [her] greatest happiness'. The question was out of Charles's hands. In Vienna, the thoughts of the imperial court centred less on Charles's admiration and Caroline's charms of mind and body than on the issue of the princess's religion.

Once, it was rumoured, Eleonore had considered conversion to Catholicism in order to marry Maximilian II of Bavaria. Now, for an infinitely greater marriage prize, Caroline's change of faith would become the sine qua non. Insistence on such a condition cannot have come as a surprise to any of the key players in this unromantic drama. Nor did any doubt Caroline's acceptance of this inevitable and overriding preliminary.

She had inherited from Eleonore, Stepney's 'princess of great virtue and piety', a sturdy Lutheranism remote from Habsburg

Catholicism. By 1703, time had tempered her unhappy mother's influence. In exchanging the dower house at Pretzsch for the palaces of Berlin and Lützenburg, Caroline found herself in an environment in which religious faith, alongside philosophy and metaphysics, formed one strand of a continuous dialogue about the nature and governance of the universe. Sophia of Hanover, one clergyman claimed, 'multiplied' questions, one leading to another: no single answer satisfied her, and she failed to convince herself of any conclusion.[92] This habit of intellectual restlessness her daughter Figuelotte shared. While religion for Eleonore had been a narrow matter of faith, Sophia's approach was discursive and, above all, pragmatic. She had delayed Figuelotte's confirmation until after her sixteenth birthday, in order to widen her marriage prospects to embrace Catholic as well as Protestant suitors. As an adult, Figuelotte disclaimed any attachment to dogma. Debate at Lützenburg centred on what she described as her 'curiosity about the origin of things', her desire 'to understand space, infinity, being and nothingness':[93] a continuous creedless disquisition about ethics, free choice, love and the soul, through which Figuelotte set out to emphasise reason over superstition and relished verbal or epistolary skirmishes for their own sake. But no one forgot that the setting for these skirmishes was the palace bestowed on Figuelotte by an indulgent husband. Hers were the freedoms of a married woman.

From Weissenfels, Caroline had returned to Berlin. She could not avoid informing Frederick as well as Figuelotte of what had taken place. From now on Vienna would communicate with Frederick directly, albeit intermittently. Ever alert to worldly advantage, Frederick described the meeting between Caroline and the archduke as 'God's providence'.[94] Nevertheless, the wheels of Habsburg statecraft revolved slowly. To her brother, the Elector Palatine, the emperor's wife entrusted supervision of the process by which Caroline's eligibility for marriage could be accomplished. Without Caroline's conversion there could be no formal proposal. Six months after her single meeting with Archduke Charles, the Elector Palatine requested that Caroline return to Weissenfels. His purpose was to apprise for himself this future imperial bride and compile a report for the empress.

To Caroline, a portionless princess, the imperial court offered no incentive bar the incontrovertible lure of a Habsburg prince. Distant were the glory days of the Empire, when Austria had defended Christian Europe against the Turkish infidel; but still an aureole of greatness clung to the imperial family. Austria's sons represented the greatest prize in the marriage market of the German-speaking world. After she had endured a six-month virtual silence, Caroline's reaction was moderate to the point of obstinacy. She resented the requirement to return to Weissenfels, and retraced her steps with an ill grace. Having done so, she lingered at her aunt's court for almost two months, awaiting the absent elector, before ignoring Frederick's protests and journeying back to Lützenburg late in August. Tardily the Elector Palatine recognised the mettle of the young woman with whom he was dealing. His departure from Vienna was days too late. Instead he sent after Caroline his Jesuit confessor, Father Ferdinand Orban, with the request that she '[be] completely persuaded that what he will lay before your noble incomparable self ... is the pure, undefiled, genuine, holy truth'.[95]

Until now Caroline's exposure to Catholicism had been scant. In 1685 the Great Elector had passed the Edict of Potsdam, offering protection in Brandenburg to French Protestants in the aftermath of Louis XIV's revocation of the Edict of Nantes. Since 1701, and the religious conversion of her improvident third son Maximilian, Sophia of Hanover had nurtured a vitriolic hatred of Jesuits, which she certainly communicated to Figuelotte. The Lutheran orphan Caroline found herself living with Calvinist guardians in a state that was tangibly and proudly Protestant. 'I feel assured that your Highness ... will ... accord [Father Orban] a patient hearing and then your fullest approval,' the Elector Palatine wrote to her.[96] It was an optimistic statement and one that, despite its measure of coercion, acknowledged likely obstacles.[97]

As summer turned to autumn, Frederick found himself on the horns of a dilemma. From an alliance with the imperial family he anticipated considerable boon; as his protests in the early 1690s against the proposed creation of a Catholic tenth electorate for 'a prince of the house of Austria' indicate, his was a Protestant outlook.[98] That he anticipated the probability of Caroline's resistance to apostasy, even in the face of arguments of powerful material persuasion, points both to aspects of Caroline's character and the strength of her religious convictions. Frederick did not resort to sophism. There is a cynical truthfulness in his appeal to her that includes, as she understood, a reminder of what she owed to him and his guardianship. 'For your part you may be able to exercise a moderating influence,' he told her, 'not to mention the advantages therefrom that might accrue to our royal and princely house. I do not very well see how your Highness can decline such an offer, since it is to be hoped that you will be so firmly established in your religion that no one need feel anxious about your soul.'[99]

For an instant, Caroline was persuaded. She yielded. To the Elector Palatine, who had sent her Father Orban, she wrote that she had perceived the errors of her Lutheranism.[100] To the authorities in Vienna, the Austrian resident in Berlin reported that she 'had already changed and was resolved to marry the King of Spain'.[101] And Caroline agreed to a second proposed meeting with the Elector Palatine, this time in Düsseldorf.

The optimism of princess and imperial diplomat was ill-founded. Caroline's meeting with the Elector Palatine never happened. Her confession of the errors of her faith masked considerable unease. Her discussions with Father Orban, attended by Leibniz, consisted of arguments 'at length' over an open Bible. Point-scoring oscillated between priest and princess, but the contest was unequal and the strain unsettled Caroline. 'Of course, the Jesuit, who has studied more, argues her down, and then the Princess weeps,' the electress Sophia explained to a niece.[102] Afterwards Caroline told Leibniz, 'I really think his persuasions contributed materially to the uncertainty I felt.'[103] The result of their discourse was anything but the 'fullest approval' for which the Elector Palatine had hoped. Orban's smooth coaxing made Caroline miserable, and reinforced all of her objections. Nevertheless, in the midst of her turmoil, mistaking the way the wind was blowing, on 25 October Leibniz claimed 'everyone predicts the Spanish crown for her'.[104]

Those more finely attuned to Caroline's state of mind saw that the matter remained unresolved. In the same week, during a visit to Figuelotte at Lützenburg, Sophia noted Caroline's vacillation: 'Our beautiful Princess of Ansbach has not yet resolved to change her religion.'[105] A fortnight later, she added, 'Sometimes the dear princess says "Yes," and sometimes she says "No"; sometimes she believes we [Protestants] have no priests, sometimes that Catholics are idolatrous and accursed; sometimes she says our religion may be the better. What the result will be ... I still do not know.'[106] Unnecessarily, Sophia explained that, as long as Caroline remained firm, 'the marriage will not take place'.[107] On 1 November Figuelotte noted that Caroline was 'still uncertain which course she will take'.[108]

In the circumstances, the doggedness of Caroline's indecision is remarkable. Prior to her 'adoption' by Frederick and Figuelotte, her prospects had been limited, as she understood, and as the insignificance of her stepsister Dorothea Frederica's match proved. In Brandenburg she had received an education and promotion beyond aspirations that she could have nurtured either at Pretzsch or, like Dorothea Frederica, fatherless in Ansbach. The result was an offer of marital jackpot, the hand of Prince Charming for this provincial Cinderella. 'Neither shall I dwell upon her high birth and station any longer than to observe, that she seems to be the only person ignorant of that superiority. She has never been heard to give the most remote hint of it,' a satirist wrote of Caroline, with vituperative irony, in 1737.[109] Whatever the truth of Caroline's self-importance at the end of her life, in the autumn of 1704 she could have been under no illusions that it was the archduke, not she, who conferred the favour in any proposed connection between them. Up to a point religious scruples and a wish to retain spiritual autonomy weighed as heavily as worldlier ambitions. Even if she was aware of contemporary views of Vienna as a region 'where mirth and the muses are quite forgott [sic]', she cannot have been anything but torn, this child of high-ranking penury alert to the frustrations of a princess's life without position or means.[110]

She found herself surprisingly alone. She knew Frederick's mind; less clear were Figuelotte's thoughts, at first apparently concealed from her. In June, Figuelotte had explained to the Hanoverian diplomat Hans Caspar von Bothmer her belief that Caroline's likelihood of marrying Charles depended on an improvement in Charles's fortunes in Spain. In September she confided to him in secret her conviction that the marriage was imminent, and stoically she resolved to enjoy Caroline's company while she could.[111] She consoled herself that princess and archduke shared a love of music: 'The Princess of Ansbach sings well. She acquits herself wonderfully [as a singer] and this will be very convenient, as the King of Spain is a skilled accompanist on the harpsichord.'[112] Possibly the older woman cherished hopes of marrying Caroline to her own son Frederick William. If so, she kept her own counsel.

Sophia's attitude was less ambiguous. She had already convinced herself of the suitability of her daughter's ward for her grandson, George Augustus, and had discussed this conviction with Figuelotte.[113] This being so, Caroline too may have been aware of the direction of Sophia's thoughts. In this case, she possessed solid grounds for refusing Charles, since she could assume the likelihood of another proposal, namely George Augustus's. Sophia, however, hardly dared to hope. 'If I had my way, she would not be worried like this, and our court would be happy,' she wrote on 27 October, 'but it seems that it is not God's will that I should be happy with her; we at Hanover shall hardly find anyone better.'[114] Meanwhile, in Ansbach, William Frederick's minister von Voit encouraged Caroline to accept Vienna's offer. Powerful tugs in opposing directions did little to mitigate her difficult decision.

Her willingness to convert, communicated to the Elector Palatine in good faith, unravelled over the course of the autumn. Anticipating opposition, in November Caroline announced to her guardians her inability to change her faith. To her surprise, Frederick commended her right-thinking in avoiding becoming the first Catholic princess in his family; Figuelotte encouraged her resolve, which Leibniz was instructed to convey in writing to Vienna.[115] For the Austrians, there could be no such comfortable reflections as Frederick's. On 4 November, Thomas Wentworth, Lord Raby, reported to Robert Harley in London the concerns of the imperial resident in Berlin about Caroline's new determination to remain Protestant.[116] A week later, Raby confirmed that Vienna's anxiety had given way to anger.[117]

Harried, bruised, a victim of nervous exhaustion but at last convinced of the conclusion she had reached, at the end of November Caroline withdrew to her brother's court at Ansbach to recover and temporarily escape observation.[118] Letters from Father Orban, the Elector Palatine and leading Habsburg courtiers followed her; each one bolstered her certainty. By contrast, Leibniz informed her that an admiring Duke Anton Ulrich of neighbouring Brunswick-Wolfenbüttel intended to include her in a romantic novel. A member of the Fructiferous Order of German literary enthusiasts as well as a reigning princeling, the ageing duke wrote poetry, oratorios and melodramatic novels of extraordinary length. As good as his word, he included passages inspired by Caroline's recent history in his doorstopper, *Octavia, a Roman Story*.

A year after their only meeting, Caroline stated her belief 'that the king of Spain no longer troubles himself about me'.[119] From Protestant Hanover, Sophia wrote to Leibniz, 'Most people here applaud the Princess of Ansbach's decision.'[120] In a letter to Bothmer, her response was delighted, her language high-falutin. 'I left Lützenburg last Monday,' she wrote, 'after witnessing a great fight in the spirit of the beautiful princess. God's love finally got the upper hand and she has scorned worldly grandeur and a prince she valued highly, in order to do nothing against her conscience, which might cause her what she describes as eternal anxiety.'[121] For reasons of her own, Sophia exaggerated. She may have been swayed by a letter in praise of Caroline's principles which she received in November from her eldest son, the elector George Louis.[122]

Caroline's own feelings, although she described herself in December as 'perfectly recovered', lacked euphoria.[123] To Leibniz, she was studiedly emollient. '[I] am glad to think that I still retain your friendship and your remembrance,' she wrote. Her references to Figuelotte and Sophia were appropriately respectful.[124] In truth she need not have worried about either. As long ago as November 1703 Figuelotte had described her as one who 'understands with good reason her own quality'.[125] Sophia too had taken the measure of that quality. She considered Caroline 'a beautiful princess of great merit'.[126]

Caroline was not in love with Figuelotte's son Frederick William. At seventeen that furious firebrand, whose upbringing she had partly shared, remained recognisably the young boy given to kicking and hair-tugging and bullying servants. In the estimation of his daughter Wilhelmina, Frederick William's temper as an adult was 'lively and hot'; he was 'suspicious, jealous and frequently guilty of dissimulation'; 'his governor had sedulously inspired him with contempt for the female sex'.[127] In spirit, and despite Figuelotte's doting, Frederick William was not the child of Lützenburg. Determinedly unlovable, he does not emerge from the sources as the grounds for Caroline declining the suit of Archduke Charles – either to gratify Figuelotte's hopes, of which she was presumably aware, or, as British diplomatic correspondence in the spring of 1705 suggests, Frederick William's own wish to marry Caroline and a similar hope on the part of her brother in Ansbach.[128] Nor is there reliable evidence that Caroline had already directed her thoughts towards the man she subsequently married, Sophia's grandson George Augustus, Hanoverian elector-in-waiting, or that Frederick offered her guidance in his role as guardian, despite his tendency to '[take] upon himself to such an extent to command her to do this, that and the other'.[129] Instead Frederick occupied himself elsewhere. Denied one august connection by Caroline's intractability, he set about planning another, a marriage between Frederick William and a sister of the King of Sweden. It was not to be, but in February 1705 diplomats reported that Frederick was sufficiently engaged with his plotting to be fully restored to good humour.[130] It proved of short duration.

Vienna's second choice fell on a princess renowned for her beauty, Elisabeth-Christine of Brunswick-Wolfenbüttel, the granddaughter of the same Duke Anton Ulrich who, in cumbersome prose, fictionalised the heroism of Caroline's sacrifice. Like Caroline the sixteen-year-old boasted a profusion of blonde hair, pale skin and what contemporaries regarded as perfectly formed arms and hands; she was 'God-fearing and graceful to all'.[131] Again the Archduke Charles was all admiration: theirs would be a genuinely loving marriage. Even in middle age, reduced by quack fertility remedies to an obese alcoholic scarcely able to shuffle unaided from chair to chair, her pale skin flushed an ugly red, her lovely arms pendulous with fat, Elisabeth-Christine would remain in Charles's eyes his *'weisse Liesl'* ('white Lizzy').

Her suit was vigorously promoted by Duke Anton Ulrich. Praise for Caroline's resolution notwithstanding, the ambitious duke made no concessions to his granddaughter's religious sensibilities. Like Caroline, Elisabeth-Christine had been brought up Lutheran. Like Caroline, she felt no inclination to convert to Catholicism. Ultimately she attributed her change of religion to family pressure: 'I feel obliged to follow the divine direction and worthy opinion of my highly honoured grandfather graciously in all things.'[132] Leibniz reassured her that salvation took no account of liturgical differences: neither Protestants nor Catholics could claim a monopoly, and in changing her faith she in no wise jeopardised her eternal prospects.

First her family set about her apostasy. Afterwards the empress, her future mother-in-law, played her part. Like Caroline in her early dealings with the Elector Palatine, Elisabeth-Christine appears to have done her best to satisfy expectations. She accompanied the empress on a pilgrimage to the statue of the Virgin Mary at Mariazell in 1706; a year later she was deemed ready for conversion. Her scruples had survived almost three years, and, as in Caroline's case, the outcome during that period was at intervals sufficiently in doubt to form a subject of conjecture across the Continent. The marriage of archduke and princess was finally solemnised in 1708, a decade after first rumours of Caroline's candidacy. In London, the Archbishop of Canterbury Thomas Tenison received a letter informing him of Elisabeth-Christine's conversion and subsequent marriage as late as July of that year.[133] Three years later, following the death of Charles's elder brother Joseph I, the Princess of Brunswick-Wolfenbüttel, zealous in her new faith, found herself Holy Roman Empress. In the short term she was also 'the most Beautifull Queen upon Earth', with the added satisfaction, since 1710, of the late-in-life conversion of her 'highly honoured grandfather', Anton Ulrich.[134]

The former accolade might have belonged to Caroline. It was not an omission she regretted; indeed she would exploit it skilfully. Over time her refusal to exchange Protestantism for Catholicism – described after her death as 'an early proof of her steady adherence to the Protestant cause' – became a key aspect of Caroline's identity and achievement.[135] Four days after the coronation of her father-in-law as George I of Great Britain, on 24 October 1714, Joseph Acres reminded his parishioners in the church of St Mary in Whitechapel, 'What a rare thing for a young Lady that has been bred up in the Softness of a Court, to decline the Pomp and Glory of the World.'[136] Caroline's upbringing had contained little of 'softness', and 'the pomp and glory' she rejected in 1704 was not the imperial crown that the Archduke Charles, as a younger son, did not then expect to inherit. Undoubtedly her decision contained its measure of religious unease. Her reservations were perhaps no more acute than those first experienced by Elisabeth-Christine of Brunswick-Wolfenbüttel. But while the latter succumbed to family pressure, Caroline, lacking parents or grandparents – and perhaps aware of likely overtures from a different quarter – resisted. As a later British encomium had it, she 'chose rather to wait with a safe Conscience, in the Exercise of the true Protestant Faith, for any remote Rewards of her Merit and Vertue, than to accept the Imperial Dignity, when it must be connected with a false and idolatrous Worship'.[137]

'He is very impertinent to suppose that I, who refus'd to be Empress for the Sake of the Protestant Religion, don't understand it fully,' Caroline later remarked when a well-meaning Bishop of London offered to 'satisfy her in any Doubts or Scruples she might have in regard to our Religion, or to explain Anything to her which she did not comprehend'.[138] Her lady-in-waiting described her on the occasion as 'a little nettled'.

For the remainder of her life Caroline took pride in her renunciation, her determination to 'slight th'Imperial Diadem'.[139] To Leibniz, as late as November 1715, she wrote, 'You know that I am not at all a Jesuit,' a reminder of her hard-fought sacrifice.[140] The vehemence of her feelings indicates the trouble it had cost her – and a certain shrewdness in her estimate of the value of her resistance that transcended Duke Anton Ulrich's elaborate fictions.

Electoral Princess

'The affections of the heart'

Caroline was wooed by a prince in disguise and in a hurry, Figuelotte's nephew George Augustus, Electoral Prince of Hanover.

His departure for Ansbach – at midnight, under cloak of darkness – suggests romance, even derring-do. He was short in stature, vain, with pale bulbous eyes, fine hair of an indeterminate colour and a peppery self-importance – or, in Toland's characteristically rosier assessment, of 'a winning countenance, speaks gracefully, for his Years a great Master of History, a generous disposition and virtuous inclinations'.[1] Unlike his intended bride he was fascinated by ghosts and werewolves, his religious outlook 'without scruples, zeal or inquiry'.[2]

It was the first week of June 1705. George Augustus travelled in the garb of a Hanoverian nobleman and called himself 'von dem Bussche'. His former tutor, Baron Philipp Adam von Eltz, a Hanoverian privy councillor, accompanied him under the alias 'Steding'. With a single manservant, they directed their tracks southwards to Ansbach. There they presented themselves at the margrave's court as travellers en route for Nuremburg. Only the elector George Louis knew their true destination and purpose. Afraid of the reaction of Frederick in Berlin, he insisted that both remain secret.

The prince was twenty-one, eight months younger than Caroline. From his grandmother, the dowager electress Sophia, and his aunt Figuelotte he had heard her charms itemised and magnified. For the better part of a decade his father had pursued fruitless negotiations with Charles XII of Sweden. His initial purpose had been to win for George Augustus the hand of the king's stubborn, musical younger sister, Ulrike Eleonore. Following a switch of tactic in 1702, he had targeted Charles's elder sister, Hedwig Sophie, recently widowed. In December Figuelotte wrote that the marriage was settled.[3] She was mistaken. In both cases George Louis's tenacity went unrewarded, and in February 1705 he had begun to look elsewhere for his son's bride, with no apparent regret on George Augustus's part.

Caroline's blonde voluptuousness was quite to contemporary German tastes. Her natural good looks made a pretty contrast to the 'rosy cheeks, snowy Foreheads and bosoms, jet Eyebrows, … scarlet lips … [and] Coal black Hair' that, with crude cosmetic help, were universal among the 'beauties' of George Louis's court.[4] Her connection to Prussia's newly royal Hohenzollerns had its value too. During the spring of 1705 the English envoy in Berlin repeatedly reported a rumour that Frederick's family intended to reclaim their ward for themselves: the prince royal, Frederick William, wanted her for his wife.[5] In Hanover the electoral family reacted with stealth and belated alacrity. 'There is in this court a real desire of marrying the prince very soon,' wrote Sir Edmund Poley.[6] Thwarted by the secrecy of George Augustus's midnight flit – 'a mystery of which I know nothing' – Poley correctly hazarded the amorous purpose of his journey. The prince's attentions, he offered, would be directed at one of three likely candidates: princesses of Hesse-Cassel and Saxe-Zeitz, and 'the Princess of Ansbach'.[7]

While Poley puzzled, George Louis's plans progressed apace. Confident in his disguise, the mysterious von dem Bussche enjoyed a conversation alone with Caroline at her brother's summer palace at Triesdorf. To what extent he hoodwinked Caroline, with her 'ready and quick Apprehension, [and] lively and strong Imagination', not to mention her familiarity with both his aunt and his grandmother, remains uncertain.[8] To his father, George Augustus reported the result as love at first sight: 'he would not think of anybody else'.[9] It was an outcome shaped less decisively by Caroline's 'uncommon turn for conversation, assisted by a natural vivacity, and very peculiar talents for mirth and humour' than her considerable physical attractions, described by one historian as 'a bosom of exemplary magnitude … encased in the fairest and pinkest of skins'.[10] As he wrote to Caroline herself, 'I found that all I had heard about your charms did not nearly equal what I saw.'[11] Job done, he returned with von Eltz post haste to Hanover.

There, discussions with George Louis lasted two hours and left the dour and fractious elector in uncommonly good humour. All that remained was for von Eltz to retrace his steps to Ansbach and, following to the letter George Louis's careful instructions, prosecute the prince's suit first with Caroline and afterwards with her brother. A single injunction dominated von Eltz's orders: that he 'guard in every way against the Princess having any kind of communication with the Court of Berlin until such time as this project of marriage is so far established as to prevent any possibility of its being upset'.[12] Fixed in his purpose, the elector did not intend his Prussian brother-in-law to thwart him.

Darkness, disguises and the utmost discretion were no shield against the compulsive gossip of courtiers and diplomats. As George Louis had predicted, speculation reached its most intense in Berlin, Caroline's home until the previous winter. From there, Lord Raby wrote to George Stepney on 5 July, 'Some are uneasy at this Court at the late journey incognito of the prince Electoral of Hanover.' Again, Raby reported, many cited the

Princess of Hesse-Cassel as George Augustus's object. Her brother had married Frederick's daughter Louise Dorothea, and 'they can't help being jealous of so audacious an allegiance for the House of Luenburg [sic]'. Others came closer to the mark. They 'say that the prince was at Ansbach to see that princess who refused last year to Change her Religion to have the King of Spain Charles the 3rd'.[13] Already, her resistance to apostasy defined Caroline. For good measure Raby enclosed a description of Figuelotte's funeral. Catching up from behind, belatedly Poley described Caroline as the 'most agreeable Princess in Germany'.[14]

What neither Raby nor Berlin's gossipmongers realised was that, two weeks before Raby's letter, both Caroline and her brother William Frederick had accepted a highly secret formal proposal of marriage on the part of George Augustus. Vienna, too, remained misguidedly optimistic. On 24 June, more than six months after Leibniz composed Caroline's written refusal, an imperial emissary requested a meeting of members of the courts of Vienna and Ansbach 'to make a final representation on behalf of the King of Spain'. To add ballast to his request, he wrote on the joint instructions of the Elector Palatine and the emperor.[15]

By the end of July the marriage contract had been signed. By early September, Wilhelmine Karoline, acclaimed in the formal documentation as 'Princess of Brandenburg in Prussia, of Magdeburg, Stettin and Pomerania, of Casuben and Wenden, Duchess of Crossen in Silesia, Electress of Nuremburg, Princess of Halberstadt, Minden and Cannin and Countess of Hohenzollern', had exchanged Ansbach for Hanover, and the uncertainty of spinsterhood for marriage to the Electoral Prince of Brunswick-Lüneburg. Generous within his means, her brother bestowed on her a dowry equivalent to around £4,000 and a trousseau that included 'a splendid outfit of jewels', items of silver and, inevitably, clothes; her later claim of having come to George Augustus 'naked' was a conventional enough exaggeration.[16] George Louis assigned to Caroline the castle of Herzberg as her dower house in the event of George Augustus's death, and a guarantee of 14,000 thalers for her widowhood.[17]

Neither Frederick in Berlin nor Sophia in Hanover had been aware of the first parries of this lightning matchmaking. Predictably, their reactions were at odds. Confirmation of the forthcoming marriage was general knowledge by late July; Frederick's 'dissatisfaction' and 'ill humour', directed at the court of Ansbach as well as that of Hanover, persisted through-out August and beyond.[18] With arch disingenuousness and in words that mimicked his own, Sophia told Poley, 'the Princess of Ansbach hath always been talked of at this court as the most agreeable Princess in Germany'. Less truthfully, given George Louis's behind-the-scenes role as puppet-master and her own contribution in focusing attention on Caroline in the first place – as early as November 1704 she reported conversations with George Augustus, and 'in talking with him about her [Caroline], he said, "I am very glad that you desire her for me"' – she added that 'the Elector had left the Prince entirely to his own choice'.[19] In the long term such fine points of equivocation proved of no importance. It suited George Augustus's preening nature to believe that ultimate credit for his 'discovery' was his own. At least Sophia did not dissemble her pleasure. Without sparing Frederick's irritation, she told him, 'I have never made a secret of loving the Princess from the moment I set eyes on her, or of desiring her for one of my grandsons.'[20] Letters from Liselotte at Versailles confirmed Caroline's exemplary reputation and ignored Frederick's wounded *amour propre*: 'A great many people here have seen the Princess of Ansbach, and they are full of praise. I hope the marriage will be a happy one … It is very lucky when such a marriage gives everyone pleasure: it is not often the case.'[21]

* * *

Frederick's fulminating was a risk George Louis was prepared to take. For Frederick, who had lived in close proximity to Caroline for almost a decade, the princess previously singled out by the emperor's younger son and forged in Figuelotte's image promised advantages to his newly royal dynasty as well as to Brandenburg-Prussia at large. In Hanover, however, the electoral family had more specific and more pressing reasons for courting Caroline.

In 1701, at an age when many of her contemporaries were dead, the dowager electress Sophia had experienced an upturn in her fortunes. With uncharacteristic but deliberate extravagance, she had welcomed to Hanover an English embassy led by the Earl of Macclesfield in mid-August that year. Its purpose was to present her with a copy of recent legislation passed by Parliament in Westminster and, on William III's behalf, to invest George Louis with England's highest order of chivalry, the Order of the Garter.

This was more than ordinary diplomatic flummery. In the Act of Settlement of June 1701, Hanover's electoral family were named as heirs to the thrones of England and Scotland in the event of the death without issue of the current heir, Princess Anne, younger daughter of the deposed James II. First in line was Sophia herself. After her, in the Act's key wording, came 'the heirs of her body, being Protestants': George Louis, then George Augustus.

This was not unexpected. William III had applied pressure to Parliament to pass a similar resolution as early as 1689. England's Dutch king was well disposed towards Sophia. His friendship with the 'good old duke', her brother-in-law George William of Celle, was warm and of long standing, and he had been impressed by George Augustus after meeting him at George William's court in October 1698. For all that, the Act's implications were momentous. Hanover in 1701 was a region of limited international profile and territorially insignificant, mostly confined between the North Sea and the Harz Mountains and bounded by the Elbe and Weser rivers. It had been granted electorate status only within the last decade. Months earlier, it had been outflanked by the promotion of neighbouring Brandenburg, now effectively the Kingdom of Prussia, a piece of political leap-frogging decried by Sophia as 'the fashion for Electors to become Kings'.[22] In return for Protestantism, however, the Act of Settlement offered Hanover's ruling family promotion to sovereigns of one of Europe's oldest kingdoms, shortly to be formally 'united' by the 1707 Act of Union between England and Scotland. That the bride of George Augustus, now fourth in line to the British throne, should already have proven so convincingly her Protestant mettle 'and in all her words and actions … declared herself to be on the most reasonable conviction, a sincere Christian, a zealous Protestant' was an obvious recommendation in the aftermath of this seismic adjustment.[23]

The significance of Caroline's stand was increased by the nature of Sophia's claim. Like England's current heir Anne, Sophia was a granddaughter of James VI and I. She was the twelfth of the thirteen children of James's eldest daughter Elizabeth, by her marriage Electress Palatinate and, briefly, Queen of Bohemia. Anne's happy marriage to Prince George of Denmark had resulted in seventeen pregnancies but only a single child who survived infancy, William, Duke of Gloucester. He in turn died on 30 July 1700, aged just eleven, of acute bacterial infection exacerbated by pneumonia and water on the brain.[24]

But his death did not make Sophia Anne's closest heir. The second marriage of Anne's father had produced a son, James Edward Stuart, who as a result of James's religious conversion in the 1670s was a Catholic. In 1688, Catholicism had accounted for James's own loss of his throne. Apparently in accordance with the will of the people, certainly in accordance with the will of sections of parliamentary opinion, James was replaced that year as England's sovereign by his elder daughter from his first marriage, Mary, and Mary's husband, the Dutch prince William of Orange, both of them Protestants, Mary devoutly so. Parliament's Bill of Rights, passed the following year, sought to legitimise this dynastic shuffle, the so-called Glorious Revolution. The Bill formally excluded Catholics from the succession in perpetuity, and damned government by any 'papist prince' as 'inconsistent with the safety and welfare of this protestant kingdom'. It was by this means that James Edward Stuart, brought up in exile on the generosity of Louis XIV of France, was stripped of his right to the throne. By the same means, more than fifty cousins and family members who were more closely related to Anne than Sophia, but who were Catholics or married to Catholics, including descendants of Sophia's elder brothers and of Charles I's daughter Henrietta, also forfeited their claims. Sophia's 'legitimacy' as England's heir stemmed from the rejection by Members of Parliament of the principle of hereditary succession. It was grounded in religious intolerance.

Her understanding of the contentious nature of her candidacy and its potential for divisiveness prompted Sophia's commission of a commemorative medal, the 'Mathilde medal', ahead of Macclesfield's embassy. Its two sides bore a profile of Sophia herself and, in a markedly similar portrait on the reverse, an English princess called Mathilde, the daughter of Henry II and Eleanor of Aquitaine. In 1156 Mathilde had married George Louis's most warrior-like forebear, Henry the Lion, Duke of Saxony and Bavaria. More than Sophia's Protestantism, the Mathilde medal celebrated former glories and the Hanoverians' specifically 'English' descent. It was among Sophia's gifts to the suite that accompanied Lord Macclesfield in the summer of 1701. The earl himself received a gold basin and ewer that had cost his hostess half her annual income, while to William III Sophia wrote tactfully, 'we await [the] event without impatience here, and pray with all our hearts "God save the King"'.[25] Periodically she took care to deny any personal desire to occupy

England's throne, a politic deceit on the part of this ambitious princess who, despite her age, was not above opportunism. Piously she wrote to Archbishop Tenison, 'I live in quiet and contentment, and have no reason for desiring a change.'[26]

Little wonder, then, that her thoughts should have turned to Caroline as a wife for George Augustus. Whatever sleight of hand was employed to convince this strutting, eager prince that the selection of Caroline for his future consort was his own, his grandmother as well as his father had reached the same conclusion ahead of him. Caroline's desirability in George Augustus's eyes was almost certainly sharpened by the interest she excited in Charles of Austria and his own younger cousin Frederick William. He also anticipated increased standing and greater autonomy at his father's court as a result of his marriage. For Sophia and George Louis, other princes' partiality mattered not a jot. Caroline's commitment to Protestantism was a powerful weapon in the dynasty's British aspirations, and an essential counterweight to family crisis.

In 1658, Sophia's own marriage contract had included a clause permitting her, in Lutheran Hanover, to continue to practise the Calvinism of her upbringing. This concession was made at her father's request rather than her own, and she did not value it highly. Later she had shown pragmatism – calculation too – in the matter of Figuelotte's faith, placing her daughter's marriageability above doctrinal allegiance. With Leibniz as her sounding block, she had since entertained herself with philosophical rather than specifically religious discourse, and read a number of key texts, including Boethius's *The Consolation of Philosophy*.[27] She was aware of Leibniz's attempts in the early 1690s to win support for a reunion of Catholic and Protestant Churches in the electorate and, equally, was not opposed to the initiative.[28] And she approved her husband's acquiescence in a plan for building a Catholic church in Hanover, as a means of wooing the good opinion of the emperor.[29]

This easy-going position inevitably changed following the Act of Settlement. There were other factors too that contributed to a religious stance on Sophia's part that appeared (although in fact it may not have been) increasingly hardline. The conversion to Catholicism of her son Maximilian in 1701 explained aspects of the permanent rupture in their relationship; until his death at the battle of Munderkingen in 1703 she was troubled by the possibility of her fifth son, Christian, following in Maximilian's footsteps. Happily George Louis's plodding Lutheranism permitted no grounds for concern. Caroline had demonstrated that she was likewise sound in her allegiances. Recent events appeared to indicate that she would buttress George Augustus's faith, an essential prerequisite since the 1701 Act. For, if George Augustus failed to provide the dynasty with Protestant heirs, the family's claims to the English crown evaporated. With Maximilian a Catholic and Sophia's youngest son, Ernest Augustus, almost certainly homosexual, the long-term position of the electoral family was scarcely less precarious than that of the Stuarts they meant to displace.

Meanwhile, the year after Macclesfield's official presentation, the English envoy extraordinary in Hanover, James Cresset, wrote to the Archbishop of Canterbury requesting the loan of communion plate, 'a dozen or two' prayerbooks and a Bible. He meant to set up a chapel in his house in Hanover and make it available to leading dignitaries. He explained his aim to Tenison as a means of 'inspir[ing] in the Court esteem for the Established Church'.[30] The archbishop, however, although he referred to himself disparagingly as 'an uncourtlie, but well intention'd, old man',[31] was already in regular communication with Hanover's court, via Sophia, and would take his own measures to convince the new heiress of the importance of religious conformity. Sophia responded in kind. On 16 August 1701 she had written to Tenison to express thanks for his support, and that of his fellow bishops in the House of Lords, for the Act of Settlement.[32]

In letters to Tenison written in French, she labelled herself with statesmanlike nicety *'votre tres affectionée amie'*. Whatever Cresset's misgivings, Sophia understood clearly that Protestant orthodoxy was paramount among her claims on England. It was a conviction she was assiduous in broadcasting, and one she did her best to impress upon her family. Evidence like Giuseppe Pignata's dedication to George Louis, in June 1704, of his anti-Catholic *Adventures with the Inquisition* suggests she succeeded.[33]

The lapse of almost a year between Caroline's rejection of Charles's suit and her marriage to George Augustus was attributable to several causes, including George Louis's reluctance to antagonise the emperor. Equally important was the death, on 1 February 1705, of Figuelotte.

Figuelotte was thirty-seven. She died of pneumonia on the journey from Berlin to Hanover, and her sudden loss inspired near-universal regret. For five days and nights a grief-stricken George Louis immured himself in his rooms, refusing to eat, kicking the walls in his misery, talking to and seeing no one; 'by hitting his Toes against the Wainscot … he had worn out his Shoes till his Toes came out two Inches at the Foot'.[34] Rumour – lurid but unsubstantiated – suggested an alternative cause of Figuelotte's death: that she had 'been poisoned, before she left Berlin, with Diamond Powder, for when [her body] was opened her Stomach was so worn, that you could thrust your Fingers through at any Place'.[35]

Frederick devoted five months to planning funeral obsequies of surpassing magnificence, as Figuelotte had known he would. More touchingly, he renamed Lützenburg 'Charlottenburg' in her memory. To Leibniz, writing from Ansbach, Caroline confided devastation on a scale with George Louis's: 'The terrible blow has plunged me into a grievous affliction, and nothing can console me save the hope of following her soon.' Her recovery from the strain of recent ordeals suffered a setback, and she was once again ill. Her letter betrays the extent to which Figuelotte had come to occupy a mother's place in her emotions. 'Heaven, jealous of our happiness, is come to carry away our adorable queen.'[36] If the rhetoric is conventional, the sentiments were sharply felt. In her illness, Caroline did not attend Figuelotte's funeral. Nor, in the short term, did she see or communicate with Sophia. But in her response to von Eltz's proposal on George Augustus's behalf in June, the baron reported to George Louis, she 'admit[ted] that she would infinitely prefer an alliance with your Electoral House to any other; and she considered it particular good fortune to be able to form fresh and congenial ties to compensate for the loss she had suffered by the death of the high-souled Queen of Prussia'.[37]

To the prospective father-in-law whom she had never met these were honeyed words. Equally accommodating was her willingness to fall in with George Louis's requirement that Frederick remain in the dark, a circumstance that reveals something of Caroline's own anxiety that the match come off. Not for the last time in their lives, Caroline's measured diplomacy contrasted with the impulsiveness of her husband-to-be. George Augustus wrote to her on the eve of her departure for Hanover, 'I desire nothing so much as to throw myself at my Princess's feet and promise her eternal devotion,' and there is puppyishness even in the copybook posturing. 'You alone, Madam, can make me happy; but I shall not be entirely convinced of my happiness until I have the satisfaction of testifying to the excess of my fondness and love for you.'[38] Undoubtedly Caroline reached her own estimate of this 'fondness and love' that was based on a single meeting. But with memories of her mother's treatment at the hands of the elector John George still painful, she could only be reassured by such effusive auguries. Like Eleonore's second marriage, Caroline's marriage to George Augustus represented a step up the ladder; her response to von

Eltz's proposal indicates her assessment of the prize at stake. At twenty-two, ambitious and clear-sighted but with a genuine attachment to the electoral family based on her affection for Figuelotte and Sophia, she was still young enough to hope for love too.

Like Hollar's etching of Ansbach, the view of Hanover by an unknown draftsman published by printmaker Christoph Riegel in 1689 depicts a Gothic town compact within its walls and dominated by church spires.[39] At intervals along the city boundaries, fortified towers bristle above undulations of the Leine river. The only building identified in the key that is not a church is the *Fürstlich haus*, the home of Hanover's ruling family called the Leineschloss. From its extensive but otherwise unremarkable façade long views unroll across the water. Behind it, hugger-mugger along busy streets cluster the tall houses of townsfolk, their steep roofs red-tiled and gabled, modest in their dimensions since Hanover's nobles lived elsewhere, in castles and country manor houses. From Versailles Liselotte remembered the market square as overrun with street urchins and, at Christmas, its box trees decorated with candles.[40]

A windmill in the foreground denotes the proximity of farmland: British diplomat George Tilson described it as 'flat Country ... very full of fir and Corn; mostly rye'.[41] It is grazed by sheep for the lucrative wool trade or set aside for hops. Out of sight, nearby forests are plentifully stocked with game. Within tranquil surrounds lies this small, unassuming town of no more than ten thousand inhabitants, 'neither large nor handsome' in the estimate of the well-travelled Lady Mary Wortley Montagu, and lacking magnificence, rich only in 'miserable' taverns.[42] The main gates were closed every night.

Despite its middling size, smaller and so much less impressive than the Dresden and Berlin of her childhood, the town that greeted Caroline at the end of her ten-day journey from

Ansbach, undertaken in the company of her brother, offered intimations of a grandeur absent from many provincial capitals. Sophia's late husband Ernest Augustus, the eldest of four brothers, had ultimately succeeded to the bulk of the brothers' joint inheritance, united under his rule as the Duchy of Hanover. Ambition had prompted his campaign for electoral status, which was granted in 1692, six years before his death. Like his Brandenburg son-in-law Frederick, he had exploited cultural initiatives to support his political aspirations, to the benefit of his old-world capital. In addition to the masquerades, gondola festivals, illuminations and Venetian-style annual carnival that raised the court of Hanover above many of its neighbours for style and splendour, these included a theatre in which French comic actors performed nightly, and an opera house within the Leineschloss hung with cloth of gold and crimson velvet and capable of seating 1,300 spectators. Lady Mary rated the latter as 'much finer than that of Vienna'.[43] Its completion at breakneck speed within a single year stemmed from competitiveness with the neighbouring court of Wolfenbüttel, which had embarked on a similar endeavour at the same time.[44] Ernest Augustus sealed his victory with an inaugural performance of Steffani's opera *Enrico Leone*, a celebration of the dynasty's superhero, Henry the Lion. Three years later the Leineschloss opera house staged 'the finest operas and comedys that were ever seen ... [including] the opera of *Orlando Furioso*'.[45] Ernest Augustus also oversaw the embellishment of a palace begun by his father in 1665: Herrenhausen.

For Caroline, as for Sophia before her, Herrenhausen would become the glory of Hanover. Two miles outside the city walls, it occupied three sides of a large courtyard, a sprawling two-storey expanse designed in its first phase by Venetian architect Lorenzo Bedoghi and completed by his countryman Hieronymo Sartorio ten years later. Where Lützenburg aimed to delight and to showcase the refinements of its savant princess, the purpose of Herrenhausen was magnificence. Its stables accommodated six hundred horses. An outdoor theatre, overseen for Ernest Augustus by Steffani, suggested an Italian opera house. Here in 1702 George Louis and Figuelotte took part in a dramatic performance based on Petronius's account of Trimalchio's banquet in the *Satyricon*, written for the occasion by Leibniz. As at the Leineschloss the palace exterior was unassuming. Within, Gobelins tapestries, damask-lined walls and coffered ceilings painted and gilded conjured the heavyweight majesty of divinely ordained princely rule.

Beyond lay the gardens. South of the palace was the Great Garden, bordered by poker-straight avenues of trees, and on three sides by an artificial canal on which gondolas floated under the watchful eye of a Venetian gondolier, Pierre Madonetto. Largely Sophia's creation, it was laid out from 1683 in conscious emulation of the baroque formal gardens she remembered from her childhood in the Dutch Republic. In 120 acres, melons grew under Murano glass cloches, a mulberry plantation fed silkworms, pomegranate and fig trees, date palms, apricot and peach trees defied a changeable climate, and hothouses warmed by tiled stoves nurtured the orange, lemon and pineapple trees which so astonished Lady Mary Wortley Montagu visiting in the chill of December in 1717.

At the garden's heart lay the Great Parterre, created by court gardener Henry Perronet to designs by Sartorio. It featured swirling arabesques of low box hedging, gravel paths and classically inspired statues by Dutch sculptor Pieter van Empthusen carved from white Deister sandstone from nearby Barsinghausen. Imported from Paris were twenty-three busts of Roman emperors. There was a grotto and a cascade, a maze, hedges and screens of hornbeam and, in time, an allée of more than 1,300 lime trees. A wooden temple, filled with doves, occupied the centre of a labyrinth. Additional designs devised by Sophia's gardener Martin Charbonnier, a Huguenot exile, extended the parterre's doily-like geometry. Like Siméon Godeau, whom Figuelotte had employed at Lützenburg, Charbonnier was a pupil of the great Le Nôtre. However powerful Sophia's attachment to the gardens of The Hague, the influence of Versailles was all-pervasive. Fountains animated circular pools – Leibniz had advised on the necessary hydraulic mechanisms. Afterwards George Louis consulted English architect and politician William Benson to create ever more spectacular jets and falls, 'great and noble' waterworks of the sort commended during his visit of 1701 by John Toland. The result was a fountain thirty-six metres high whose installation cost George Louis the enormous sum of £40,000.

In her widowhood Sophia occupied one wing of the palace. Daily she made a lengthy circuit of the gardens she described as her life, 'perfectly tiring all those of her Court who attend[ed] in that exercise', a promenade of two or three hours which one English visitor considered the sole 'gaiety and diversion of the court'.[46] Herrenhausen was not, as her niece Liselotte assumed, Sophia's dower house. In 1699 she had made over to George Louis the income willed to her by Ernest Augustus for its upkeep, and the palace continued to serve as the court's summer residence from May to October.[47] In the year of Caroline's marriage, George Louis embarked on an extensive refurbishment. Under Sophia's influence furniture, tapestries and objets d'art were commissioned from the Dutch Republic. For the large building in the garden called the Galerie, a little-known Venetian painter, Tommaso Giusti, created a fresco cycle depicting the story of Aeneas, that epic tale of filial piety and the foundation of an empire.[48]

In Dresden and Berlin, Caroline had learned to recognise visual culture as a conduit for princely agendas. The Saxon Kunstkammer, with its collection of dynastic portraits, and the marvels of the Green Vault, had first stirred in her an aesthetic awakening continued by Frederick and Figuelotte. Sophia's collection of paintings in Hanover rivalled her daughter's. Her cabinet of curiosities was rich in jewels and gemstones, and her garden was the foremost in Germany. Compared with that of his father, George Louis's court lacked panache, peopled by 'such leather-headed things that the stupidity of them is not to be conceived'.[49] The court opera was closed, and celebrations, including that of Caroline's marriage, missed the flourish prized by Ernest Augustus and Frederick. Court routine was dully repetitive: 'We have not much variety of Diversions, what we did yesterday & to day we shall do tomorrow'; the daily 'drawing room', or formal reception, did not daily delight.[50] Even Sophia's gatherings of learned and distinguished men, albeit they included after 1710 the composer George Frederick Handel, employed as George Louis's *Kapellmeister* or master of court music, wanted the sparkle of Figuelotte's effervescent sodality. After the dowdiness of Berwart's shadow-filled palace in Ansbach, Herrenhausen and the Leineschloss were splendid enough.

Caroline's married life began in Hanover itself. At the Leineschloss Sophia formally welcomed her, on 2 September 1705, 'with all the expressions of kindness and respect that could be desired'.[51] Her wedding took place the same evening, in the palace chapel, in a service notable for its simplicity. Caroline wore a dress of coloured silks. There was a ball and a French play, the former accompanied by modest quantities of alcohol, Caroline's introduction to the abstemiousness that was a feature of Hanoverian court life.[52] George Augustus slept through the wedding sermon, provoking predictably ribald comment. 'What good news for the bride that he should be well rested,' Liselotte wrote, the sort of quip that, a century later, earned her the epithet of the *'most improper* Letter-writer in *Europe'*.[53] From England Queen Anne wrote too, letters of congratulation to Sophia and her family. Days later Sophia still remembered the faces of the congregation as 'wreathed in smiles when we looked at the young couple'.[54] George Louis was almost certainly the exception. Acrimony and impatience dominated his feelings towards his only son, and would colour aspects of his relationship with Caroline. He acknowledged her good looks but as yet made no further approaches to intimacy.

It is also possible that Caroline's smiles lacked conviction. Both she and George Augustus had anticipated from the elector a more generous wedding present. She 'really could not help taking notice', wrote Lady Mary Wortley Montagu, 'that the presents made to her on her wedding were not worthy of [George Augustus's] bride, and at least she ought to have had all his mother's jewels'.[55] With a degree of subtlety, Caroline's complaint was not on her own account. She protested at the suggestion of any slight to George Augustus.

A living ghost shared with Caroline and George Augustus the quarters allocated to them in Hanover's town palace. She was the prince's mother, Sophia Dorothea of Celle, and though very much alive, dead to the court and the electoral family, by whom her name was never mentioned. Not for the first time in our chronicle, her story is one of conflicted emotions, double standards and novelettish melodrama that nevertheless impacts on events to come.

Sophia Dorothea was George Louis's first cousin. Her father was Ernest Augustus's younger brother, George William, Duke of Celle. Her mother, Eléonore d'Olbreuse, was a Huguenot noblewoman of striking good looks, whose commoner blood earned from Liselotte the pithy dismissal of 'mouse droppings in the pepper'.[56] Neither love nor romance played its part in forging the cousins' disastrous union. At the time of their marriage in November 1682, Sophia Dorothea was sixteen; spoilt, self-willed, preoccupied with dress and luxuries, but notably pretty in the curvaceous, pale-skinned manner of the times, and, if an early portrait by Jacob Ferdinand Voet can be trusted, lacking in confidence and anxious to please.[57] George Louis was twenty-two. By the terms of their marriage contract, kept secret from Sophia Dorothea, he received straight away her entire dowry; at her parents' death, their revenues and property became his too. It was an arrangement guaranteed to deny George Louis's bride the possibility of financial independence.

Opportunities for acquaintance had recurred throughout the cousins' childhoods; decided antipathy predated their marriage. Although G.K. Chesterton exaggerated in describing George Louis in 1917 as 'the barbarian from beyond the Rhine', his preoccupations were strenuously masculine.[58] Off the battlefield he enjoyed hunting. 'Low of stature, of features coarse, of aspect dull and placid', he inherited few of his mother's rarefied interests, only walking and music, and no aptitude at all for the role of romantic swain.[59] Like many German princelings, including his lecherous father, he began as a busy fornicator, though his momentum would slow with increasing responsibility. He was otherwise undemonstrative and emotionally costive. He was sixteen when Figuelotte's under-governess fell pregnant with his first child: Sophia castigated him as a 'progenitor of bastards'.[60] His first full-time mistress shortly afterwards was Maria Katharine von Meysenburg, the sister of his father's redoubtable mistress Countess von Platen. With no eye to psychological complexities, this curious arrangement had been brokered by Ernest Augustus himself.[61] His mother insisted that George Louis would 'marry a cripple if he could serve the house', but in the event this was not required of him.[62] Instead, despite rumours that Sophia's English family wished him to marry Princess Anne of York, the future Queen Anne, and, in 1680, an inconclusive trip to London apparently to that end, his father chose for George Louis his pretty young cousin in neighbouring Celle.

It was an arranged royal marriage like others before and since, and compatibility between the partners was an after-thought. Ernest Augustus's plan was twofold: to bring together the disparate territorial possessions of his family, and to ensure their long-term security by introducing primogeniture in the next generation. George Louis's marriage enabled Ernest Augustus to knit together Calenburg, Celle and Hanover. In time both George Louis and his eldest son would inherit outright the contiguous raggle-taggle of all three duchies, as well as the fourth segment in the patrimonial jigsaw, the prince-bishopric of Osnabrück.

It was unfortunate that George Louis's response to the prospect of marrying Sophia Dorothea combined delight in her good looks with 'repugnance' at aspects of her character, and that her own reaction was something akin: of such was the stuff of political necessity.[63] The glister of Sophia Dorothea's inheritance outweighed her temperamental and emotional unsuitability to play the parts of George Louis's wife and Hanover's electress, outweighed even the £40,000 dowry of Princess Anne, with additional annual promises of £10,000. A portrait of the mid-1680s by Henri Gascar depicts the married Sophia Dorothea with flowers in her curly hair. Her dress of richly woven fabric slips alluringly from her shoulder. A garland of flowers in her hand represents fertility and the promise of springtime, but nothing in this seductively decorative image suggests gravity.

As the marriage approached, Sophia wrote tactfully to the bride's father that she had never imagined George Louis capable of so violent a passion.[64] Three of his four younger brothers were similarly smitten, with Frederick Augustus serenading his sister-in-law as 'bellissime', 'most beautiful'. For her part Sophia Dorothea hurled a diamond-set miniature of George Louis against the wall. But the couple's first child and only son, George Augustus, was born a year after their wedding. At the outset, irrespective of bridal aversion, youthful sexual excitement contributed its precarious bond.

Even taking into account George Louis's repeated absences during the first years of his marriage, on campaign with the

imperial army fighting the Turks, the interval between Sophia
Dorothea's two pregnancies – in 1683 and 1688 – tells its own
tale of marital harmony unravelling. In 1689, the year after she
gave birth to a daughter named after her, Sophia Dorothea met
the man who three years later became her lover, Count Philip
Christopher von Königsmarck. Their relationship tracked a
familiar course: acquaintances, correspondents, bedfellows. The
pretty electress's infatuation was stoked by boredom, a comprehensive rejection of every aspect of her married life from
Hanoverian court etiquette to behaviour on George Louis's part
that encompassed neglect, overt hostility and even acts of fright-
ening physical violence, described in some accounts as close to
attempted strangling. Above all she was jealous.

Infidelity was a prerogative of princes. Sophia tolerated
Countess von Platen, Figuelotte mostly overlooked Madame von
Wartenburg; Ernest Augustus indicated to his daughter-in-law
that she must make similar concessions. In 1690, George Louis
had acquired the mistress to whom he would remain faithful for
life, tall, thin, plain Melusine von der Schulenburg, whom his
mother disparaged as a 'malkin', a picturesque noun applied
equally to scarecrows and slatterns.[65] Within three years Madame
Schulenburg had two daughters, referred to as her nieces, and,
like the elector John George IV in his affair with Billa von
Neitschütz, George Louis all but lived with her. Sophia Dorothea's
retaliation had a tit-for-tat quality, but husband and wife inhabited a world in which men and women were not judged as
equals, and women's faithlessness, with its danger of pregnancy
and illegitimacy, threatened the integrity of royal succession.
'Does the young duchess not know that a woman's honour
consists of having commerce with no one but her husband, and
that for a man it is not shameful to have mistresses but shameful
indeed to be a cuckold?' Liselotte asked rhetorically.[66]

A predictably tight-lipped nineteenth-century verdict casts
Königsmarck as a 'handsome, wicked, worthless reprobate'; his

sister judged him 'an equal mixture of Mars and Adonis'.[67] To Sophia Dorothea, the raffish Swedish mercenary provided an exhilarating contrast to George Louis, with his brusque neglect, eruptions of physical violence and, when it suited him, perfunctory love-making. In suggestive French, in letters written in code in invisible ink, Königsmarck wooed his princess. He called her his 'divine beauty', he signed his name in blood. He courted her lady-in-waiting, Eleonore von dem Knesebeck, who acted as go-between for the lovers, concealing Sophia Dorothea's replies to his letters in hats and gloves and stitching his own letters into curtain linings safely out of sight. He also cultivated the good opinions of Sophia and Ernest Augustus. In 1692 Stepney reported Königsmarck directing 'splendid ballets ... all in maskeradings' in the Leineschloss opera house.[68]

'Maskeradings' on the electoral stage were an apt metaphor. Princess and count progressed from artless dalliance to desperate longing, fuelled in part by their shared talent for self-dramatisation. In their letters and dizzy assignations they slipped between the worlds of fairy tale and melodrama, their emotions heroic in intensity, in daring, in urgency. Königsmarck labelled himself 'a poor butterfly burnt by the flame'; he confided to Sophia Dorothea a terrifying but prophetic dream in which his actions were punished by execution; he was exaggeratedly jealous of George Louis's continuing conjugal rights and begged God to kill him if Sophia Dorothea failed him.[69] Neither lover accepted responsibility for behaviour they knew to be perilous. But Sophia Dorothea's posturing included a measure of genuine unhappiness.

That she crossed the Rubicon from flirtation to infatuation was plainly ill-advised. That she disdained discretion or concealment was still more injudicious. Sophia and Figuelotte were among those who counselled against the dangers of transgression. Determined to divorce George Louis and marry Königsmarck, she ignored their warnings. Unaware of the impossibility of her financial position, she fixated on the idea of elopement. 'Let us love one another all our lives and find comfort in one another for all the unhappiness brought on us,' she pleaded.[70]

Four years after their first exchange of letters, desperate measures brought to an end the romance of Sophia Dorothea and her dashing Swede. On the eve of his departure for Dresden to take up a position as major general in the Saxon army, Königsmarck was murdered en route to his mistress's apartments in the Leineschloss. Orders for his killing probably originated with Ernest Augustus or, on his behalf, Countess von Platen. A particularly gruesome version of events has a vengeful and incensed countess grinding his face beneath her high-heeled shoe. George Louis was absent on a visit to Figuelotte in Berlin.[71] The deed itself, on 1 July 1694, was the work of a quartet of Hanoverian loyalists, including von Eltz and an architect called Nicolò Montalbano, who shortly received from Ernest Augustus an enormous one-off payment of 150,000 thalers.[72] Königsmarck was stabbed over and again. His body was concealed in a weighted sack and thrown into the Leine river, where it settled into muddy wastes alongside general debris and the drowned carcasses of cattle. Sophia Dorothea knew nothing of this squalid butchery. With mounting apprehension, she continued to await her lover.

In her ignorance she was not alone. The best the ever-vigilant George Stepney could manage was to describe the circumstances of Königsmarck's disappearance as 'doubtfull' and, with a degree of accuracy, point to the probability of 'daggers and poyson' in Hanover.[73] But the nature of the count's infraction was widely understood: 'I believe his amours made that court too hot for him,' Stepney wrote during one of Königsmarck's regular absences the month before Montalbano's blow.[74]

Sophia Dorothea retreated to Celle and her parents; she refused to return to George Louis. Anxious about the effect of such a scandal on Hanover's standing in the Empire, Ernest Augustus took refuge in cod legalities. In a punitive divorce settlement finalised in December, Sophia Dorothea alone was accounted culpable. Cresset reported that 'the sentence was pronounc'd upon malicious desertion'.[75] The Englishman considered the elector guilty of sharp practice: 'Hannover has made a pretty good hande of this match. She brought 'em in land of purchas'd estate 50,000 crowns, besides jewels which they are now takeing from her and she is pack'd off with about £800 a year in bad rents.'[76]

Sophia Dorothea was banished to the castle of Ahlden, a timbered and moated manor house in Celle, more than thirty miles from the town of Hanover. She spent the remainder of her life as a prisoner there, writing 'most patheticall letters' to her mother, who visited sporadically, but denied any contact with her children or the possibility of marrying again.[77] To preserve an illusion that the newly styled 'Duchess of Ahlden' had retired voluntarily after forsaking her marriage, she was provided with an annual income of eight thousand thalers and a roster of servants appropriate to her rank as former electress: ladies-in-waiting, two pages and gentlemen-in-waiting, two valets, a butler, three cooks, a confectioner, a head groom, a coachman, fourteen footmen, twelve maids and a garrison of forty infantry- and cavalrymen to ensure her confinement.[78] A handful of visitors were closely supervised.

George Louis embraced tranquil domesticity with Madame Schulenburg and a princely establishment that, in one contemporary estimate, eventually ran to more than 1,100 servants and retainers.[79] The ravages of smallpox, which left Melusine pockmarked and virtually bald, in no way diminished George Louis's affection. She wore a red wig and a thick varnish of make-up, and gave birth to the couple's third and last daughter, Margarete Gertrud, known as 'Trudchen', in 1701. In stark contrast to his relationship with George Augustus and the younger Sophia Dorothea, the elector was devoted to all three of his mistress's 'nieces'. For her part, Sophia Dorothea had imagined she would continue to see her children following her divorce, and wrote to Sophia as intermediary, begging that she be allowed to embrace them once more. Her surviving correspondence does not otherwise lament their loss: her daughter is mentioned in a single letter, George Augustus not at all.[80] At intervals she implored her father-in-law to reconsider the terms of her confinement: other courts, her mother reported to her, condemned their harshness and injustice. All in vain. Sophia Dorothea remained at Ahlden for thirty-two years, 'lead[ing] a very solitary life, but all the same … splendidly dressed', in one of Liselotte's less sympathetic observations.[81]

Shorter in duration was the confinement in the state prison of Scharzfelz Castle of Eleonore von dem Knesebeck, who was tortured for her part in the lovers' perfidy. She narrowly escaped a charge of attempting to poison George Louis with nitric acid after explaining her possession of the chemical as a beauty aid. In 1701, William III's patience with Duchess Eléonore finally snapped. For seven years she had lobbied him on her daughter's behalf, and with no wish to antagonise George Louis or risk the loss of Hanoverian support in his campaigns against the French, he forbade her to broach the subject any longer.[82]

Over the Leineschloss and Herrenhausen settled an immoveable silence. Sophia Dorothea was never mentioned again, her name excised from state prayers. Her portraits were banished to storerooms, including Jacques Vaillant's confusing image of her with her children, of 1690, in which a heavily jewelled electress embraces George Augustus while her dress parts to disclose tantalisingly full pink-white breasts. At a stroke both her children were motherless. George Louis and Sophia restricted the time either spent alone with Duchess Eléonore.

In chancelleries across Europe Sophia Dorothea's story electrified idle prattlers. As late as 1732, it inspired the rapidly suppressed shilling-shocker *Histoire Secrette* [sic] *de la Duchesse D'Hanover*. Gossip came close to the mark nevertheless. Stepney based his final explanation for Königsmarck's vanishing on rumours that dogged Ernest Augustus's court: 'a great lady ... (with whom he is suspected to have been familiar) may have been cause of his misfortune'.[83] And steps were taken to put the curious off the scent, beginning with Königsmarck's sister Aurora, mistress of Augustus the Strong of Saxony. 'His sister raves like Cassandra and will know what is become of her brother,' Stepney wrote, 'but at Hanover they answer like Cain that they are not her brother's keeper.'[84] Only Duke Anton Ulrich, habitually at odds with his Hanoverian neighbours, successfully uncovered the full facts of the murder, laid bare in his correspondence with a Danish diplomat called Otto Mencken.[85] To *Octavia, a Roman Story*, he added a sixth volume. In his tale of 'Princess Solane', Sophia Dorothea is a romantic innocent fatally outmanoeuvred by George Louis and Countess von Platen.

'Her natural feelings for the pains and distresses of others are not to be described,' wrote Dr Alured Clarke, the author of *An Essay Towards the Character of Her late Majesty Queen Caroline*, in 1738. 'They were so strong that she became a fellow sufferer with them, and made their cases ... much her own.'[86]

If there is any truth in this posthumous panegyric, it seems likely that the story of George Augustus's mother, known to Caroline before her marriage, provoked her fellow feeling – and not only with Sophia Dorothea but with George Augustus. Sources have not survived that document either short- or long-term effects on George Augustus of his mother's fall from grace, only a series of assumptions made by successive historians. How much the eleven-year-old prince understood in 1694 is not clear. Nor is the nature of his response in the decade ahead. The abruptness of his severance from his mother was surely traumatic, as was his exposure to the bitter recriminations against Sophia Dorothea which consumed the electoral court. Rich in pathos, a story of George Augustus attempting to catch a glimpse of his vanished mother by stealing away from a hunting party, only to be caught four miles from Ahlden, is almost certainly a sentimental invention. His grandmother Sophia became the dominant female presence in his childhood, a role to which, by nature and inclination, she was ideally suited. George Louis's attitude, by contrast, suggested at best detachment.

A response to Sophia Dorothea's history was required of Caroline from the beginning of her marriage, in her several roles of wife, daughter-in-law, sister-in-law and granddaughter-in-law. The younger Sophia Dorothea categorised her mother's error as one of imprudence, and, following her own marriage and departure from Hanover, wrote to her regularly. Such leniency would have been impolitic on Caroline's part. Nevertheless, unspecified 'courtesies' apparently paid by Caroline and George Augustus to the widowed Duchess Eléonore, living modestly outside Celle at Wienhausen, indicate a joint response to the dilemma by husband and wife.[87] Sophia, by contrast, regarded her former daughter-in-law with hostility, while on the subject of recent family history George Louis maintained a discouraging silence.

In the autumn of 1705, Caroline cannot have shared for long Toland's view of Hanover's court as *even* in Germany accounted the best both for Civility and Decorum'.[88] With Sophia Dorothea's disgrace and, in 1698, Ernest Augustus's death had vanished much of 'the old gay good humour'.[89] Animus between George Louis and his grown-up son was deeply ingrained. A tradition of hostility between ruler and heir had been a feature of Hanover's ruling family as far back as the Middle Ages, but its absence from George Louis's relationship with Ernest Augustus invited questions concerning its re-emergence in the current generation.[90] It was unavoidable that Caroline should look for explanations in the collapse of George Louis's marriage, as well as in the undoubted physical resemblance of George Augustus and his mother, both slight in build, impulsive, quick to blush. Caroline's loyalty to George Augustus in his disputes with his father indicates that, in Clarke's words, the case she made her own was not Sophia Dorothea's or George Louis's, but that of her husband. In 1705 this attitude proved important in consolidating their affection: an awareness of the ties that bound them would characterise their marriage. Caroline too felt the shadow of Sophia Dorothea's transgression. George Augustus's compulsion for orderliness, his need to control and obsessive focus on small details – afterwards thorns in Caroline's side – traced their roots to the vacuum created by his parents' divorce, and his resulting uncertainty and disorientation.

Caroline recognised in addition warnings for herself in her predecessor's downfall. By 1705 her exposure to the vagaries of royal marriage was broad. Too young to remember her mother's happy marriage to John Frederick, she was unlikely to forget the unhappiness of Eleonore's second marriage. She had witnessed Figuelotte's unconventional management of Frederick and the latter's admiration. And the case of Sophia Dorothea implied aspects of the electoral family's views of the role of wives. Having spent her entire life in courts, Caroline understood the necessity, in such an environment, to temper her behaviour to the prevailing clime – as Stepney had once intimated in Eleonore's case, if necessary to the point of dissembling. She was aware that 'in courts ... the affections of the heart are as much conceal'd as its substance', and that there 'even trifles, elegantly expressed, well looked, and accompanied with graceful action ... ever please beyond all the homespun, unadorned sense in the world'.[91] Her success in Berlin, her conquest of the Archduke Charles at Weissenfels, her resistance to Father Orban and the Elector Palatine, and her seamless,

discreet management of her engagement to George Augustus
testify to something remarkable in Caroline's character. From
the outset her fidelity to George Augustus was more than sexual
or emotional. She kept faith with something in herself too.

In April 1708, once more bound for war against the French, the
Duke of Marlborough, commander in chief of Queen Anne's
forces, described his reception at the court of Hanover.[92] Present
at the audience granted him were Sophia – who considered
Marlborough 'as skilled as a courtier as he is a brave general',
'his manners ... as obliging and polished as his actions are glorious and admirable' – George Louis and George Augustus.[93]

As electoral princess, the Hanoverian equivalent of Princess
of Wales, Caroline played a visual role in court ceremonial: her
primary function was dynastic, a provider of heirs and progeny.
That she was not present at Marlborough's audience indicates
the perimeters of her sphere of activity. For Caroline, the decade
before Queen Anne's death and the family's move to London
was overwhelmingly domestic in character. George Louis vigorously excluded George Augustus from politics. By continuing to
oversee court entertainments, Sophia as effectively barred
Caroline from key aspects of a consort's role.[94] With the exception of Sophia herself and Caroline's favourite of Sophia's ladies-
in-waiting, intelligent, beautiful Johanna Sophia, Countess of
Schaumburg-Lippe, afterwards Countess of Bückeburg, whose
husband, like George Louis, preferred the company of his
mistress, Caroline mostly lacked rewarding female friendship.
She had little in common with rapacious and dreary Melusine
von der Schulenburg; she knew enough of courts to maintain
friendly relations with her father-in-law's favourite and her
'nieces'. Although Leibniz had been urged in 1705 to 'cultivate
her good qualities assiduously, for there you have a spirit naturally beautiful, and an intellect completely disposed to reason',
the philosopher's frequent absences from Hanover meant

Caroline also lacked intellectual stimulus.[95] The period was not without its strains.

Her husband and her sister-in-law were her closest contemporaries. Neither had benefited from the irregularities of their childhood. George Augustus was splenetic, irritable and prickly in his self-esteem. In his grandmother's eyes he lacked good sense.[96] His aunt Liselotte attributed his bad temper to Duchess Eléonore's inferior bloodlines; he was niggardly, boastful and, at moments of strain, intemperate.[97] Toland excused his restlessness as 'great vivacity' of a sort that did not 'let him be ignorant of anything'.[98] An indifferent portrait by Kneller, painted in 1716, captures something of his Cock Robin self-regard.[99] George Louis preferred his daughter. Superficial but spirited, Sophia Dorothea the younger shared her mother's want of serious-mindedness. 'All the pride and haughtiness of the House of Hanover are concentrated in her person,' her own daughter wrote in the early 1740s, when Sophia Dorothea was in her fifties. She insisted her mother was 'benevolent, generous and kind', but also claimed 'her ambition is unbounded; she is excessively jealous, of a suspicious and vindictive temper, and never forgives those by whom she fancies she has been offended'.[100]

If even part of this assessment was true in 1705, Caroline can hardly have found proximity easy. She was closer in temperament to the dowager electress, whose interests resembled Figuelotte's, but the two women initially saw little of one another. George Augustus's early attentiveness to Caroline was marked. 'The peace of my life depends upon … the conviction of your continued affection for me,' he would write to her. 'I shall endeavour to attract it by all imaginable passion and love, and I shall never omit any way of showing you that no one could be more wholly yours.'[101] He did not conceal his preference for her company above that of the court, and he and Caroline spent as much time as possible together. As late as May

1712, an English agent reported, 'the Court is all gone to Herrenhausen for the whole summer, *only* the Prince electoral and his wife the princess remain here'.[102] Such uxoriousness – influenced in part by the aimlessness of George Augustus's life, which George Louis ensured lacked official responsibility – inspired mixed reactions, including in Caroline herself. Liselotte dismissed her nephew's cosy behaviour as inappropriately unprincely, another malign legacy of non-royal Duchess Eléonore.[103] Within weeks of their marriage Sophia wrote to Baron von Schütz, 'I have never seen a lovelier friendship than that between the Prince Electoral and his wife. It appears as if they were made for one another, which causes us great joy.'[104] But, despite earnest protestations of devotion, the prince struggled to suppress argumentative instincts.

Whenever possible, Caroline sought out fleeting opportunities for time alone with Sophia at Herrenhausen. Their shared interests were wide-ranging and included philosophy, music and politics. During these first months of adjustment, disjointed encounters placed even this relationship under strain. Sophia's letters to Liselotte make clear her frustration and disappointment: Caroline's presence failed to staunch the older woman's grief for Figuelotte, and the new electoral princess was cast firmly on her own resources. She oscillated between gratitude for George Augustus's attachment and the need to cultivate, or indeed placate, others of her new family. Reading and singing offered her an outlet of sorts. Like Sophia she took lengthy walks in the palace gardens. In 1711, Handel wrote a set of twelve chamber duets for Caroline, described by his first biographer in 1760 as 'a species of composition of which the Princess and court were particularly fond'.[105] That Caroline hazarded the challenging soprano part is testament to the success of the singing lessons begun in her childhood at Ansbach by Antonio Pistocchi.[106]

A phantom pregnancy during the first year of her marriage, reported by Sophia as early as November, indicates Caroline's anxiety to provide the necessary heir.[107] At twenty-two she could anticipate more than a decade of childbearing; it was George Augustus's determination to play his part in the long-running War of the Spanish Succession that contributed a note of urgency. Supported by his privy council, George Louis had consistently thwarted his son's military aspirations. To date the latter's nearest approach to the theatre of war was a journey to the Dutch palace of Het Loo, undertaken in the autumn of 1701 with his grandfather, the Duke of Celle, as part of William III's efforts to create a coalition against Louis XIV. Following his marriage, George Augustus again requested permission to join the fight against the French. 'The court is against it and will not give their consent to let him go into the field until he has children,' noted a British envoy.[108] Repeated prohibitions failed to depress his ardour. Instead his resentment of his father mounted, adding a further note of asperity to a fissured relationship, with inevitable implications for Caroline.

On 31 January 1707, despite gainsayers who attributed her increasing girth to distemper or even wind, and 'the court having for some time past almost despaired of the Princess Electoral's being brought to bed', Caroline succeeded in her primary task.[109] Early in the evening, with the windows shuttered against the cold and the doors barred to court flunkeys, she gave birth to a delicate-looking baby boy, Frederick Louis. Unusually – and ill-advisedly, given speculation that Caroline's pregnancy was once again imaginary – only a midwife and the court surgeon, de la Rose, were present at the birth in the Leineschloss. Responsibility for this break with tradition lay with George Augustus, whose concern was for Caroline's comfort. His actions irritated the British envoy Emmanuel Scrope Howe and, in the absence of the usual crowd of official witnesses, facilitated lurid rumours that the baby's father was not George Augustus but one of George Louis's Turkish valets. Portraits of the prince throughout his life refute such spiteful calumnies. Lady Mary Wortley Montagu afterwards noted in Frederick 'the fine fair Hair of the Princesse' and 'an Air of Sprightliness' reminiscent of George Augustus's volatile fidgetiness.[110] Introduced to her first great-grandchild at the perfunctory service of baptism held in Caroline's bedroom two weeks later, Sophia commended both his liveliness and his laughing eyes; erroneously she described him as 'strong and robust'.[111] She stood as one of three godparents, all of them members of the baby's immediate family.

At George Louis's insistence, invitations to the baptism were not extended to foreign officials. In England, this second departure from tradition was interpreted as a slight to Queen Anne, whose throne the baby stood to inherit. It was left to George Augustus to untangle the knot of ill-feeling predictably wrought by the double omission. In a dispatch of 25 February, Howe noted with some scepticism divisions in the electoral family and George Augustus's anxiety to exonerate himself from blame. A measure of his disgruntlement, the envoy tarred elector and electoral prince with the same broad brush: 'I think the whole proceeding has been very extraordinary. Wherever the fault is, I won't pretend to judge.'[112]

Howe's prickly equivocation notwithstanding, Anne's view of George Augustus was principally coloured by her ambivalence towards his father and, especially, his grandmother. To George Louis her attitude was remote, in the account of a French spy resentful, because, in 1680, he had 'refused to marry [her] because of the humble birth of her mother', Anne Hyde, like Duchess Eléonore a commoner.[113] Her resistance to Sophia was shaped by her conviction that the older woman coveted her crown, and was not above meddling in British politics to stir up trouble to serve her own ends. In the short term, Anne set aside her ire and most of her misgivings.

To Howe, a smooth-talking Duke of Marlborough described news of Frederick's birth as 'received here [at Anne's court] with great joy and satisfaction'.[114] In its aftermath Anne conferred on George Augustus the titles Duke and Marquess of Cambridge, Earl of Milford Haven, Viscount Northallerton and Baron Tewkesbury, with precedence above all other British peers; she also invested him with the Order of the Garter. The gift of titles was partly made at the request of Sophia. Her response nevertheless was to dismiss her grandson's elevation as 'meaningless', an attitude that neither George Augustus nor Caroline shared.[115]

George Louis reacted with predictable jealousy. He confirmed Anne's disaffection by refusing to permit the appropriate cere-monial in the formal presentation of the patents of nobility. With hindsight George Augustus's assurances to his royal bene-factress, via Howe, of 'the most perfect veneration and ... the most zealous and respectful sentiments' sound increasingly strangulated, the response of a man aware that his family's atti-tude towards its future prospects lacked coordination.[116]

Anne's emissaries in 1706 included, as secretary to the Lords Justices, the future *Spectator* essayist and playwright Joseph Addison. Addison's admiration for Caroline, first encountered then, would prove long-lasting; it was reciprocated in full. In November 1714 he dedicated his tragedy *Cato* to her. He remem-bered her as a 'bright Princess! who, with graceful Ease/And native Majesty, are form'd to please'.[117] She in turn told Leibniz that Addison shared all the good qualities of his Cato, though his writing about gardening, especially his advocacy of a 'natu-ral' or non-formal approach, ultimately influenced her more than his drama.[118]

Soon, however, George Augustus's priority was not the querulous Anne but Caroline. Six months after she gave birth to Frederick, Caroline contracted smallpox. It was the disease that had killed her father as well as her greatly disliked stepfather John George of Saxony and his mistress Billa von Neitschütz. How she reacted is not recorded, and she was fortunate not only to survive but, after a lengthy period of illness culminating in pneumonia, to emerge at the end of August relatively unscathed. To the younger Sophia Dorothea, newly married to her cousin Frederick William in Berlin, Sophia confided that she found Caroline's appearance greatly altered. She had previously described her as 'much more beautiful than her portraits', since paintings failed to convey accurately the luminescence of her skin.[119] Others considered the damage to her complexion minimal, and Caroline's good looks would remain a source of flattery: a decade later she was described as 'of a fine complexion'.[120] Despite the opposition of George Louis and Sophia, George Augustus had remained at her bedside throughout, a well-intentioned but predictably restless attendant. Like John George, his reward was to contract the disease himself, though his recovery from what was evidently mild exposure was quicker than Caroline's and without setbacks. This proof of his devotion had a symbolic quality. The experience of potentially life-threatening illness served further to cement the couple's affections, in their own minds as well as their attendants', and Caroline's future tolerance of her husband's foibles would be coloured by gratitude for such evidence of courage and attentiveness.

The following year, with the succession assured, George Louis relaxed his prohibition against George Augustus joining the allied troops. With clear guidelines on suitably princely behaviour in the field, he allowed him to take part in a campaign by English, German and Dutch forces in the Low Countries. Beginning in May 1708, George Augustus was absent from Hanover for six months. His companions in arms included von Eltz, who had accompanied him incognito to Ansbach in 1705. It was the only significant period of time he and Caroline would spend apart until 1729, and they wrote to one another twice or three times every week.

First-hand experience of armed combat offered George Augustus responsibility and princely *gloire*: a commendation for bravery from the Duke of Marlborough after his horse was shot from under him during heavy fighting near Oudenaarde on 11 July. Not for the last time, his actions inspired indifferent verse, variously attributed to Jonathan Swift and William Congreve. In a sign of the electoral family's rising profile in England, the poem in question was published in London: by John Morphew, at a printing press near Stationers' Hall. George Augustus appears in *Jack Frenchman's Lamentation* as 'Young Hanover brave': 'When his warhorse was shot/He valued it not,/But fought it on foot like a fury.' For obvious political reasons the poet ascribed the prince's courage to his blood ties to Queen Anne. In a battle fought against the Catholic French, George Augustus's bravery was a useful weapon to advocates of the Hanoverian succession. Afterwards he was described as having 'distinguished himself early in opposition to the Tyranny which threatened Europe'.[121] The next day, exhausted after twenty-four hours without sleep but eager to share his elation, George Augustus wrote an excited letter to Caroline.

Caroline would not be alone in detecting in him a newfound confidence. Short of his twenty-fifth birthday, he had sampled the military daring that remained central to a prince's role in the Empire. It brought him lasting fulfilment, and the memory of Oudenaarde, including his own part as 'Young Hanover brave', was one he cultivated assiduously.

In conversations with Sophia, Caroline expressed her pride in George Augustus's bravery; during their lengthy separation she was more often prey to fear and anxiety. But the events of Oudenaarde would serve wife as well as husband. As late as 1734, *An Ode to be Performed at the Castle of Dublin, On the 1st of March, being the Birth-Day of Her Most Excellent and Sacred Majesty Queen Caroline* celebrated Caroline's role as loving wife to the conquering hero: 'What Shouts of publick Joy salute her Ears!/ See! see! the Reward of her Virtue appears./From Audenard's Plain/Heap'd with Mountains of Slain,/The Dread of Gallic

Insolence,/Grac'd with Spoils,/Reap'd by Toils/In Godlike Liberty's Defence,/The Hanoverian Victor comes,/Black with Dust, and rough in Arms,/From the Noise of Fifes and Drums,/ He comes, he comes, he comes/To gentler Love's Alarms.'[122]

Caroline's satisfaction in the fulfilment of her own public role, as mother of a new generation of the electoral house, was less straightforward. With the self-containment habitual to her, she kept her own counsel. 'I thank you from the bottom of my soul, that her Royal Highness, whom I value above all persons liveing, continues in so good health, and, as I am inform'd, in as good humor & temper as ever,' John Toland wrote to Leibniz on 6 October.[123] Her good humour was an aspect of Caroline's infectious zest for life: she had learned long ago the value of counterfeiting even-temperedness.

Three further children completed the nursery in Hanover. Daughters Anne, Amelia – whom Caroline called 'Amely' – and Caroline were born at two-yearly intervals from 1709. Although Caroline would later tell one of her ladies of the bedchamber that 'she thought the principal Duty of a Woman was to take care of her Children', and at least one contemporary account claimed 'she took infinite pleasure in amusing herself with the sportings and innocence of young children', she was not consistently cosily maternal with her children when young.[124] Even a sympathetic observer like her future woman of the bedchamber Charlotte Clayton protested at Caroline's preference for 'settling points of controversial divinity' over vigilance in the matter of her children's development; she was attentive to discipline, and the royal schoolroom included lessons in Latin, German, French, Italian and the work of ancient historians.[125]

Caroline's apparent failure to react either swiftly or effectively to the infant Frederick developing rickets suggests negligence, but should be read within the context of contemporary parenting habits and widespread medical ignorance, and balanced by

George Augustus's assurance to her, in a letter written two years later, of his instinctive love for their new baby Anne, a clear indication that she valued affection between parents and children.[126] In the event, credit for Frederick's recovery mostly belongs to Sophia, who, by directing that 'Fritzchen' spend time outdoors in the gardens at Herrenhausen, exposed him to the light and fresh air which effected a cure around the time of his third birthday. In her letters, Sophia intimated that her contribution extended to supervising Fritzchen's wetnurse and feeding regimen: first smallpox then pneumonia had separated Caroline from her baby.[127] A subsequent appraisal would absolve Caroline of the besetting flaw of royal and aristocratic parenting, that 'Parents of rank … have so little regard to … the happiness of their children, as by leaving them in the hands of their servants, to suffer them to receive their earliest impressions from those, who are commonly taken from the dregs of their people.'[128] In Caroline's case it was an assessment of variable accuracy, and Frederick benefited from the doting ministrations of his still energetic great-grandmother.

Caroline had miscalculated Frederick's delivery date. Two years later, she made the same mistake with her second pregnancy. Ernest Augustus, Sophia's youngest son, complained that the combination of Caroline's muddle-headedness and George Augustus's secrecy in relation to his *'petite famille'* had left him again unsure whether Caroline was in fact pregnant. Perhaps she had lately miscarried or was on the brink of miscarriage?[129] All doubts were resolved on 2 November 1709.

George Augustus was absent from the birth of his first daughter. Mindful of the restlessness of his nursemaiding two years earlier, Caroline had encouraged him to join the remainder of the court at the recently renovated electoral hunting box at Göhrde in the Celle forests. In his absence, he committed to paper effusions of love. 'I am only a little bit angry that it [the birth] has caused you pain,' he wrote with clumsy fondness.

'You should know me well enough, my very dear Caroline, to believe that everything that concerns you attaches me the more deeply to you, and I assure you, dear heart, that I love the baby without having seen it. I pray you, take care of yourself, that I may have the pleasure of finding you well, and that still greater joy may be conferred upon a heart deeply desirous of it.'[130] Sophia's letters from Göhrde, full of the coldness of the weather and the splendour of the palace's remodelling, echoed a similar strain, proof of an improvement in the women's relationship since 1705. 'I am sure you do not doubt that my heart is completely yours,' the older woman wrote, 'and that I defy even your Prince to love you more than I will do all my life.'[131] To Bothmer she described the speediness of Caroline's second labour.[132]

With a view to the family's future prospects, the baby was christened Anne. At George Augustus's invitation, the queen agreed to stand as godmother to her infant namesake. Further missives from Hanover prompted a christening gift of Anne's own portrait miniature set in diamonds. To Caroline she wrote, 'I take keen pleasure in giving, as often as I am able, proofs of the perfect friendship I bear for your husband as well as the whole electoral family,' and added, 'I believe the diamonds are very good.'[133] Neither Sophia nor George Louis accepted either of these statements at face value, and indeed the gift had only been forthcoming after a number of tactful reminders. Loftily, Sophia dismissed Anne's trinket as 'the sort one gives to ambassadors'. Like her son, she was predictably irked by the queen's request that Duchess Eléonore stand proxy for her at the baby's baptism.

Anne's stipulation may well have been a piece of calculated mischief-making. Certainly it was a reminder to her Hanoverian heirs that, for the moment at least, the balance of power tilted in her favour. The prize represented by the British throne was a considerable one. It had lately been augmented by the passing

of the Act of Union, which prevented Scotland's Parliament
from nominating its own successor to Anne, thereby guarantee-
ing her heirs the double inheritance. Correctly Anne estimated
Sophia's greed for her crown, revealed in the elaborate courtesies she extended to British visitors to Hanover and her 'many
questions about [British] families, customs, laws, and the like',
noted by Toland as early as 1701.[134] Diplomats kept the queen
informed of efforts made by members of Sophia's family to
prepare themselves for coming apotheosis: lessons in English;
the acquaintance of British politicians, men of letters and military men like Marlborough assiduously cultivated; Leibniz's
faulty attempts to master the intricacies of parliamentary opinion, including the divisions between those 'vile enormous
factions', the Whigs, who supported the Hanoverian succession,
and the Tories, who included those opposed to it, as well as the
nature and extent of support for Jacobitism; the reception of a
delegation from the University of Cambridge in 1706 and,
following his appointment in the autumn of 1713, new English
books dispatched from London by the Hanoverian resident
George von Schütz. George Augustus had begun to learn English
in 1701, soon after the Act of Settlement; Sophia extolled his
speedy progress the following spring.[135] Bilingualism would
form a cornerstone of Frederick's education. At necessary intervals Sophia also protested her fondness for her British niece: 'I
believe that it would be for the good of England that the Queen
should live for a hundred years,' she wrote cumbrously to the
Duke of Marlborough.[136] Out of earshot she grumbled at the
failure of Anne's government to grant her a pension or civil list
payments, or to invest her with the title Princess of Wales. 'I
quite agree, "*Altesse Royale*" [Royal Highness] has become very
vulgar now, much more common than "Your Electoral Serene
Highness",' Liselotte consoled her.[137]

In this process of preparation, Caroline acted independently.
Sophia was thirty-five years older than Anne. For all she

invoked a Dutch proverb about creaking wagons going far, her chances of surviving even so sickly an individual as Anne were slight. George Louis was a man of middle age, dogmatic, unenthusiastic about leaving Hanover. He shared Liselotte's view that 'what one is familiar with is always better than anything strange, and the fatherland always appears best to us Germans', and perhaps also her sense of foreboding that, as king, he would 'find more worry and trouble than pleasure in his regal condition, and ... often say to himself, "If only I were still Elector, and in Hanover."'[138] As Caroline recognised, it was she and George Augustus who stood to profit most from imminent changes. Deliberately she set out to demonstrate a comprehensive embracing of all things British, establishing the pattern to which, in public, husband and wife adhered for the foreseeable future. In her own case this extended even to her name. While she signed her early correspondence with Leibniz, for example, 'W. Caroline', by 1710 she was simply 'Caroline', Wilhelmine abandoned, as it would remain. The English-sounding 'Caroline' allied her with earlier Stuarts. Caroline and Charles shared a common Latin root in 'Carolus': the coincidence of name was capable of suggesting continuity between dynasties. It seems likely that this double recommendation outweighed a similar link between Wilhelmine and William. Architect of the Hanoverian succession, champion of both Sophia and George Augustus, the Dutch-born William III lacked the native appeal of Charles II.

In her self-anglicisation Caroline was helped by increasing numbers of British travellers who made their way to Hanover. On 11 September 1710, Mademoiselle Schutz, niece of George Louis's minister Baron Bernstorff, wrote to a friend in London that the electoral court contained quantities of English visitors.[139] Others wrote to Caroline, like Edmund Gibson, chaplain to Archbishop Tenison, who in March 1714 sent her a copy of his *Codex juris ecclesiastici Anglicani*, on the government and discipline of the Church of England, accompanied by fulsome compliments.[140]

Caroline first tasted tea at her own request from English visitors to Herrenhausen. She employed a Miss Brandshagen to talk and read to her every day in English, unaware that the thickness of the latter's German accent would leave her with a heavy Hanoverian burr for the remainder of her life. Her English was never perfect, although one commentator credited her with mastering the language 'uncommonly well for one born outside England', and in July 1712 Sophia claimed she had begun to speak the language very prettily, and was amusing herself reading everything she could lay hands on either in support of, or against, the Hanoverian succession.[141] Alured Clarke's claim that her 'uncommon turn for conversation' was 'assisted by … her skill in several languages … [and] art of compounding words and phrases, that were more expressive of her ideas than any other' suggests a distinctive patois of mixed origin, almost certainly including elements of English, French and German.[142] At Herrenhausen she spoke English to the Countess of Schaumburg-Lippe, whose own written English survives as flawless, and in the summer of 1714 to the poet John Gay, whose relief at being spared speaking French as a result was tangible.[143] Both women, Gay wrote, 'subscrib'd to Pope's *Homer*, and her Highness did me the honour to say, she did not doubt it would be well done, since I recommended it'.[144] Caroline also requested from the poet a copy of his own recent verse, *The Shepherd's Week*. Earlier, in another instance of her grasp of cultural developments, Caroline had asked a visiting diplomat to obtain for her in London the works of exiled French essayist Charles de Saint-Evremond, which had been published for the first time in 1705, following Saint-Evremond's burial in Poets' Corner in Westminster Abbey.

Thanks in no small measure to Caroline, the spring after her marriage, Howe was able to report the enthusiasm of the electoral family for celebrating Queen Anne's birthday. 'The Electoral Prince and Princess ... told me the night before that they would come and dance. Half an hour before the ball began, they brought me word that the Electress was also coming. The Electress gave the Queen's health at supper, and stayed till two o'clock.'[145]

Anne's response to such heavyweight flattery was muted. The value she attached to it can be judged from the silence with which she greeted news of the birth of Princess Amelia in 1711 and that of Princess Caroline in 1713. Her 'perfect friendship' proved, in appearances at least, decidedly variable. By contrast the Duke of Marlborough wrote to George Augustus following Amelia's birth of 'the joy that comes to mind from the increase of your illustrious house. It is a subject of rejoicing to all who have at heart the interests and satisfaction of Your Highness.'[146] Meanwhile Caroline's assiduous anglophilia looked beyond Anne's lifespan. While her second daughter had been named for members of her German family Amelia Sophia Eleanor, her third daughter was christened Caroline Elizabeth. It was a clear indication of the direction of her parents' thoughts.

In describing George Augustus as possessing 'rather an unfeeling than a bad heart', Lord Chesterfield expressed the opinion of his more generous contemporaries.[147] The Jacobite Lord Strafford dismissed him as 'passionate, proud and peevish'.[148] The prince had inherited in some measure the 'honest blockhead' instincts of his father, 'more properly dull than lazy'; he shared with his father and his wife the fixation, widespread at German courts, with 'pedigrees that were of no more signification than Pantagruel's in Rabelais', familiar with the antecedents 'of every reigning prince then in Europe'.[149] George Augustus lacked the 'penetrating eye' Lord Egmont noted in Caroline, lacked too her penetrating mind.[150] Yet husband and wife were affectionate and companionable. In different ways, each was devoted to their growing family. Unlike George Louis, both were straightforwardly ambitious about their British prospects. And Caroline's good looks had mostly survived her brush with smallpox. At a court where the women were so heavily powdered that the custom of kissing on greeting had been abandoned, Caroline was naturally pale-skinned, with a pink-and-white glow captured in 1714 in a portrait miniature by Swiss artist Benjamin Arlaud.[151] Her physical charms inspired in her highly sexed husband a giddy sort of libidinous infatuation, which would prove of long duration.

They were not, however, equals in temperament, intellect or outlook. George Augustus was described as 'of a small understanding', while Caroline possessed 'a quickness of apprehension, seconded by a great judiciousness of observation'.[152] Her love of reading, which extended to rereading favourite texts like Leibniz's *Theodicy*, based on conversations between the philosopher and Figuelotte, stirred her husband to boorish spite. He dismissed her instincts as those of a schoolmistress, 'often rebuked her for dabbling in all that lettered nonsense (as he termed it), called her a pedant' – but on the evidence of her plan, in November 1715, to have *Theodicy* translated into English, failed to sway her mind.[153] He was quick to pique, crimson-faced in his fury. His tantrums exploded and receded like August thunder, and accounts of him venting his anger by kicking his wig around the room like a football inevitably suggest Rumpelstiltskin. By contrast one gushing newspaper labelled Caroline of 'majestic mien ... extraordinary sense ... greatness of soul'.[154] Her self-control points to a nature more moderate or more calculating, either the 'low cunning' Lady Mary Wortley Montagu disliked in her or the 'softness of behaviour and ... command of herself' applauded elsewhere.[155] As we will see, there are strong grounds for challenging Lady Mary's view that Caroline's 'extravagant fondness' for George Augustus was 'counterfeited'; and if we accept her statement that 'his pleasures ... [Caroline] often told him were the rule of all her thoughts and actions', the grounds for such behaviour are easy enough to identify in the sexual politics of the period, as the history of Sophia Dorothea amply demonstrates.[156] George Augustus had the vanity of a royal first-born, a double entitlement of sex and status. Caroline was spouse, orphan, poor relation, as conscious of her disadvantages as of her strengths.

Leibniz wrote that he 'admired the equability and honour, the kindness and moderation, which this princess maintains amidst such great prosperity'.[157] There were gaps within the couple's marriage. Caroline combined clear-sightedness about her husband's limitations with emotional warmth commended by George Ridpath, editor of the *Flying Post*, as 'exemplary'.[158] George Augustus himself said that 'her sweetness of temper ... check[ed] and assuage[d] his own hastiness and resentment'.[159] Her later behaviour would indicate her pride in his sexual thraldom. She did not forget that she owed her 'great prosperity' to him.

We should not be surprised that George Augustus took mistresses, nor that the woman he ultimately chose for this role was modest and self-effacing and, like Caroline, sufficiently sensible to shield him from exposure to his own shortcomings. He did not love her, and her sexual allure never eclipsed Caroline's. Like heroics on the battlefield at Oudenaarde, George Augustus's acquisition of a mistress was another facet of princely *gloire*, 'a necessary appurtenance to his grandeur as a prince [more] than an addition to his pleasures as a man' – important twice over in the case of this posturing, insecure prince-in-waiting, whose father denied him purpose or employment.[160] Horace Walpole suggested he was motivated by the 'egregious folly of fancying that inconstancy proved that he was not governed [by his wife]' and that he, not Caroline, had the upper hand in their relationship.[161] If so, as we shall see, he failed.

Henrietta Hobart was a woman of good family, good-looking without beauty and forced by the early deaths of her parents to hasten into marriage, which she did, aged seventeen, in March 1706. Unlike Caroline in a similar position, she badly miscalculated. 'Wrong-headed, ill-tempered, obstinate, drunken, extravagant, brutal', Charles Howard was an impoverished good-for-nothing despite aristocratic connections. He swiftly reduced his teenage wife to penurious misery and, in his cups, a state of near-constant fear for her own safety.[162]

Like Caroline, however, Henrietta Howard was resourceful and courageous; she was serious-minded and intelligent, 'a complete treatise on subjects moral, instructive and entertaining … [her] reasoning clear & strong'.[163] Adversity had schooled her in compliance and made her cynical too. Seven years of humiliating marriage had reduced her to the cunning of an adventuress. In 1713 she conceived a plan to escape the disastrous financial straits to which her husband's profligacy had reduced them. For a year in dreary London lodgings she scrimped and saved; she sold the last of their possessions, including even their bedding; she received from a maker of periwigs an offer of eighteen guineas for her 'extremely fair, and remarkably fine' hair; and with heroic self-sacrifice, she entrusted to the care of relations her adored seven-year-old son, Henry.[164] Then husband and wife, bound together only by need and intense mutual dislike, crossed the North Sea from England to Hanover. Their intention was to salvage their fortunes by securing paid employment with Britain's future rulers.

Henrietta's target was the dowager electress Sophia, heiress to the throne. Her introduction, easily procurable for a well-born Englishwoman, was a success. Henrietta's natural emollience, pleasing appearance and, most of all, her knowledge and reading, commended her rapidly. Her visit to Herrenhausen was repeated, then repeated again. She met Caroline. Henrietta's professed admiration for Leibniz, possibly a careful deceit, impressed both princesses. Caroline offered her a position as *dame du palais*, or lady-in-waiting, beginning immediately; Sophia extended the promise of a greater prize, an appointment as bedchamber woman in the event of her accession to the British throne, with a salary of £300. More surprisingly, the unprepossessing Charles Howard – 'a most unamiable man, sour, dull and sullen' – secured a promise of equivalent employment from George Louis, as groom of the bedchamber.[165]

Caroline considered herself fortunate in the acquaintance of this charming, cultivated English gentlewoman, like the Countess of Schaumburg-Lippe close to her in age, with apparently sympathetic interests. In her thoughts was no idea of pleasing George Augustus. She had not intended to welcome a cuckoo into her nest. Nor was the role of mistress one Henrietta had planned or coveted: her motives began and ended with financial stability. Given the nature of Caroline's marriage, in which husband and wife were frequently together, and the relative intimacy of scale of their apartments in the Leineschloss, it was inevitable that Henrietta's employment by Caroline should also bring her to George Augustus's notice. In the first place, she proved one of several objects of his ambulant cupidity.

They did not become lovers in Hanover, nor, later, straight away in London. So gradual was Henrietta's transition from lady-in-waiting to prince's mistress that Caroline had time to accustom herself to her husband's infidelity. By then he had taken other lovers; by then Caroline knew enough of Henrietta, and George Augustus's attitude towards her, to assess with confidence the limits of her rival's influence. But a telling detail suggests that such equanimity may not have been her first response, recognising in Hanover the way the wind was blowing. Sophia told her that the liaison would improve George Augustus's English.[166] This wry dismissal, offered by the older woman to the younger, was perhaps her means of setting aside Caroline's resistance, and seems to point to initial objections on

Caroline's part. Sophia's intervention reminded her of unchanging truths about princely marriage. Stoically Eleonore had endured Billa von Neitschütz, Sophia the Countess von Platen; George Louis, of course, had Madame Schulenburg. Even Frederick of Prussia, who had so little interest in Madame von Wartenburg that their relationship remained unconsummated, understood that the status of a prince demanded a mistress; Figuelotte's revenge had consisted of addressing her exclusively in French, a language Madame von Wartenburg did not understand. Mistresses were simply accessories to a crown. For a princess of Caroline's ambition, it was a debit to be weighed against credits. With George Augustus's complicity, she would prevent Henrietta from becoming his confidante. Strenuously Caroline would deny her younger rival any exercise of influence. Sensibly she swallowed Liselotte's advice: 'Once jealousy has taken root there is no getting rid of it.'[167]

On 16 December 1713, prompted by rumours of Anne's rapidly worsening health, Leibniz sent Caroline assurances of his 'perpetual devotion'. More revealingly, he wrote, 'I pray ... that you may one day enjoy the title of Queen of England so well worn by Queen Elizabeth, which you so highly merit.'[168]

It was a striking connection to draw. England's Elizabeth I was synonymous with strong female rule. Skilfully she had resisted encroachments on her power by male politicians; she had allowed herself to appear a Protestant champion; she had participated in a court culture in which the figure of the queen inspired poets, playwrights, painters; she was a figurehead for English victory over the Spanish; as the Virgin Queen she posed as a divinely endowed mother of her people. Bar the last her roles were adjuncts of sovereignty, pretensions that lay beyond Caroline's remit as consort. As ever, Leibniz's purpose was flattery. In spotlighting Elizabeth over more recent female rulers Mary II and Anne, his compliments ignored the wifely submission of Mary and Anne's vexed struggles to dominate bitter political factionalism. They overlooked Marlborough's victories against the French and the effectively publicised Protestant piety of both Stuart women, their grounds for usurping their Catholic father, James II. Instead Leibniz aligned Caroline within what was already a more mythologised tradition, regarded in eighteenth-century Britain as a golden age. Within his courtly sycophancy lay a statement of aspiration.

Leibniz said just enough to acknowledge Caroline's dependence on George Augustus: 'Consequently I wish ... good things to his Highness, your consort, since you can only occupy the throne of that great Queen with him.'[169] His defining of George Augustus as the agent of Caroline's promotion – 'his Highness, your consort' – is significant. Leibniz had first encountered Caroline a decade earlier. His intuition was fallible, as we have seen in the matter of her proposed marriage to the Archduke Charles, but his knowledge of her character was extensive. His association of Caroline with Elizabeth I was highly charged, even if the seed had been sown by Caroline herself, six months earlier, in naming her daughter 'Caroline Elizabeth': inevitably it invited comparisons between the two women. If such a comparison represents a distortion of Caroline's true nature, it reveals much of how Leibniz regarded her.

In her response, Caroline demurred without conviction. Elegantly she shuffled Leibniz's compliment on to Sophia. Still her reply uncovers facets of her self-perception and, undeniably, something of her longing for the British throne: 'I accept the comparison which you draw, though all too flattering, between me and Queen Elizabeth as a good omen. Like Elizabeth, the Electress's rights are denied by a jealous sister with a bad temper [Anne] and she will never be sure of the English crown until her accession to the throne. God be praised that our Princess of Wales [Sophia] is better than ever, and by her good health confounds all the machinations of her enemies.'[170] A spirited exercise in humbug, Caroline's letter accurately reflects her nervousness about the Hanoverian succession. 'You do well to send me your good wishes for the throne of England, which are sorely needed just now, for … affairs there seem to be going from bad to worse. For my part (and I am a woman and like to delude myself) I cling to the hope that, however bad things may be now, they will ultimately turn to the advantage of our House.'[171]

Twelve years had elapsed since Parliament had passed the Act of Settlement for Anne's brother-in-law, William III. Without fondness or relish Anne had been forced to accept her German cousins as her heirs, even before she succeeded to the throne. After seventeen fruitless pregnancies she found the succession issue vexatious and distasteful. At intervals, flashes of impatience and irascibility had spliced her 'perfect friendship' for the electoral family. Sophia's demands for further acknowledgement provoked outbursts of frustration, even hostility. Among Britain's political classes, opinion was as divided over the Act as Anne's. Whig supporters favoured its terms, while among Tories and Jacobites were those loyal to the queen's half-brother James Edward Stuart, already recognised by Louis XIV as James III. Daniel Defoe showed that similar divisions existed throughout British society: 'If you cho[o]se to listen to your cookmaids and footmen in the kitchen, you shall hear them scolding and swearing and fighting among themselves, and when you think the noise is about beef and pudding, the dishwater or the kitchen staff, alas, you are mistaken; the feud is about who is for the Protestant Succession and who for the Pretender.'[172]

Inside and outside Parliament partisans and troublemakers contributed to acrimonious debate. To the electoral family this suggested that, after more than a decade, their prospects remained unsettled. Beyond reminding George Louis that she had given 'on all occasions, proofs of my desire that your family should succeed to my crowns', Anne withheld any sop to

Hanoverian nervousness.[173] She would not countenance a single member of the family setting foot in England, 'it being a thing I cannot bear to have any successor here though it were but for a week'.[174] Her half-brother's court was at St Germain-en-Laye, north of Paris, a focus for Jacobite loyalty; she refused to permit a second focus for opposition closer to home, within her own capital. In interpreting her aversion as personal, Sophia and George Louis mistook her.

The political turbulence of Anne's reign further stoked persistent anxiety in Hanover. Parliamentary elections in 1710 returned an increase in the number of Tory members of the House of Commons; the ministry of Robert Harley and Henry St John was more decidedly Tory in persuasion than its predecessor. In 1713 its leaders canvassed for peace with France. Via the Treaty of Utrecht, Britain formally withdrew from the War of the Spanish Succession. Her allies, including Hanover, remained at war, proof in Hanoverian eyes that the British government had ceased to regard the electorate's fortunes as contiguous with its own. George Louis considered the peace an act of betrayal. It provided grounds for dislike of the Tories for both George Louis and George Augustus for years to come.

Beginning in the autumn of 1713, dispatches from the new Hanoverian resident in England, George von Schütz, bolstered George Louis's uncertainties. Like his employers, Schütz bluntly misread Anne's intentions. He described the queen as 'totally prejudiced against us': 'she will endeavour to leave the crown to the greatest stranger rather than ... the Electoral family'. His explanation of her motives lay in belated feelings of filial guilt: 'It is certain she attributes the loss of her children to the dethroning of her father.'[175] Letters from Liselotte echoed the strain. 'Queen Anne must be well aware in her heart of hearts that our young king [James Edward Stuart] is her brother; I feel certain that her conscience will wake up before her death, and she will do justice to her brother,' she wrote on 12 January 1714, after a winter in which gout, erysipelas and recurrent fever had undermined Anne's battered health.[176]

Under the circumstances, George Louis's response, made with the support of all his family, could not have been more provocative. Among requirements of the memorandum he dispatched to England at the beginning of May 1714 was Anne's agreement to residence in Britain for a member of the electoral family. Anne's rejection was curt, categorical, furious: letters dispatched separately to Sophia, George Louis and George Augustus, each uncompromising in its rebuttal. Among their disavowals was any possibility of George Augustus taking his place in the House of Lords as Duke of Cambridge, which she described as an 'infringement ... on my sovereignty ... a project so contrary to my royal authority'.[177] 'The Electoral Prince ... is practically in despair about going to take his seat in the English Parliament according to his right,' Caroline wrote afterwards. 'I fear for [his] health, perhaps even his life.'[178] Equally emotionally, the eighty-three-year-old Sophia claimed the affair would be the death of her, but retained sufficient vim to hope that Anne's angry rejoinders might be published to discredit her. Caroline's subsequent letter to Leibniz reads like a public manifesto, its smooth denial of private intent a slick piece of political self-effacement. 'I do not know how the world may judge our conduct,' she writes of George Louis's request and George Augustus's dashed hopes. 'I do not regret the loss we may personally suffer from it so much as having in some measure to abandon the cause of our religion, the liberty of Europe, and so many brave and honest friends in England.'[179] Once before she had demonstrated the strength of her Protestant convictions. Beneath the pious afflatus was truth in her mistrust of James Edward Stuart's Catholicism.

Of course George Augustus did not die of his despair. Sophia's demise, by contrast, three days after receipt of Anne's searing rejoinder, may have been hastened by the intemperance of her reaction to that missive and the extent to which 'the miserable affair weighed on her mind', overwhelming serener thoughts.[180] She was walking in the gardens of Herrenhausen after dinner, with Caroline and a company of her ladies, including the Countess of Schaumburg-Lippe, when she collapsed quite suddenly. She died as the first spatterings of rain darkened the manicured pathways, and every effort to revive her, including bleeding her feet and cutting her stays, failed. Anne's weary dismissal of the news of her death as 'chipping porridge' – a thing of no significance – represents a final defeat for Sophia's vanity.

In the event, Anne survived her German heiress by six weeks before she too died, infinitely fatigued and, at forty-nine, preternaturally aged, on 1 August 1714. 'Sleep,' wrote her doctor, 'was never more welcome to a weary traveller than death was to her.'[181] At St James's Palace the accession of George Louis as George I was trumpeted to crowds of the curious soon after one o'clock in the afternoon. Later the same day, similar announcements were made across the country, including in York, where Lady Mary Wortley Montagu witnessed 'greater Crouds of people than I believ'd to be in York, vast Acclamations and the appearance of a general satisfaction, the Pretender afterwards dragg'd about the streets and burnt, ringing of Bells, bonfires and illuminations, the mob crying liberty and property and long live K[ing] George'.[182]

Thanks to Anne's intransigence, neither George Louis nor any other member of his family was present in London to witness the age-old spectacle or hear the sonorous proclamation; they were similarly absent from proclamations in Edinburgh and Dublin on 5 and 6 August. To his daughter Sophia Dorothea, thanking her for her congratulations, the new king stated his intention of frequently returning to Hanover. In London, the insertion into the prayerbook of the names of the new royal family was accomplished as a matter of urgency.

At a stroke, Caroline's husband became heir to the thrones of England, Scotland and Ireland, as well as the electorate. Her fears, carefully communicated to Leibniz, proved empty. 'The cause of our religion, the liberty of Europe, and so many brave and honest friends in England' would not be abandoned after all. In George Louis's fifty-fifth year, she dared anticipate a greater prize than George Augustus's seat in the House of Lords as Duke of Cambridge: that sumptuous inheritance that first Sophia, afterwards George Augustus himself, had nurtured in her thoughts since the autumn of 1705. No longer were her aspirations the womanly delusions she had once dismissed so coyly.

But sadness at Sophia's death tempered every expectation. In her correspondence Caroline turned to Liselotte and Leibniz, last links in the gilded chain that, two decades earlier, had rescued her in the aftermath of Eleonore's death. 'It is true that HRH the Princess of Wales does me the honour of writing very diligently,' Liselotte noted. 'Her shortest letters are five sheets long, written on four sides; yesterday I received seven sheets, making twenty-eight pages, the previous one was thirty-five, and an earlier one was forty-three sheets.'[183] Her letters were an outlet for Caroline's feelings. Liselotte's long-distance companionship offered partial compensation for the loss of Figuelotte and Sophia. Her view that Caroline possessed a heart, 'a rare thing as times go', is a valuable assessment.[184] Unlike the public effusions that greeted Caroline after 1714, it is based on personal knowledge in a private context, albeit an epistolary version of herself that Caroline constructed in a lengthy correspondence, writer and recipient destined never to meet. With gloomy relish, the older woman would warn her 'there have been few queens of England who have led happy lives'.[185]

On 4 September 1714, the deputy earl marshal, the 6th Earl of Suffolk, published 'A Ceremonial for the Reception of His Most Sacred Majesty George, By the Grace of God, King of Great

Britain, etc, Upon His Arrival from Holland to his Kingdom of
Great Britain'. Suffolk's 'publick notice' stipulated times and
places where 'the Nobility, the Lord Mayor, Aldermen and
Citizens of London, etc, are to meet in order to attend His
Majesty'. In celebration it called for conduits to run with wine
and 'the great guns' at the Tower of London to be discharged
twice in bold salute. On the new king's arrival at St James's
Palace, it required 'the Foot Guards in the Park [to] fire three
volleys, and the Cannon in the Park ... to be discharged'.[186] The
document made no mention of Caroline, who at George Louis's
request remained in Hanover for several weeks after his own
departure.

The king was accompanied on his journey to London by his
son, his mistress Madame Schulenburg, the latter's three
'nieces', key ministers and courtiers, including his vice master
of the horse (and husband of his illegitimate half-sister Sophia
Charlotte), Johann Adolf von Kielmansegg, whom he meant to
oversee his English hunting, a tailor, two trumpeters, two physicians, footmen, pages, a complete kitchen staff and a dwarf of
surprisingly stentorian tones called Christian Ulrich Jorry,
whose particular requirements, given his size, included the skills
of George Louis's tailor: in total a flotilla of four frigates, twenty-
two warships and six transports for personnel aside from the
royal yacht.[187] Satirical opinion dismissed the entire pack as
'pimps, whelps and reptiles'.[188] Caroline's suite the following
month was smaller and correspondingly less incendiary. It
included the Countess of Schaumburg-Lippe, who, after a
lengthy separation, left behind her neglectful husband Frederick
Christian and assumed the title Countess of Bückeburg, and
another favourite lady-in-waiting, Baroness von Gemmingen.
Princesses Anne and Amelia travelled with her.

On George Louis's instructions, Frederick stayed behind in
Hanover with his great-uncle, Ernest Augustus. His grandfather
had decided that Frederick would serve as the family's

permanent representative in the electorate. He was seven years old. Only in January, Sophia had written to Liselotte of his excitement that Christmas. 'I have no doubt that your Prince Fritzchen was absolutely delighted with the Christchild, because I still remember so well how I loved it,' Liselotte replied.[189] To enforce a permanent separation from his parents and siblings on so young a child was an act of terrible cruelty, from which neither prince nor parents would fully recover. Caroline's immediate response has not survived, but it is unlikely that George Louis invited discussion of his decision; he had previously asserted his right to make key choices regarding Frederick's upbringing in the educational programme he devised for the boy in September 1713, entrusted to his chamberlain J.F. von Grote. Nor did Caroline confide her feelings to Henrietta Howard, who had left behind in England her own seven-year-old son only the previous year. Instead she consoled herself that her case was less extreme than that of her mother: in the 1690s, Eleonore had temporarily lost both of her children to the court of Berlin.

Further delayed by the illness of her youngest daughter, who remained for the time being in Hanover, Caroline travelled as far as the Dutch coast with her brother, William Frederick. Both correctly surmised that they would never see one another again, and henceforth William Frederick's outward focus reverted to the localised concerns of his forebears. In 1729, his son Charles married his Hohenzollern kinswoman Frederica Louisa of Prussia, Figuelotte's granddaughter and George Augustus's niece. His passion for hunting, especially falconry, earned him the moniker the 'wild' margrave. Among those who made valedictory visits to Herrenhausen to take leave of Caroline and her daughters was George Augustus's grandmother, the 'mouse droppings in the pepper' Duchess Eléonore.

Before her departure, Caroline appointed her first two English ladies of the bedchamber. They were Louisa, Countess of

Berkeley, and Elizabeth, Countess of Dorset, whose husband was described in terms certain to endear him to George Augustus as 'in spite of the greatest dignity in his appearance ... in private the greatest lover of low humour and buffoonery'; he would later be rewarded with a dukedom.[190] Four years earlier, through foresight or simple calculation, Mary, Countess Cowper, had opened a correspondence in French with Caroline, apparently with a view to a similar appointment; with her children, she claimed, she had taken to nightly drinking '[George Augustus's] Health by the Name of *Young Hanover Brave*'.[191] Following Anne's death, she dispatched a 'Letter of Congratulation ... [and] another Letter to offer her my Service, and to express the perfect Resignation I had to whatever she would think fit to do, were it to choose or refuse me'.[192]

Caroline's reply was evasive. Its suggestion that the decision rested ultimately with George Augustus was deliberate and significant. In her letter to Mary Cowper, Caroline constructed the conceit with which she would keep faith lifelong, of a partnership between husband and wife, in which the latter deferred to the former; it was only partly misleading. 'This Letter she answered,' wrote Lady Cowper, 'telling me she was entirely at the *Prince's* Disposal, and so could give me no Promise; but that she did not doubt the *Prince's* Willingness to express his Friendship to me upon all Occasions.'[193] Little wonder that the poet Stephen Duck, seeing only what Caroline wanted him to see, could later describe her as the 'most submissive Wife;/Who never yet her Consort disobey'd'.[194] Caroline's career as Princess of Wales had begun.

PART TWO

Britain

I

Princess of Wales

'Majesty with Affability'

On 13 October 1714, to the crack of gun salutes at the Tower of London and in St James's Park, Caroline arrived in a city described only six years previously as among 'the most Spacious, Populous, Rich, Beautiful, Renowned and Noble … that we know of at this day in the World: 'Tis the Seat of the *British* Empire, the Exchange of *Great Britain* and *Ireland*; the Compendium of the Kingdom, the Vitals of the Commonwealth, and the Principal Town of Traffic …'[1] She would never leave.

Two days previously she had arrived at Margate on the Kent coast, escorted by a squadron of English men-of-war. Her passage, aboard the royal yacht *Mary*, had taken ten days. 'Speaking of the Princess's comeing', on 21 September to George Augustus, the new lord chancellor, William Cowper, had 'wish'd she was here while the Weather was good, lest she sho'd be in Danger in her Passage; he [George Augustus] [had] said, Providence had hitherto so wonderfully prosper'd his Family's succeeding to the Crown in every Respect … that he hoped it wo'd perfect it' – a hope that was realised in Caroline's uneventful crossing.[2] After a ceremonial welcome at Rochester she travelled to London with George Augustus at her side and accompanied by her elder daughters. Their journey to St James's Palace was cheered by representatives of all seven classes of Englishman recently identified by Daniel Defoe, from 'the *great*, who live profusely' to 'the *miserable*, that really pinch and suffer want'.[3] It was a fitting first exposure to her husband's future subjects.

For their part, the British applauded Caroline's manner while judging her appearance less to their tastes than did her countrymen; she drew compliments for her 'native Majesty' and easy comportment.[4] An occasional visitor to court described her as 'fat ... of a fine complexion, & ... very ugly'; subsequent gifts of clotted cream from a lady-in-waiting may point to a sweet tooth.[5] The same observer judged her height at somewhere between that of George Louis and the shorter George Augustus, but acknowledged that she seemed 'very good natur'd & obligeing'. The *Daily Courant* informed its readers that 'the whole conversation' of those who encountered Caroline 'turn[ed] upon the charms, sweetness and good manner of this excellent princess, whose generous treatment of everybody, who has had the honour to approach her, is such that none have come from her without being obliged by some particular expression of her favour'.[6] Similarly anodyne was an early commemorative print by John Simon. Even in this conventional image of poodle curls and ermine furbelows lurks a glimmer of shrewdness in Caroline's unblinking gaze.[7] The publisher labelled the portrait 'Wilhelmina Charlotta, Princess of Wales', evidently unaware of Caroline's change of name. A contemporary German version of a related image used the same names.[8]

At thirty-one, a mother of four children, her early bloom dulled by smallpox and her figure beginning to thicken, Caroline would chiefly be appraised not on her looks but her religious soundness and her fecundity – according to John Gay, 'the lovely parent of our royal race ... The tender mother, and the faithful wife.'[9] She was the first Princess of Wales since Catherine of Aragon married Henry VIII's elder brother Arthur in 1502. Not since the birth in 1367 of the future Richard II, a grandson of Edward III, had a royal succession been assured over three generations. And since the death in 1708 of Queen Anne's husband, Prince George of Denmark, Britain had lacked a royal spouse. Descriptions of George as 'very fat, loves news, his bottle and the Queen' offered Caroline limited guidance in creating a role for herself.[10]

Within weeks of her arrival, Joseph Addison, who had first seen Caroline in Hanover in 1706, could claim, 'No longer shall the widow'd Land bemoan/A broken Lineage, and a doubtful Throne;/But boast her Royal Progeny's increase,/And count the Pledges of her future Peace./O Born to strengthen and to grace our Isle!'[11] She was praised as the mother of 'hopeful issue' by the Bishop of Oxford, William Talbot, in a sermon that anticipated 'many more pledges of the lasting happiness of these kingdoms'.[12] In his *Royal Progress* of 1714, poet Thomas Tickell celebrated the fruitfulness of Caroline's marriage to George Augustus: 'A train of kings their fruitful love supplies.'

Her copper-bottomed Protestantism contrasted favourably with the Catholicism of recent female consorts: buck-toothed proselyte Henrietta Maria, the wife of Charles I; Charles II's barren Portuguese queen, Catherine of Braganza; and Mary of Modena, James II's teenage bride, reviled as the 'Pope's daughter'. 'In your most tender years,' offered the *Saturday Evening Post*, 'you despis'd with so much courage and firmness those dazzling grandeurs which combated the duties you ow'd to conscience that there's nothing too great for the Protestant religion to expect from so noble a soul.'[13] The General Assembly of the Church of Scotland praised her as 'a princess that has signalled her zeal for the Protestant religion, and hath shown to the world that nothing can with her come in competition with the honour of her God and redeemer, and the peace of her own conscience'.[14] Echoing what was clearly already a commonplace, a Welsh schoolboy called John Morgan described Caroline as one 'who rather for the sake of Piety, Our Princess than an Empress chose to be'.[15] And approval of Caroline's Protestantism inspired a wider celebration of her virtues. With appealing asperity, the poet Mary Jones singled out her sincerity: 'This Virtue, 'tis said, was first brought over by Wilhelmina-Carolina, Daughter of Frederick, Marquis of Brandenburg-Anspach: but as it was a Plant perfectly exotic, and could never be brought to flourish in this Soil; that illustrious Princess did not much attempt to cultivate it, except in a few warm Bosoms like her own.'[16] A reissue of John Toland's *An Account of the courts of Prussia and Hannover*, published in 1714 with passages about Caroline added since the first edition of 1705, signified the rise in her prominence and her central place in the new royal family.[17]

At the outset commentators understood Caroline's role as primarily reproductive, guarantor of future stability by securing the succession. Save in their impact on her children's education, her cultural and intellectual achievements were ignored. None remarked on her pleasure in discovering for herself the libraries assembled by William and Mary at St James's Palace and at Kensington. A single unusual unsigned print of this period places Caroline's portrait between seated figures of Religion and Knowledge.[18]

In her first official portrait, by Sir James Thornhill, in a medallion on the painted ceiling of the Queen's Great Bedchamber at the palace of Hampton Court, completed in 1715, the princess is invested with more typical – and more typically bland – symbolic attributes. A spray of pink roses denotes love and England; she is associated with good sense and, critically, with plenty and ripeness, represented by grapes and a pumpkin.[19]

That Caroline had been forced to leave behind in Hanover the most dynastically important of her children, Frederick, does not appear to have given rise to undue comment: Frederick's portrait also featured on Thornhill's painted ceiling. Rather, engravings like Michiel van der Gucht's triptych 'Our Present Royall Soveraign L[or]d', in which a portrait of George Louis is flanked by images of George Augustus and Frederick, and a mezzotint of Caroline's four eldest children, published by Edward Cooper, in which a spear-carrying Frederick is surrounded by his pretty sisters, celebrated the strength of the royal line, overlooking Frederick's absence and the family's fragmentation.[20] Airily, a song of 1714 hymned 'Prince Frederick, the Rose that in Hanover grows,/And now springs with delightful Bloom'.[21] On the eve of their sailing, watchers in The Hague had drawn attention to princesses Anne and Amelia, whose 'excellent behaviour … showed much above what their age could promise, one being but three and a half and the other but five years old', a compliment to Caroline in her role of mother and preceptress.[22] Lady Cowper likewise noted, 'the little *Princesses* are Miracles of their Ages, especially *Princess* Anne, who at five Years old speaks, reads and writes both German and French to Perfection, knows a great deal of History and Geography, speaks English very prettily, and dances very well'.[23] Bar the prettiness of Anne's English, all were talents inherited from, and insisted upon by, her capable mother. So too was the trait soon identified by one of Caroline's bedchamber women. Anne, she wrote, 'displayed from an early age a most ambitious temper'.[24]

Three years later, Thornhill again painted the princess, as part of the huge mural of the Hanoverian succession in the dining hall at Greenwich Naval Hospital. He presented her in the figure of Prudence. Again she was accompanied by her children.

Despite differences in scale, London in the early eighteenth century was every bit as cramped as Ansbach or Hanover, tight within their ancient walls. Unlike either, home to more than half a million inhabitants, it had overspilt its medieval boundaries, amazing in its 'prodigious size and length', according to German diarist Zacharias Conrad von Uffenbach, who visited in 1710.[25] It boasted startling pockets of newness and modernity. Half a century before, the Great Fire of London had swept away a Tudor town of jerry-built half-timberings, medieval churches and tenements. From the ashes had arisen new squares and thoroughfares, including the neighbourhood of St James's Palace, where George Louis made his court, depicted by Wenceslaus Hollar in 1660 as a venerable country retreat amid tall trees and broad meadows. In the first days of her arrival, wherever Caroline looked she glimpsed a city in the throes of muscular rejuvenation. The rebuilding of St Paul's Cathedral by surveyor-general Sir Christopher Wren had been completed only three years previously: visible from the palace gardens, its mighty dome dominated London's skyline. In 1714, in Greenwich, Spitalfields and Limehouse, work began on handsome new churches designed by Nicholas Hawksmoor in line with provisions of Queen Anne's Fifty New Churches Act. Shortly work commenced on the tactfully named Hanover Square. Equally tactfully it would displace Soho Square, Leicester Fields and Golden Square as a centre of aristocratic living; householders included the lord chancellor. Ministers and courtiers also settled in Arlington Street, a stone's throw from the palace.

The needs of this enormous, refashioned city were titanic, as Defoe boasted in his *Tour Through the Whole Island of Great Britain*: 'This whole Kingdom, as well as the people, as the land, and even the sea, in every part of it, are employ'd to furnish something, and I may add the best of everything, to supply the city of London with provisions.'[26] London was a centre of consumption. It offered its new royal family every conceivable luxury and all essentials, from the cherries, apples and oysters daily dispatched in season from Kent to the mixed catch of sprats, whiting, herrings and mackerel that arrived from the coast of East Anglia. From Norfolk and Suffolk, poultrymen drove turkeys to London's markets, geese and chickens too; sheep travelled from Lincoln and Leicester, cattle from Scotland, Wales and Kent, including the isles of Skye and Anglesey; sheep for mutton journeyed from Essex. From Herefordshire came bacon and cider, from Cheshire, Gloucester and Warwick cheese, butter from Suffolk and oats from Surrey. Newcastle dispatched sea coal, Shooters Hill faggots. Shoes, gloves, leather, lace, cloth, clocks and everything pertaining to self-adornment and easy living were in greater demand in London than anywhere else in Britain. Among wares offered by the hawkers and street-sellers of Marcellus Laroon's *The Cryes of the City of London Drawne after the Life*, published in 1688, were flounders and 'biskets' and 'ripe speragus' and caged birds, 'long threed laces', 'fine writeing inke', 'lilly white vinegar', 'delicate cowcumbers to pickle' and second-hand 'satten', 'taffety' and velvet.[27] Chimneysweeps, tightrope-walkers, mendicant preachers and, unavoidably, the 'London beggar' and the 'London curtezan' plied their varied trades.

Greedy and unceasing demand created a vibrant market, which in turn, despite extremes of wealth and poverty, shaped the city's buoyant outlook. Like every metropolis, the London Caroline first encountered attracted tricksters and charlatans; it was also home to artists, poets, savants and divines. As John Bancks offered in his *Description of London*: 'Many a Beau without a shilling;/Many a widow not unwilling;/Many a Bargain, if you strike it:/This is LONDON! How d'ye like it?'

In Caroline's case, she had determined to like it long before she arrived. In conversations with Sophia, in the plans she had made with George Augustus, in her diligent and determined espousing of all things British during the decade of her marriage in Hanover, she had prepared herself for this moment when she would emerge as George Augustus's consort upon a different, larger, grander stage. History has depicted early Georgian London, much as it saw itself, as a city of cut-throat optimism and crude scatology, of growing political maturity, hard-drinking brutality and vicious religious polarities, of commercial zeal, financial resourcefulness and skulduggery, of double-dealing among all classes, of artists and writers beady-eyed in their exposure of the follies and foibles of court, Parliament, low life and foreigners, of freedom of speech held dear: a volatile, effervescent, engaged urban culture chauvinistic in its predilections, its citizens, in the eyes of one foreign visitor, in love with 'their nation, its wealth, plenty, and liberty, and the comforts that are enjoyed'.[28]

'The greatest Part of the People do not *Read* Books, Most of them cannot *Read* at all,' lamented the Jacobite pamphleteer Charles Leslie. 'But they will Gather together about one that can *Read*, and Listen to an *Observator* or *Review* (as I have seen them in the Streets).'[29] Those who could read, even among the artisan class, according to an account of the 1720s, kept themselves up to date by 'begin[ning] the day by going to the café to read the news'.[30] Londoners had views, noisily expressed. 'Englishmen are mighty swearers,' noted the Swiss visitor Cesar de Saussure.[31]

Accustomed from girlhood to the toxic 'softness of a Court', Caroline knew enough to take little on appearances as she journeyed through cheering crowds and streets of brick-built houses black with soot on that mild October day. From the beginning she set out to win over this teeming microcosm of the kingdom whose length and breadth would remain hidden from her in the three decades she dwelt exclusively in London and its fringes.

With a combination of affability and regal dignity she impressed the denizens of George Louis's capital. Courtiers had already noted George Augustus's approachability. As early as 12 October they were described as 'backward in speaking to the King, tho' they are ready enough to speak to the Prince'.[32] Clearly husband and wife had evolved between them a deliberate policy of openness, especially as George Augustus was later regarded as one who 'never could put on when he was not pleased' any 'air of good humour'.[33] Lord Hervey, a gentleman of the bedchamber to George Augustus who became one of Caroline's closest friends, later reported Caroline as claiming 'popularity always makes me sick'; her early behaviour seemed designed to just that end.[34] And her approach, in which consciousness of her position was balanced by ebullient warmth, won plaudits. A song written in 1714 by a Mr Durfey claimed that Caroline had possessed all hearts, 'and will more every Age ov'rcome,/By her Temper, that Charms and adorably Warms'.[35]

The coordinated attitudes of the new Prince and Princess of Wales kindled memories of the double monarchy of William III and Mary II, itself the template of Protestant parliamentary kingship prescribed by the Act of Settlement. In the case of Caroline and George Augustus the comparison was accurate insofar as it indicated a shared profile, with aspects of their royal role assigned by gender. Robert Molesworth's dedication to Caroline in 1716 of *Marinda: Poems and Translations upon several occasions* suggests that she benefited from the likeness. Admiringly, Molesworth described her in glowing comparison to Queen Mary: an 'incomparable Consort' who '(like your Royal Highness) understood how to joyn *Majesty* with *Affability*, how to make *Magnificence* consistent with *Oeconomy*, the strictest *Virtue* with the most *Obliging Freedom*; the *Highest Wisdom* with the least *Pretences* to it'.[36] With its focus on royal accountability, it was a distinctively Whig appraisal.

In the event, affability, virtue, wisdom, majesty and a frugal approximation to magnificence would define Caroline's public persona until her death, her version of queenship. Like Mary, her religious faith was key to her standing, as John Gay indicated: 'Religion's cheerful flame her bosom warms,/Calms all her hours, and brightens all her charms.'[37] To bedchamber woman Charlotte Clayton the Bishop of Oxford wrote in the summer of 1714, 'I see ... in her Royal Highness, our blessed Queen Mary revived.'[38] A year later, on the anniversary of George Louis's accession, clergyman Joseph Acres preached that, in Caroline, 'much of the late Queen Mary is revived, who was the best, God knows, the much best Part of us all'.[39] Caroline's early gift of communion plate to one of Westminster's seven Huguenot churches was a philanthropic gesture of support for Protestant exiles from France, possibly prompted by the Huguenot blood George Augustus had inherited from Duchess Eléonore; the political astuteness of the gesture is an indication of Caroline's shrewdness.[40] She was punctilious in her churchgoing and, despite initial mutterings about her Lutheranism, earned praise for her religious observance, 'the devoutest in the World'.[41] She maintained the recent tradition of churchgoing on 'the anniversary of the martyrdom of King Charles the First ... and appeared in mourning, as is usual on that day'.[42] Like Mary, she publicised visible piety alongside programmes of cultural patronage; beneficiaries of her charity included the Corporation of the Sons of the Clergy. And Caroline would be more fortunate than Mary, whose sudden death from smallpox, aged thirty-two, prevented the completion of her plans.

Caroline made her first court appearance the evening after her arrival, at the King's Drawing Room, or formal assembly, at St James's Palace. Entering the crowded room at seven o'clock, she remained for three hours. Of the card games on offer she chose piquet in preference to ombre and basset, both of which were distinguished by high stakes and high losses (on 22 February 1718, for example, the *Original Weekly Journal* reported George Louis losing three thousand guineas playing ombre with the Duchess of Monmouth and the Countess of Lincoln[43]). Among her fellow players was Sarah, Duchess of Marlborough, mistress of the robes to Queen Anne, to whom a tactful Caroline had addressed an introductory letter as obliging 'as if I had been

her equal'.[44] Later the duchess's jealousy, added to her dislike of
Robert Walpole, the politician with whom Caroline was most
closely associated as queen, made her the most astringent of
Caroline's critics. On this occasion there were no dissenting
notes. Nor were eyebrows raised too obviously at Caroline's
choice of cumbersome, lace-trimmed headdress, heavy silk
frock and her preferred embroidered silk 'slippers' – backless,
low-heeled shoes resembling mules – in place of more fashionable shoes with high wooden heels.[45] She had yet to acquire the
'old leather fan' that afterwards exasperated her ladies.[46]

From the card table, Caroline appears not to have discerned
the difference in deportment between British and Hanoverian
women that so troubled the Countess of Bückeburg: 'the English
Women did not look like Women of Quality, but made themselves look as pitifully and sneakingly as they could; ... they
[held] their Heads down and look[ed] always in a Fright,
whereas those that are Foreigners hold up their heads and hold
out their Breasts, and make themselves look as great and stately
as they can, and more nobly and more like Quality than the
others'.[47] While players at nearby tables broke off their games
and formed an attentive circle around Caroline and Lady
Bückeburg, Caroline occupied herself with pleasantries to the
galaxy of new faces, intent on making friends even to the point
of simulating enjoyment: 'In matters of lightest moment she
had so entire a command of herself, that whenever she pleased,
she seemed to enjoy even trifles, as if she was quite unbent, and
had nothing else to attend.'[48] Meanwhile a habitually drunken
peeress would take the earliest opportunity to apprise the countess that, in Britain, noblewomen showed their 'Quality by ...
Birth and Titles, and not by sticking out [their] Bosoms'.[49]

Not only Caroline's stamina for court entertainments but her
willingness, like George Augustus, to speak English – albeit
heavily accented and larded with French – contrasted with the
behaviour of her father-in-law. A report of March 1718 described

George Augustus as speaking English well and correctly on all occasions.[50] George Louis did not disguise his preference for the company of his Hanoverian entourage or the less vapid demands of the business of government, conducted mostly out of sight in a small private room off his bedchamber, inaccessible from the main palace staircase. He declined to play cards. His conversation, in French, was confined to a handful of intimates. Unconcerned either to cultivate the good opinion of his new courtiers or to challenge his dismissal by Jacobites as 'a foreigner ignorant of the language, laws and customs of England', and averse to 'outward Pomp and gaudy Attendance', he spent no more than an hour at the drawing room.[51] He brought with him to England that habit of abstemiousness that Caroline had first noted at the Leineschloss on the evening of her wedding.

Unlike George Augustus and Caroline, he did not walk in St James's Park in the morning or at midday, escorted by yeomen of the guard and accompanied by courtiers, although a painting by Marco Ricci of around 1710 depicts the park, with its three tree-lined avenues, as London's most fashionable promenade – as Lady Hertford remembered it in a letter to her mother in May 1721, the place where 'all the fine folks' exchanged news and gossip, attended by tiny lapdogs, lovers, hangers-on.[52] Nor did he betray by word or deed that relish for his new kingdom that George Augustus and Caroline publicised so studiedly. At a ball at Somerset House in December, 'the Prince and Princess ... danc'd our English Country Dances'.[53] It was a characteristic gesture, this proof of the trouble they had taken to master these distinctively unGerman measures, and was acknowledged the following year when dancing master and choreographer John Essex dedicated to Caroline the second edition of his manual *For the Further Improvement of Dancing*, which included instructions for country dances.[54] Wholly unconvincing, George Augustus's declaration that 'I have not one drop of blood on my veins dat is not English,' and Caroline's only marginally less misleading insistence that she would 'as soon live on a dunghill as return to Hanover', were guaranteed crowd-pleasers.[55] The care Caroline took to publicise her love of British history served the same end: in July 1715 she was reported as stating that 'she was always v[ery] angry with the English when she was reading their history to see how violent and raging they were against one another'.[56] By contrast, the Comte de Broglie described George Louis as without any 'predilection for the English nation, and never receives in private any English of either sex'.[57] Broglie's view was inaccurate – Mary Wortley Montagu was among the new king's intimates – but serves as a reflection of popular perceptions even among court insiders.

The new reign, like court life in Hanover, began with a series of drawing rooms. Caroline's presence at each, she protested lightly, threatened to prevent her from assembling suitable clothes for the coronation. This took place on a bright October day a week after her arrival. The service was a revised version of Queen Anne's, adapted by Archbishop Tenison, its single flourish William Croft's new setting of an anthem first used at the coronation of William and Mary, 'The Lord God is a sun and a shield'. At £7,287, George Louis's coronation cost around half the sum spent by Queen Anne in the previous decade, a result of rapid preparations and the new king's preference for simplicity.[58]

Characteristically, George Louis played his part without marked aplomb. Uninspired verse in the *Flying Post*, London's leading Whig newspaper, turned even this lack of demonstrativeness into a virtue: 'We now the gold and jewels cease to view,/And find the truest jewel lodged in you;/The crown no brightness to the monarch brings,/The Crown takes lustre from the best of kings.'[59] Implicit was a criticism of Stuart monarchy, with its grandeur, theatricality and vainglory. For Britain's new dynasty it was a commendation but also a warning, this rhetoric of just deserts and exemplary behaviour. Tangible enthusiasm on George Louis's part focused on the performance of *Rinaldo* by his former Hanoverian *Kapellmeister* Handel, which was included in the celebrations at his own request. A conciliatory choice, it was the first opera the composer had written in England, in 1711. Handel had dedicated it to Queen Anne, labelling it 'a Native of your Majesty's Dominions, and ... consequently born your Subject'.[60] Enthusiasm for Handel, shared by Caroline and George Augustus and a feature of the last years of Anne's reign, provided connective tissue between old and new regimes.

As Princess of Wales rather than queen consort, Caroline had no place in the formal processions inside Westminster Abbey. She sat beneath a velvet canopy of state, close to the sacrarium, a ringside spectator of goings-on. Her dress was probably that of embroidered silk, worn beneath ermine-lined crimson velvet robes of state fastened with diamond stomacher brooches, in which Kneller painted her in 1716, a stiff and unprepossessing image that nevertheless became Caroline's chief official likeness. It is a less attractive, less informative portrait than that produced at the same time for George Augustus by Swiss miniaturist Christian Friedrich Zincke. Zincke's doll-like figure does full justice not only to Caroline's bosom but to her long pointed nose, inherited from her father, and a steely fixity in her gaze.[61] The relative simplicity of her coronation clothes in both paintings lends credence to Caroline's suggestion that she had had less time than she needed to organise either dress or jewels, and had resorted to careful improvisation. The contrast with the magnificence of the dress she wore at her own coronation thirteen years later – a faithful copy of that worn by Mary II – is pronounced. She is absent from the account of the service Lady Cowper committed to her diary, a sign of her secondary role. The sermon made much of her vocation as mother.

Instead, the religious significance of George Louis's accession formed Mary Cowper's principal focus: 'I own I never was so affected with Joy in all my Life; it brought Tears into my Eyes,

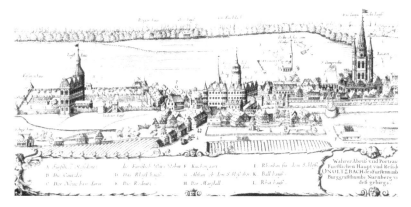

The little town of Ansbach, by Wenceslaus Hollar, c.1630, dominated by the margrave's palace and the Gothic church of St Gumbertus.

Caroline's parents, Eleonore Erdmuthe Louise of Saxe-Eisenach and a doting John Frederick, Margrave of Brandenburg-Ansbach.

Sophia Charlotte, queen in Prussia, known as Figuelotte, by Friedrich Wilhelm Weidemann – a second mother to Caroline, intelligent, irreverent, beautiful.

Frederick III, Elector of Brandenburg, afterwards king in Prussia, who became Caroline's self-appointed guardian in 1696: a man who, in his own words, possessed 'all the attributes of kingliness and in greater measure than other kings'.

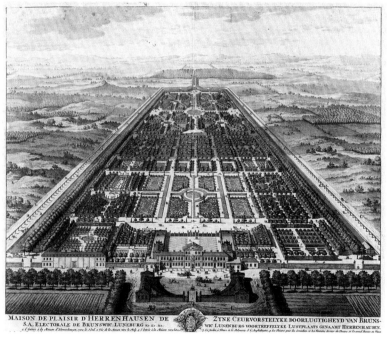

MAISON DE PLAISIR D'HERRENHAUSEN DE S.A. ELECTORALE DE BRUNSWIC LUNEBURG &c. &c. &c.

ZYNE CEURVORSTELYKE DOORLUGTIGHEYD VAN BRUNS-WIC LUNENBURG VOORTREFFELYKE LUSTPLAATS GENAAMT HERRENHAUSEN.

The palace of Herrenhausen, the glory of Hanover, begun in 1665, its garden a series of poker-straight avenues, with gondolas floating on a man-made canal.

Electress Sophia, the dynastic link
between the thrones of England and
Scotland and the Hanoverian electorate.
To her delight, she would become
Caroline's grandmother-in-law.

The man who became Caroline's father-in-law, George Louis, Elector of Hanover, afterwards George I, intractability in every line of his stubborn profile.

This portrait of 1691 by Jacques Vaillant of Sophia Dorothea of Celle depicts the hapless princess with her children, George Augustus, the future George II, and the younger Sophia Dorothea.

The man Caroline married, George Augustus, Electoral Prince of Hanover, afterwards, as seen here, King of Great Britain: cocksure, strutting and a little foolish, but deeply attached to his remarkable bride.

St James's Palace and Pall Mall as they would have appeared in Caroline's lifetime, a reach-me-down setting for royal life.

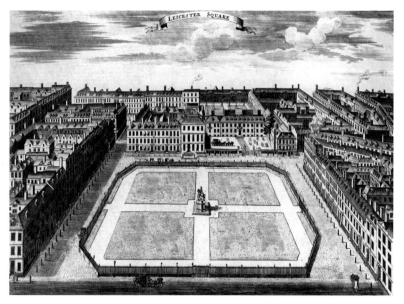

Family feuding forced Caroline and George Augustus to find a home of their own –
Leicester House, in Leicester Square.

Caroline's most devoted female
courtier, woman of the bedchamber
Charlotte Clayton. Caroline told her,
'You know me, & know that I love
people of wit & merit.'

Maid of honour Molly Lepell, one of the
beauties of Caroline's household. Her
marriage to John, Lord Hervey, proved
unhappy.

Henrietta Howard, the rival Caroline skilfully managed, an intelligent adventuress who became George II's mistress through financial necessity – and simultaneously served Caroline as woman of the bedchamber.

Until her death in 1722, Elisabeth Charlotte, Duchess of Orléans, a German princess married to Louis XIV's brother, acted as epistolary confidante to Caroline. They never met.

Described as 'the Queen's Minister' for his closeness to Caroline, Sir Robert Walpole proved himself a puppeteer of genius in his manipulation of both Caroline and George Augustus.

James Thornhill's huge painting of the family of George I in Greenwich Naval Hospital places Caroline, dressed in gold, immediately behind her father-in-law.

and I hope I shall never forget the Blessing of seeing our holy Religion thus preserved, as well as our Liberties and Properties.'[62] Contemporary doggerel suggests alternative viewpoints: 'God in his wrath sent Saul to punish Jewry;/And George to England in greater fury.'[63] Coronation Day riots in some twenty large and small English towns, including Bristol, Chippenham, Canterbury, Norwich and Reading, made disaffection manifest; in Birmingham rioters advocated 'pull[ing] down this King and Sett[ing] up a King of our own'.[64] But inside the abbey all passed smoothly, albeit Jacobite aristocrats, 'looking as cheerful as they could, [were] very peevish with Everybody that spoke to them', or notable through their absence, like the Earl of Kinnoull, who excused himself on grounds of gout.[65] George Augustus's hastily altered coronet had last been worn by Mary II. In place of coronet or diadem, Caroline looped pearls through her fair hair. Her jewels included the so-called 'Hanover pearls' which George Louis had inherited from Sophia.[66] She was denied the opportunity to wear the 141-carat Pitt Diamond by the successive refusal that summer of George Louis and George Augustus to purchase it from its owner Thomas Pitt.[67] This huge jewel was subsequently acquired by the French royal family.

Any record of Caroline's emotions has not survived, but her thoughts surely included the older woman whose jewels she wore and whose ambition for the British throne had inspired her own; Sophia had been dead less than six months. She must have thought too of Frederick, George Augustus's heir, and the decision she had taken a decade ago to decline the Archduke Charles's proposal, 'scorn[ing] an empire for religion's sake', as John Gay imagined it.[68] All around her in the abbey glittered intimations of her future rewards. She was aware on this occasion of the gulf between the positions of consort-in-waiting and consort, and reminded of the extent to which her own position depended entirely on George Augustus. In the short term, she would find few reasons for dissatisfaction. George Louis had no

intention of releasing Sophia Dorothea from incarceration in
Ahlden to resume her place at his side. In her absence Caroline's
position was considerable. Official female royal patronage lay
exclusively within her gift, despite the king's attachment to
Madame Schulenburg and unsubstantiated rumours that the
couple had married morganatically, as well as the privileged
position enjoyed by George Louis's half-sister Sophia Charlotte
von Kielmansegg, who was frequently mistaken for his mistress
though 'as corpulent and ample as [Madame Schulenburg] was
long and emaciated'.[69] As Lady Cowper's letters of the summer
had indicated, the scramble for places in Caroline's household
would be determined and energetic.

Moreover, in the aftermath of the coronation, with George
Louis's consent, Caroline and George Augustus took over
important aspects of the king's entertaining. From now on,
evening assemblies were held not in George Louis's drawing
room but Caroline's, twice a week throughout the first winter,
supplemented by a series of balls held in the palace and at
Somerset House. At every entertainment the new Prince and
Princess of Wales were prominent. John Essex claimed that, in
reviving balls, which had not featured in Anne's entertaining,
Caroline 'retriev'd the Grandeur & Gayety of the Court'.[70] At a
ball in February 1715 the couple were joined by five-year-old
Anne. 'She was admired by all, for her ability surpassed her age
and her dance was performed with surprising grace,' wrote the
Dutch ambassador.[71]

Caroline and George Augustus's apartments lay in Paradise
Court, on the opposite side of a quadrangle to George Louis's,
separate beneath the same roof.[72] In the short term, George
Louis undertook the brief journey to Caroline's drawing room.
He seldom remained long. He preferred to spend his evenings
unobserved in Madame Schulenburg's apartments, 'lock[ing]
himself up', as a groom of the bedchamber described it, or else
at the theatre. Unlike the Leineschloss, St James's Palace boasted

neither opera house nor theatre for courtly diversion. Instead, that first winter George Louis attended twenty-two of the forty-four opera performances staged by the King's Theatre, Haymarket.[73] Unlike George Augustus and Caroline he avoided the royal box, and so, unlike them, failed to make any lasting impact on his theatregoing subjects. George Louis's poor English did, however, alter the nature of theatre managers' offerings, with an emphasis on visual spectaculars and 'other things which divert the senses more than the mind'.[74] Given the gaps in their own English in 1714, Caroline and George Augustus may have shared some of the king's relief. Undertaken without fanfare, his absences from the palace were rarer than their own.

The engraving of 'St James's Palace and Parts adjacent' made in 1707 by Johannes Kip for *Britannia Illustrata, Views of Several of the Queen's Palaces and also of the Principal Seats of the Nobility & Gentry of Great Britain*, depicts a muddled grid of rectilinear buildings of uninspiring Tudor aspect. After dining there alfresco with Charles II in 1686, the diarist John Evelyn described the palace's French-style formal gardens as 'a very delicious paradise'. Beyond their boundaries, in Kip's version, stocks of deer gambolled.

By 1714 such commendations were rare. Elizabeth I's surveyor John Norden had claimed of the palace, a former women's leprosy hospital, 'the situation is pleasant, indued with a good ayre and pleasant prospects', while a French visitor in 1638 had marvelled at its 'great number of chambers, all covered with tapestry and superbly furnished with all manner of furniture … [It] is very ancient, very magnificent, and extremely convenient.'[75] The building's subsequent neglect in favour of the nearby Palace of Whitehall until the latter was razed by fire in 1698 resulted in a structure that was ill-equipped both internally and externally to support the pretensions of majesty, despite the new suite of state apartments commissioned in 1703 by Queen Anne from Sir Christopher Wren and Sir John Vanbrugh, and advice on the privy garden from André Mollet, an assistant of Le Nôtre. Visitors agreed on its inadequacy: 'The whole is an irregular pile. But the very confusion in its plan, with its antiquity ... ministers to the fancy, making amends for its want of good architecture.'[76] Used to Herrenhausen, elegant and expansive within its elaborate tracery of hedges and ornamental waterways, and the bandbox charms of Lützenburg, Caroline must have shared a view closer to that of Daniel Defoe: 'The Palace of St James's, though the ... receptacle of all the pomp and glory of this kingdom, is really mean in comparison of the glorious Court of Great Britain. The splendour of the nobility, the wealth and greatness of the attendants, and the real grandeur of the whole Royal Family, outdo all the courts of Europe, and yet this palace comes beneath those of the most petty princes in it.'[77] It was smaller than the Leineschloss, less coherent than Berwart's palace in Ansbach. In 1732, the author of the *Critical Review of Public Buildings* insisted the palace had 'no beauty to recommend it, and was the contempt of foreign nations and the disgrace of our own'.[78] Caroline's view has not survived. Later she built a library at St James's Palace; as king and queen, she and George Augustus used it extensively for court functions. For reasons that will become clear, it was not a building for which she otherwise expressed great attachment. Her preference was for Kensington Palace and Hampton Court.

Extensive alterations began soon after George Louis's accession. Most were confined to the palace's service quarters – new cellars, sculleries, laundries, even a new confectionery kitchen – although George Augustus and Caroline also enlarged and redecorated their apartments, to designs by Nicholas Hawksmoor, and commissioned a kitchen of their own. (This was not completed until 1719, by which time the couple had left the palace.[79]) The state apartments remained unchanged. Throwbacks to the last reign in their decoration and picture

hang, they suggested to visitors visual continuity with Anne's
court. This may have arisen from apathy on George Louis's part.

Pressure of space forced the bulk of royal servants and retainers to live elsewhere, lodged in Somerset House and buildings
around Whitehall. Hugger mugger, three generations of the
royal family found accommodation in the antiquated precincts,
while George Louis, George Augustus and Caroline each set
about assembling the entourage of courtiers which comprised
the top rung of their households. George Louis's British household eventually extended to 950 people, including, by 1720,
seventeen gentlemen of the bedchamber, a harpsichord-maker,
herb strewer, master of the tennis court and keeper of the lions
in the royal menagerie at the Tower of London. Annually it
consumed an estimated one-eighth of the national budget.[80]
More modestly, Caroline provided herself with six ladies of the
bedchamber, all peeresses, six women of the bedchamber and
six maids of honour, serving on a rota. All were British bar the
Italian-born Duchess of Shrewsbury, Adelaide Talbot. She owed
her place to George Louis's repeated intervention. As much as
her husband's position as the king's lord chamberlain, her
'wonderful Art at entertaining and diverting People' and her
willingness to 'exceed the Bounds of Decency' may well have
swayed his favour; Sir Gustavus Hume recorded George Louis's
enjoyment of polite bawdy: 'the freer the conversation the more
to the King's mind'.[81] Since Caroline's own conversation
included its measure of indelicacies, lapses in the duchess's good
taste are unlikely to have proved a stumbling block.

The highest-ranking office, the incongruous-sounding post of
groom of the stole, fell to the Duchess of St Albans, one of the
eight 'Hampton Court Beauties' whose portraits by Kneller
Mary II had commissioned in 1691; her presence suggested a
link between later Stuart courts and that of the new dynasty.
The position was mostly ornamental. Scarcely more was
expected of ladies of the bedchamber. Women of the

bedchamber faced more onerous responsibilities, akin to well-born ladies' maids, although all those 'in waiting' could expect lengthy days in the royal presence with consequent vulnerability to fatigue, boredom and royal caprice. A supporting cast of sempstresses and laundresses maintained the princess's wardrobe. Apothecaries and physicians ministered to other needs.

The choice of her household was among Caroline's first tests, and gave rise to speculation and concern. On 23 October a disdainful Lady Mary Wortley Montagu dismissed three rumoured nominees, Lady Townshend, Lady Hinchinbrooke and Lady Mary Lumley. 'She must be a strange princesse if she can pick a favourite out of them, and as she will one day be Queen ... I wonder they don't think fit to place Women about her with a little common sense,' she told her husband.[82] By 26 October Caroline had finalised key appointments, excluding all three of Lady Mary's bugbears; she postponed choosing her maids of honour, a junior post for younger, unmarried women. As in her letter to Lady Cowper, written from Hanover, she maintained the fiction that in each instance the casting vote belonged to George Augustus. Her protestations may have rung hollow. As Mary Wortley Montagu indicated, gossip that Caroline 'ha[d] an influence over her Husband' had preceded the princess's arrival.[83]

Particularly anxious for a place in Caroline's household was the Countess of Bristol, 'hard as flint' and 'the oddest, and I fear the worst woman that ever lived', in her daughter-in-law's estimate.[84] The devoted wife of a staunchly pro-Hanoverian politician, and the mother of seventeen children, Lady Bristol failed to find favour until some years later, when necessity forced Caroline's hand. She '[spoke] to the Princess to be Mistress of her Robes ... She [Caroline] answered her that she did not design to have any, but that if she was obliged to take one, the Prince had made her promise it should be Mrs Coke [a former maid of honour to Queen Anne, married to Anne's vice chamberlain].'[85] Such was Lady Bristol's zeal – not to mention what sounds like pique – that she promptly embarked on a scheme to disgrace Mrs Coke. The failure of this response on Lady Bristol's part is unsurprising. Its mixture of rancour and temerity in challenging what Caroline had insisted was George Augustus's prerogative temporarily sealed the fate of the eager noblewoman.

Other women, equally tenacious, behaved with greater circumspection. Mary Cowper reported the Duchesses of Bolton and St Albans, Henrietta Howard and Charlotte Clayton, together at St James's Palace in the aftermath of the coronation in order to pay their respects to Caroline and win the coveted appointment. Persistence and a measure of impudence, Mary Wortley Montagu asserted, were the way to get ahead at court; Lady Cowper's brother, John Clavering, concluded that only by 'tormenting' those with influence could he be anything but 'the worst sollicitor for my self in the World'.[86] In Henrietta Howard's case, the need was especially pressing. Lady Frederica Schomberg wrote that 'Mrs Howard had had a Promise … from Hanover in the Princess Sophia's Time', an understanding Caroline had reiterated.[87] Given her parlous finances and the loathing she felt for her reprobate husband, it was essential that Henrietta successfully translate kind words into solid emolument and an offer of accommodation.

Her success in securing a place as one of Caroline's women of the bedchamber should not be underestimated. Henrietta Howard was unusual among royal attendants in lacking either a powerful champion or strong claims to royal attention. Five of Caroline's bedchamber ladies – the Duchesses of St Albans and Shrewsbury, Lady Dorset, Lady Cowper and Lady Berkeley – were married to prominent Whig politicians, while the sixth, the Duchess of Montagu, was a daughter of the Duke of Marlborough, energetic over a number of years in his efforts to assure the electoral family of his support. Charlotte Clayton, a fellow bedchamber woman with Henrietta, also enjoyed Marlborough sponsorship: her background was humble, her origins obscure. In the absence of worldly advantages, Henrietta's appointment suggests genuine liking on Caroline's part. Alternatively, if we accept the contemporary view that insisted Caroline was 'exact in her knowledge of the Characters and Merits of Persons', she made a correct assessment of Henrietta's virtues.[88] A measure of attachment to Sophia's plans for this resourceful but unassuming Englishwoman may also have swayed the princess, who was still in mourning for her former mentor and adopted matriarch.

Inevitably politics played its part in nominations to Caroline's household: likewise similar decisions taken by George Louis and George Augustus. Father and son shared pronounced antipathy for the Tories, whom they considered responsible for the anti-Hanoverian Peace of Utrecht as well as traitorously inclined to Jacobitism. In George Louis's case, anti-Tory bias in his household appointments was increased by the role of his German advisers. 'From the top to the Bottom,' wrote courtier Peter Wentworth, 'they have a great stroak in recommend[ing] Persons that are fit to serve his Majesty. Most, nay All the Addresses are made to Mons[ieur] Bothmar [George Louis's Hanoverian envoy to Britain]. He having been so long in England is suppos'd to know all the English.'[89]

In line with their policy of cultivated 'Englishness', Caroline and George Augustus were careful to avoid providing grounds for such accusations (added to which, Caroline's only German attendants, the Countess of Bückeburg and Baroness von Gemmingen, were as ill-versed as she in British aristocratic society, and incapable of venturing pertinent opinions); George Augustus openly criticised his father's dependence on his German advisers. Past behaviour and political allegiance, rather than the intervention of Bothmer, appear to have governed the choices made by husband and wife. George Augustus's appointment of the 2nd Duke of Argyll as groom of the stole recognised the duke's long-term support for the Hanoverian succession, as well as a war record that included, like George Augustus's, fighting at the battle of Oudenaarde. By contrast, Mary Granville 'had been brought up with the expectation of being a maid of honour' to Queen Anne. Thanks to her family's suspected Jacobite sympathies and despite an influential uncle who had served as Anne's treasurer, she found herself ineligible for the same position in Caroline's household. Lady Nottingham's ambition to become royal governess foundered on her husband's Tory loyalties and her own occasionally theatrical High Church sympathies, which jarred with Caroline's Low Church outlook.[90] Maid of honour Sophy Howe owed her place to a connection to the electoral family: she was a great-great-niece of Sophia's through the electress's brother, Prince Rupert. Personal regard also played its part. Lady Cowper reported the brief ceremony of kissing hands on accepting Caroline's invitation, and 'the Princess when I had done it took me up and embraced me three or four times and said the kindest things to me far beyond the value of any riches'.[91] On Caroline's part it was characteristic effulgence. To Charlotte Clayton she wrote, 'I know your good heart is join'd with an infinite wit accompany'd with all the good sense in the world, things and qualities that are very rare, particularly found together.'[92]

Three days after finalising her choices, Caroline attended Lord Mayor's Day in the City, in company with George Louis, George Augustus, Anne, Amelia and a handful of her ladies. The previous day, Lady Cowper recorded, had been 'passed in Disputes amongst us Servants about the Princess's kissing my Lady Mayoress, and quoting of Precedents ... Queen Anne not having kissed her when she dined in the City, my Mistress did not do it either'.[93] It is a telling detail. On this, one of her first public appearances, Caroline sought advice on correct procedure. That she chose to model her behaviour on that of Queen

Anne and did not kiss the lord mayor's wife on meeting can be interpreted variously. Anne was her most recent female role model; unlike Caroline, she was a reigning monarch. Invited by Caroline to offer guidance, the Duchess of Marlborough had suggested that appropriate protocol for the new Princess of Wales was that outlined for a royal princess. Ignoring the duchess, Caroline preferred the more exalted model, a clear indication of how she viewed her position and intended to be treated.

Sarah Marlborough scoffed at the pretensions of 'a little German princess ... that some people called Madam Ansbach', but her own pretensions – of such magnitude that Caroline later referred to the Marlboroughs as 'the imperial family' – make her an unreliable witness.[94] Self-importance was unquestionably a facet of Caroline's character, so too an attachment to convolutions of etiquette. Her decision that peers' daughters at court kiss her hand rather than being kissed by her in greeting inspired resentment among those on the receiving end of a 'lessening ... of their privileges': 'All the Lords' daughters were much dissatisfied with this alteration in the Honour they used to have in former courts, and it made a great noise in the Town,' the duchess suggested.[95] On 3 January 1716, Lady Loudoun described the princess's response to a satirical poem by Lady Mary Wortley Montagu, 'Monday; Roxana or the Drawing Room'. Caroline failed to recognise the poem's irony, which transformed it from criticism to endorsement of the new princess and her court. As a result she was decidedly not amused.[96]

Caroline's elevated sense of her royal status was a characteristic of German royalties, with their exaggerated absorption in bloodlines, and at one with George Augustus's. Lord Hervey would note that 'the pageantry and splendour, the badges and the trappings of royalty were as pleasing to the son as they were irksome to the father', etiquette and ceremony a clear substitute for influence or responsibility.[97] Praise for Caroline's refusal to convert to Catholicism invariably suggested that she 'preferr[ed] a sound faith to the pomps of the world'.[98] In truth she shared George Augustus's predisposition, which had also been Anne's: the late queen was described as mindful of 'very little besides ceremonies and customs of courts and suchlike insignificant trifles'.[99] Prince and princess embraced key aspects of Anne's court ceremonial, including, in George Augustus's case, the minutely choreographed ritual of dressing in the presence of privileged attendants, a morning meeting of the main household officers known as the *levée*.[100] For the moment Caroline's ardour kept pace with her husband's: he 'had not more at heart all the trappings and pageantry of sovereignty than she the essential parts of it'.[101] Like much of the couple's policy of anglicisation, the *levée* – offering an exclusive forum for informally expressing opinions and requests – asserted continuity between Stuart and Hanoverian practice: it deliberately adhered to precedents established in Anne's reign.[102]

In German courts, royal women typically balanced the political and military pursuits of their menfolk by shaping their cultural and social lives; they played their part in court ceremonies which upheld the unique status of royalty. Jointly the roles of husband and wife comprised twin aspects of royal 'leadership'. Even Figuelotte, dismissive of Frederick's absorption in protocol, provided for chosen members of his court lively entertainments and inspiring cultural direction at Lützenburg. At Hampton Court and Kensington Palace, Mary II had adopted a similar role in relation to the chilly (and frequently absent) William III, shaping the structure of day-to-day court life.[103] Insofar as she was able, living under her father-in-law's roof, Caroline pursued a similar agenda. Vigorously she reignited a court calendar moribund since the dull days of Queen Anne's continuing ailments, beginning with the appointment of her household, the entertainments she provided in George Louis's stead, and her decision to be treated with the kind of formalised deference previously restricted to reigning queens. The change was rapid. Lord Chesterfield reported in 1716 that 'the gay part of the town' was 'much more flourishing': 'balls, assemblies and masquerades have taken the place of dull formal visiting days'. A new liveliness coloured fashion and behaviour, even attitudes to sex. 'Women,' he added 'are become much more agreeable trifles than they were designed … Puns are extremely in vogue and the license very great.'[104]

Few women merited the label of 'agreeable trifles' more than Caroline's maids of honour. Her tolerance of their frivolous behaviour points to the same open-mindedness with which she regarded George Augustus's philandering. As in other aspects of their lives, in determining the tone of their court husband and wife acted together, and George Augustus's approval can be assumed. Caroline took pleasure in her female household. Her ladies partnered her at cards and dice games like hazard, at which she and the Duchess of Montagu won £600 on Twelfth Night 1715. Complacently she wrote to Leibniz that her ladies 'served her with all the attention in the world'.[105] Letters to Liselotte about etiquette at Versailles indicate her fascination with royal ceremony at its grandest and most prescriptive.[106]

Her women's usefulness to Caroline was comprehensive. In most cases connected to the political establishment by ties of marriage or family, they offered her a channel of information and, potentially, influence. Her friendships with elite women built bridges between the monarchy and aristocratic society, and helped maintain a political dimension to court life. 'Mama is so impatient about the business that is in the house [of Commons] today that she desires your opinion about the turn it will take,' Princess Anne wrote on Caroline's behalf in 1730, to a lady-in-waiting who was married to a government minister.[107] This process also worked in reverse, with ladies able to request favours of the princess on behalf of husbands, brothers and remoter connections. In addition, in 1714, to a newcomer in a foreign city, Caroline's attendants supplied companionship and, occasionally, guidance. Supportive female friendship had been a feature of her life since the years with Figuelotte in Berlin. Naturally warm, she craved and excelled at such closeness. 'I wait for that moment with impatience, that I may with my own mouth assure you how very tenderly I am yours,' she told Charlotte Clayton during an illness of the latter's. 'I am easy on my part if I can have you preserv'd, & if you always are the same to me, as I shall be to the last moment of my life wholly yours.'[108]

Overwhelmingly the young women she chose as her maids of honour were vivacious, flippant, pretty and pert. Despite an age gap of more than a decade, Caroline took pleasure in the robust charms, 'merry pranks' and vigorous flirtations of Molly Lepell, Mary Bellenden, Mary Meadows, Sophy Howe, Mary Howard and their colleagues, whose enticements Alexander Pope celebrated in his 'Court Ballad' of 1717.[109] Mary Wortley Montagu expressed surprise at 'a virtuous Princesse with a Court so lewd'; another contemporary described Caroline's relationship with the young women as that of 'Mistress, Friend and (I may say) a Parent'.[110] In those around her Caroline prized liveliness of spirit, virtue and intelligence, but not necessarily all three in combination, and she valued those companions able to entertain her. 'You know me, & know that I love people of wit & merit,' she admitted.[111] Save when their behaviour threatened her own reputation, she avoided interference in her maids' lives.

In accordance with the diktats of etiquette, the women of Caroline's household performed countless small acts of public reverence. Each curtsey, every bowed head and bob offered visible proof of her status as pre-eminent royal female. Their daily duties were bookended by her dressing and undressing; they accompanied her outings, served her at the dining table, attended her at formal assemblies, read and talked to her in the privacy of her rooms; they handed her the cups of chocolate of which she was so fond and the 'long hoop petticoats' of crimson linen, stiffened with whalebone, that gave her heavy silk underskirts their distinctive silhouette.[112] On occasion they represented Caroline in public, as in the autumn of 1725, when Lady Pomfret stood royal representative at the christening of one of Lord and Lady Hertford's children.[113] Their tasks were trivial, menial, repetitive; alternatively decorative and undemanding. Unfettered access was their reward.

An account supplied to Caroline of the contrasting but complementary duties of ladies of the bedchamber and women of the bedchamber in the reign of Queen Anne indicates the nature of their tasks and the difference in status between the two groups of attendants, as well as Caroline's determination to be guided by royal precedent.

If her Majesty shifted [put on her clothes] at noon, the Bedchamber-Lady being by, the Bedchamber-Woman gave the shift to the Lady without any ceremony, and the Lady put it on. Sometimes, likewise, the Bedchamber-Woman gave the fan to the Lady in the same manner, and this was all the Bedchamber-Lady did about the Queen at her dressing.

When the Queen washed her hands, the Page of the Backstairs brought and set down upon a side-table the basin and ewer; then the Bedchamber-Woman set it before the Queen, and knelt on the other side of the table over-against the Queen, the Bedchamber-Lady only looking on. The Bedchamber-Woman poured the water out of the ewer upon the Queen's hands.

The Bedchamber-Woman pulled on the Queen's gloves when she could not do it herself.

The Page of the Backstairs was called in to put on the Queen's shoes.

When the Queen dined in public, the Page reached the glass to the Bedchamber-Woman, and she to the Lady-in-Waiting.

The Bedchamber-Woman brought the chocolate, and gave it without kneeling.[114]

Every action and gesture was regulated and prescribed. In her role of lady of the bedchamber, Lady Cowper recorded an occasion when 'the Duchess of St Albans put on the Princess's Shift, according to Court Rules, when I was by, she being Groom of the Stole', the lower-ranking countess deferring to her superior.[115]

While women of the bedchamber served on bended knee, pouring water over Caroline's hands for washing, ladies of the bedchamber were of loftier status. The bedchamber women dressed the princess's hair under the supervision of the bedchamber ladies, who discussed with Caroline her choice of jewellery. Even in the latter's case, intimacy need not extend beyond the handing from attendant to mistress of a fan. But intimacy was not the point. Each permission was symbolic, each arcane distinction a means of enacting royal superiority and enforcing loyalty. It sounds an irksome business for all concerned, but was not universally regarded as such. Caroline understood that its effectiveness depended on its wholeheartedness and the strength of her own relationship with the women involved.

For Caroline, who believed unshakeably in the sanctity of royalty and the gulf between those of royal blood and 'mouse droppings in the pepper', traditional court ceremonies, accomplished with the willing cooperation of an aristocratic household, confirmed her own legitimacy and maintained appropriate dignity for the crown. She saw that her attentiveness to precedent suggested a continuum encompassing both Hanoverian and later Stuart rule. She was also afforded opportunities for patronage among her new countrywomen.

George Louis, by contrast, at first dispensed altogether with the position of groom of the stole. He dressed in private with the assistance of two Turkish valets brought with him from Hanover, Mohammed and Mustapha. Two years after his accession he ennobled the former, allowing him to select his own title. Mohammed's choice of 'von Königstreu', meaning 'true to the king', suggests his loyalty to George Louis and George Louis's ability, like Caroline, to inspire partisanship when he chose to do so. Although George Louis added to the number of his bedchamber attendants over time, responsibility for his wigs, hats, shirts and other clothing remained Mohammed's. Despite difficulties of distance and with no idea of patronising British manufacturers, Mohammed continued to place orders with the same suppliers he had used in Hanover.[116]

By contrast Caroline's private account books indicate that, if her patronage was not exclusively British, she at least obtained Continental goods through British sellers, like her purchases of 'Black frinch Lace' from 'E Tempest, Milliner', and a 'compleat head of Brussels point' from lace merchant John Denay.[117] In other instances, including purchases from Mr Stockers and Mr Reeds, both provincial lace-makers, she bought British goods direct from the manufacturer.[118] Her participation in a formal-ised dressing ritual, assisted by her English waiting women, may also have helped to 'anglicise' her clothes choices. Liselotte described the 'peculiar headdresses' worn by Caroline's daugh-ters in 1715 as looking 'exactly like the folded table-napkins which are produced at German Courts when company is expected'.[119]

Caroline's letters to Charlotte Clayton, and Mary Cowper's account of her treatment by Caroline, prove that her conviction of royal superiority did not preclude warmth or bonds of affec-tion between mistress and ladies. Thoughtful in her present-giv-ing, she 'sent for Amber out of Germany, for Boxes for her Ladies'. To Mary Cowper she gave 'a fine gold Box ... with Words which far exceeded its Value'.[120] As Lady Cowper concluded following her first waiting, 'I am so charmed with her good Nature and good Qualities, that I shall never think I can do enough to please her.' Two years later she described Caroline as 'a most charming, delightful Friend, as well as Mistress'.[121] Similar opinions would be repeated. Caroline's charm – both instinctive and diligently cultivated – was a powerful tool in her armoury. By employing a majority of women with personal links to George Louis's government she ensured, insofar as she was able, that their desire for the regime's success matched her own.

As mistress and attendants would discover, Caroline soon had need of all the friendship she could muster.

The portrait of Caroline by Thornhill in the coved ceiling of the Queen's Great Bedchamber at Hampton Court was George Louis's commission. His choice of a scheme of painted decoration, incorporating portraits of three generations of the new dynasty, followed a visit to the Thames-side palace with George Augustus in November 1714. Completion of the Queen's State Apartments, unfinished since Mary II's death twenty years earlier, would provide the prince and princess with accommodation appropriate to their rank. In addition, Thornhill's decoration promised a piece of powerful visual propaganda in a handsome new setting for the ceremonial *levée*, which George Louis himself avoided. He approved the painter's preparatory sketches personally.[122]

This inclusive mural iconography was not a sign of family unity. In 1714, Leibniz received a letter from Melusine von der Schulenburg's brother Frederick William informing him that 'the father treats the son with excessive rigour, not wishing to satisfy his most insignificant wish'.[123] By the end of the following year, rumours of a rift had reached Versailles. 'People say here,' Liselotte wrote, 'that the Prince [of Wales] is on very bad terms with his father, and that they won't speak to one another.'[124] A cousin of George Louis's, a former confidante of

Sophia's and a correspondent of Caroline's, she did not express surprise.

The tension between father and son was of long standing, a dark penumbra over Caroline's marriage from the outset. If George Louis had intended Tommaso Giusti's fresco cycle at Herrenhausen, based on the story of Aeneas, to promote respect between father and son – the 'pietas', or devotion to family, of Virgil's *Aeneid* – he was to be disappointed. The fault was in large measure his own. His cuckolding by Sophia Dorothea and the collapse of family life following her disgrace stamped George Louis for the rest of his life. Physical similarities between George Augustus and Sophia Dorothea have been noted. Despite a loving relationship with his own father, and the influence of Sophia with her highly developed sense of family and dynasty, George Louis does not appear to have attempted to rebuild his fractured relationship with his only son. From his accession as elector in 1698, he excluded George Augustus from any approach to power; he restricted his military experience to a single campaign in 1708. In doing so, he consigned him to a life of aimlessness: an excessive fondness for hunting and a preoccupation with princely genealogy and convolutions of etiquette. Resentment was the inevitable consequence. St James's Palace afforded fewer opportunities for separate living than Hanover, where, at least once, Caroline and George Augustus had chosen to remain at the Leineschloss while George Louis and his court removed to Herrenhausen. In London enforced proximity intensified family friction. Caroline's role as wife included providing George Augustus with an outlet for the recurrent frustrations that dominated his relationship with his intractable parent.

George Louis's behaviour did not alter following the move to Britain. In October 1714 he created George Augustus Prince of Wales – 'our most dear son, a Prince whose eminent filial piety hath always endeared him to us', an acclamation that would

swiftly gain in irony.[125] He allowed him to attend meetings of
the privy council and the cabinet, both bodies of key ministers
with important decision-making powers. In May 1715 he agreed
to Parliament's financial settlement of a £700,000 annual civil
list payment (made up of customs, excise and postal duties). He
did not refuse Parliament's suggestion that £100,000 of this sum
be earmarked for the Prince of Wales and his family, a portion
for Caroline's use, the whole sum set aside for Caroline in the
event of George Augustus's death.[126] None of these concessions
translated into either purpose or patronage for George Augustus,
who was barred from the king's private audiences. In March
1715 he took his seat in the House of Lords. Caroline's journey
to Westminster with her daughters to witness this spectacle,
which husband and wife had anticipated even in the last reign,
was widely reported. Together they sat in state on chairs placed
to the right of the throne. George Louis regarded the ceremony
as empty rigmarole, without implications for the younger man's
profile. He made clear his displeasure at Caroline's keen interest
in politics. Undeterred, she attended parliamentary debates
whenever she considered the issue sufficiently pressing. In April
1716, for example, despite George Louis's disapproval, she
watched the progress of the Septennial Act, by which the Whig
ministry gathered around the king prolonged its term in office
from three to seven years.[127]

A crumb from the royal table, George Louis permitted his son
and daughter-in-law to receive foreign ambassadors on his
behalf. Neither was hoodwinked that their role was more than
decorative. With his impatience of ceremony, his taciturnity and
something frigid in his manner, George Louis disdained the
formalities of diplomatic receptions. Caroline embraced the
opportunities offered for regal condescension, and performed
her part with warmth and conviction. In 1717 the Irish-born
estranged wife of the Portuguese ambassador, Catherine da
Cunha, a Catholic Jacobite, was disarmed by the easy charm of

Caroline's welcome: 'I've been three times at Court and alwayes the Princesse has treated me with a more than ordinary distinction; in short to soe great a degree that its a shame to repeat al the kind and obligeing things she sayes to me, and were she my mother she coud not doe more.'[128] A diplomatic memorandum records Caroline's attentiveness to the wife of the Venetian ambassador: 'After the Ambassadress had been brought to bed a fortnight, Her Royal Highness sent a message that she would come to see her, which the ambassadress excused herself from at that time, her House not being yet in Order to receive that Honour.'[129] Opportunities for Caroline to showcase her charm did not amount to meaningful employment for the restive George Augustus.

In north and south-west England and across Scotland in the autumn of 1715 the anti-Hanoverian feeling apparent at the time of the coronation erupted into an uprising. In York, Lady Mary Wortley Montagu had observed, 'all Protestants here seem unaminous [sic] for the hannover succession'; others were less convinced.[130] The observant had noted the signs: mourning clothes worn on George Louis's birthday, skirmishes and window-breaking on the anniversary of Anne's coronation, an efflorescence of scurrilously disrespectful balladry. 'A Sacred Ode to King George' denounced George Louis's accession as offensive to God and a usurpation: the balladeer addressed the king as 'thou who sits upon the Throne/Of STUART's Ancient Race,/Abandoning thy Rightful own,/To fill another's Place'.[131] In 'An Excellent New Ballad' the king appeared as 'a Turnip-Hoer ... [who] reap'd where [he] ne'er sow'd'.[132]

As the turnip-hoer's daughter-in-law, Caroline was not exempt from the fluctuating popular mood, nor an object of affection among Jacobites. In April 1715, Liselotte reported Jacobites lobbying her: 'The Princess of Wales is supposed to have received a sort of petition asking her to consider, just and God-fearing as she is known to be, that the only rightful heir to the kingdom is the one known as the Pretender, as he was King James II's son as surely as her husband was Count Königsmarck's. How unspeakably insolent, if this really was said to the Princess! England is a mad country.'[133]

The insurrection provided an obvious opportunity for a member of the new dynasty to join government troops and serve as a focus for loyalty. Given George Louis's age and position as king, and Frederick's absence, George Augustus was the only candidate. Instead, command of government forces was entrusted to his groom of the stole, John, Duke of Argyll, gazetted the previous September as 'Generall of our Foot in Scotland', while George Augustus continued to chafe in London.[134]

The Scottish duke's suppressing of the uprising demonstrated afresh his commitment to George Louis's family. He described Jacobite forces as 'ten times more formidable than our friends in England ever believed', and their 'vigilance and furious zeal' as 'inexpressible'.[135] As a result, although Argyll claimed victory, the outcome of the battle of Sheriffmuir in November was regarded as ambiguous, both sides suffering losses, both initially believing they had won. To Lord Townshend, secretary of state for the Northern Department, Argyll explained the impossibility of pursuing a later offensive: 'The weather here is extremely severe; the frost is great; and there is deep snow upon the ground.'[136] Neither his equivocal 'victory' nor this failure to seize any subsequent initiative impressed George Louis, and Argyll was replaced as commander by William Cadogan.

All too soon, the king vented his disappointment in a manner calculated to goad George Augustus to fury. He voiced no sympathy for his son's enforced inertia at so critical a juncture, nor for the Jacobite peers condemned to death for their part in the rebellion. Caroline, by contrast, petitioned on behalf of the youthful traitor Lord Carnwath at an evening entertainment at St James's Palace, 'hasten'd out of ye drawing room into her owene rooms and cryed' – grounds for later celebrations of her compassion like that of the poet Richard Savage, who wrote of her as queen, 'Your heart is woman, though your mind be more', and Walter Scott's fictional Caroline, who in *The Heart of Midlothian* promises to intercede with George II to obtain a pardon for the sister of Jeanie Deans for a wrongful conviction of murder.[137] Other appeals begged Caroline's intervention for those who had 'the misfortune to engage in unnatural rebellion against their rightful and lawful sovereign ... and now have an unfeigned sorrow and abhorrence for so Unnatural an Attempt'.[138] The warm-heartedness remarked on by her ladies-in-waiting was not simply a matter of calculation.

It was not yet the case that George Louis's treatment of George Augustus amounted to unrelieved hostility, rather that the father discounted the son's claims to greater responsibility or prominence. Coolness, observers noted, obtained on both sides. 'The late King,' remarked the politician Robert Walpole in 1730, 'did not like that his son should be preferred to him.'[139] Confining George Augustus to trivialities was George Louis's means of denying him opportunities for popularity in a period before the development of those civic and charitable duties that subsequently constituted royal engagements.

In this the king reckoned without Caroline. Her charm offensive, 'the warmth and goodness of her Heart [that] irresistibly broke out on every occasion, and on subjects of every kind', ranged from learning country dances to winning over the wife of the Portuguese ambassador and crying at the fate of condemned Jacobite nobles, and reaped dividends for husband as well as wife.[140] As early as 1705, requesting the new English edition of Saint-Evremond's essays, she had indicated her commitment to her husband's British prospects; within those essays she encountered Saint-Evremond's dictum that 'he who sets out to write the History of *England* must write the History of Parliaments', with its clear warning note.[141] Caroline's anglophilia is too consistent and wide-ranging to be other than deliberate. It was a policy forged in Hanover, in an atmosphere of uncertainty over the likelihood of the electoral family's succession. Publicly she had never wavered. Her first motives were to prove, in the only way available to her, the family's fitness to rule. Only in Britain, where the difference between Caroline's approach and George Louis's became clear, did this outlook appear to challenge the monarch.

From now on, her polished flattery of her new countrymen was achieved at the expense of the king, who withheld such niceties. While the older man appeared assertively German, despite the trickle of Stuart blood he inherited from Sophia, Caroline and her husband – whose claims were correspondingly less (and in Caroline's case non-existent) – posed as would-be Britons. This was more than sham. Caroline's absorption in February 1716 in Sir John Germaine's collection of 'rarities, consisting of seals and reliefs' was an early indication of her fascination with Tudor history. This would later see her acquire biographies of all five Tudor monarchs, as well as their portraits, beginning with a copy of Anthonis Mor van Dashort's strikingly austere image of Mary I, which was identified in Caroline's collection by 1724.[142] Unable to view his whole collection in a single sitting, she invited Sir John to return the following day. 'Amongst other Things,' reported Lady Cowper, 'he showed us the Dagger of King Henry VIII, which he always wore and is pictured with.'[143]

Undoubtedly these fragments of Tudor posterity appealed all the more since Caroline herself had recently been associated with sixteenth-century politics. In 1715, against the backdrop of Jacobite dissent, dramatist Nicholas Rowe dedicated to Caroline his final play, *The Tragedy of Lady Jane Gray* [sic]. A Whig supporter of the new regime, Rowe presented Jane Grey as a Protestant martyr, 'the Noblest Subject ... a Heroine, a Martyr, and a Queen'. In Rowe's hands she becomes a mouthpiece for feminine virtue: 'No wandring Glance one wanton Thought

confess'd,/No guilty Wish inflam'd her spotless Breast:/The only
Love that warm'd her blooming Youth,/Was Husband, *England*,
Liberty and Truth.'[144] It was a neat piece of theatrical propaganda, uniting at a stroke Protestantism, chastity and the benefits of the Hanoverian succession embodied by Caroline.
Ironically, given later characterisations of Caroline as domineer-
ing, John Gay wrote to Pope's friend John Caryll, 'Mr Rowe's
Jane Gray is to be play'd in Easter Week when Mrs Oldfield [the
actress Ann Oldfield] is to personate a Character directly opposite to female nature, for what Woman ever despised
Soveraignty.'[145]

Caroline had surely played her part in shaping the sentiments
with which George Augustus stunned a dinner party of mixed
British and Hanoverian courtiers in March 1716. 'Mrs Clayton
in Raptures at all the kind Things the Prince had been saying of
the English, – that he thought them the best, the handsomest,
the best shaped, the best natured, and lovingest People in the
World, and that if Anybody would make their Court to him, it
must be by telling him he was like an Englishman.'[146] The result
was 'the violentest, silliest, ill-mannered Invective against the
English that ever was heard' on the part of the disgruntled
Germans present.[147] Unsurprisingly, Lord Hervey recorded,
'everybody imagined this Prince loved England and hated
Germany'.[148] No one could attribute similar feelings to George
Louis. Versions of George Augustus's conversation, inevitably
reported to his father, did little to check the two men's escalating dislike. But it was the son who had more accurately taken
the measure of their new subjects. 'I do not think there is a
people more prejudiced in its own favour than the British
people,' wrote Swiss traveller César de Saussure in February
1727. 'They look on foreigners in general with contempt, and
think nothing is as well done elsewhere as in their own country.'[149] To ignore such prejudice was foolhardy. While George
Augustus's feelings towards the British would change,

eventually resembling those of his father, Caroline consistently behaved in a manner that suggests a correct estimate of her adopted countrymen.

In 1715, while disaffected Scots dismissed George Louis as a 'turnip-hoer' and George Augustus as Königsmarck's bastard, a group of Welshmen living in London established a charitable foundation to provide poor relief for the capital's exigent Welsh and to demonstrate their 'uncommon zeal' for the Hanoverian settlement.[150] The inclusion of 'loyal' in the name of the Most Honourable and Loyal Society of Antient Britons deliberately contrasted the peaceable Welsh with Jacobite Scots. George Augustus accepted an invitation to be the society's president. 'After this the Society waited upon her Royal Highness the Princess ... [who] received them very graciously; and declared, *That the Society was very acceptable to her.* And as such gave them the Honour to kiss her Hand.'[151] Caroline's graciousness on that occasion evidently hit the mark. The society's chronicler, Thomas Jones, acclaimed her just as she intended: 'How lovely is her Mien, her Temper sweet,/Majestick, but serene, and humbly great.'[152] Later she appointed two Welsh maids of honour, Margaret and Anne Williams.

The society merged celebration of Caroline's birthday, on 1 March, with the festival of St David, Wales's patron saint, which fell on the same day. Prince and princess returned the compliment, marking St David's Day at court by wearing leeks. Not everyone was as beguiled by the coincidence as Caroline or the society's founders. Lady Cowper's daughter Sarah dismissed it as political humbug: 'it is a superstitious Conceit of some Whigs who say it did portend that she shou'd Become princess of Wales'.[153] In 1717, Nehemiah Griffiths's 'The Leek. A Poem on St David's Day' was 'most humbly inscrib'd to the honourable society of Antient Britons, establish'd in honour of Her Royal Highness's birthday, and the principality of Wales'. Encouraged by her sturdy Protestantism, her winning manner and examples of her charity – like the donation she had made in January 1716 for the relief of Thames boatmen suffering as a result of the river's two-month freeze, with their consequent loss of livelihood – Griffiths acclaimed Caroline as a 'Princess of superior grace'.[154] An unnamed poet asserted on the society's behalf, 'Tho on her Vertues I should ever dwell,/Fame cannot all her numerous Vertues tell.'[155]

In the following decade Caroline was also the dedicatee of *Orpheus Caledonius; or, a Collection of the best Scotch Songs,* including seven songs attributed to David Rizzio, private secretary to Mary, Queen of Scots.[156] No mention was made of George Louis or George Augustus. It was Caroline, regarded as an archetype of feminine virtues, apolitical and devout in her religion, who attracted praise from such diverse quarters. Notwithstanding the partial inaccuracy of this view, she became in this way a means of extending support for the dynasty into Wales and even Scotland: 'Ev'n Tongues disloyal learn her Praise'.[157] It was the role Whig poet Thomas Tickell identified for Caroline in his poem 'Kensington Gardens', in which Caroline is presented as winning support for George Louis's regime through her appearance and her manner: 'Form'd to gain hearts that Brunswick's cause denied,/And charm a people to her father's side'. She did it without ever leaving the capital.

Her marriage to George Augustus in 1705 had come about with George Louis's support. George Louis had even guided George Augustus towards 'choosing' the Ansbach princess, and closely supervised formal prosecution of his suit. His purpose does not appear to have been his son's happiness. Rather he considered the advantages to the electorate of an alliance prominent on account of Caroline's well-publicised rejection of Archduke Charles, as well as her suitability as a future British consort, given the Act of Settlement's assertive Protestantism; to his mother he commended the strength of her convictions. Subsequent expressions of admiration for Caroline on George

Louis's part were notable for his punctiliousness in distinguish-
ing between admiration and liking. He described her as *'cette
diablesse, madame la princesse'*, a diabolical woman, a she-devil or
a fury.[158] But he was not immune to her ample physical allure,
and Liselotte reported a rumour 'that the King is himself in love
with the Princess', which she discounted in the same breath on
the grounds that George Louis was incapable of love. 'I consider
that the King has in no ways a lover-like nature; he only loves
himself ... he never had any consideration for the mother who
loved him so tenderly.'[159] Caroline's pink and white amplitude
contrasted with the stringier charms of Madame Schulenburg.
George Louis's exasperation at the daughter-in-law he failed to
cow mostly included a grudging sort of praise. The view of her
contemporaries was that 'he never cordially loved her'.[160]

On the surface their relationship was sufficiently cordial for
Lady Cowper to attribute her own flattering treatment by the
king in December 1714 to her place in Caroline's household: 'I
was sure,' she reported herself as telling Caroline, 'it must be
from my having the Honour to be about her Person that I had
received such a Favour.'[161] She does not record Caroline's
response. That Caroline felt able openly to rebuke George Louis
demonstrates at least a degree of candour in their relationship.
In February 1716, irritated by a growing popular view that the
king was the puppet of a junta consisting of his Hanoverian
advisers and the leading Whig ministers Stanhope, Sunderland,
Walpole and Townshend, Caroline 'chid the King ... and told
him he was grown lazy. He laughed, and said he was busy from
Morning to Night. She said, "Sir, I tell you they say the Ministry
does Everything, and you Nothing." He smiled, and said, "This
is all the Thanks I get for all the Pains I take."'[162] The blandness
of George Louis's reply precluded discussion. It suggests his
unwillingness openly to disagree with Caroline. And realising
the dependence she and George Augustus shared on George
Louis's goodwill, Caroline was careful to maintain a semblance

of harmony. More than once George Louis entertained his companions at the supper table with anecdotes about Versailles, taken from Liselotte's letters to Caroline, proof of an ongoing dialogue between them.[163] Correctly Caroline considered Liselotte's garrulous buoyancy safely neutral territory.

By 1715, however, it was evident that George Augustus could expect little from his father. The robustness of the older man's health added to the son's despondency. After a year in London the prospects of his inheritance felt no closer than a decade previously. Ambitious and strong-willed, Caroline shared her husband's restlessness. It was no surprise that George Augustus concluded, as Lord Hervey reported, that 'his father had always hated him and used him ill'.[164] Affection between ruler and heir was decidedly at a premium.

In the summer of 1716, despite the protests of his ministers and continuing Jacobite dissent, George Louis returned to Hanover. On 5 July, in a letter addressed to his 'Dearest Son', he appointed George Augustus 'guardian and lieutenant of the realm' in his absence. The arrangement took into account the younger man's inexperience; it granted George Augustus responsibility for minor aspects of government, with bigger questions referred to Hanover. The prince's powers included presiding at cabinet meetings; he was prevented from making senior cabinet or military appointments. Predictably, George Augustus inferred a slight in his father's withholding the title of regent. There was worse to come. Of his 'dearest son' George Louis demanded a concession: he must dispense with the Duke of Argyll as his groom of the stole, or forfeit the guardianship to his uncle Ernest Augustus, Prince Bishop of Osnabrück. Both monarch and ministry had been troubled by Argyll's anger at being passed over for Cadogan after the battle of Sheriffmuir. In the king's absence they mistrusted his influence on George Augustus.

With no alternative and 'in an Agony', George Augustus concurred and dismissed his friend. Diplomatically he had

announced himself 'resolved to sacrifice Everything to please
and live well with the King', a statement that in itself points to
the extent of ill feeling between father and son.[165] He acted with
a bad grace, after consulting Caroline. Caroline's own reaction
was scarcely so moderate. Argyll's removal left her 'all in a
flame'. She did not scruple to disguise her feelings from courtiers and intimates, and Lady Cowper, reading her mood, decided
Caroline would 'hardly forgive what is past'.[166] As an indication
of Caroline's response to opposition it offers unrosy insights into
her character, something more than strength of purpose. Fiery
outbursts of temper intermittently rocked her self-control; her
memory for slights was sharp. Jointly Caroline and George
Augustus decided not to join the king at Kensington Palace,
west of Piccadilly, where apartments had been prepared for
them.

In the interests of public harmony George Louis attended
Caroline's drawing room at St James's Palace the evening before
his departure. The following morning, similarly prompted,
George Augustus accompanied his father as far as the royal
yacht at Gravesend for a public leave-taking. And in recognition
of the prominence George Louis's absence granted them, prince
and princess sat for portraitist Sir Godfrey Kneller. Over a
lavishly embroidered silk gown, Caroline wore ermine-trimmed
robes of state.[167] A consort's crown stands at her elbow, a chair
of throne-like proportions behind her. Similarly regal is George
Augustus's likeness. Both were images of aspiration, heavy with
intent.

In the New Year of 1716, Caroline fell pregnant. In April she
confided to her ladies, 'it [was] twelve Weeks ... since she reck-
on[ed] herself with child'.[168] The discovery delighted her. She
could not accustom herself to her separation from Frederick.
'The Princess sent for me in private and asked me a thousand
questions about her little Frederick,' Lord Polwarth wrote that

year, after Caroline learned of his visit to Hanover. Polwarth's description of 'the finest young prince in the world' both re-assured and unsettled his anguished mother.[169]

A new baby offered Caroline distraction from her longing for her son. She was frequently in the company of her three daughters. Their daily routine – 'prayer, coiffe, and breakfast' at seven, walking in St James's Park until nine, lessons before and after a plain midday dinner of unspiced meat, music lessons for Anne with Handel, in time drawing lessons with artist Philippe Mercier – culminated in an hour spent with Caroline in needle-work or 'talk[ing] of sensible things'.[170] At Caroline's instigation 'sensible things' included Frederick, although only Anne among the three princesses was old enough to remember the brother they had left behind.

Evidence, even at this stage, suggests something inconsistent in Caroline's attitude to her eldest child. Between 1718 and 1721 the artist Martin Maingaud painted three portraits of the royal children, including, in 1720, a double portrait of Frederick with his middle sister Amelia.[171] If these commissions originated with Caroline and George Augustus rather than George Louis, it is possible to interpret them as proof of the royal parents' determination to maintain family unity despite enforced sepa-ration. In truth, Frederick and Amelia were strangers to one another after a six-year parting – the portrait was an affection-ate fiction, an exercise in wish fulfilment. But Caroline does not appear to have written to Frederick, though he was a precocious child and capable of sustaining a correspondence with his mother. How much solace she can have derived either from misleading portraiture or conversations with daughters who did not remember their brother is questionable. Nevertheless, evidence suggests she resisted nearer approaches to contact, and it was left to intermediaries like Liselotte to obtain and forward regular bulletins concerning Frederick's health as a means of giving 'his poor mother that much comfort'.[172] Later the relationship of mother and son broke down irretrievably. Seeds for future dislike were sown in the first years of their parting.

In her unhappiness, Caroline may have drawn some comfort from Lady Mary Wortley Montagu's report of a conversation with Frederick in Hanover in November 1716, if the Countess of Bristol, Lady Mary's correspondent, passed on her account. 'I am extreamly pleas'd that I can tell you without either flattery or partiality that our young Prince has all the Accomplishments that tis possible to have at his age, with an Air of Sprightlynesse and understanding, and something so very engaging and easy in his behaviour, that he needs not the advantage of his rank to appear charming. I had the honour of a long conversation with him last night before the King came in. His Governour retir'd on purpose ... that I might make some judgement of his Genius by hearing him speak without constraint, and I was surprised at the quicknesse and politenesse that appear'd in every thing he said, joyn'd to a person perfectly agreable and the fine fair Hair of the Princesse.'[173]

Despite Frederick's absence and George Augustus's worsening relationship with George Louis, during the king's return to Hanover it was as a royal 'family' that the Prince and Princess of Wales and the infant princesses impressed themselves on the British public. The straightforwardness of this youthful family unit contrasted starkly with George Louis's scabrous-seeming inner circle, which was described by Mary Wortley Montagu as his 'German ministers and playfellows male and female', and by Horace Walpole as 'so uncommon a seraglio': the king's Hanoverian advisers; the beanpole Madame Schulenburg, 'by no means an inviting object' with her enamelled make-up and unconvincing wig; Mustapha and Mohammed the Turks; and George Louis's elephantine half-sister Baroness von Kielmansegg, 'altogether inclined to work evil ... vicious, intriguing', whom many suspected of being his second mistress and whom Pope, in 'Artemisia', accused of rancid personal hygiene: "'Twere well if she would pare her Nails,/And wear a cleaner smock'.[174] Following his father's departure, George Augustus moved his court, including his children, to Hampton Court for the remainder of the summer. Londoners saw their royal family-in-waiting in barges rowed by liveried oarsmen; they saw them in carriages or walking; those with a mind to it saw them together in playful holiday amity.

Henry VIII's leviathan palace lies on the banks of the Thames at a remove from central London. Extended and remodelled by William and Mary, in the summer of 1716 it stood within large gardens refashioned in the previous reign by Henry Wise for Queen Anne. In place of box trees, whose scent Anne had hated, were rows of clipped yews; as at Herrenhausen, the garden included extensive formal areas – within a wilderness stood a hornbeam maze. Beyond the parterres and artificial waterways, outside its walled perimeter, unfurled the open and wooded spaces of Home Park and Bushy Park. Through copses and spinneys sliced twenty miles of rides, cut to enable the hunting enthusiast Anne to drive her two-wheeled chaise in pursuit of hounds and quarry. In St James's Park, Anne had introduced a herd of the 'finest coloured deer'; here, in an area still rural, game abounded, including partridge for shooting. Within the garden itself, around an oval bowling green, stood a quartet of square pavilions ideal for small-scale entertaining.

The previous year, Liselotte had written from Versailles, 'From what I hear of the air in London, I don't believe I could last there for twenty-four hours without falling ill. I'm told there is a constant smell of coal; I couldn't stand that, and the air is said to be quite thick.'[175] Thomas Tickell referred to 'the Town [that] in damps and darkness lies'.[176] Not at Hampton Court. Throughout August 1716 the sun shone day after day, and the huge palace provided an idyllic setting for the extended *fête champêtre* that Caroline oversaw with George Augustus. It was not their first visit. Surviving accounts, including Mr Brinkman's bill of October 1715 for 'A proportion of Table linen to serve Their Royall Highnesses the Prince and Princess of Wales and Family for fourteen days as the service was at Hampton Court', suggest they lived there in some style.[177] Lady Cowper referred to a summer of 'great Splendour', the most glittering that Caroline and George Augustus would enjoy in George Louis's lifetime; maid of honour Molly Lepell remembered an interlude of 'a thousand agreeable things'.[178] For entertainment courtiers took to the river in a flotilla of velvet-lined barges. There were balls and drawing rooms and gambling at cards and, as at Herrenhausen, lengthy walks in the gardens, which provided a concourse for flirtation – in court argot of the period, 'frizzelation'.

It was to be a season of contrasts. Prince and princess set about establishing a court utterly at odds with George Louis's cloistered existence and fustian-clad reserve. Lavishly they celebrated the second anniversary of the king's accession at the beginning of August. They 'dined in public every day in the Princess's apartment. The Lady in Waiting served at table,' a spectacle visible to anyone sufficiently tidy in their dress to gain admission to the palace, 'even of the lowest sort and rank in their common habits', and, according to the Countess of Bristol, 'a most glorious sight'.[179] Whatever the truth of the couple's feelings, government ministers and their adversaries were received with equal warmth. 'The King was no sooner gone, than the Prince took a Turn of being civil and kind to Everybody, and applied himself to be well with the King's Ministers, and to understand the State of the Nation,' wrote Lady Cowper.[180] Even distracted by court ceremonies, George Augustus was not consumed by fripperies. He demonstrated a keen interest in politics, 'very intent upon holding the Parliament, very inquisitive about the revenue'; he asked 'daily for papers'.[181] The couple's guests included the Duke of Argyll, no longer a member of George Augustus's household.

Lady Cowper described the course of Caroline's days. 'In the afternoon the Princess saw company or read or writ till the evening, and then walked in the garden, sometimes two or three hours together, and then went into the pavilion at the end of the bowling green and played there [at cards].'[182] At Caroline's invitation, small supper parties took place in the Countess of Bückeburg's rooms. Her guests included members of her household – the Duchesses of St Albans and Shrewsbury, Lady Cowper and the countess; politicians' wives and the octogenarian Duchess of Monmouth, widow of Charles II's eldest illegitimate son, James, Duke of Monmouth, who had died in 1685 for his part in an armed rebellion against James II. Encouraged by Caroline, the elderly duchess regaled her companions with 'stories of King Charles's Court and Death' and his last mistress, Louise de Kérouaille, Duchess of Portsmouth, a 'tool [of] the Court of France'.[183] Courtiers not invited held supper parties of their own. Among Henrietta Howard's guests in her rooms on the floor above Caroline's were Alexander Pope and George Augustus himself. In the summer of 1716 the prince's immediate target was not Henrietta but his wife's pretty maids of honour, in particular Mary Bellenden. Happy in her pregnancy, Caroline did not dwell on his dalliances, actual or imaginary.

She made no concessions to her condition save the time set aside for quietly writing letters and 'reading such Books as are rarely attempted but by persons of much leisure and retirement, whose thoughts are not taken up with any of the cares or solicitudes of the world'.[184] Reading was George Augustus's least favourite of her pastimes, and Caroline confined it to that part of the afternoon when he slept off his midday dinner. With the exception of continuing unhappiness over Frederick, her cares and solicitudes were diminished by the king's absence: she did not share her ladies' fear that excessive walking in the palace gardens jeopardised her unborn baby or threatened miscarriage, although she humoured their concerns to the extent of 'tak[ing] some good things [her doctor] Sir David Hamilton gave her'.[185] Even George Augustus's heavy-handed flirtation failed to ruffle her equanimity.

Amid lavish entertaining, the royal couple also indulged philanthropic instincts. For the children of the locality they organised running races with prizes of smocks, petticoats and scarlet stockings provided from the royal purse. The gates of the palace gardens stood open to any who chose to enter. The result, as one visitor noted, was the presence of 'all sorts of people', granted 'free admission to see [the prince and princess]'.[186] In this way, *Saturday's Post* reported, George Augustus and Caroline encountered 'numerous Crowds of Country People'. All delighted in the 'easie Deportment and Affability of the Princess of Wales, who would even condescend to talk to a Country-Lass, in a Straw-Hat, with the same gracious Air her Royal Highness entertains Persons of the first Distinction; and yet, at the same time, lose nothing of her native Grandeur'.[187] Such ease and affability, added to the couple's deliberate visibility, won widespread approval. As a shrewd observer noted, 'they gain very much upon the people by that means'.[188] Among courtiers a fashion for straw hats sprang up, inspired by these encounters and the informality of the late-summer days.

Of course George Louis received detailed reports of goings-on at Hampton Court. Instructed 'to give an Account of Everything that was doing', Bothmer made sure of that.[189] The absent monarch's chief concern was not with country sports or millinery. George Augustus and Caroline's open-handedness in their treatment of Whigs and opposition Tories made them a magnet for the disaffected. Leading Whig ministers Lord Townshend and chancellor of the exchequer Robert Walpole sensed danger. Walpole objected to the private audiences both prince and princess continued to grant the Duke of Argyll. In Caroline's

ostentatious friendship with the disgruntled Scotsman, anger at
what she considered George Louis's unreasonable request
undoubtedly played its part. 'Coldly', averse to criticism or
instruction, she defied the Duchess of Richmond's plea that she
behave with greater circumspection. These audiences, Walpole
told Townshend, 'have such an effect ... as draws the tories from
all part of the neighbourhood, gives such a disgust to the Whigs
as before Michaelmas I may venture to prophecy the company
here will be two to one of the King's enemies'.[190]

Townshend responded by assiduously cultivating George
Augustus. His was an uphill task. Caroline regarded him as 'the
sneeringest, fawningest Knave that ever was', an impression he
shortly consolidated through a foolish error of judgement.[191] He
assumed that the fastest route to George Augustus's favour was
through Henrietta Howard or Mary Bellenden's commendation.
Accordingly he decided to ignore Caroline, even to show her 'all
the Contempt in the World'.[192] Caroline, Lady Cowper judged,
'had too much Quickness not to feel this as much as possible';
unshakeable was the lady-in-waiting's conviction of 'how much
it was for [Townshend and Walpole's] Interest and Advantage
to get her on their Side'.[193] Hastily, Townshend 'quite altered his
Conduct to the Princess'. For her part, a cynical Caroline chose
to accept his blandishments at face value. And unsurprisingly,
Lady Cowper concluded, the change in his behaviour 'brought
the Princess into perfect Tranquillity'.[194]

If accurate, this is a revealing view of Caroline's determination not to be sidelined. She had repeatedly asserted her compliance with George Augustus's will – as Walter Scott's fictional
Caroline tells the Duke of Argyll in *The Heart of Midlothian*, 'I can
only be the medium through which the matter is subjected to
[my husband's] superior wisdom.'[195] Her sway was considerable
nevertheless; at no point in her marriage did a mistress's influence exceed her own. Other men would repeat Townshend's
miscalculation. None of Caroline's waiting women ever did so.

To Charlotte Clayton, Lady Cowper suggested the summer's struggles had taken their toll. 'The Princess has been mightily out of order,' she wrote on 18 August. 'She was in great danger of miscarrying.'[196]

In the last week of September, while Caroline rested in anticipation of an October confinement, George Augustus made a four-day trip to Kent, Sussex, Surrey and Hampshire. He visited leading statesmen at home, the Earls of Dorset and Scarborough and the Duke of Newcastle; he attended military and naval reviews in Portsmouth; buoyant civic receptions greeted him in Farnham and Guildford; he took the waters in Tunbridge Wells. In every public encounter 'bounty and charity ... was very liberally bestowed'.[197] Such regal junketings had not been George Louis's intention. He deplored what he considered his son's deliberate pursuit of popularity. Privy not only to Bothmer's reports but to the conviction of his private secretary Jean de Robethon that George Augustus 'only wanted Power to displace Everybody the King liked, and dissolve the Parliament', he suspected his political intentions.[198] Cautiously he had restricted George Augustus's temporary power; he could not regulate long-distance against the younger man's influence on either public opinion or the voting habits of members of his household. As peers or MPs, several of George Augustus's household were eligible to vote in Parliament – against the government if persuaded to. George Louis's concerns were acute. They were shared by Walpole, who told Stanhope that he worried George Augustus planned 'to keep up an interest of his own in Parliament independent of the King's'.[199] The gaiety and splendour of George Augustus and Caroline's summer court masked entrenched mistrust between political factions as well as royal generations. Wittingly, husband and wife had set sail on dangerous seas.

While his father fulminated at Herrenhausen, George Augustus's focus was Caroline. Her confinement would take

place at St James's Palace. From Hanover her former midwife
was summoned. Again Caroline appears to have mistaken her
dates. A letter written by Lady Cowper on 9 October suggested
her labour was imminent, but nothing happened, and the court
did not return to London until the 28th.[200] By then, there had
been troubling warning signs. To Liselotte Caroline stated 'she
had suffered from bleeding and such pains'.[201] More bleakly, she
was described as 'extremely weak and subject to continual faint-
ings'.[202] Inevitably her doctors were at a loss to help her. She
made the return journey to London by barge, accompanied by
George Augustus and her ladies, on a day of bright autumn
sunshine.

The first of Caroline's children born in Britain was a stillborn
son. Her five-day labour was dominated by squabbling over the
manner of delivery. Prince and princess preferred to trust again
to the ministrations of the German midwife. Familiarity and
modesty probably swayed Caroline's viewpoint. Her British
attendants, including Lady Cowper, who had recommended his
appointment, argued in favour of the physician Sir David
Hamilton. Since Hamilton spoke no German and the midwife
no English, and each side regarded the other with suspicion
bordering on hostility, cooperation proved impossible. 'The
good Princess had symptoms of labour on Sunday evening, and,
tis thought, might have been safely delivered of a living son that
night, or any time before Tuesday morning, if Sir David Hamilton
… might have been admitted to her,' wrote clergyman White
Kennett with patriotic loyalty. 'But the Hanover midwife kept
up the aversion of the Princess to have any man about her …
notwithstanding the importunity of the English ladies, and the
declared advice of the Lords of the Council.'[203]

At length, fractiousness gave way to panic as Caroline
succumbed to 'a shivering Fit, which held her a good While, and
violently'.[204] For an interval her position was precarious. 'Hurly-
burly' between the warring factions continued nevertheless,

and 'the Midwife ... refused to touch the Princess unless she and the Prince would stand by her against the English "Frows", who, she said, ... had threatened to hang her if the Princess miscarried'.[205] Meanwhile Caroline's suffering persisted. She was not the first princess whose wellbeing was sacrificed to disagreements between antagonistic attendants. Only George Augustus's angry intervention resolved the impasse. In 'a passion', he 'swore that he would fling out of Window whoever ... pretended to meddle'. His threats were too late for Caroline's baby. 'The poor Princess continued in a languishing Condition till Friday Night, when she was delivered of a dead Prince' – in White's account 'between one and two, when the midwife alone delivered her of a dead male child, wounded in the head'.[206]

For days afterwards, Caroline continued to languish. 'Ye backstairs', Mrs Boscawen told Lady Evelyn, were 'always soe crowded' with well-wishers.[207] In bed she distracted her grief by reading letters. Belatedly contrite, her ladies-in-waiting took fright at her glancing encounter with death. Their reactions reveal fondness for their mistress, and more: a view of Caroline's central place within the new regime. To Lady Cowper, Anne Paulet wrote on 10 November, 'ye happyness of England depends upon her life'.[208] Only Caroline, it seemed, could bridge an ever-widening gulf between the king and his heir.

In the evening of 2 November 1717, the sound of cannon fire ricocheted through St James's Park and at the Tower of London. One year on from her stillbirth, Caroline was safely delivered of a son, her first child successfully born on British soil. In keeping with royal precedent the baby emerged into a crowded bedchamber. Alongside George Augustus, the Duchesses of St Albans, Shrewsbury, Montagu and Monmouth, Ladies Dorset, Hinchinbrooke, Grantham and Cowper, the Countess of Bückeburg and the Archbishop of Canterbury availed themselves of their right to be present at the birth. With greater felicity than the previous autumn, British and German doctors worked side by side. George Augustus reacted with 'transports' of joy to this second male heir. George Louis shared his elation to the extent of a £1,000 reward for the messenger who conveyed the news to him at Hampton Court; afterwards, to '[see] the child suck', he visited the royal nursery.[209] When the news was made public, the *London Gazette* reported 'a universal joy ... among all sorts of people throughout London and Westminster, of which the greatest demonstrations were shown by ringing of bells, illuminations and bonfires'.[210] 'Universal joy' proved as short-lived as the fireworks. In the words of one ballad, the 'royal babe' was 'born of Blood,/Which some call good,/Yet much ill Blood created'.[211]

A disagreement over the baby's godparents resulted in a rift between George Augustus and his father that, formally resolved in 1720, never properly healed. The parents chose a trio of godparents: aside from George Louis himself, the king's unmarried brother Ernest Augustus, and George Augustus's sister Sophia Dorothea, Queen of Prussia. Royal christenings took place in the mother's bedchamber, with courtiers or family members standing proxy for absent godparents, the royal mother still in her bed, as at Frederick's christening in Hanover a decade earlier. Protocol provided no outlet for anger that, on George Augustus's part, had attained explosive proportions.

George Louis's decision, at the insistence of his ministers, to name his grandson George William, proved a tinderbox assertion of power. So too his replacement of Ernest Augustus as godparent with his lord chamberlain, the Duke of Newcastle, and of Sophia Dorothea with Caroline's groom of the stole, the Duchess of St Albans, wife of the captain of the band of gentlemen pensioners in George Louis's own household. On the surface the king followed recent precedent in including his lord chamberlain among the baby's sponsors; he was well aware of animosity between Newcastle – 'as jealous of his power as an impotent lover of his mistress' – and George Augustus.[212]

Caroline shared her husband's irritation at her father-in-law's heavy-handed meddling. Like him she understood the convention in relation to the lord chamberlain as a matter of tradition rather than a requirement. She had almost certainly anticipated material benefits from her choice of godparent, an important consideration in the case of a second son unlikely to inherit the crown. Her request that Newcastle merely stand proxy for Ernest Augustus was firmly rebuffed, as was her suggestion that the service be postponed to allow time to reach a compromise. She was exasperated that her preferred name of William, held by three English kings, including the hero of the Glorious Revolution, was to be preceded by 'George', which she considered unhelpfully German. Unusually, given her pride in her own rationality – her legacy from Figuelotte, Sophia and Leibniz – she was also troubled by an unhappy prediction about the name.[213] Both husband and wife suspected George Louis of deliberate antagonism.

As it happened, intemperate behaviour on George Augustus's part gave his father the opportunity for which he was apparently looking. At the service of baptism on the evening of 28 November, the prince stood opposite his father. Caroline's ladies-in-waiting flanked him on one side of her bed, the Duke of Newcastle shadowed the king. The miasma of resentment between them erupted following George Louis's departure. 'No sooner had the Bishop closed the ceremony, than the Prince crossing the feet of the bed in a rage, stepped up to the Duke of Newcastle, and holding up his hand and forefinger in a menacing attitude, said, "You are a rascal, but I shall find you."'[214] Or in the words of a ballad-writer: 'the Prince did wax full wroth,/ E'en in his Father's hall: "I'll be reveng'd on thee (he cry'd),/ Thou rogue and eke rascal!"'[215] He accused the statesman of dishonesty. Unnerved by the force of his anger and confused by the thickness of his German accent, the duke claimed George Augustus had challenged him to a duel: 'I shall *fight* you.' It was this that he reported to the king. 'The Peer thus provok'd in a high indignation/Limpt forthwith away to the Head of the Nation;/To complain of the abuse shew'd to one of his Station.'

George Louis's decision to believe his servant above his son indicates the collapse of good relations following his return from Hanover in December 1716. Politics provided the short-term cause. 'How like the English to come between father and son,' wrote Liselotte, after noting with understatement, 'it seems there is trouble between the King of England and the Prince of Wales'.[216] Other irritants were of maturer vintage.

In 1717 a schism had unfurled at the heart of government. Townshend and Walpole opposed Sunderland and Stanhope over policies devised by George Louis to gain for Hanover the Swedish territories of Bremen and Verden, partly through the costly deployment of the Royal Navy in the Baltic. After extensive contact during the previous summer, and in discussion with Caroline, George Augustus chose to side with Walpole and Townshend. Accordingly, members of the prince's household voted against measures proposed in Parliament by Stanhope and Sunderland, while George Augustus himself pointedly stayed away from cabinet meetings.

Such overt opposition within his own family inevitably unsettled George Louis, who did his best, during the early months of 1717, to persuade his son to a reconciliation. To the same end he made approaches to Caroline too, through a series of intermediaries, including Stanhope and his mistress Madame Schulenburg. Neither husband nor wife yielded. Amiably but politely Caroline resisted Melusine's plea that she encourage George Augustus to change his mind. She gave the same response to Stanhope, whose angry reaction to her stonewalling included threatening to persuade Parliament that the prince's income of £100,000 be made dependent on George

Louis's acquiescence. Coolly Caroline countered this bluster with teasing. Once Stanhope had chosen to overlook her; now he lost his temper and presumed to threaten her. But she lacked neither courage nor quick thinking. Of the hot-headed minister, lately married to the daughter of the wealthy merchant Thomas Pitt, she requested, as a further incentive for George Augustus, that he add his father-in-law's magnificent diamond.[217]

If all this resembled calculated defiance, the couple do not seem to have meant to alienate the king completely. Instead they acted naïvely in anticipating tolerance on George Louis's part of a course of action so contrary to his own best interests. George Augustus's obstinacy matched his father's, but the fate of Sophia Dorothea was proof of the ruthlessness of the older man's response to challenge. Headstrong, impulsive and listless – in the words of one courtier 'so little master of Himself' – in the spring of 1717 George Augustus correctly hazarded government weakness.[218] What he failed to see – and Caroline failed to impress upon him – was the impossibility of George Louis allowing him to make political capital from the crisis.

In this climate of uncertainty and mistrust, Stanhope and Sunderland persuaded George Louis to abandon a second trip to Hanover. Instead, like the prince and princess the previous year, he spent the summer at Hampton Court, where George Augustus and Caroline joined him. Caroline's behaviour suggested emollience, walking in the palace gardens with her father-in-law; George Augustus routinely avoided his father. George Louis expressed his displeasure by refusing to invite George Augustus to share his table when he dined in public; George Augustus retaliated by declining to attend George Louis's shoot. Of the famous 'water party' in July 1717, at which fifty musicians in a barge premiered Handel's *Water Musick*, Prussian diplomat Friedrich Bonet noted, 'Neither the Prince nor the Princess took any part in this festivity.'[219] The atmosphere could not have been more different from twelve months earlier, when even the weather had seemed to shine on the efforts of the prince and princess to assert themselves as sovereigns. As if to erase memories of their former sway, George Louis had exerted himself to provide a programme of court entertainments more splendid than anything since his accession.

In 1714, Melusine's brother had written that George Augustus 'behaves in such a manner that the king has good reason to complain', a reflection of the view of George Louis's inner circle.[220] Three years on and George Louis's attitude had hardened. In the aftermath of the unhappy baptism, he investigated George Augustus's challenge to a senior member of his household testily. At the same time, abandoning compromise, he placed his son under house arrest. Barricaded for days in his apartments by armed yeomen of the guard, George Augustus wrote his father two submissive, apologetic letters. Less submissively, he told the king's emissaries that it was the right 'of every subject in England to chuse who should be Godfathers to their Children'.[221] A distressed Caroline sought reassurance from Liselotte: 'The Princess assures me that her husband did everything in his power to conciliate the King's good graces; he even begged his pardon, and owned that he had been to blame as humbly as if he had been addressing himself to God Almighty.'[222] It was not enough. Encouraged by ministers who saw in George Augustus's downfall a means of robbing their opponents of a figurehead, George Louis decided to banish his son from St James's Palace. To make clear his fall from grace he stripped him of his royal guard. The younger man obeyed only when the command was put in writing: 'The Vice Chamberlain is ordered to go to my Son, and to tell him from me, that he and his Domesticks must leave my House.'[223]

To Caroline, George Louis offered a choice: 'Notwithstanding the order sent to my Son, she may remain at St James's, until her health will suffer her to follow her Husband.' But that was not all. Once before he had been party to a settlement that forbade Sophia Dorothea contact with her children; now he claimed possession of Princesses Anne, Amelia and Caroline, and their baby brother too: 'It is my Pleasure, that my Grandson and Granddaughters remain at St James's, where they are, and that the Princess is permitted to come to see them, when she has a Mind; and that the Children are permitted from Time to Time to go and see her and my Son ... In the present Situation of my Family, I think, that whilst she stays at St James's, she would do well to see no company.'[224] It was an impossible choice, as George Louis knew, and a shaken Caroline declined to remain under the royal roof on such terms. Again she confided her predicament to Liselotte.

Of course she followed her husband. Her position depended upon him, and she, who understood too well the fragility of women's security, would not jeopardise this certainty. George Louis was an old man, and such unprecedented rage within the royal family must surely abate. Caroline told him she was 'under the highest obligations to [George Augustus] for having made her the happiest woman in the world; and that though her children were entirely dear, they were not as a grain of sand to her, in comparison of Him'.[225] Her stand, as she understood, had a bravura quality. In abandoning to George Louis's arbitrary pleasure her daughters and the infant son who was still only weeks old, she ensured that popular sympathy rested with George Augustus at his father's expense. It was a point scored at inestimable cost to all concerned.

Let Liselotte's verdict stand for the response of Caroline's contemporaries, even if she underestimated the extent of Caroline's involvement in George Augustus's defiance: 'The King of England is really cruel to the Princess of Wales. Although she has done nothing, he has taken her children away from her. Where could they be so well and carefully brought up as with a virtuous mother?'[226]

In March 1718, George Louis invested the Duke of Newcastle with the Order of the Garter. The following month he conferred an earldom on Stanhope.

II

Leicester House

'Not a Day without Suffering'

'A very handsome large square, enclosed with rails and graced on all sides with good built houses, well inhabited and resorted to by the gentry,' Leicester Square – still, in the first quarter of the eighteenth century, in some accounts referred to as Leicester Fields – lay north-west of Charing Cross, within walking distance of St James's Palace.[1] In the north-east corner of the square, behind a courtyard screened from the public way, stood early-seventeenth-century Leicester House – in Sutton Nicholls's view of around 1720, a large brick-built structure of unremarkable aspect with views over formal gardens, small shops and rows of genteel townhouses, its own gatehouse and tall gates.[2] Behind it lay a modest formal garden of statues and clipped yews, and a ribbon of deciduous trees offering spreading shade. In Alexander Pope's account it boasted green-painted doors. It suffered infestations of bedbugs.[3]

In the wake of their expulsion it was here, on 25 March 1718, that George Augustus and Caroline installed the remnants of their court, after a short but unsatisfactory interval of homelessness spent partly at Grantham House, in nearby Dover Street. It remained their London home until George Louis's death, the setting for the rival court they assembled in opposition to the king. For the house that had briefly belonged to his paternal great-grandmother, the 'Winter Queen', Elizabeth of Bohemia, George Augustus paid £6,858; he set in train year-long alterations supervised by architect Nicholas Dubois.[4] Its immediate surrounds, altered by new building since Elizabeth's death in 1662, were the haunt of footpads, ruffians and hoydens, noisy during waking hours, a lively, dark-seamed neighbourhood of night-time menaces. 'Here lives a Person of high Distinction; next door a Butcher with his stinking Shambles! A Tallow Chandler shall front my Lord's nice Venetian window and two or three brawny naked Curriers in their Pit shall face a fine Lady in her back closet and disturb her spiritual Thoughts,' wrote a correspondent of the journal *Old England* about London in 1748.[5] So it was three decades earlier in the vicinity of Leicester Square. Less charitable observers noted the proximity to Leicester House of middling shopkeepers' premises, the row of lock-up shops at its gatehouse entrance.[6] For its new incumbents, the house's association with Elizabeth outweighed nicer drawbacks. It was to Elizabeth, the eldest daughter of James I, that George Louis traced his claim to the throne. In her later collecting, Caroline underlined the significance of this connection. Her purchases included a painting of 1634 by Bartholomeus van Bassen, *The King and Queen of Bohemia Dining in Public*.[7]

Caroline was thirty-five years old. Nearly four years had passed since she last saw her eldest child. Since December she had been parted from her daughters. In leaving behind St James's, she even lost access to the royal library, a greater deprivation for this princess than many; George Louis had forbidden prince or princess to remove from their apartments in the palace a single piece of furniture. One month ago, husband and wife had sat at the bedside of baby George William and helplessly watched as life slipped away from the tiny child whose birth had occasioned so much anger. 'His illness began with an oppression upon his breast, accompanied with a cough, which increasing, a fever succeeded with convulsions,' one newspaper reported.[8] As his condition worsened, George Louis had ordered the baby's removal from smoke-lagged St James's to the cleaner air of Kensington Palace. From the end of January he had relaxed his severity to the extent of granting Caroline permission to visit all four children. In the case of baby George William it was too late. There was no consolation for Caroline in his night-time burial in Westminster Abbey, accomplished with the full panoply of yeomen of the guard and a procession of royal coaches – 'in Royal Tomb The little Bones you'll find', lamented one ballad-eer.[9] Nor in the autopsy ordered by George Louis to prove that the child's death could not be blamed on separation from his mother.

It was an older, sadder, grieving Caroline who set about establishing at Leicester House a setting for a princely court she modelled in part on Figuelotte's lively Lützenburg. Less than two years earlier she had sat for Kneller's official portrait, contentment in the smile that gently plays about her lips in that otherwise stiff and formal image. For the moment, equanimity failed her. In the aftermath of George William's death, public sympathy was strongly in George Augustus and particularly Caroline's favour. George Sewell's *Verses to Her Royal Highness the Princess of Wales, Occasion'd by the Death of the Young Prince* blamed political factionalism for the family rift, the children's separation from their parents and the loss of the infant prince: 'the Royal Infant bleeds;/The Royal Mother weeps for British Deeds'.[10] Of little solace to Caroline, such sentiments reverberated across the Continent, where memories of George Louis's vengefulness towards Sophia Dorothea persisted. Liselotte was predictably unconstrained. 'My God, how I pity our poor dear Princess of Wales!' she wrote on 24 February. 'I heard from England yesterday that her last-born little prince died of catarrh on the chest. She saw him at Kensington just before the end. I wish she hadn't seen him, for it will be even more painful for her now.

God grant that this Prince's death may extinguish all the flames kindled at his christening! But alas, there is no sign of that yet.'[11]

Signs would remain scant. Four months earlier, neither husband nor wife had anticipated the scale of George Louis's anger and implacability. If she regretted at all failing to dissuade George Augustus from opposing his father, it was a chastened though unrepentant Caroline who, in Leicester Square, began the process of rebuilding the couple's lives in the face of private suffering and public humiliation. At the same time, and without encouragement from George Louis, she kept up a sporadic attendance at the king's drawing rooms.

Her challenge was considerable. Pressure of space at Grantham House had prevented prince and princess from holding court in their customary style. This, combined with George Louis's order that anyone who wished to work or be received at his own court sever all connection with the households of George Augustus and Caroline, had eventually robbed their gatherings of any but their closest friends and the neediest hangers-on. 'Many waited on them at their first going to Lord Grantham's,' it was noted, 'but few since.'[12]

The Duchesses of St Albans and Montagu, both married to men close to the king, were first to leave Caroline's service. The hastiness of their departure appeared akin to abandonment. The Countesses of Bristol and Pembroke replaced them. Lady Cowper, wife of the lord chancellor, and Mrs Clayton, married to a treasury official, shortly followed, in both cases reluctantly, Mrs Clayton, compelled by financial exigency, dependent on her husband's exchequer salary of £1,500. For the wealthy Duchesses of St Albans and Montagu Caroline conceived a lasting enmity.

Caroline's circle shrank accordingly, but she was not left wholly alone. William Wake, Archbishop of Canterbury since January 1716, defied George Louis's proscription and continued to visit both prince and princess in his role as spiritual mentor.

Edmund Gibson, dean of the Chapel Royal, referred to Wake's 'intire interest in the prince and Princess' – Wake himself had attributed a decisive role to Caroline in his promotion to the archbishopric.[13] Throughout her marriage, Caroline had taken care to maintain amiable relations with Melusine von der Schulenburg. Now, pressed by the Cowpers, the king's mistress intervened on Caroline's behalf. Informally Lady Cowper was advised that she might continue to see Caroline until the princess was fully restored to health. This concession lasted only until December, when she was instructed 'not to attend her any longer, having had leave to do it only during her illness'.[14] Princess and bedchamber lady contrived to meet discreetly. Among Lady Cowper's surviving papers is an undated letter detailing arrangements for one such secret meeting.[15] Happily this cloak-and-dagger deception was of short duration. In April Lord Cowper resigned as lord chancellor, enabling his wife to return to Leicester House. From the country he urged her in vain to encourage 'that good and serious disposition you found in ye Prince and Princess during your last waiting to submit to his Majesty and to live as becomes ye most dutiful children'.[16]

A similar leniency to that temporarily granted Mary Cowper was not extended to others of Caroline's ladies, and Caroline resorted to further subterfuges. 'The Princess ... loves you mightily, and desires you would not come hither unless you find you can do it with safety,' Lady Cowper wrote to Charlotte Clayton. 'She has ordered me to tell you, that if you do think of coming, she desires ... that you would be here by nine o'clock in the morning, and if you will give her notice of the day you will come, she will meet you in the garden-house, at the end of the terrace, that nobody may see you.'[17] Caroline's response to such an assignation suggests her longing for former companionship. On 30 July 1719 she wrote to Mrs Clayton, 'the four hours you was with me past as two, I long for the time that will give me the satisfaction of seeing you without constraint as often as I can'.[18]

To both women Caroline continued to write regularly. In adversity she proved the sincerity of that affection she had expressed in happier times. She described Charlotte Clayton as 'the best friend I have, whom I shall love as long as my heart has sense or motion'.[19] A circumspect note colours several letters. Soon after leaving St James's Palace, she requested of Mrs Clayton information from her husband about George Augustus's financial position. 'Your letters shall be burnt,' Caroline reassured her, 'you may send it by my son's nurse who comes sometimes to see Geminghen [Baroness von Gemmingen].'[20] A much-needed spark of humour was added by Mrs Clayton finding herself unable to decipher Caroline's letters. 'I laugh'd heartily that you could not read one of my letters, the Prince said to me, You write like a cat,' Caroline replied to her.[21]

Of her women who remained eligible to visit St James's Palace, or Kensington Palace, where George Louis had embarked on a programme of improvement and renovation, including apartments for Princesses Anne, Amelia and Caroline, the girls' mother begged that they 'goe & see my children' and pass on to her all the news they could, much as she quizzed visitors to Hanover about Frederick.[22] Her need of such reassurances redoubled following George Louis's decision in May to replace as royal governess Caroline's friend the Countess of Bückeburg with his own appointment, Jane, Dowager Countess of Portland, noted in court circles for her intelligence and the mother of a large family. George Augustus expressed the couple's disapproval of the switch by offering Lady Bückeburg an annual pension of £500.

Those who remained with Caroline shared with their mistress an unavoidable sense of diminishment. In a letter of 12 July 1718, Baroness von Gemmingen confided to Lady Cowper how much she missed her.[23] But Caroline, according to a posthumous verdict, was able 'to bear up with patience and resolution against undeserved calumny or reproach'; from the outset, there was nothing funereal in the atmosphere at Leicester House.[24] Indeed she had determined to create a court glittering and vibrant and, restraints notwithstanding, at least enjoyed in this her own house a degree of independence she could not have exercised under George Louis's roof. Like Sophia and Figuelotte, she meant to attract not only politicians and noblemen, but the leading minds of the day.

She valued high spirits too; among the household installed at Leicester House in the spring of 1718 were a gaggle of Caroline's maids of honour, including the court beauties Mary Lepell and Mary Bellenden, as well as woman of the bedchamber Henrietta Howard. A popular ballad claimed of the first that her charms 'could warm an old monk in his cell', and suggested that 'Should Venus now rise from the ocean/And naked appear in her shell,/She would not cause half the emotion/That we feel from dear Molly Lepell.'[25] Caroline's relationship with the young women was of straightforward warmth, and was reciprocated in kind. Her maids of honour proved a lure for male visitors, including the poets whose tributes she craved. The young women's enjoyment of their role in Caroline's court says much for its vivacity, even at this low point. To Henrietta Howard, flighty Sophy Howe wrote of a visit to her parents in the country, 'One thing I have got by the long time I have been here, which is the being more sensible than ever I was of my happiness in being maid of honour.'[26] Walpole described Caroline's 'new court' as made up of 'the liveliest and prettiest of the young ladies'.[27]

At Hampton Court in the summer of 1716, Lord Townshend had suspected Henrietta Howard of an influence over George Augustus that she did not possess, mistaking her for the prince's mistress. Over the course of 1718, Townshend's misapprehension became fact. Determinedly, George Augustus had endeavoured to press his attentions on Mary Bellenden, exploiting his knowledge of her straitened finances to cajole her into his bed.

She resisted with vehemence. 'The Prince's gallantry was by no means delicate,' commented Horace Walpole, who described him ostentatiously emptying his purse and counting gold coins in front of Mary; his indelicacies – and the contents of his purse – failed to impress. Physically she defended herself against him by folding her arms across her breasts at his approach. Making her feelings clear, she 'told him [she] was not cold, but … liked to stand so'.[28] George Augustus did not feign love. Lust – and a desire for an amorist's reputation – prompted him. More convincing proof of where his true affections lay that spring was offered by Caroline's latest pregnancy.

To Mary Bellenden, with a characteristic lack of couthness, George Augustus had suggested possible financial rewards for sex. Still entirely dependent on her court appointment for security, and frightened by any prospect of a return to her husband's bullying, Henrietta Howard accepted the challenge her younger colleague had rebuffed. Neither affection nor physical attraction played any part in her decision. A memorandum of 29 August 1716 details Henrietta's views on her own marriage: Charles Howard's brutishness, she concludes, has invalidated their marriage contract, and so 'I must believe I am free'.[29] Lord Hervey considered that Mary Bellenden's rejection 'left Mrs Howard, who had more steadiness and more perseverance, to try what she could make of a game which the other had found so tedious and unprofitable that she had no pleasure in playing it and saw little to be won by minding it'.[30] The decision that her own marriage had been effectively terminated by mistreatment helped Henrietta to reconcile herself to what would be a lengthy liaison based on limited compatibility.

That George Augustus was highly sexed is clear from Caroline's willingness during her pregnancies to countenance his wandering attentions. So it had been in the summer of 1716 at Hampton Court, and so it proved two years later. With careful self-control she reacted to this liaison she had expected for five years. A courtier's claim that 'tho' [Henrietta Howard] was at that time very handsome, it gave her Majesty no jealousy or uneasiness', is a tribute to Caroline's public demeanour as much as an accurate reflection of her state of mind.[31] Certainly Henrietta's eventual recognition as George Augustus's mistress appears to have caused Caroline discernible distress only intermittently. A handful of instances survive of her exploiting her superior rank to score points at her rival's expense. Lord Hervey records the iciness of her response to discovering a love letter from George Augustus to his mistress, accidentally dropped from its hiding place in her bodice.[32] He quotes Caroline's tart dismissal of Henrietta: 'For my part, I have always heard a great deal of her great sense from other people, but I never saw her in any material great occurrence in her life, take a sensible step.'[33] Such comments, querying Henrietta's intelligence, arose from the double nature of the women's rivalry. Not only was Henrietta George Augustus's mistress, she was Caroline's cultural rival too, a friend of Pope and Swift and the prominent Tory satirist and creator of John Bull Dr John Arbuthnot, whom she entertained in her apartments in the royal palaces. Like Caroline, Henrietta aspired to a literary salon; like Caroline, she would commission artists and architects. 'I intend to improve myself in terms of art, in order to keep pace with you this winter,' a friend wrote to Henrietta in 1724, 'otherwise I know I shall make but a scurvey figure in your room.'[34] Such commendations aggravated Caroline's jealousy.

In her defence, and aside from her envy, Caroline shielded Henrietta from Charles Howard, firmly denying him access to his estranged wife. Throughout the royal quarrel she enabled Henrietta to remain a member of her household – and therefore George Augustus's mistress – notwithstanding Charles's place in George Louis's employ. Initially George Louis acquiesced in this arrangement, an indication that his relationship with Caroline, however strained, was not consistently spiteful. In his later efforts to reclaim his wife Charles Howard would invoke the king's approval.

Aphoristically, Hervey summed up George Augustus as 'a man incapable of being engaged by any charm but habit, or attached to any woman but his wife'.[35] The prince's relationship with Henrietta never lessened his dependence on Caroline. His emotional attachment to her was undiminished, as was his overwhelming physical attraction to her, which she reciprocated in full. Horace Walpole later confirmed the prince's preference: 'King George II has often, when Mrs Howard, his mistress, was dressing the Queen, come into the room and snatched the handkerchief off [Caroline's shoulders while her hair was being dressed], and cried, "Because you have an ugly neck yourself, you love to hide the Queen's!"'[36]

By 1718, Caroline knew enough of discreet, unassertive Henrietta – acclaimed for her reasonableness by both Pope and her besotted admirer Lord Peterborough – to be certain she would never supplant her in George Augustus's esteem. Undoubtedly she was gratified by something tepid in their relationship, grounds for Hervey's mischievous suggestion later that George Augustus had never 'entered into any commerce with [Henrietta], that he might not innocently have had with his daughter'.[37] And she understood that it was George Augustus's vanity that demanded the publicity of a mistress as much as he craved another woman's sexual enticements. The previous summer, Caroline had chosen to ignore advice from Liselotte, based on her marriage to the Duke of Orléans – the older woman had described her relief when her husband had suggested separate sleeping arrangements.[38] Caroline's marriage was of a different complexion, her enjoyment of sex marked. She would fight to maintain George Augustus's uxoriousness.

At the end of May, Caroline miscarried. It was not as a result of anxiety at Henrietta's elevation, or the news that George Augustus had awarded her a generous annual pension of

£2,000: more highly than simple sexual fidelity, Caroline prized emotional dependence. Instead, a large elm tree felled close to her window by a violent storm had startled her. Her decision to dismiss peremptorily a nursemaid who claimed that George Augustus had ogled her was just as likely prompted by her sense of the girl's impertinence as jealousy at her husband's roving eye.[39]

Caroline's success in creating at Leicester House any sort of alternative to George Louis's court at St James's, Kensington or Hampton Court points to her decided strength of character, as well as wide-ranging social, cultural and intellectual interests. The interdiction on so many courtiers, added to the constraints of the prince and princess's income – the latter exacerbated by George Augustus's parsimony – made the competition between the two courts potentially a one-sided affair. While Caroline embraced the challenge energetically, George Louis – saturnine and retiring – triumphed through deliberate open-handedness. Lady Hertford described to her mother the lavish picturesque-ness of his birthday celebrations in June: 'The ball was in the greenhouse, ... the way to it being through a garden of orange, lemon and bergamot trees ... There was a great deal of new clothes and most of them as fine as the season would allow of.'[40] Each evening that summer he entertained fifty to sixty guests to dinner, with balls held twice weekly.[41] Such was royal hospital-ity at a ball at St James's in the winter that the king's vice cham-berlain described 'the room where the Side Board was kept' as so 'stained with claret [that] it was necessary to provide Sayl cloth against another ball to prevent like damage'.[42]

Locked into a competition for courtiers' allegiance with George Louis that she could not win, cut off from her children and friends and publicly stripped of many of the trappings of her rank, Caroline found the period 1717 to 1720 one of consider-able strain. Those who encountered her noticed her distraction.

In April 1718, Archbishop Wake referred to an oversight on her part towards a struggling writer. 'I shall ... wait upon the Princess tomorrow, and will put her in mind of this charity, if her present trouble has made her forget it,' he wrote.[43] The couple lacked money. Caroline's income of £18,000 a year was less than that of leading courtiers. Her grounds for not acquiring a set of Dutch tapestries that had previously belonged to Charles I – the sort of purchase that appealed to her sense of historical continuity – were almost certainly financial.[44]

Caroline's thoughts were frequently occupied with her own more immediate problems. In the face of protests from within his family and hostile public opinion, George Louis remained determined to retain control over his grandchildren. In January 1718 he instituted legal proceedings described by the lord chancellor as deciding 'whether the Education, and Care of the Persons of His Majesty's Grandchildren, and ordering the Place of their Abode, & appointing their Governors, Governesses and other Instructors, Attendants and servants, and the Care and Approbation of their Marriages when grown up, belong of right to His Majesty, as King of this Realm, or not?'[45] Unsurprisingly, a majority of the judges consulted concluded that they did. Equally unsurprising is Caroline's tearful reflection to Lady Cowper, inspired by longing for Frederick, Anne, Amelia, Caroline and the unfortunate George William: 'I can say, since the Hour I was born, that I have not lived a Day without Suffering.'[46]

At first too proud to accept the king's offer of limited access to her children, and determined to make good her stand at George Augustus's side, Caroline relied on intermediaries. Chief among them until her replacement by Lady Portland was the Countess of Bückeburg, whom George Louis allowed to visit Caroline every evening to deliver a daily report.[47] No want of affection prompted Caroline's decision not to visit her children in person. Several years later, an illness of Amelia's left her

frequently overwhelmed by worry; as it survives in her correspondence, her response is typical of her attitude to her daughters. 'You cannot believe the anxiety I am in,' she wrote. Her
anguish brought on 'a sore throat which hinders me from
goeing today [to see Amelia] & ... a little touch of feavour & a
cold', and her frustration at what she regarded as doctors'
incompetence provoked vigorous flashes of temper. Appalled by
George Louis's choice of physician and the latter's ineptitude,
she wrote disgustedly, 'I believe I could ... have pull'd out his
eys.'[48]

As the eldest of the princesses, albeit only eight at the time of
their separation, Anne took upon herself the task of writing to
her parents. From Kensington she sent George Augustus a
basket of cherries with assurances of all three girls' affection:
'their hearts, souls and thoughts were with their dear parents
always'.[49] To Liselotte, Caroline reported George Augustus's
tearful receipt of this gift. But there was no comfort for Caroline
when Anne protested at the lovelessness of the princesses' lives
under their grandfather's roof: 'we have a good father and a
good mother, and yet we are like charity children'.[50]

Anne's brief notes to her mother were continual pinpricks,
like the plaintive 'j'espere ... que vous seres en etat de venir se soir ce
qui nous fera beaucoup de plaisir' (I hope that you can come this
evening, which will give us much pleasure).[51] For all Caroline's
deliberate 'Englishness', parents and children communicated in
French, which both parents found easier. Caroline's letters were
directed 'pour ma chère fille Anne', and written with a studied
brightness that cost her dear.[52] 'You know too well how much I
love you,' she told her eldest daughter when illness prevented
her from visiting.[53] Parents' and daughters' notes reveal a crav-
ing on both sides for a close and loving family life, as does Lord
Hervey's claim that towards Lady Portland, who had usurped
their place in the princesses' lives, Caroline and George Augustus
nurtured 'a most irreconcilable hatred'.[54]

Fleetingly, Caroline was distracted by the acquisition of a house in the country, an escape from the heat and stench of London summers. 'Very neat, very pretty', the former Ormonde Lodge stood in parkland that had once surrounded the old Richmond Palace near Kew, a pedimented classical box rebuilt in the last reign. It had previously belonged to the Duke of Ormonde, a prominent Jacobite. For his well-known political sympathies the duke had forfeited his estates and hastily escaped to France. In his midnight flit he left behind a house fully furnished even down to the large Delft flowerpot in the dining-room fireplace, a 'Yellow Damask bed compleat' and, in the closet within the Yellow Dressing Room, 'a Fine Turkey work carpet' valued at £4.[55] A contemporary verdict found 'everything in it and about it answerable to the grandeur and magnificence of its great master' – boon indeed for the couple who had been prevented from removing a single piece of furniture from George Louis's palace.[56]

At a remove from the capital and bordered by the Thames, the house offered Caroline and George Augustus reminders of happier times at Hampton Court. Its setting resembled that of Pope's villa at nearby Twickenham: 'Our River glitters beneath an unclouded Sun ... Our Gardens are offering their first Nosegays; our Trees, like new Acquaintances brought happily together, are stretching their arms to meet each other ... The Birds are paying their thanksgiving Songs.'[57] The duke's garden, however, offered a vision of nature perfected, ornamented with trees in wooden planters: pomegranates and orange trees as at Herrenhausen; myrtle, bay and nut trees. In his *Journey through England* of 1714, John Macky judged it 'a most delicious habitation'.[58]

George Louis was predictably displeased with the couple's discovery. In a letter of July 1719 the Countess of Bristol referred to the 'no small pains' he had taken to 'disappoint' them in their hopes of ownership, and their friends' happiness at the frustration of those pains. 'Everyone,' she noted, 'took part in the Prince and Princess's pleasure in having this place secured to them when they almost despaired of it.'[59] For £6,000, George Augustus bought the house and its extensive gardens; for its contents, including fire shovels, blankets and a barn still stocked with peas, rye and wheat, he paid a further £709.1s.2d.[60] Renovations were undertaken, and Caroline would set about constructing a sizeable library wing north of the main house. Up-to-the-minute sanitary arrangements are indicated by subsequent yearly payments to one John Bell for cleaning the 'bathing copper' and pipes.[61]

In early September 1719, in line with current thinking that 'there is some sort of pleasure in shewing one's own fancy upon one's own Ground', Caroline invited gardeners and garden-makers, including royal gardener Henry Wise, Charles Bridgeman and Pope, to discuss plans.[62] Bridgeman won the royal imprimatur. He planted a series of avenues lined with trees, dug a rectangular duckpond, constructed viewing mounts, one overlooking the river, built an amphitheatre within an elm copse. In line with emerging theories of 'natural' design, he dotted about 'morsels of a forest like appearance'; he created wildernesses and a snailery. A riverside terrace planted with elms stretched as far as the village of Kew. 'The beauties of the most stately Garden or Palace lie in a narrow Compass, the Imagination immediately runs over them and requires something else to gratify her,' Joseph Addison had written in the *Spectator* in 1712. He contrasted such 'stateliness' with 'the wide Fields of Nature [where] the Sight wanders up and down without confinement and is fed with an infinite variety of Images, without any Stint or Number'.[63] In Richmond, for the first time Caroline put into practice these emerging theories. Extended, altered and set in modishly remodelled gardens, the house became the setting for the couple's summers until the king's death, a rural idyll shorn of the formalities of Hampton Court.[64] Smaller than any existing royal residence, it required Caroline to build a terrace of four houses on Richmond Green to accommodate the overflow of her household.[65]

For George Augustus, Richmond Park and its surrounds provided extensive hunting, of foxes as well as stags. Husband and wife canvassed a comic actor called William Pinkethman, who made his fortune performing short plays or 'drolls' at Bartholomew and Richmond Fairs, to erect a temporary theatre. As at Hampton Court, prince and princess took an interest in the local community. They called the house Richmond Lodge and, to one another, simply 'the Lodge'. In December 1719 the *Weekly Journal* reported the rat-catcher John Humphries clearing the house of more than five hundred rats and taking them all 'alive to Leicester House as a proof of his art'.[66] On a practical level, their Richmond summers became for George Augustus and Caroline an opportunity for retrenchment, the prince targeting the royal table as a focus for economies. 'His diet', reported one unimpressed visitor, was 'so plain and the quality of his roasts and dishes so little and the ingredients for dressing them so little'.[67] One-off household expenses included 'a Dutch Fire Engine'.[68]

1718 was a year of rumours and denials. Claims of reconciliation were rapidly succeeded by counter-claims. On 10 February, *The Criticks: Being papers upon the times* interpreted Caroline's appearance at a royal drawing room as proof of 'the near prospect there is of a reconciliation between his Majesty and his Royal Highness. The Princess of Wales's appearance at court can bode no less.'[69] By contrast, in March, Liselotte wrote that the men's quarrel 'gets worse every day. I always thought [George Louis] harsh when he was in Germany, but English air has hardened him still more.'[70] Despairingly she told a correspondent, 'There is not a word of truth in the story that the King of England gave the Princess of Wales a present of lace. Unfortunately, everything is still in a very bad way.'[71] So bad, in

fact, that on 22 April George Augustus cancelled a visit to the
Drury Lane Theatre to attend a performance of Dryden's *The
Indian Emperor*, after hearing that George Louis had threatened
to dismiss every actor who performed in front of him. In May,
the Earl of Oxford stated that 'any persons that are turned out
of doors at St James's are sure to find entertainment at Leicester
Fields, so that the happy reconciliation is as near as ever'.[72] An
attempted amnesty in the summer failed. Meanwhile, as part of
his policy of eclipsing Leicester House socially, and also because
he had conceived an instant liking for the house, George Louis
set in motion plans for new state apartments at Kensington
Palace.

The prescriptiveness of George Louis's terms for reconciliation points to his angry intolerance: 'Provided the Prince would
dismiss such of his servants as were disagreeable to the King,
and that for the future he would take none but such as should
be approved of by His Majesty. That he should give up his children and such a sum for their education as His Majesty should
appoint. That he should neither see nor keep correspondence
with any but such as His Majesty should approve of, and lastly
that he should beg the Dukes of Roxburgh and Newcastle's
pardon.'[73] George Augustus's rejection was comprehensive; he
refused to offer assurances of better conduct in the future. His
response reflected a decision reached jointly by husband and
wife.

In supporting his continuing stand against his father, Caroline
may have had reasons of her own. Liselotte wrote that George
Louis had spread injurious rumours about his daughter-in-law,
suggesting possible infidelity. 'He will get laughed at by everybody for doing this,' she wrote on 28 July, 'for the Princess has
a spotless reputation.'[74] Poets including Nahum Tate acclaimed
Caroline as 'Cynthia', an alternative name for Artemis, a goddess
associated with chastity as well as wisdom. As the recipient of
Caroline's confidences, Liselotte was baffled by George Louis's

reported stance. She described Caroline as one who had 'never done anything against him and has always honoured, respected and indeed loved him as if he were her own father'.[75] The words may be Caroline's own, parroted by the older woman. If so, they tell us the impression Caroline was determined to convey to the outside world.

In May 1719, George Louis embarked on the visit to Hanover he had unwillingly abandoned two years earlier; among those who accompanied him were the composer Handel. So far were father and son from any restoration of normal relations that George Augustus was denied his former role of guardian and lieutenant of the realm. Instead the king drew up a Council of Regency: he excluded his son from its number. He did, however, formalise arrangements for increasing access to the royal children. On 4 May he instructed Lady Portland: 'We do allow our ... most Dearly beloved Son and our most Dearly beloved Daughter-in-law, the Princess of Wales, to see our said Grandchildren as often as they shall think fit, provided it be only in the Apartment of our said Grandchildren, & that whenever our said Son and Daughter-in-law, or either of them, repair thither for that purpose, they bring with them none but their Servants of their Bedchamber actually attending in the course of Duty upon their Persons, & not any other Person or Persons who are forbid Our Royal Presence.'[76] To Caroline he extended the opportunity of spending the summer with her daughters at Hampton Court. This concession did not apply to George Augustus, and Caroline declined.

An undated letter to Charlotte Clayton, probably written in the first half of 1719, seems to demonstrate Caroline's conviction that George Louis's attitude was softening, with compromise increasingly a possibility. 'The King himself is troubled,' she wrote, '& these are his very words that He can't forgive himself.'[77] Whatever the accuracy of her assessment, it was for this reason, as much as a desire to maintain appearances, that

Caroline later waited on George Louis to congratulate him on his safe return from the electorate. Wherever possible, and regardless of the truth of her feelings, she acted to sustain the fragile discourse between the warring households.

In the meantime, and sensibly, she provided herself with diversions. At Leicester House the adoptive daughter of Figuelotte established the equivalent of a salon. 'She loved a repartee; was happy in making one herself, and bearing it from others. And as this talent was rendered ... amiable by the greatest good nature and chearfulness of disposition ... she was (without respect to the dignity of her rank) the life of every company' – useful qualities in a saloniste.[78] Even Sarah, Duchess of Marlborough, acidulated in her jealousy of Caroline, granted her such personal qualities that she would 'never want a full court of the best sort of people that this country affords'.[79]

Poets Thomas Tickell, John Gay and Joseph Addison paid court to her. She had met Addison, a Whig enthusiast, and Gay separately at Herrenhausen, and all three men had written poetry in celebration of the Hanoverian succession. Gay's motives were pecuniary. Habitually cash-strapped, in 1724 he dedicated to Caroline his play *The Captives*. Her attendance at the first night, added to a financial gift, contributed to its £1,000 profit, proof of the value of royal endorsement. The following year Gay addressed a sequence of fables to her younger son, but no satisfactory court appointment was forthcoming, and acrimony supplanted partisanship.

A handful of intermediaries may have led Caroline to Alexander Pope: candidates include Henrietta Howard, Lady Mary Wortley Montagu and the architect Earl of Burlington, whom Caroline had met in Hanover in 1714, and whose wife would become a lady-in-waiting. Later, Henrietta's perseverance was a factor in persuading Jonathan Swift briefly to play his part in Caroline's circle. (Swift himself would tell the Duchess of Queensberry that only after eleven invitations from Caroline

did he finally 'yield her a visit'.[80]) Swift's attitude to Caroline
was one of wariness. 'I have no complaint to make of her Royal
Highness,' he wrote to Henrietta with rebarbative equivocation,
'therefore I think I may let you tell her that every grain of virtue
and good sense in one of her rank, considering their bad education among flatterers and adorers, is worth a dozen in inferior
persons.'[81] Swift gave Caroline a dress length of gold-threaded
Irish silk; he composed throwaway lines on the subject of breakfast at Richmond Lodge. But Caroline's attempt to introduce to
early-eighteenth-century London the salon culture she had
encountered in Berlin and Hanover yielded mixed results. Key
players protested at the meretricious nature of royal patronage:
'Her Majesty never shall be my exalter/And yet she would raise
me, I know by – a halter,' Swift wrote.[82]

Pope's ambivalence was undisguised. In *The Dunciad* he
mocked what he considered Caroline's lumbering intellectual
pretensions. Following a misunderstanding over a broken
promise about a present, Swift's feelings proved similarly ambiguous. With heavy-handed irony he described Caroline as 'a
perfect goddess born and bred,/Appointed sovereign judge to
sit/On learning, eloquence and wit'.[83] Such bitter implications
earned him Caroline's lasting aversion. Aspersions on her intelligence provoked angry rejoinders, whatever Robert
Molesworth's claim of her combining 'the *Highest Wisdom* with
the least *Pretences* to it'. Caroline found fewer faults with versi-
fying courtiers Lord Stanhope (from 1726 Lord Chesterfield)
and Lord Peterborough, though a suspicion that the former had
included her among objects of his ridicule, mimicking the thickness of her accent and certain gestures, earned a stinging rebuke:
'You may have more wit, my lord, than I, but I have a bitter
tongue, and always repay my debts with exorbitant interest.'[84]

Less vexed was Caroline's acquaintance with Ann Oldfield, a
leading actress and the mistress of an illegitimate nephew of the
Duke of Marlborough. 'Engaging Oldfield, who, with grace and

ease,/Could join the arts to ruin and to please' had taken the part of Lady Jane Grey in Rowe's tragedy of 1715.[85] *The Catalogue of All the English Plays in Her Royal Highnes's* [sic] *Library*, compiled in 1722 and extending to several hundred entries, indicates the scope of Caroline's interest in the theatre.[86] Her conversations with Antonio Conti, a Venetian philosopher-scientist who was a protégé of George Louis's half-sister Sophia Charlotte, ranged farther afield: they discussed Newton, Plato and Descartes. Conti's knowledge of theology, mathematics and medicine recalled those men of learning Caroline had encountered at Lützenburg and Herrenhausen, chief among them Leibniz.[87] In his breadth of knowledge he offered Caroline an intellectual stimulus absent from her marriage – like another distinguished Leicester House visitor, the French philosopher Voltaire. In memory of their meetings in 1726, two years later Voltaire dedicated to Caroline his eulogy of the French king Henri IV, *La Henriade*. 'It was the fate of Henry IV to be protected by an English Queen,' he addressed Caroline. 'He was assisted by the great Elizabeth, who was in her age the glory of her sex. By whom can this memory be so well protected as by her who resembles so much Elizabeth in her personal virtues?'[88] It was neither the first nor the last time Caroline's name was linked with Elizabeth I's.

Voltaire's commendations aside, Caroline was fortunate that her interests extended beyond the brittle praise of poets and the syllabub froth of court gossip. In 1728, in his dedication to Newton's posthumously published *The Chronology of Ancient Kingdoms Amended*, John Conduitt wrote, 'all Your hours of leisure are employed in cultivating in Your Self That Learning, which You so warmly patronize in Others'.[89] One visitor to Leicester House described Caroline's gatherings as 'a strange picture of the motley character and manners of a queen and a learned woman ... learned men and divines were intermixed with courtiers and ladies of the household; the conversation turned upon metaphysical subjects, blended with repartees, sallies of mirth and the tittle-tattle of a drawing room'.[90] Formal receptions frequently included similarly 'motley' elements of new learning. Sir John Evelyn described demonstrations at Leicester House drawing rooms of a new sort of military device and a machine that produced colour printing.[91]

From her arrival in Berlin Caroline had been exposed to extensive theological and philosophical debate. Left behind in Hanover, Leibniz remained among her correspondents after 1714. Influenced by Figuelotte and Sophia, as well as by memories of Eleonore's strong faith, she maintained an active interest in religious discourse; as queen she would involve herself in Church patronage, even recommending a bishopric for her clerk of the closet, Joseph Butler, on her deathbed.[92] 'The tittle-tattle of a drawing room' was never enough for Caroline. In her first week in waiting, Lady Cowper reported Caroline's request of works by Jacobean philosopher and politician Francis Bacon; weeks later the princess read John Locke's *Essay Concerning Human Understanding* of 1690.[93] Bacon had championed scientific enquiry, a rational and sceptical mindset. He claimed that 'the inquiry, knowledge and belief of truth is the sovereign good of human nature', a view compatible with Locke's argument that understanding is acquired through experience.

A fortnight after embarking on her study of Bacon, the dispute-loving Caroline was visited at St James's Palace for the first time by heterodox divine Dr Samuel Clarke.[94] Clarke was rector of the nearby church of St James's, Piccadilly. A controversial figure, his religious views engaged with, and in part endorsed, findings on natural philosophy published by Newton, whose *Opticks* he had translated into Latin. He presented Caroline with books he had written. Of his *Demonstration of the being and attributes of God* of 1705, he claimed his argument was 'as near to Mathematical as the Nature of such a Discourse would allow', a line of reasoning guaranteed to intrigue the book's recipient. Clarke shared Newton's qualified belief in the doctrine of the Trinity, and in 1712 had published *The scripture-doctrine of the Trinity: wherein every text in the New Testament relating to that doctrine is distinctly considered*. His own view celebrated God's transcendence: 'The Father alone is Self-Existent … Independent.'[95] For the unorthodoxy of these views, Church authorities had compelled from him a promise that he cease publishing on the subject of the Trinity. No such constraints curtailed his private conversation.

In November 1714 there was nothing accidental in Clarke's visit to Caroline at St James's Palace. In a letter to Caroline written earlier that year Leibniz had attributed a decline in religious belief in England to the writings of Isaac Newton. Newton, who considered his work as bolstering belief in God despite his private reservations about the Trinity, called on Clarke as go-between once he learned of the accusations against him. In refuting Leibniz on Newton's behalf, Clarke could count on support from several of Caroline's new household, including the Low Churchwomen Mary Cowper and Charlotte Clayton.

Caroline read Clarke's books virtually at once, evidence of the extent of her interest. Not only read but approved. To the Countess of Nottingham, who dismissed Clarke as a heretic, she described him on 19 November as 'one of my favourites', his writings 'the finest things in the world'.[96] Yet neither Clarke's treatises nor the intervention of her ladies played a persuasive part in the debate between Leibniz and Newton, in which both men embroiled a willing Caroline. The philosopher-scientists' disagreement was only superficially theological. Its roots lay in a contest of longer standing concerning the invention of differential calculus. Newton dated his discovery to 1666, though he did not publish his findings until 1693. Leibniz also claimed the breakthrough, having published his own account in 1684.

For two years Caroline arbitrated in an epistolary debate in which Clarke took Newton's part and letters passed nominally between Clarke and Leibniz, seen by Caroline. Her own first sympathies lay with Leibniz, a valued link to Figuelotte. It was he who in 1704 had been present at Caroline's discussions with Father Orban and who had written her formal rejection of Archduke Charles's suit. Shortly after her arrival in London, Caroline proved her attachment in an unsuccessful attempt to persuade George Louis to offer Leibniz a position as British royal historiographer. Now, however, with increasing exposure to Newton's views, her position altered. This was partly attributable to the charisma of the man himself. Aged and infirm, carried by chair the short distance from his house in nearby St Martin's Street to Leicester House, Newton was nevertheless a giant, compelling presence in Caroline's drawing room. She 'frequently desired to see him, and always expressed great satisfaction in his conversation', wrote a relation of Newton's by marriage; in February 1716, accompanied by Clarke, he made an afternoon visit to St James's Palace to explain his 'system of philosophy' to her.[97] Caroline's shifting allegiance recognised Newton's eminence in British life. Consistent with so much of her public behaviour, she understood the impossibility of championing Leibniz at the expense of his British counterpart.

Certainly Leibniz's disdain for his rival was unremitting. On 10 May 1715 he decried Newton's position to Caroline by drawing an analogy between the eucharist and gravity and concluding that, in relation to the former, Newtonian science undermined Lutheran doctrine. Caroline was unpersuaded by what sounds like sophistry. Such was the gulf between the men that Clarke refused to translate into English Leibniz's *Theodicy*, although Leibniz intended to dedicate the translation to Caroline, and Clarke could have anticipated disappointment on her part at his refusal. In the event Caroline did not react amiss – Lady Cowper's diary indicates that, far from a rift with Clarke, the princess's household consulted him as scientist as much as divine. On the night of 6 March 1716, Lady Cowper records

Clarke explaining the phenomenon of 'an extraordinary light' so irregular it inspired terror in the men carrying her sedan chair.[98] According to Clarke's first biographer 'seldom a week passed' in which, when in London, Caroline did not see him or read material he sent her.[99] She 'used frequently to pit Dr Samuel Clarke ... on subjects of literature' against the scholar and royal librarian Richard Bentley, despite Bentley's aversion to such exchanges, and in allowing Clarke to publish his correspondence with Leibniz, she endorsed a dedication to herself and the accompanying statement that the letters had been written at her instruction.[100] Her affection for the clergyman is indicated by later acts of charity. 'If you see Dr Clarke,' she wrote to Charlotte Clayton in 1718, 'pray tell him in my name that I design 100 guineas per annum for his chair hire, & it shall begin at Christmas & pass through your hands.'[101] That she discussed her encounters with all three men with her eldest daughter Anne is apparently indicated in a letter written in 1738 by the future Frederick the Great to Voltaire: 'I spoke at length with the Princess about Newton; from Newton we moved on to Leibniz and from Leibniz to the late Queen of England [Caroline].'[102]

She allowed Clarke a degree of frankness in their dealings. According to one anecdote, Caroline 'once pressed ... Dr Clarke strongly to acquaint her with her faults. After evading this delicate business as long as he could without giving offence, he at length said; "As I am compelled, your Majesty must pardon me for saying that when people come from the country to St James's chapel for a sight of the royal family, it is not a very edifying example to them, to see your Majesties talking during the whole time of divine service." – The Queen blushed; told the Doctor he was right, and a hearty laugh ensued.'[103] And Caroline was candid in her dealings with Leibniz. In the month of the 'extraordinary light', she described herself to him as 'nearly converted' by Newton's theories on the 'reflexions, refractions, inflexions and colours of light'; in May she explained, 'I am in on the experiments, and I am more and more charmed by colours.'[104] For Leibniz, such admissions were so much worm-wood and gall.

The triangular dialogue of Leibniz, Caroline and, in the role of Newton's amanuensis, Clarke, continued until Leibniz's death in November 1716. A year later, when the letters were published as *A Collection of Papers which Passed between the Late Learned Mr Leibnitz and Dr Clarke in the Years 1715 and 1716 Relating to the Principles of Natural Philosophy*, they bore Clarke's statement that their publication was validated by Caroline's patronage. Her participation in this altercation, which was complex and conten-tious, demonstrates her excitement at developments in contem-porary thought. It also indicates the longevity of the influence of Figuelotte and Sophia. Caroline understood the critical importance of appearing to embrace Anglican orthodoxy, particularly given Queen Anne's public record of wholehearted and rigorous piety. 'As she knew she had the reputation of being a little heterodox in her notions, she often ... denied herself the pleasure of seeing and conversing with men who lay under that imputation,' recorded Lord Hervey; consistently she questioned religious truisms.[105] In line with current thinking, her curiosity blurred distinctions between science, theology and philosophy. She enjoyed the company of those who shared her interests. In 1716 she granted audiences lasting up to three hours to Benjamin Hoadly, absorbed by the ideas on authority within the Church of this controversial Low Church bishop and his unwa-vering support for the Hanoverian succession.[106] In turn, her own enthusiasms inspired those around her. Lord Hervey mocked Lady Deloraine's absorption in philosophy in 1731, writing, 'she has taken of late into the sweet fancy to study philosophy and talks all day, and I believe dreams all night of a plenum and a vacuum. She declares of all philosophers Dr Clarke is her favourite and said t'other day if there was any justice in Heaven, to be sure he took place there of the twelve apostles.'[107] It was recognisably one of Caroline's fancies.

Caroline's earliest encounters with the Anglican priesthood date from the beginning of George Louis's reign. Diligent in demonstrating the level of religious devotion she knew was expected of royal women, she nevertheless engaged in exchanges of views with priests of wide-ranging outlook. As a result of her Lutheranism, her instinctive sympathies were for Low Churchmen and Latitudinarians – those within the Church of England who favoured a liberal approach to liturgy and doctrine, like Clarke, Hoadly, who edited Clarke's *Sermons*, and Robert Clayton. She also included among her circle High Churchmen: Archbishop Wake, who aspired to closer relations between Anglicans and French Catholics; leading Tory Churchman Dr Thomas Sherlock, Dean of Chichester, reported in 1727 as having 'oftner access [to Caroline] in private than anyone of the clergy'; and the cleric who became her chaplain, Joseph Butler.[108] For the remainder of her life, at Leicester House and beyond, Caroline continued to explore aspects of theological debate within informal conversation and in her reading. Lord Egmont concluded, 'she reads and converses on a multitude of things more than [her] sex generally does'.[109] It was a further instance of the continuing legacy of her first mentors.

As with his contempt for 'boets' and 'bainters' (poets and painters), George Augustus did not share his wife's interest in religion. The couple were closer in their political outlook and their attitude to George Louis.

From the beginning, each understood the conditions necessary for ending the royal quarrel. Without an apology on George Augustus's part, they recognised that reconciliation would remain impossible. The king was determined on control. Sunderland reported him as asking, with biblical rhetoric, 'Did you not always promise to bring me the Prince bound hand and foot?'[110] As early as February 1718 one journal pointed out that, without the prince's submission, "tis absurd to think of healing the breach'.[111] The same publication identified Caroline as the ideal mediator, on the grounds of her 'consummate conduct and goodness' as well as her particular interest in the issue. A petition from 'several loyal subjects, Englishmen and Protestants' proposed 'none so proper as your Royal Highness to assuage these jealousies and reduce both parties to a reunion'.[112] And far from being damaged by the ongoing schism, Caroline's popularity remained high: she was widely regarded as an innocent victim in the conflict between father and son, her task of intermediary a delicate one. In April 1719 a Catholic sedan-chair carrier, or chairman, called Moore insulted Caroline in her sedan chair. According to the report in the *Weekly Journal* of his trial and its aftermath, he found himself jeered by angry crowds, who followed him from Somerset House to the Haymarket. 'The respect her Royal Highness has among all parties was remarkable in the general cry there was all the way he pass'd of "Whip him", "Whip him"; and by the great number of people that caressed and applauded the executioner after his work was over.'[113] In the event, however, it was not Caroline, working alongside her husband, who brought about the uneasy truce unconvincingly enacted on St George's Day 1720, but a go-between of a different complexion.

Throughout the winter of 1719, 'every Day ... once, if not twice', Caroline had been visited at Leicester House by Robert Walpole.[114] Walpole was the political leviathan of the age, an abrasive, opportunistic Norfolk squire of redoubtable intellect, excluded from office since his quarrel with Stanhope and Sunderland but still a dominant presence in the House of Commons. In 1719 he helped defeat a government Peerage Bill meant to prevent George Augustus from creating new peers after his accession and thus perpetuate indefinitely the ministry's own political hegemony.[115] Displays of oratorical mastery, however, were not enough for Walpole, nor were George Augustus's best interests his primary motive. He intended a full return to power and saw the long-term political dangers of a continuing royal rift. Assiduously he cultivated Caroline's good opinion. Defeat of the Peerage Bill lay close to her heart. 'The Prince & I work like dogs, & perhaps to as little purpose,' she wrote as the Commons debate approached, a statement that indicates both the extent of the couple's political engagement and their partnership.[116]

Walpole's intervention ensured the outcome Caroline wanted. He avoided the mistakes of other politicians in paying court to Henrietta Howard or, like Stanhope, personally berating and offending Caroline. Instead, day after day through that long winter, in his own words he took the 'right sow by the ear'. His behaviour included its measure of flattery. Through Caroline he was confident he could bend George Augustus to his will. For all Caroline's initial misgivings – her dismissal of Walpole's 'gros corps ... jambes enflées, et ... villain ventre' (fat body, swollen legs and vile belly) – politician and princess had much in common. Both inclined to coarseness of expression and strength of purpose; both were earthy, bold, determined. To Walpole, Caroline represented a shortcut to the future king. He was not a man to consume his energies looking backwards. It was another trait they shared.

Walpole successfully persuaded Caroline of the overlap in their interests. By the spring of 1720, a resentful Lady Cowper lamented that 'Walpole has engrossed and monopolised the Princess to a Degree of making her deaf to Everything that did not come from him.'[117] Walpole's planned reconciliation between the royal combatants included a proposal for repaying George Louis's £600,000 civil list debt and George Augustus's debts of around £100,000. As immediately appealing to Caroline was the prospect of a politician at the heart of government sympathetic to prince and princess and the possible return of her daughters.

Walpole recommended the dispatch of a letter from George Augustus to his father. It was an idea the prince had previously rejected: a sufficient expression of contrition and a guarantee of future obedience. For Lady Cowper, who found herself summarily supplanted as Caroline's adviser, it smacked of self-serving: 'all this to procure Walpole and Townshend the Benefit of selling themselves and their Services at a very dear Rate to the King'.[118] Caroline's pragmatic response acknowledged that Walpole's gain was likely to prove her own. She understood the vulnerability of her own and her husband's position. She described herself as 'oblig'd to the lower house for all the Prince enjoys of his possessions', recognising Parliament's power over them financially.[119] To Charlotte Clayton she wrote of the proposal to cancel George Augustus's debts, 'You can easily judge … what I feel upon this head both as the wife and the mother of the persons who will reap the fruit.'[120] Correctly she surmised that a quarrel at the heart of the royal family would ultimately benefit only the regime's opponents, chief among them trouble-making Jacobites.[121] 'The Reputation of a Quarrel,' wrote Lady Mary Wortley Montagu, 'is allways so ridiculous on both sides.'[122]

In the second week of April, Walpole made Caroline his 'Offers of Reconciliation'. To Lord Cowper he explained, 'the Princess was to have her Children again, and … the Prince was to write to the King … and should return to live again at St James's; that Lord Sunderland had promised to come into all Measures of the Court, and in particular that of raising [£600,000] to pay the Debts of the Civil List, and that this was the only Opportunity for the Prince to make an advantageous Bargain for himself'.[123] Despite Walpole's daily and twice-daily visits to Leicester House, neither Caroline nor George Augustus accepted these assurances as certain. George Augustus insisted 'he would write Nothing that should tie his Hands', prepared to voice the bare minimum by way of apology.[124] Nor did the inter-vention of the Archbishop of Canterbury or the Bishop of Norwich, Charles Trimmell, sway either husband or wife. 'The Bishop of Norwich offered to swear upon his Knees to the Prince and Princess that all terms should be made good and satisfactory to them; that all the Princess's Friends were to be restored.'[125] George Augustus remained sceptical, and Caroline correctly, upsettingly and frustratingly estimated her powerlessness in the whole process. According to Lady Cowper, she 'cried and said, "I see how all these Things must go; I must be the Sufferer at last, and have no Power to help myself."'[126]

And so it was. So it had been for Eleonore, so too for Sophia Dorothea and, save in the patronage she exercised at Lützenburg, for Figuelotte. If Lady Cowper's account is trustworthy, both she and her husband implored Caroline's resolution in insisting on the return of her children; behind the scenes Lord Cowper investigated the possibility of dismissing Lady Portland and replacing her with a governess of Caroline's choice. Mary Cowper reported Caroline as telling Walpole, 'This will be no jesting Matter to me; you will hear of me and my Complaints every Day and Hour, and in every Place, if I have not my Children again.'[127] Walpole persuaded her that nothing could be gained from George Louis through demands; instead she must trust.[128] On 15 April the Archbishop of Canterbury, William Wake, visited Caroline. That she 'said Nothing of the Affair to him' proved to concerned courtiers the extent of Walpole's influence over her: 'the Archbishop ... was entirely kept out'.[129] Encouraged by Walpole and Caroline, George Augustus wrote to his father. Lady Cowper described him as 'governed by the Princess as she is by Walpole', a verdict that would persist.[130]

Lady Cowper considered the couple had been 'half frighted, half persuaded' by Walpole, but the letter Caroline wrote to Charlotte Clayton on the eve of George Augustus's formal reception by his father indicates both excitement and relief: 'I

give you, my dear Clayton, the good news that the reconciliation will be made today, & that I shall soon have the satisfaction
of naming you, my dear Clayton, without constraint mine.'[131]
Three years was a long time to have been separated from virtually everyone bar George Augustus of whom she was fondest.
The prospect of closure, even without gain, was a welcome one
for Caroline.

By contrast, George Louis's response does indeed suggest
'half' persuasion. He received his son coldly, Caroline not at all.
In return for his pains, on his departure for Leicester House
George Augustus was once again attended by beefeaters, 'drums
and guards and fine things', as Walpole commented dismiss-
ively.[132] With some vehemence – and to the relief of George
Louis – he refused to move back into St James's Palace. Caroline's
tears notwithstanding, and despite the warnings of the Cowpers
and Walpole's asseverations, mother and father were not
reunited with their children, and Lady Portland continued as
governess. Four days earlier, Princess Anne had been diagnosed
with smallpox, 'in such a dangerous way that I very much
feared for her life', wrote royal physician Sir Hans Sloane.[133]
George Louis allowed Caroline to visit her daughter, but no part
in her treatment. 'Every Day, from Eleven to Three, and from
Six to Eleven', Caroline sat at Anne's bedside until she recovered.[134] Her illness, with its attendant anxieties, exposed just
how unsatisfactory for Caroline Walpole's compromise was,
particularly when a letter from Archbishop Wake to Lord
Sunderland, requesting permission to visit Caroline, 'not knowing how soon he might be sent for to do his Duty to the afflicted
Mother in her comfortless State', found its way accidentally into
Caroline's hands. It was proof of the very powerlessness she had
bewailed. A reflection of her resignation, 'the Princess said
Nothing but "Voyez quel Homme!"'[135]

Her own reconciliation with her father-in-law took place on
24 April, in a small closet off her daughter's sickroom. Unlike

George Augustus's five-minute exchange with his father, their conversation lasted an hour and ten minutes. To Lord Cowper, Walpole reported that 'the King was very rough with the Princess – chid her very severely in a cruel Way. He told her she might say what she pleased to excuse herself; that she could have made the Prince better if she would, and that he expected from henceforward she would use all her Power to make him behave well.'[136] Caroline's response has not survived. With her customary concern for appearances, as well as her pride, she 'came out transported at the King's mighty kind Reception, and told the Doctors and Everybody how mighty kind he had been to her'.[137] 'The Germans used to say,' Lady Cowper noted, 'the Princess of Wales was *"grandissime Comédienne"* [a great actress].'[138] At her mother's knee, Caroline had learned that royalty was a performance art. On 24 April 1720, maintaining the dignity of her rank demanded dissimulation. She had no intention of advertising her humiliation, nor would she acknowledge publicly any justness in Lady Cowper's argument that prince and princess had been made a 'cat's foot' by Walpole to serve his own ends. Instead she wrote to George Augustus's sister Sophia Dorothea in Berlin, informing her of her pleasure in the happy outcome.[139]

She did not attend the premiere of Handel's *Radamisto* at the King's Theatre, Haymarket, three days later. King and prince made what was probably a carefully orchestrated first public appearance together, albeit in separate boxes.[140] Popular excitement ran high. Inside the theatre the crowd was sizeable, proof of public interest in the royal peace-making. 'Many [women], who had forc'd their way into the house with an impetuosity ill suited to their rank and sex, actually fainted through the excessive heat and closeness of it,' remembered Handel's biographer Mainwaring in 1760. 'Several gentlemen were turned back, who had offered forty shillings for a seat in the gallery, after having despaired of getting any in the pit or boxes.'[141]

If they hoped for visible signs of affection between monarch and heir, the eager audience was as thoroughly disappointed as the courtiers who had thronged George Louis's drawing room two nights earlier, when 'the King spoke not to the Prince nor none of his Friends'.[142] George Louis had recently answered a letter from his daughter. As Caroline had known she would, Sophia Dorothea had reported Caroline's expressions of joy at the royal reconciliation. The king's reply betrays the full ambivalence of his feelings for Caroline by this stage. 'I do not know if the joy the Princess has indicated to you is sincere,' he wrote. He explained his conviction that, had she been of a similar mind previously, there were several occasions when she could have taken care not to have made things worse.[143] It was a clear apportioning of blame, and accurate insofar as it recognised Caroline's support for George Augustus's opposition to his father. This view was shared by others among George Louis's intimates. Mary Wortley Montagu claimed that Caroline 'never resented anything but what appeared to her a want of respect for [George Augustus]', the light in which she presented to the prince his father's intransigence.[144] In truth, in their mutual mistrust and antipathy, there was little to choose between the feelings of all three senior royal figures. George Louis suspected that Walpole and Townshend had forced his son into a reconciliation; George Augustus and Caroline knew they had been manipulated. At least George Louis's dislike fell short of Sunderland's. The minister, George Louis's groom of the stole since 1719, toyed with plans for having George Augustus transported overseas.

'I fear I am with child,' Caroline wrote simply to Charlotte Clayton that July.[145] She was thirty-seven years old, and greeted the discovery with mixed emotions. Two years had passed since her miscarriage at Richmond Lodge; still vivid were her memories of George William's death and the protracted labour that had resulted in a stillborn son the year before that. Referring to the unhappy outcome of all three recent pregnancies, she added, 'the accidents which have lately happen'd give me noe encouragement'. As ever, gossip in Caroline's household uncovered the news almost before the princess herself was aware of it. 'I hear she is a-breeding,' wrote one of her ladies, 'but I believe nobody knows she is, so that at most it is but suspicion.'[146]

In this instance Caroline would prove more fortunate in her pregnancy. Her thoughts, however, dwelt on her two last births. A letter written by Lady Cowper shows Caroline questioning the right of members of her household to entry to her bedchamber for the delivery. 'I spoke to [Lord Cowper] last night, according to the Princess's command, about the people proper to be present at the labour; he bids me say that the Princess is at her perfect liberty in that point to do as she pleases, neither the law, nor any rule or custom, having fixed upon anybody to be present.'[147] On 15 April 1721, without attendant duchesses, Caroline gave birth to her fourth baby boy.

On this occasion no opposition met her decision to call him William Augustus, nor her choice of godparents: husband and wife Frederick William and Sophia Dorothea of Prussia and, as previously, George Louis's brother Ernest Augustus. Sophia Dorothea learned of the compliment from her father. In a letter written at the beginning of May, George Louis communicated news equivalent to that which, four years earlier, had provoked the royal rift. That he did so may point to a softening – however mild – in his attitude to George Augustus and Caroline.[148] For their part the royal couple's names for their son indicate anything but conciliation.

At best the news of her pregnancy was a distraction from Caroline's disappointment at the outcome of events in April, described by the Duchess of Marlborough as 'deficien[cies] in the late reconcilement'.[149] To British representatives at foreign courts and foreign ministers at St James's, George Louis had sent notice of the restoration of family harmony. Stubbornly, with a zeal born of love, Caroline had held out for the return of her daughters, only to be thwarted by Walpole and George Louis.

At least the nursery regime devised by Lady Portland was in accord with Caroline's own priorities. Surviving exercise books belonging to Princess Anne point to ambitious aspirations in the royal schoolroom: extracts from Plutarch, Herodotus and Thucydides translated into French, German transcriptions of theological texts, the history of the Roman Empire rendered in Italian.[150] To the music lessons for which Handel received £200 a year were added lessons in drawing and painting from artist Philippe Mercier, afterwards responsible for the best-known image of Caroline's children, *The Music Party* of 1733. Crucially, however, and devastatingly for Caroline, the girls remained in their grandfather's care, in apartments close to his own, or with access to those of Madame Schulenburg, at St James's, Kensington and Hampton Court. George Louis required control over the princesses; more than that, he expected their affection. To Anne, he wrote, 'all that I wish my dear granddaughter is that you further nurture your friendship towards me'.[151] From an early age, Anne, Amelia and Caroline struggled to balance conflicting loyalties. Forgiveness or no forgiveness, apologies accepted or otherwise, family 'unity' would remain elusive.

After William, there would be two more children for Caroline and George Augustus: Mary, born in February 1723, and Louisa in December 1724, when Caroline was forty-one. A letter written by maid of honour Bridget Carteret after Louisa's birth demonstrates the extent to which Caroline's principal function continued to be seen as securing the royal line: 'It is with great pleasure that I congratulate dear Mrs Clayton upon her Royal Highness's safe delivery. We think it such a blessing her being safe and well, that we do not repine at not having a Prince at some proper time.'[152]

By 1724 there would be no 'proper time' left for Caroline: William was the couple's last son. Caroline's recovery from Louisa's birth was unusually protracted. More than a month later, George Louis described her as almost ready to leave her bedroom, following an unspecified 'violent attack' either of pain or of illness.[153] Like even those closest to Caroline, he had no idea that his daughter-in-law had suffered an umbilical rupture following Louisa's delivery. It was a secret Caroline would guard determinedly, concealed from all but George Augustus, who agreed never to mention it, and one for which she paid dearly. Six months later, in July 1725, her eleventh and final pregnancy ended in another miscarriage. A letter of 27 July from the Countess of Pomfret to Charlotte Clayton highlights concern among her female attendants about her health in the aftermath.[154]

The absence of the three eldest princesses, added to Frederick's continuing residence in Hanover, divided Caroline's family permanently. Not only age but location separated the children of Leicester House from their older siblings. William, Mary and Louisa were a decade younger than Frederick, Anne, Amelia and Caroline. They had no experience of electoral life in Hanover, and lived full-time with their parents. Frederick's upbringing had been entrusted to courtiers and George Louis's Hanoverian ministers: his governor, Johann Friedrich Grote, was the brother of a treasury minister.[155] Attempts by George Augustus in 1718 to secure Frederick's transfer to London had predictably failed. For Anne, Amelia and Caroline, regular visits from their mother contrasted with constant exposure to a court environment in which their father was regarded with contempt, Caroline with suspicion. For each princess George Louis provided a gentleman usher, dresser, chambermaid, page of honour and page of the back-stairs. All were his own appointments.[156] While the regime's adherents would continue to celebrate George Augustus and Caroline's royal 'family', the togetherness of siblings and parents was illusory. Inevitably it was Caroline's happiness that suffered most.

With no alternative, she responded pragmatically. She visited her elder daughters as often as she was able, and took a close interest in the upbringing of her 'second' family of William, Mary and Louisa. According to Stephen Philpot's *Essay on the Advantages of a Polite Education joined with a Learned One*, published in 1747, Caroline was usually present at the children's lessons; on other occasions she requested a report from their tutor.[157] The younger princesses' routine was based on that of their sisters, and included an hour-long walk each morning between seven and eight, and regular prayers.[158] George Augustus shared aspects of his wife's involvement. At Leicester House, according to Sir Hans Sloane, husband and wife 'always took most extraordinary, exemplary, prudent and wise care of the health and education of their children'.[159] An associate of Isaac Newton's commended Caroline's 'singular Care for the education of the Royal Issue, and earnest desire to form their minds betimes, and lead them into the knowledge of Truth'.[160] Unsurprisingly, the woman whose own handwriting was disastrously self-taught employed a writing master for her youngest daughters, a Mr Palairet.[161]

The input of Caroline and George Augustus extended to discipline, as Sarah, Duchess of Marlborough discovered on a visit to Leicester House. The duchess's arrival coincided with Caroline physically punishing one of her daughters. When the visitor attempted to console the child, George Augustus responded by remarking, 'Ah, see there, you English are none of you well bred because you were not whipped when young.'[162] Momentarily overlooking the couple's habitual masquerade of Britishness, he identified Caroline's parental severity as distinctively German. But British childhood too contained its measure of brutality. The cause of death of a four-year-old girl in the family of diarist John Evelyn was identified as her corset: the child's ribs were broken by over-tight lacing. She died when her broken ribs pierced her lungs.[163] And George Augustus shared Caroline's strictness. In 1751, he remembered, 'I know I did not love my children when they were young: I hated to have them running into my room.'[164]

Set against this severity, Caroline and George Augustus commissioned a third portrait from Martin Maingaud soon after the reconciliation. Completed in 1721, Maingaud's image of Anne, Amelia and Caroline, aged eight to thirteen, depicts the princesses as the Three Graces in a composition that points to a degree of parental pride.[165] A letter from Caroline to the youngest of the princesses shows a mother's concern for good behaviour, coloured by the mildest asperity: 'Caroline, I pray you quit your indolence which prevents you from expressing your pretty thoughts and makes you act as if you had neither feeling nor reason.'[166] In addition, a verdict of the Duchess of Buckingham, illegitimate daughter of James II, concerning 'the little care and regularity that is taken in the prince's family' with regard to the tidiness and arrangements of Leicester House, points to parents more interested in family life than the appearances of rooms or a visitor's good opinion.[167]

With some success, Caroline took pains to encourage the six siblings in Britain to think of themselves as a single family. A letter translated by Mary from Latin into English as part of a series of exercises set by the royal tutor Jenkin Thomas Philipps reports, 'The Duke, your Brother [William], has this morning caught a great Fish two foot long, which he gave to his sister Amelia for her Dinner.'[168] In another letter in the same series, Mary translated 'His serene Highness William, your most dear Brother, has turned the Roman History of Sextus Rufus into English, which he designs to dedicate to your Highness, that it may be a Monument of his Brotherly love towards you.'[169] Family togetherness is a constant theme of the 'letters' William and Mary exchanged under Philipps's tuition – the emphasis surely arose at Caroline's request. 'I pray God that it may not rain tomorrow, but be a fine day,' Mary translated, 'that your Highness may go out in the Coach with the Queen and your Sisters, to catch a great Buck, who is swift of feet, but the Dogs are swifter.'[170] A similar emphasis on the siblings' good fortune, although conventional enough, may also have arisen at their parents' request. 'You live a very happy life, you see horse races,' Mary translated, in a letter that contrasted the blessings of her own life with the 'privations' of her tutor's. 'I am forced to stay at home for I have no Coach nor horse, & I cannot walk, because it rains very fast.'[171]

The education of the younger royal children also included specific sops to their mother's predilections. On 5 December 1727, Philipps set six-year-old William the following translation: 'When first I knew you, you seemed to have a great Quickness of Wit & you was not born for Trifles, as other Boys are, but for learning. Yesterday you asked me a very curious Question but hard to be explained, for Instance you asked me if everything could return to Nothing?'[172]

This was precisely the sort of philosophical speculation Caroline had encountered at Lützenburg and Herrenhausen, a question of the sort debated by the mixed company at Leicester House. It was a question she might have asked herself, this Princess of Wales at odds with her king, denied the company of her older children, still – when the formalities of reconciliation were done – exiled to Leicester Square.

Caroline's affection for her children was shortly tested by an undertaking that engrossed and appalled her contemporaries. In April 1722, at their mother's instigation, ten-year-old Amelia and eight-year-old Caroline were inoculated against smallpox. Two years earlier, Caroline had kept an anxious bedside vigil as Anne battled the disease that she herself had suffered early in her marriage. So serious was Anne's condition that the

Archbishop of Canterbury anticipated her death; her recovery left her badly scarred. The following year, in February, began a two-month smallpox epidemic in London. One doctor reported that it seemed 'to go forth like a destroying Angel'; it was 'epidemical and very mortal'.[173]

Its terrible toll among acquaintances and her extended family galvanised into action Lady Mary Wortley Montagu, recently returned from Turkey, where she had encountered the process of inoculation that she described as 'engrafting'. Into the skin of a healthy patient, matter from the pustules of a smallpox victim was inserted; the recipient, in subsequently succumbing to a mild dose of the disease, acquired lasting immunity from its severer forms. Lady Mary's four-year-old son Edward had been inoculated in 1718. In 1721 her infant daughter Mary was also successfully treated.

Little Mary's inoculation was performed by Charles Maitland and witnessed by a handful of members of the College of Physicians, as well as 'Several Ladies, and other Persons of Distinction'.[174] Inevitably the procedure attracted public attention. Physicians petitioned George Louis for permission to experiment with the miraculous process on condemned inmates of Newgate Gaol; royal physician Sir Hans Sloane directed the king's attention to the breakthrough. For her part, Lady Mary attributed the medical men's interest to Caroline. She claimed the princess 'was her firm support and stood by her without quailing'.[175]

At George Louis's agreement, Sloane oversaw the inoculation by Maitland of six prisoner volunteers at the end of August. Five survived. (The sixth was already ill at the time of the inoculation.) Their reward was a royal pardon. Maitland wrote an *Account of Inoculating the Small Pox*, but deferred publishing. Inspired by Sir Hans and Lady Mary, Caroline had conceived a plan to inoculate 'all the Orphan Children belonging to the Parish of St James's, Westminster'.[176] Opposition was widespread – from an incredulous public, sceptical physicians, and clergymen who considered the disease 'a divinely instituted check against sin'.[177] In the event only six charity children were inoculated, and Maitland published his account in February 1722. Caroline consulted Hans Sloane following the successful treatment of his own grandchildren. Cautiously, the doctor refused to commit himself. 'The Princess then asked me if I would dissuade her from it,' he recorded, 'to which I made answer that I would not, in a matter so likely to be of such importance.'[178] Added to the Wortley Montagus, Newgate prisoners and Westminster orphans, it was endorsement enough for Caroline. With George Louis's permission, Princesses Amelia and Caroline were inoculated on 17 April. Caroline's response to what happened next has not survived, but any anxiety she may have felt was soon dispelled by her daughters' full recovery. Lady Mary described herself as 'so much pull'd about and solicited to visit people' due to fashionable interest in the experiments, 'that I am forc'd to [run] into the Country to hide my selfe'.[179]

From Versailles, where medical practice was bungling even by contemporary standards, Liselotte expressed concern. 'I must confess that I worried a great deal about the Princess of Wales and the two Princesses. I am not so brave, and if my children were quite well I couldn't possibly steal myself to make them ill, even though it was for their own good.'[180] Hers was the prevailing view of the times, that of Caroline and George Louis, who took an active interest in scientific research promoted by the Royal Society, considerably in advance.[181] 'God grant ... that the dear little Princesses are protected for the rest of their lives from this horrible disease,' wrote Liselotte. 'My doctor doesn't think this remedy is safe, he says he doesn't understand it.'[182]

In 1723 Maitland travelled to Hanover to inoculate Frederick, whose indifferent health, including glandular pains and 'fevers' treated by bleeding and a diet of asses' milk, was a further cause of Caroline's concern. For his efforts Maitland received handsome payment of £1,000. The younger royal children were inoculated in 1726. 'A great Part of the Kingdom follow'd her Example, and since that Time ten thousand Children, at least, of Persons of Condition owe in this Manner their Lives to her Majesty,' Voltaire wrote in 1733.[183] Acknowledging the vital importance of royal sponsorship in overcoming objections, in 1724 James Jurin of the Royal Society dedicated to Caroline his *Account of the Success of Inoculating the Smallpox*.[184]

The formalities of reconciliation accomplished, George Louis had returned to Hanover in the summer of 1720. In his absence, he allowed the three elder princesses to rejoin their parents. It was a lone concession, made with Caroline in mind. For all his reservations, George Louis did attempt to rebuild his relationship with his daughter-in-law, greeting her at a drawing room in May with the unequivocal '*Je suis ravi de vous voir ici*' ('I am delighted to see you here') and, on another occasion, singling her out for conversation when he 'said not a Word to the Prince, nor any Soul belonging to him'.[185] Lady Cowper recorded a conversation between Caroline and Archbishop Wake's wife at the beginning of July: '"Our Children we shall have, and the Regency they promise us, but the Last I don't believe; and I tell you naturally, my dear Mrs Wake, I will venture my Nose we shan't have it." I was pulling on her Gloves, and said, "Yes, Madam; if your Highness had thirty Noses you might venture them all without the least Danger to them."'[186]

For three years during the courts' split, George Augustus and Caroline had provided a focus for opposition politicians. With Walpole, along with Townshend, restored to the ministry, the couple's closest political associate returned to George Louis's service. The king's visit to Hanover was the first of four he would make before his death; on each occasion he denied his son powers of regency or guardianship. Mistrustful of Walpole on account of his part in the reconciliation, George Augustus turned instead for political advice to his treasurer Sir Spencer Compton, speaker of the House of Commons. But Compton was an ally of Walpole's: he cautioned compromise. Caroline's mistrust of Townshend predated the family split.

Compton's advice was intended for both prince and princess, and was probably unnecessary. For Caroline, as well as George Augustus, stark lessons emerged from their three-year estrangement from the king. Both understood the futility of continuing opposition. After April 1720, a number of disaffected politicians renounced Leicester House for St James's Palace, their defection proof of the real centre of patronage and influence. To George Augustus's lasting chagrin, Walpole and Townshend headed the stampede. Lacking an alternative, and with his father embarked on his seventh decade, the heir to the throne settled down to play a waiting game in the unlikely company of Walpole's Tory opponents, Lords Bolingbroke and Bath. At Richmond Lodge each summer George Augustus put behind him the politics of the capital for up to six months at a stretch, returning in late autumn for official celebrations of his birthday on 30 October. The retirement of the couple's life in Richmond, in an environment of family and friends without courtly ceremonial, reflected their efforts at increasing detachment. Few official images of either George Augustus or Caroline survive from this period. With retirement came a decline in their public profile. There was some comfort for Caroline in the return to the 'publick' days at Leicester House of those courtiers George Louis had forbidden to visit either prince or princess. In May 1720 Sir John Evelyn noted 'a great deal more company than used to be here before ye reconcilement of ye King and Prince'.[187]

Instead husband and wife made political capital by alternative means. Unlike George Louis, his mistress Madame Schulenburg, created Duchess of Kendal in 1719, and half-sister Sophia Charlotte, Countess of Darlington from 1722, George Augustus and Caroline emerged largely unscathed that year from the collapse of the South Sea Company. Established in 1711 to secure government borrowing at a fixed rate, the company had become an El Dorado scheme offering investors the profits on a trade monopoly with South America as a means of servicing the national debt. Serendipitously, in 1718 the disgraced George Augustus had lost his position as governor of the company, to be replaced by his father. George Louis's holdings of South Sea Company stock represented at least £20,000. Bribes of shares worth £15,000 apiece netted support from Melusine and Sophia Charlotte, while two of Melusine's daughters were each given shares worth £5,000. But the fabled trade with South America was virtually non-existent. Stoked partly by the company's association with George Louis, Melusine and members of the ministry, the manic speculation of the summer of 1720 was founded, as one commentator marvelled, 'upon the machine of paper credit supported only by imagination'.[188] Share prices rocketed almost tenfold. The fortunate profited mightily. And the inevitable bursting of the South Sea Bubble in September reduced others, including John Gay, to beggary.

The involvement of monarch, mistress and ministers in so catastrophic a financial fraud shattered confidence in government probity. Allegations of corruption centred on leading players. Lady Cowper borrowed money secretly to acquire stock that swiftly plummeted. It is in this context that we ought to measure her claim that Walpole had won Caroline and George Augustus's support for reconciliation with bribes of share handouts: 'pleas[ing] the Princess ... by making her a Stockjobber in the South Sea'.[189] If this statement is true, the gift represented a change of heart on the part of politician and princess, according to a letter written by Caroline late in 1719: 'I can assure you upon my honour that Walpole is sincere & has not entered into that ugly scheme,' she insisted. 'He is furious in the affair & violent against all those who have bought.'[190] In February 1720,

Walpole had attacked government plans to make use of the South Sea Company to lessen the national debt; in December he won parliamentary support for proposals to deal with consequences of its collapse. Although he was not the sole architect of the government's response, it was Walpole who, politically, would benefit most from recovery efforts that included shielding George Louis from censure. The aftermath of the crisis sealed his pre-eminence. Ditto the death from a cerebral haemorrhage of Stanhope in 1721, and that of Sunderland from pleurisy the following April. Neither man had proved himself a friend to George Augustus and Caroline. For the moment their successor was George Louis's first minister, and distasteful to George Augustus for this reason; he called him 'rogue and rascal without much reserve, to several people, upon several occasions'.[191] Caroline's response was surely mixed. For Lady Cowper, at whose expense Walpole had achieved his ascendancy over Caroline, the relationship between mistress and bedchamber lady would not recover.

Meanwhile, in 1722 Walpole embarked on the rebuilding of his family home at Houghton in Norfolk to designs by Colen Campbell. The work was funded by profits of his South Sea Company stock, of which Caroline apparently knew nothing. Like Caroline at Richmond Lodge, he employed as landscapist Charles Bridgeman. And Caroline maintained a polite interest in the after-effects of speculating. In July 1729, hapless equerry Peter Wentworth recorded her 'ask[ing] me if I was not in the Bubbles. With a sigh I answered: "Yes, that and [other mishaps] had made me worse than nothing." Some time after, when I did not think she saw me, I was biting my nails. She called to me and said: "Oh, fie! Mr Wentworth, you bite your nails very prettily."'[192] Later still, a Colonel Graham is recorded as delivering to Caroline an account of George Louis's South Sea stock, compiled by Sir Charles Vernon.[193]

* * *

Lady Mary Wortley Montagu described the pastoral revelry of Richmond Lodge: racing boats on the Thames, outdoor entertainments in the new gardens Caroline had commissioned from Bridgeman following her garden-makers 'summit' in 1719, and, as summer gave way to autumn, 'His Royal Highness hunts in Richmond Park, and I make one of the Beau monde in his Train.'[194] 'On Monday night last,' reported the *Daily Post* on 23 August 1721, 'Mr Penkethman [sic] had the honour to divert their Royal Highnesses, the Prince and Princess of Wales, at his theatre at Richmond, with entertainments of acting and tumbling, performed to admiration; likewise with his picture of the Royal Family down from the King of Bohemia to the young princesses, in which is seen the Nine Muses playing on their several instruments in honour of that august family.'[195] Undoubtedly Caroline was better pleased with this flattering dynastic *tableau vivant* than with any amount of acting and tumbling, however admirably performed.

'The Prince, and everybody but myself, went last Friday to Bartholomew Fair; it was a fine day, so he went by water,' wrote one of Princess Amelia's maids of honour on 31 August 1725. 'After the Fair, they supped at the King's Arms, and came home about five o'clock in the morning.'[196] For her part Caroline was described as 'walk[ing] about there all day' when at Richmond Lodge.[197] Indoors she indulged the taste for ceramics, including Chinese and Japanese porcelain, that she shared with Mary II. On 12 June 1724 Lady Hertford reported the East India Company making 'the Princess a present of Japan which they say cannot be equalled by any in the world. It is indeed the finest that, I believe, ever came to England.'[198]

In a contemporary engraving of the house by Joseph Goupy, it appears a Watteau-esque backdrop to holiday diversions. Gate piers frame long views over lawns that are swept and raked by gardeners. Pockets of courtiers disport themselves languidly. High walls and banks of trees shelter decorous enclosures and,

behind the matchbox house, with its steep roof and heavy triangular pediment, sunlight washes suggestively. 'Nothing can be
pleasanter than this place. Every field looks like a garden,' Lady
Hertford wrote to her mother.[199]

Intimations of princely bliss were only partly misleading.
Future sovereigns, George Augustus and Caroline retained
influence and consequence. 'I write to you at this time piping
hot from the Birth night, my Brain warm'd with all the
Agreeable Ideas that fine Cloths, fine Gentlemen, brisk Tunes
and lively dances can raise there,' wrote Lady Mary to her sister
after the ball to mark George Augustus's fortieth birthday in
1723.[200] Celebration of Caroline's forty-first birthday the following spring was equally enthusiastic. In honour of her position as
Princess of Wales, representatives of the Society of Antient
Britons presented leeks at Leicester House. The *Weekly Journal*
described the formal birthday reception as 'the most splendid
and numerous that has been known, the concourse being so
great that many of the nobility could not obtain admittance and
were obliged to return without seeing the Prince and Princess'.[201]
A roster of bishops, judges and ambassadors from as far afield as
Morocco offered congratulations. 'At one o'clock the guns in
the park proclaimed the number of her Royal Highness's years,
and at two their Royal Highnesses went to St James's to pay
their duty to his Majesty, and returned to Leicester House to
dinner, and at nine at night went again to St James's, where
there was a magnificent ball in honour of her Royal Highness's
birthday.'[202] A year later, at his house near Greenwich the Duke
of Leeds marked Caroline's birthday with night-time illuminations. Bonfires, fireworks and flaming obelisks provided a setting
for toasts drunk to royal family and government.

It was not only royal birthdays that provided diversion. The
endowment of a Royal Academy of Music in 1719, the list of
subscribers headed by George Louis and George Augustus, made
London for a decade the operatic centre of the world. To a

succession of new operas by Handel were added works by the newly resident Giovanni Bononcini and Attilio Ariosti; Caroline had encountered both composers previously at Figuelotte's court in Berlin. In February 1724, Handel's librettist Nicola Francesco Haym dedicated to Caroline the word-book to the composer's latest opera, *Giulio Cesare in Egitto*, with its contrasting feminine paradigms: Pompey's faithful widow Cornelia and the ambitious seductress Cleopatra. Haym praised Caroline's *'perfetta e giudiziosa conoscenza della Musica'* ('perfect and judicious knowledge of music'), which he attributed to Pistocchi's early teaching.[203] Notwithstanding the period's perfidious flattery, it is clear that Caroline had maintained her early interest in music. The royal dedication in this instance was happier than Handel's dedication to George Augustus, three years previously, of *Floridante*. This middling work dramatises the challenges of a Thracian prince whose jealous father attempts to strip him of his rights to the throne.[204]

Caroline witnessed an undignified spat between supporters of rival sopranos Faustina Bordoni and Francesca Cuzzoni at a performance of Bononcini's *Astianatte* on 6 June 1727. The *British Journal* reported that 'on Tuesday-night last, a great Disturbance happened at the Opera, occasioned by the Partisans of the Two Celebrated Rival Ladies, Cuzzoni and Faustina. The Contention at first was only carried on by Hissing on one Side, and Clapping on the other; but proceeded at length to Catcalls, and other great Indecencies: And notwithstanding the Princess Caroline was present, no Regards were of Force to restrain the Rudenesses of the Opponents.'[205]

On 16 April 1726, Jonathan Swift noted a new resident at Leicester House. In the words of less enlightened commentators 'more of the Ouran Outang species than of the human', the feral child offered as a gift by George Louis to Caroline walked on all fours, laughed, snorted and whinnied and, publicly and unconcernedly, soiled himself. He was called Peter. Villagers had discovered him in woodland close to Hanover, a child of twelve or thirteen who lived among the trees, fending for himself and foraging. He spoke no German and gave no evidence of previous exposure to humans. On George Louis's orders he had been brought to St James's Palace. There, at a crowded drawing room on 7 April, he encountered Caroline, resplendent in black velvet and heavily jewelled. Entranced, he listened to her 'gold watch that struck the hours ... held to strike at his ear'.[206] She was equally entranced, this princess absorbed by science, philosophy and religion. Peter had no soul, observers insisted; he was a savage, accustomed to eating acorns and moss. He had leapt, Daniel Defoe commented, 'from the woods to the court; from the forest among beasts ... to the society of all the wits and beaus of the age'.[207] There is no indication that George Louis's courtiers identified Defoe's irony.

At Leicester House, Caroline invited Dr Arbuthnot – physician, satirist, mathematician, philosopher and a 'character of uncommon virtue and probity' – to educate Peter.[208] The boy resisted. Arbuthnot diagnosed him as mentally handicapped; courtiers tired of antics that ceased to charm. So Peter was lodged in Hertfordshire with a family paid for their surrogacy. For sixty years he worked as an agricultural labourer, spared the scarlet stockings royal courtiers had wrestled him into. At Caroline's intervention and thanks to the efforts of Dr Arbuthnot he avoided a return to the house of correction in Celle where he had first been brought to George Louis's attention. His reign as court jester was brief.

Briefly Peter's misrule had recalled the high spirits of the first years of Caroline and George Augustus's court. His departure was one of several from Leicester House. By the mid-1720s the households of the middle-aged prince and princess lacked their former effervescence. Maids of honour Mary Bellenden and Mary Lepell had left Caroline's service on marriage, the latter to fellow courtier Lord Hervey. Sophy Howe had lost her post in

1720 after an ill-judged elopement, disguised as a boy, and an illegitimate pregnancy. Appointed in Miss Howe's place in February 1721, Mary Howard was beautiful but foolish – Hervey refers to her 'wretched head' – and failed to inspire the admiration her predecessors had excited. Caroline's later appointments, although she continued to value intelligence, suggest her primary requirement from her ladies was seamless integration into the increasingly domestic court circle. Of a new lady of the bedchamber, Henrietta, Countess of Pomfret, she wrote in October 1725, 'I am very well satisfied with Lady Pomfret. She seems as if she lov'd me, & has wit & the experience of the world, & the advice of a good friend will make her a real woman of quality. She behaves wonderfully well in the family, & everybody is satisfied with her.'[209]

Among remaining royal attendants there were murmurs of dissent. As early as November 1714, 'ill from standing so long upon my feet', Lady Cowper had protested against the physical strain of court appointments.[210] After 1720 her resentment of Walpole, attributable to his part in the royal reconciliation, corroded her admiration for Caroline. Relations between the women were further strained by Caroline's choice of the Countess of Dorset as the Duchess of St Albans's replacement as groom of the stole.[211] Mary Cowper had coveted the position herself; she considered herself slighted. Certainly Caroline's handling of the new appointment lacked transparency. Following Lord Cowper's resignation in 1718 against George Louis's will, Lady Dorset was a less contentious choice than Cowper's wife for the senior position in Caroline's household, and perhaps, given pressure on her from George Louis to re-instate the duchess, Caroline's only alternative. Lady Cowper remained at court until her death in 1724; a rancorous note colours her later diary entries. 'Nothing was more evident than the Transports of Joy in which the Princess was with this new Accession of Flatterers, and Mr Walpole had so possessed her

Mind, there was no room for the least Truth,' she wrote on 20 May 1720.[212] Inevitably such all-consuming sourness tarnished the atmosphere of the royal bedchamber.

Lady Cowper was not alone in her disenchantment. After George Augustus's birthday in 1726, the Honourable Mrs St John wrote a poem to Caroline's lady of the bedchamber, the Countess of Hertford: 'My rambling thoughts are strayed from home, –/Why need they farther than St James's roam?/When now perhaps, you're stifled in the crowd,/On hearing P[rince]'s jokes so coarse and loud;/Or else retired behind the Chair of State,/Where you're compelled to praise what most you hate,/Or listen to some idle page's prate/Till midnight strikes.'[213] In the same year the Duchess of Shrewsbury died. Caroline's account of her death, which she attributed to the incompetence of royal physician Sir John Shadwell, indicates dry humour: 'He gave her something very strong to ease her stomach, & when that was too strong, he gave her laudanum, which laid her asleep for this world.'[214] The death of the spirited, louche-tongued duchess further diminished the stock of cheer at Caroline's court.

Henrietta Howard, described as 'much in the vapours', felt it sooner than most. As early as 1722 Mary Bellenden, now Mrs Campbell, had written to her, 'I was told before I Left London, that somebody that shall be nameless, was grown sour & crosse & not so good to you as usual.'[215] The relationship of Caroline's bedchamber woman and George Augustus was built on flimsy foundations: Henrietta's desire to escape her dislikeable husband and the prince's need, via the face-saving measure of a mistress, to counter suggestions of an emasculating attachment to Caroline. In sensibility, outlook and motive mistress and prince were misfits. Even George Augustus's sexual attraction to Henrietta failed to rival the earthy passion Caroline still inspired in him. Recent events had not altered him. He remained of a testy, exacting nature, preoccupied with what Figuelotte had once dismissed as 'littleness', 'calm when great points go as he would not have them ... but when he is in his worst humours and the devil to everybody ... it is always because one of his pages has powdered his periwig ill or a housemaid has set a chair where it does not use to stand'.[216] His 'love' was a routine matter. He 'was the most regular man in his hours: his time of going down to [Henrietta Howard's] apartment was seven in the evening: he would frequently walk up and down the gallery, looking at his watch, for a quarter of an hour before seven, but would not go till the clock struck'.[217]

In letters to her friends, Henrietta expressed her longing to escape her life at court and a position she had embraced through expediency; she described herself as 'Jealous for Liberty and property'.[218] Ongoing, occasionally violent attempts by Charles Howard to reclaim his wife, his motives pecuniary, malevolent, trouble-making, added to her strain. He involved Caroline in his threats – in April 1726 he warned her that George Louis commanded that Henrietta 'immediately retire from her employment under Your Royal Highness'.[219] For reasons of her own, namely her determination that George Augustus retain this mistress she controlled, Caroline stood her ground. Later Henrietta described the 'malicious pleasure' with which Caroline showed her a letter from Archbishop Wake, urging her to relinquish Henrietta to her lawful husband, an instance of Caroline making clear to her rival her power over her.[220]

First impressions long abated, the women cherished little warmth for one another. Caroline was not above reminding Henrietta 'that it was in my power, if I had pleased, any hour of the day, to let her drop through my fingers – thus –'.[221] Unsurprisingly, Henrietta felt the indignity of her role as bedchamber woman. Her less congenial tasks included holding a bowl of water on bended knee while Caroline washed her hands or cleaned her teeth. Henrietta minded enough to investigate past precedents to provide her with grounds for refusal. In her frustration she chose, Caroline wrote, to 'quarrel with me about holding a basin of ceremony at my dressing, and to tell me, with her fierce little eyes and cheeks as red as your coat, that positively she would not do it; to which I made her no answer in anger, but calmly, as I would to a naughty child: "Yes, my dear Howard, I am sure you will; indeed you will."'[222] Precedents went against Henrietta, and Caroline's calm patronising did little to win her rival's affection.

For his part, as time passed, George Augustus derived scarcely more satisfaction than she from his relationship with the woman Caroline labelled his 'trull'.[223] To his credit, in an unusual act of generosity, in 1724 he gave Henrietta the enormous sum of £11,500. She would use it to build Marble Hill House, a Palladian villa close to Pope's house in Twickenham, on the opposite bank of the Thames from Richmond Lodge, a two-hour barge journey from central London. Like Caroline, Henrietta employed Charles Bridgeman as landscapist. In October 1728 she heard from Lord Chesterfield of an 'extreme fine Chinese bed, window curtains, chairs, etc, to be sold for between 70l and 80l: if you should have a mind to it for Marble Hill'.[224] Lady Hervey refers to Henrietta stealing nights away from court at Marble Hill in 1729.[225]

Condemned to enforced intimacy with husband and mistress, the smooth running of her household periodically shattered by Charles Howard's malign bluster, Caroline can hardly have avoided the dampening effect of their shared disaffection. Yet she relied on Henrietta for respite from George Augustus – the hours he spent in his mistress's rooms each evening, their walking together in the morning – and she did not intend to relinquish her. In this difficult atmosphere her children provided distractions, so too the interior life she stimulated with 'the reading of choice authors ... always one of her greatest pleasures'.[226] 'When I had the honour to see [the Princess of Wales] She was Reading Gulliver, & was just come to the passage of the Hobbling prince, which she Laughed at,' Dr Arbuthnot wrote to the author of *Gulliver's Travels*, Jonathan Swift, on 5 November 1726.[227]

In the same letter, Arbuthnot indicated the success of Swift's recent present to Caroline of Irish plaid: 'The princess immediately seizd on your plade for her own use, & has ordered the young Princesses to be clad in the same.'[228] Still separated from her elder daughters, Caroline could enjoy nevertheless the affinity of dressing alike. Testament to her considerable physical girth by this stage, she ordered twenty-five yards of Swift's Irish silk for her own dress, and twenty to provide dresses for her three elder daughters.[229] Behind her back, she learned, the corpulent Walpole described her as 'a fat old bitch'.[230]

Caroline's marking time ended on 11 June 1727. In the early hours of the morning, in the town of Osnabrück where he had been born, George Louis died. He had broken his journey en route to Hanover, following a stroke brought on by indigestion from the surfeit of strawberries or oranges or melons he had eaten two nights earlier at a hefty supper in the Dutch town of Delden. For the sixty-seven-year-old monarch it was a straightforward, unheroic death.

Too straightforward in the event to escape the lurid impulses of romancers. Legend attributes George Louis's death to fear. A letter, it was rumoured, was handed to him in his travelling coach. Its author was his estranged wife Sophia Dorothea, whose death on 13 November 1726 George Louis had marked by going to the theatre on two consecutive nights. He had forbidden court mourning for her in London or Hanover, and prevented George Augustus from acknowledging in any manner his unhappy mother's demise. So slow were his orders concerning her burial that the River Ahler surrounding the dismal manor house of Ahlden had overflowed its banks in winter storms by the time his instructions arrived. Logged with water, the manor garden could provide no burial place for the lead coffin, which threatened to float away. For want of an alternative it was removed to a church in the town of Celle, where the simplest of plaques commemorates this unfortunate princess.

Perhaps those responsible for the story of a letter from beyond the grave imagined that Sophia Dorothea had anticipated just such an ignominious end. In the bitterness of her final days she reminded the man who had destroyed her happiness of a prophecy that within a year of her death, he too would die.

Flaming torches lit the procession that bore George Louis's body into Hanover. Trumpeters 'rest[ed] their trumpets bottom upward', silent in respect. Even at one o'clock in the morning 'a great concourse of people from all parts [of the electorate]' had gathered to witness, 'with tears in their eyes, this last honour paid to their late sovereign, once the joy and delight of his subjects'.[231] He was buried in the church within the Leineschloss, close to his mother Sophia. Sixteen colonels of the Life Guards carried his coffin.

Days later, the news reached London. Roused by Robert Walpole from his afternoon nap at Richmond Lodge, his breeches in his hands, his mood discouraging, George Augustus succeeded his father as George II in a vignette that lacks dignity. His accession was proclaimed at Leicester House, Charing Cross, Temple Bar, Cheapside and the Royal Exchange. And Caroline became queen. Among the new king's first actions, according to Horace Walpole, was to hang at Leicester House two portraits of his mother, against walls draped in purple and black. He placed the larger portrait in Caroline's dressing room – out of sight of the crowds of politicians and place-seekers who Lord Hervey described as rapidly thronging George Augustus's house until it resembled the floor of the Royal Exchange in the middle of a busy trading day.[232] 'All the nobility of both sexes now in town attended at Leicester House and had the honour to kiss their Majesties' hands,' wrote Lord Polwarth.[233] It was in stark contrast to the doldrums of the royal split.

III

Queen

'Constancy and Greatness'

Caroline's sentiments on George Louis's death were those of Swift's 'Lilliputian Verse', *A Poem to his Majesty King George II on the present State of Affairs in England, with Remarks on the Alterations to be expected at Court, after the Rise of the Parliament*: 'Smile, smile,/ Blest Isle./Grief past/At last./Halcyon/Comes on./New KING,/ Bells ring,/New QUEEN,/Blest scene!' Like Henry Newman witnessing 'a vast Concourse of Boats' accompany George Augustus and Caroline down the Thames weeks later, she allowed herself a moment of optimism: 'nothing will be wanting in so gracious a Prince to endear himself to his People'.[1]

She could hardly feel differently. Since 1705, George Louis's acrid relationship with George Augustus had coloured every aspect of her life. In 1714 she had been forced to leave behind in Hanover her seven-year-old only son. Three years later she had lost her home, her remaining children and a handful of those trappings of rank by which she set such store. Reconciliation had failed to restore her daughters to her, and George William's brief life had ebbed its fleeting course beyond his mother's reach. More than a match for her father-in-law's stolid intellect, Caroline had been condemned to obedience nevertheless, compelled by her own pride to endure with unruffled public calm whatever indignities he reserved for her. She was not consumed by poignancy at his death. During the days of black bombazine at Leicester House, her thoughts dwelt instead on possibilities.

Caroline's coronation portrait by Enoch Seeman registers few changes in the eleven years since Kneller's official likeness of 1716. Sarah, Duchess of Marlborough had derided what she regarded as the inane happiness of Caroline's expression during the service at Westminster Abbey that represented for her, after almost a quarter of a century of waiting, a personal apotheosis; nastily she referred to Caroline's hair 'clotted all over with powder'.[2] Seeman's portrait, and its many copies by Charles Jervas, offers an alternative narrative. His Caroline's fixed expression lacks the sweetness of Kneller's serenely smiling princess, but avoids inane happiness or complacency. She has a high colour. Her eyebrows are heavier, as are the shadows beneath her eyes. There is a fullness to the legendary embonpoint that tactfully suggests struggling corsetry. But this Caroline has become the quintessence of magnificence, and the hand that in Kneller's portrait toys with a single ringlet of hair, in Seeman's refuses to relinquish the consort's crown on the table beside her. It was exactly as Caroline intended.

She was still recognisably the flaxen-haired, pink-and-white princess with whom George Augustus had fallen in love in disguise at Triesdorf in the summer of 1705. For the moment of Caroline's crowning, Handel – like his predecessor Henry Purcell at Mary of Modena's crowning in 1685 – composed a setting of words from Psalm 45, 'My Heart is Inditing', performed on instruments including the large new organ specially installed in the abbey at a cost of £130 by Christopher Shrider. 'Upon thy right hand did stand the Queen in vesture of gold/And the King shall have pleasure in thy beauty,' sang the combined choirs of Westminster Abbey and the Chapel Royal, supplemented by

'Italian Voices' from the opera house.[3] And so it was. Caroline wore a dress of silver and gold tissue. Its underskirt was embroidered in gold and scarlet with exotic blooms and scrolls of swirling foliage. Swathes of velvet, including the lengthy train carried in the coronation procession by her three elder daughters, were edged in deep bands of ermine and densely wrought embroidery of gold metallic thread. Eyewitness accounts describe 'royal robes of purple velvet', though in surviving portraits the colour is blue.[4] Festoons of pearls threaded her pale, powdered hair; in heavy bunches they hung from the shoulders of her dress. On her velvet sleeves, outlining her décolletage, ornamenting her bodice and in tiers across her sparkling kirtle trembled brooches of large diamonds, their flat, dark facets magnets for every ray of sunshine or candlelight, so that she appeared to glitter from head to foot. Bar carping Sarah Marlborough, spectators were literally dazzled. 'The Golden Tissue veil'd the dazling [sic] Air/ Of Light, too strong for vulgar Eyes to bear,' wrote the author of 'To the Queen', published in *Verses on the Coronation of King George II and Queen Caroline*.[5]

It was, in every particular, the costume Mary II had chosen for her coronation in 1689, save that, in Caroline's case, the gewgaws that contributed so materially to her splendour were mostly borrowed. Hervey claimed she was 'as fine as the accumulated riches of the city and the suburbs could make [her] ... for she had on her head and shoulders all the pearls she could borrow from the ladies of quality at one end of the town and on her petticoat all the diamonds she could hire of the Jews and jewellers at the other'.[6] At George Louis's coronation, Caroline had been forced to content herself with Sophia's Hanoverian pearls. Her father-in-law's generosity in the meantime towards his mistress and his half-sister had done little to replenish the royal jewel box. Remembering with a courtier's cynicism, Hervey unravelled a metaphor in Caroline's pillaged finery, a 'mixture of magnificence and meanness not unlike the éclat of royalty in many other particulars when it comes to be nicely examined and its sources traced to what money hires or flattery lends'.[7]

Hervey missed the deeper symbolism of Caroline's imitation of Mary. Mary had been crowned joint ruler with her husband William III, the parity of their public partnership recognised in their double sovereignty. But Caroline was George Augustus's consort, not his equal. Her behaviour throughout their marriage had demonstrated her understanding that her eminence derived from him. In the design by William Kent for a temporary triumphal arch for Westminster Hall, setting for the coronation banquet, which George Augustus approved personally, a carved medallion tops the pediment. It features bust portraits in profile of husband and wife. Uppermost is George Augustus's image; Caroline's lies half-obscured below. The arrangement of the portraits identified the relative status of both players. The double image nevertheless suggests a partnership, shared purpose, echoed in the inscription 'Georgius II Rex et Carolina Regina', and this celebration of royal marriage marked a contrast with George Louis, his divorce, rapacious Madame Schulenburg and a cabal of Hanoverians and Turks. As the choir sang at Caroline's anointing, 'Kings shall be thy nursing fathers/And queens thy nursing mothers.' Among coronation addresses to Caroline were verses by the professor of poetry at Oxford University, Thomas Warton the elder. The verses' title – *To Her Majesty Queen Caroline on her Accession to the Throne* – appeared to accord Caroline's 'accession' significance equal to George Augustus's.

As with her earlier espousal of etiquette devised for Queen Anne, and her rejection of Sarah Marlborough's advice that she follow ceremonial guidelines for a princess rather than a reigning queen, Caroline's coronation day appearance revealed twin ambitions: her desire to imply continuity between Stuart and Hanoverian regimes as a means of underlining her own legitimacy, and to establish her intention to be treated beyond doubt as the highest-ranking woman in her husband's kingdom. Deliberately she excelled herself in splendour. In May, 'a merchant had sent for a very rich silk and gold brocaded cloth from France, and had offered it to the Princess of Wales, who refused to purchase it, finding it too brilliant and costly'.[8] On 11 October, brilliance was her aim, costliness disregarded.

The service followed the format of James I and Anne of Denmark's crowning more than a century earlier. In Caroline's case, the peeresses who customarily carried a queen's train were replaced by Princesses Anne, Amelia and Caroline: 'with equal Steps attendant on the Queen/Three Royal Virgins in the Train were seen'.[9] In keeping with this impulse to grandeur – which may also have been meant for a public show of restored family unity following a decade-long separation between parents and daughters – records at the College of Arms preserve Caroline's wish that, in medieval fashion, her styles and titles be proclaimed alongside those of George Augustus at the coronation banquet.[10]

Foreign guests marvelled. They considered that the service exceeded in magnificence the coronations of Louis XV and Caroline's first suitor, Archduke Charles, since 1711 the Holy Roman Emperor Charles VI.[11] At £8,720, expenditure was modest compared with future celebrations, notably the £238,000 frittered on George IV's behalf in 1821, but the increase of £1,500 on the cost of George Louis's coronation in 1714 was in line with George Augustus's desire for a service of appropriately regal fandangle.[12] In the unremitting focus on George Augustus and Caroline's royalty there was nothing pinchpenny. Thomas Kingsman of Westminster School referred to 'a magnificence, than which the Roman Capitol never boasted greater'.[13] Caroline's role in embodying majesty was key. In *Caroline of England*, Peter Quennell records a story that her jewel-encrusted skirt was so heavy 'that it was found necessary to contrive a sort of pulley that enabled her to raise the hem when she knelt down'.[14] The value of those weighty jewels was estimated at

£100,000, equivalent in 2017 to £13.5 million.[15] In the venerable spaces of Westminster Abbey, the image of the glittering queen, her attendant princesses and ladies-in-waiting recalled the women of the court of the Emperor of Lilliput described by Swift in *Gulliver's Travels*: 'The Ladies and Courtiers were all most magnificently clad, so that the Spot they stood upon seemed to resemble a petticoat spread on the Ground, embroidered with Figures of Gold and Silver.'[16] Little wonder John Evelyn rated it 'the finest Coronation that ever was in England'.[17]

Caroline had consistently emphasised her subsidiary role to George Augustus's. Even in letters to her closest attendants she outlined his primacy, writing for example to Charlotte Clayton in May 1719, 'He [George Augustus] will look over your letters himself not trusting me.'[18] Yet she had never disguised her enjoyment of the prospect of power, or her relish for elevated rank. A letter written by Swift to Henrietta Howard in 1730 refers to conversations with Caroline in the summer of 1726 at Richmond Lodge. Irishman Swift had explained to the princess the problems of his native country, as he saw them. She 'ordered me', he wrote to Henrietta four years later, that 'if I lived to see her in her present Station [that of Queen], to send her our Grievances, promising to read my letter, and do all good offices in her power for this miserable and most loyall Kingdom, now at the brink of ruin'.[19] Since 1714, Caroline's individual acts of charity had demonstrated her compassion: her donations to river boatmen suffering in the great freeze of 1716; her grant to Samuel Clarke of an allowance to cover the costs of sedan-chair hire. Her interest in the smooth running of every aspect of British government, including Ireland, was equally strong, albeit coloured by dynastic opportunism. And the rhetoric of authority, as recorded by Swift, undoubtedly appealed to her.

As throughout her marriage, Caroline would be forced to circumspection if she meant to realise the implications of her coronation dress preserved in Seeman's portrait, or the will to power implicit in her response to Swift. To date, her marriage had been markedly successful by princely standards. What Sophia had described in 1708 as 'the loving friendship between newlyweds' had been replaced by less rosy illusions, but neither husband nor wife doubted the depth of their affection for one another, and Caroline remained George Augustus's closest confidante.[20] Snapshots like Lady Hertford's memory of Caroline reading aloud to George Augustus 'when he lay down after dinner' from Rabelais's gutsy scatological romp, *The Life of Gargantua and of Pantagruel*, highlight the comfortable intimacy of their mature relationship, and the prevailing view of Caroline's 'most extravagant fondness for [George Augustus's] person' testifies to the strength of their shared physical attraction.[21]

For twenty-one years, from George Augustus's battlefield exploits at Oudenaarde in 1708 to his first return to Hanover in 1729, husband and wife were seldom separated. Long proximity, aided by Caroline's dominant character and the need she recognised of flattering George Augustus's vanity, had served to align their thoughts on many subjects. Hervey recorded a discussion about Whig loyalty with Caroline. 'During the conversation the King came in, and the Queen telling him what she had been talking of, the whole came over again, the King repeating almost word for word what the Queen had urged before.'[22] When husband and wife sat for portraits by Zincke, Caroline advised the artist, out of earshot of George Augustus, 'to make the King's picture look young, not above twenty-five'.[23] In an identical clandestine impulse, George Augustus instructed Zincke to paint Caroline as if she were no more than twenty-eight.

Soon after his accession, with Walpole's assistance, George Augustus formalised the value he attached to Caroline in the document of financial provision he made for her for his lifetime and after. This jointure, dated 10 August 1727, recognised the insolubility of the royal marriage in the new king's eyes. It celebrated 'the Sincere and Perfect Love and Affection which his Majesty bears to Her Majesty'; it nodded to her intelligence: 'a Constancy and Greatness of mind peculiar to herself'. But its tenor was that of acclamations which had greeted Caroline on her arrival in Britain in 1714. In its focus on her motherhood and steadfast Protestantism – the 'long succession of Princes derived from her Majesty' and 'her zeal for the Protestant Religion' – the record of Caroline's jointure clearly implied, at the outset of George Augustus's reign, a traditional interpretation of the role of queen consort.[24]

It was the message of *Carmen Corunarium: or, a Gratulatory Poem on the Coronation of King George II and Queen Caroline*, in which, in October 1727, Caroline was addressed as 'QUEEN, Bride, and Fruitful Mother All in One/Surrounded with your Bright and Royal Train'.[25] It was the same message repeated by Welsh poet Jane Brereton, with an added emphasis on Caroline's imagined absorption in domesticity: 'O Wife! More happy in thy Lord alone/Than in the Pow'r, and Splendor, of his Throne./O Mother! blest in your illustrious Race,/The Guardian Angels of our future Peace'; and by the author of Verse 43 of the *Verses on the Coronation of King George II and Queen Caroline*, who described Caroline as 'more proud her Monarch's Heart than Throne to share'.[26] It was the message of a silver coronation medal by John Croker, on which a flatteringly wasp-waisted Caroline is depicted between figures of Religion and Britannia framed by the motto '*hic amor haec patria*' (this my love, this my country), indicating her appropriately queenly double allegiance to piety and patriotism.[27] It was the message of an essay to Caroline, in which the author reminded her that 'to enjoy, together with the highest state of publick Splendor and Dignity, all the retired Pleasures and domestick Blessings of private life; is the perfection of human Wisdom, as well as Happiness'.[28]

Six months later, Caroline's first birthday as queen was marked by William Bisset in a poem of uncompromising title:

Verses Compos'd for the Birth-Day of our Most Gracious Queen Caroline: The First Birthday of a Protestant Queen Consort for One Hundred and Ten Years. Bisset's poem was read aloud 'the same Day in the Great Drawing-Room before Several of the First Quality', including Caroline herself. Caroline was never at liberty to define her role exclusively in line with her own inclinations. She could be in no doubt concerning the expectations of her contemporaries, nor the limited compass of a queen consort's sphere of activity. In January of that year she had proved her understanding of popular requirements. To twelve persecuted French Protestants who had escaped from gaol and crossed the Channel to begin new lives in Britain, she gave £1,000. To a 'deserving' cause it was largesse on an appropriately regal scale.[29]

By contrast, muscular concepts of kingship were central to the opera Handel premiered on 11 November 1727, his first of the new reign. *Riccardo Primo, Rè d'Inghilterra*, with a libretto by Paolo Rolli, celebrated in romantic fashion the life of Richard the Lionheart. Italian master to Princesses Anne, Amelia and Caroline, Rolli wrote a dedicatory sonnet linking the Crusader king to George Augustus. Rolli's Richard was soldier and amorist, much as George Augustus liked to consider himself.[30]

Despite poets' careful separation of the relative spheres of husband and wife, submission and self-effacement played no part in the version of Caroline recognised by many of her contemporaries. Nor is this the version history has preferred. The best-known published sources, notably recollections of Walpole and the memoirs of George Augustus's lord of the bedchamber and, from 1730, vice chamberlain, John, Lord Hervey, depict a woman determined in her ambition and skilful in manipulating appearances and a foolish husband. 'Her power was unrivalled and unbounded,' wrote Hervey. 'His Majesty lost no opportunity to declare that the Queen never meddled with his business, yet nobody was simple enough to believe it; and few besides himself would have been simple enough to hope or imagine it could be believed, since everybody who knew there was such a woman as the Queen, knew she not only meddled with business, but directed everything that came under that name, either at home or abroad.'[31] In a similar spirit, Edmund Gibson, Bishop of London, invited in 1727 to draw up a list of Whig clergy meriting preferment, concluded that the invitation was 'no less ye Queen's motion because it comes immediately from ye King'.[32] Visual sources are equally clear. In a satirical print of March 1737 called *The Festival of the Golden Rump*, it is Caroline who inserts into the anus of a satyr-like George Augustus enema-style injections of a flavoured brandy that will restore him to her guidance, while Walpole and Bishop Hoadly look on approvingly.[33]

Such accounts represent distortions and exaggerations. The forcefulness of Caroline's character lent them credence, like her description of dealing peremptorily with doctors treating Princess Amelia: 'these animals have propos'd a flannel shift to make her sweat, upon which I dismissed them'.[34] The truth is inevitably more complex. A report compiled for the French government early in 1728 by Johann Daniel Schöpflin identified Caroline's sphere of activity as the equivalent of public relations. Schöpflin described her chief role as contributing to George Augustus's popularity, like Thomas Tickell in his poem 'Kensington Gardens' and Richard Savage in *The Bastard*, written the same year as Schöpflin's report, in which he claimed that a people 'who ne'er before/Agreed – Yet now with one Consent *adore*!'[35]

Within this role Schöpflin evidently included diplomatic activity on Caroline's part, which far outstripped that which George Louis had once allotted her and George Augustus jointly. It was Caroline, for example, who in late September 1727 received the Prussian envoy Wallenrodt at Kensington Palace and for two hours discussed plans begun by George Louis for a double marriage between the two reigning families: that of Caroline and George Augustus's son Frederick to his Prussian cousin Wilhelmine, and of Wilhelmine's brother, another Frederick (the future Frederick the Great), to one of Caroline and George Augustus's elder daughters. In October, Caroline received on the king's behalf Count Conrad von Dehn, the Wolfenbüttel special envoy. The import of this meeting outweighed the duchy of Wolfenbüttel's territorial insignificance, thanks to provisions of George Louis's will, which George Augustus intended to overrule. Afterwards, it was Caroline who acted as her husband's mouthpiece in an hour-long interview with the elector of Saxony's envoy, Jacques Le Coq. On that occasion she explained to Le Coq George Augustus's hopes, as elector of Hanover, for a Saxon alliance.[36] The possibility of hostility towards Hanover on the parts of his brother-in-law, Frederick William of Prussia, and the Emperor Charles VI troubled George Augustus; he had begun making noises about a defensive alliance of German states. To Caroline he entrusted a role in preliminary negotiations. Like her meeting with von Dehn, it was a clear statement of his faith in her skills.

Throughout her marriage, Caroline's concern with power had emerged in large- and small-scale actions. In 1712, Sophia had described her voraciously consuming pamphlets debating the Hanoverian succession, acquainting herself with the political outlook of the country she and George Augustus would inherit. Two years later, Caroline had requested from John Gay a copy of his verses *The Shepherd's Week*. Her interest in this instance was not English pastoralism, or even Gay's advancement. Her aim was the visible espousal of a culture, and the promotion of her own interest in that culture as a means of establishing her fitness – and by extension that of her husband – to occupy a position of eminence in Gay's country. She meant to win Gay's plaudits, and for a while succeeded. Caroline's skill during the long years of waiting was to exploit the means available to her in a political climate and within a family structure that offered her limited access to power on grounds of her sex. Her acts of patronage and her attempts to understand Whig, Tory and Jacobite arguments about the Act of Succession indicate the extent to which she actively involved herself in George Augustus's prospects. They suggest a wife clearly aware of her husband's future position. In themselves they do not inevitably reveal an intention to encroach on the power that position entailed.

This was not the verdict of many of those closest to Caroline, or of journal writers or caricaturists. They interpreted her 'masculine' interests and the influence she exercised over her husband as automatically tending to a personal agenda. This is the vision of Caroline preserved in Hervey's memoirs, with their cruelly forensic portrait of the royal marriage and woodpecker-style belittling of a pettifogging, pernickety George Augustus. Similar impressions emerge from surviving statements by Walpole. In the case of vice chamberlain and leading minister, who both enjoyed Caroline's favour and support, their partly fictionalised versions of her served their own ends, proof of the extent of their intimacy with the king and queen. Observers further from the political hub contented themselves with acknowledging something redoubtable in their new queen. The Earl of Middlesex was reminded of Elizabeth I: 'Your honour'd Name shall each revolving Year,/The Muses' Tribute with Eliza share./For Gloriana does again appear.'[37] Middlesex conjured memories of the Tudor virgin of a vanished golden age, married to her kingdom: a secular goddess inspiring poets, artists, courtiers. The comparison recalled a letter written by Leibniz more than a decade earlier. Beyond artistic patronage, Middlesex did not suggest that Caroline shared Elizabeth's sovereign power.

*   *   *

On 3 June 1727, a week before George Louis's unexpected death, *Applebee's Original Weekly Journal* had sounded a prophetic note. To ambitious politicians it offered a warning: 'as their power only depends upon the breath of their sovereigns, an angry blast of that flings them at once from the summit of their glory and the height of their ambition; or at most their authority generally determines with the life of their Prince, it being very rarely found that the most expert statesman can continue a favourite to two Princes successively'.[38]

Foremost among expert statesmen in the summer of 1727 was Robert Walpole. Predictably, George Augustus dismissed him with some dispatch on that June afternoon at Richmond Lodge when the reluctantly woken prince greeted his father's minister with irritable disbelief, clutching as tenaciously to old grievances as to the pair of breeches in his hands. Instead George Augustus placed the government in the hands of his trusted treasurer, Spencer Compton.

It was as the wary had anticipated. 'Everybody expected, that Mr Compton the Speaker would be the Minister, and Sir Robert thought so too, for a few days,' noted MP Arthur Onslow, in an account transcribed by his son four decades later. 'The new king's first resolution ... was certainly for Mr Compton ... who had long been his Treasurer, and very near to him in all his counsels. It went so far as to be almost a formal appointment, the king, for two or three days, directing everybody to go to him upon business.'[39]

For days Walpole tasted the invisibility of the ex-favourite. Meanwhile Compton floundered under responsibility he had not sought. He enlisted Walpole to draft the new king's accession speech; at his request Walpole scripted amendments too. Each morning, as speaker of the Commons, Compton attended to parliamentary business. In these daily absences Walpole waited on the new sovereigns, so that it was he, not Compton, who shortly won George Augustus's confidence. Caroline nailed her colours to the mast at one of the first drawing rooms of the reign by singling out Walpole's wife for special attention.

Walpole reassured the new king of his willingness to serve. Discussion touched on the civil list. Walpole offered George Augustus £800,000 a year. It was £100,000 more than George Louis had received, and his settlement of £100,000 for Caroline was double the grant to any previous queen consort (and the figure suggested by Compton). Implicit was Walpole's ability as chancellor of the exchequer to steer this settlement through Parliament. A new reign necessitated new elections. These returned a significantly enlarged majority of Walpole's supporters. Rewarded with a peerage for fleeting ineptitude and promoted to the House of Lords as Baron Wilmington, Compton discovered he had lost the glittering prizes. Walpole would remain George Augustus's first minister until Caroline's death and beyond.

Contemporaries attributed Walpole's rapid ousting of the new king's loyalist to Caroline. Swiss visitor to London César de Saussure recorded what was evidently a widespread view that Caroline, who 'possesses many qualities, amongst them prudence', was the more politically sagacious of the royal couple.[40] Arthur Onslow concluded, 'by the Queen's management, all this was soon over-ruled', an impression Walpole was happy to confirm. In conversation he traced the source of 'the great credit' he had with the king to 'the means of the Queen, who was the most able woman to govern in the world'.[41] It was a self-serving conceit, this suggestion that his authority derived from Caroline, a source of power therefore denied his opponents or any outside the golden circle of her approval. It gained currency from the belief already common of Caroline's influence over her husband, the doggerel that taunted 'You may strut, dapper George, but 'twill all be in vain;/We know 'tis Caroline, not you, that reign –/... if you would have us fall down and adore you,/Lock up your fat spouse, as your dad did before you.'[42]

From the political jockeying in the first months of George Augustus's reign – before Hervey embarked on his memoirs or Horace Walpole published recollections of his father – emerged the idea of the new king as Caroline's puppet that has coloured so many subsequent accounts. It rapidly became an *idée fixe* as prevalent among politicians like Onslow as among the readers of broadsheets in London coffee houses. 'As soon as ever the Prince became King the whole world began to find out that [Caroline's] will was the sole spring on which every movement in the Court turned,' Hervey wrote later, in a typically grandiloquent vision of Caroline as the new regime's presiding genius.[43] With partial veracity he claimed, 'it was now understood by everybody that Sir Robert was the Queen's minister'; he reduced the contest between Walpole and Compton to a matter of queenly whim.[44]

But the outcome of the Walpole-brokered royal reconciliation of 1720, which had failed to win for Caroline the return of her daughters, had proved how little Sir Robert was 'the Queen's minister', for all Lady Cowper's mutterings at the time. Instead, it had demonstrated to Caroline the firmness of the grip on power of the man she labelled '*le gros homme*'. George Augustus, she knew, represented her sole legitimate access to influence. In the summer of 1727 she saw in Robert Walpole, who had misled her, broken his promises to her and alienated her husband, a politician capable of wielding and retaining power, and as such a potential asset to the crown and a conduit for her own and George Augustus's views and wishes. Walpole's success at Compton's expense – personally pleasing to Caroline – forced from her a pragmatic response. Over time, queen and minister would find common ground in apparent mutual admiration. Carefully Walpole flattered Caroline. He encouraged in her a belief in her own power, telling her, 'Madam, I can do nothing without you. Whatever my industry and watchfulness for your interest and welfare suggest, it is you must execute. You, Madam, are the sole mover of this Court.'[45] They did not always agree, and their tussles more often ended in victory for Walpole. It was a reflection of the balance of power in their relationship, and, by and large, that of crown and Parliament.

In the account of Compton's fall from grace written by the lord chancellor Peter King there is no mention of Caroline. Instead Lord King attributes Walpole's success to his cunning: 'By his constant application to the King by himself in the morning when the Speaker, by reason of the sitting of the House of Commons, was absent, he so worked upon the King, that he ... established himself in favour with him.'[46] Historians have pointed additionally to pressure on George Augustus from abroad, particularly France and the Dutch United Provinces, to retain his father's ministry to ensure continuity of foreign policy. Correctly, Hervey concluded that Walpole manipulated Caroline rather than the other way round. He saw that she, in turn, won George Augustus's agreement to Walpole's plans: 'that whoever [Walpole] favoured, she distinguished; and whoever she distinguished the King employed'.[47]

Even this assessment overlooks any suggestion that George Augustus, a man peppery in defence of his own prerogatives, intended to exercise power personally. The Earl of Strafford reported the new king 'talk[ing] of ruling by himself'. Another account claimed, 'all that can be gathered for the present is that, whatever side be uppermost, they will not have the same authority, that the last ministry had, since the King seems resolved to enter into all manner of affairs himself'.[48] Neither king nor queen was easily manipulated. Hervey and Walpole agreed on 'the difficulty there is in persuading either of them to get the better of their pride in most cases'.[49] Both he considered 'unmanageable and opinionated'.[50] Neither tolerated opposition. To disagreement, Hervey claimed, Caroline returned 'very short and very rough answers'.[51]

A picture coalesces of a triad at the centre of royal government: king, queen and minister in a courtly ballet of overlap-
ping interests, prickly egotism and routine mutual hoodwinking.
In 1733 an opposition newspaper called the *Craftsman* explained
their relationship using a metaphor drawn from chess, with
Walpole as the knight: 'see him jump over the heads of the
nobles ... when he is guarded by the Queen, he makes dreadful
havoc, and very often checkmates the King'.[52] So skilfully was
this managed that George Augustus came to commend Walpole
as 'a brave fellow'. Walpole and Caroline devised secret signs for
conversations in the king's presence as a means of directing him
to their ends: Walpole taking snuff, playing with his hat, fidget-
ing with his sword.[53]

The power that Caroline exercised through this mummery
was over her husband rather than the government of Britain.
George Augustus 'lived in dread of being supposed to be
governed by her', wrote Horace Walpole. 'That silly parade was
extended even to the most private moments of business with
my father, who, whenever he entered, the Queen rose, curtsied
and retired, or offered to retire – sometimes the King conde-
scended to bid her to stay – on both occasions she and Sir Robert
had previously settled the business to be discussed.'[54] As it had
in the reign of George Louis, real power belonged to Walpole.
Caroline was as much a servant of Walpole's premiership as its
beneficiary. And she achieved her ends at a cost to her self-
esteem, prostrating her greater intelligence before the husband
she loved but could not respect intellectually. Hervey identified
her 'dominant passion' as pride; he described 'the darling pleasure of her soul' as power. In his account, Caroline can realise
the latter only by sacrificing the former, a painful barter: 'She
was forced to gratify the one and gain the other, as some people
do health, by a strict and painful regime, which few besides
herself could have had patience to support, or resolution to
adhere to ... She used to give [George Augustus] her opinion as

jugglers do a card, by changing it imperceptibly, and making him believe he held the same with that he first pitched upon.'[55] In doing so, she became 'as great a slave to him thus ruled, as any wife could be to a man who ruled her', an irony that would have appealed to Caroline's detractors.

Despite a lapse of four months since George Louis's death, Frederick was absent from his parents' coronation. On 9 September he had acted as principal mourner in his grandfather's funeral procession in the Leineschloss. Obsequies satisfied, no communication from George Augustus or Caroline summoned him to London. Instead Frederick fronted coronation celebrations in Hanover, presiding over a feast in the palace attended by 'all the people in the town who were cleanly dressed'.[56] On the palace balcony he presented himself to crowds enjoying spit roasts and fountains of wine in the Holzmarkt below. Commemorative verses acclaimed him as 'Prince Friedrich, our King's son, he is our joy, he is Europe's star of hope and our country's son'.[57] Meanwhile across the Channel, Lord Middlesex referred to Londoners 'imag[ing] absent Frederic in our Mind'.[58] Although Caroline had described Frederick to the Duchess of Wolfenbüttel as recently as June as the dearest of her children, no evidence points to the prince's presence in his parents' minds.[59] 'Fred'ric, distant from the British Coast,/ Part of the Pomp was by thy Absence lost,' an anonymous poet commented tactfully.[60] It was not, apparently, Caroline or George Augustus's view.

The separation of parents and eldest child had come about at George Louis's insistence. In 1714 Caroline's unhappiness at their parting had been extreme. At intervals both husband and wife had petitioned in vain for their son's return, including in 1718, at the height of the family rift. Caroline had begged visitors to Hanover for accounts of her Fritzchen, the minutiae of his days, his health, height, happiness. In 1716 she and George

Augustus were privy to a scheme initiated by the lords chief justice, Thomas Parker and Peter King, to commission from royal librarian Richard Bentley new editions of the works of classical authors for Frederick's education, a plan not realised for another decade.[61] Portraits commissioned from Martin Maingaud either by Caroline and George Augustus or by George Louis had endeavoured to preserve the appearance of family unity, partnering Frederick with his sister Amelia. And until 1721 Frederick had remained the couple's only son. Without consulting his parents, George Louis had planned his marriage to Wilhelmine of Prussia, the daughter of George Augustus's sister Sophia Dorothea.

Today no letters survive between Caroline and Frederick for the period of their separation, albeit this lasted fourteen years and both were naturally affectionate. The Dutch royal archives preserve remnants of a correspondence between Frederick and his nearest sister Anne, in which Frederick confides his sadness at George Louis's death, his regret for the loss of the 'most particular tenderness and friendship' between monarch and grandson, and a 'consolation in this sad affliction [in] the knowledge of my dear parents' goodness' that would prove misplaced.[62] No equivalent exchange of letters between mother and son has yet been traced. The disappearance of both sides of such a correspondence makes possible an assumption that it never in fact existed.

Why Caroline should have adopted such a course in 1714 is unclear. Evidence does not indicate any prohibition by George Louis. Caroline was a prodigious letter-writer. That she failed to maintain any direct communication with her eldest child was certain to shape their relationship in the long term. Her own childhood had been marked by a series of painfully truncated relationships, including separation from her mother and, afterwards, the latter's death, and from her adored brother William Frederick, as well as the unsettlement of a series of uprootings:

Ansbach, Crailsheim, Dresden, Pretszch. In the event, for both parties the consequences of severance between mother and son proved astonishingly painful.

Frederick played no part in the celebrations of 11 October 1727, the coronation procession on a raised walkway between Westminster Hall and Westminster Abbey, witnessed by Lady Mary Wortley Montagu among others: George Augustus and Caroline each beneath a glittering canopy of cloth of gold attended by courtiers, choristers, judges and heralds, the king's herb woman, a drum major, spear-bearing yeomen of the guard and, for the eagle-eyed, the 'Delightfull Spectacle' of William III's mistress Elizabeth, Countess of Orkney, 'a mixture of Fat and Wrinkles, and ... a considerable pair of Bubbys a good deal withered, a great Belly that preceeded her; ... the inimitable roll of her Eyes, and her Grey Hair which by good Fortune stood directly upright'.[63] For one observer it was Caroline's finest hour, at which she demonstrated to the full her understanding of monarchy as public spectacle: 'The queen never was so well liked ... she walked gracefully and smiled on all as she passed ... I could hardly see the King, for he walked so much under his canopy, that he was almost hid from me by the people that surrounded him; but though the Queen was also under a canopy, she walked so forward that she was distinguished by everybody.'[64] Nor did Frederick's parents recall him to London after the ceremony, when Caroline succumbed unmajestically to gout. Unquestionably Frederick was surprised by their continuing neglect, especially given the removal of obstacles following George Louis's death. He would not discover an explanation for their silence for another year.

Within days of receiving news of George Louis's death, the new king and queen left Leicester House. Their destination was Kensington Palace, where Caroline would spend extended periods until 1736.

Apartments for George Augustus and Caroline had first been prepared at Kensington more than a decade earlier, in the summer of 1716, despite reports describing areas of the palace exterior as 'much Crakt and out of Repair'.[65] On that occasion the unravelling of the couple's relationship with George Louis prevented them from occupying the rooms made ready for them. Prince and princess instead subsequently evolved a calendar that saw them moving winter and summer between Leicester House and Richmond Lodge. With George Louis dead and George Augustus's inheritance of Kensington, Hampton Court, Windsor Castle and St James's Palace, these arrangements altered. At Richmond Lodge the new king was reminded of the frustrations of his lengthy apprenticeship, the long summers of idleness following the frigid détente with his father. His preference during Caroline's lifetime was for Hampton Court. In 1727 he gave Richmond Lodge to her, although a letter written by Princess Amelia to Lady Portland indicates that Richmond remained a fixture in royal routine: 'Papa and Mamma ... are gone again to Richmond as the custom proves to be every Wednesday and Saturday. We stay them days comfortably at home [i.e. at Kensington Palace] and rest.'[66] Beginning in 1728, Windsor provided excellent hunting at the end of the summer, though, like his father, George Augustus was reluctant to live there. Not sharing her husband's enthusiasm, and grown too fat for riding, Caroline followed the chase, as Queen Anne had done, in a horse-drawn four-wheeled chaise.

Thomas Tickell celebrated the beauty of Kensington Palace's setting, 'midst greens and sweets', and its greater salubriousness than St James's Palace in summer, when the rising stench of the crowded city clogged the Tudor courtyards and 'epidemical distempers' flourished.[67] In 'Kensington Gardens' he imagined Caroline and 'the Dames of Britain' walking in front of the palace, their frocks as bright as flowers: 'Each walk, with robes

of various dyes bespread,/Seems from afar a moving Tulip-bed,/
Where rich Brocades and glossy Damasks glow,/And Chints.'[68]

Caroline would develop a particular attachment to Kensington
Palace. It lay within walking distance of St James's, across Hyde
Park along the road known as Rotten Row. This was the house
in which Anne, Amelia and the younger Caroline had spent
periods of the last decade. Altered, restored and redecorated by
George Louis, who had also set in train the re-landscaping of the
gardens by Henry Wise, it was a higgledy-piggledy structure of
some elaboration. Externally it lacked grandeur. A dynastic
propagandist brought up amid the *Wünderkammern* (rooms of
curiosities) and portrait collections of German princely courts,
Caroline personalised its interiors with her own distinctive
picture hang. Her choices included a copy of Cornelis van
Poelenburgh's *Seven Children of the King and Queen of Bohemia*,
which she acquired for her closet. Like her earlier purchase of
Bartholomeus van Bassen's *King and Queen of Bohemia Dining in
Public*, it underlined George Augustus's hereditary right to rule,
one of numerous instances of Caroline decorating with political
intent.[69] And aided by Charles Bridgeman, she remodelled the
palace's immediate surrounds.

The late king's garden plans had included a menagerie. On
the site of Queen Anne's hunting ground lived three tigers and
a pair of civet cats in iron enclosures. Introductions of 'outland-
ish' and 'East Indian' birds were planned at the time of his
death, so too a snailery in imitation of Caroline's at Richmond
Lodge. In its semi-rural outlook and absence of architectural
bombast, Kensington had reminded George Louis of
Herrenhausen; as at Herrenhausen he invested its garden with
spectacle and theatre. Caroline's garden plans, by contrast,
targeted a contrived naturalness. She was encouraged by praise
for her gardens at Richmond Lodge. The future Lord Egmont
reported a conversation in 1727 in which 'Sir John Rushout
[told] her that we owe our best taste in gardening to her'.

According to Egmont, Caroline replied, 'Yes indeed I think I may say that I have introduced that in helping nature, not losing it in art.'[70]

She relocated the big cats to the royal menagerie at the Tower of London. She purchased additional land to the north of the palace. Bridgeman constructed the Broad Walk, called the 'Grand Walk'; he laid down paths and created uninterrupted views across the new Serpentine Lake.[71] 'Well judg'd Vistos meet th'admiring Eyes:/A river there waves thro' the happy Land,/And ebbs and flows, at *Caroline's* Command.'[72] More prosaically there were 'Feeding Houses for Fowls' within reach of the kitchens, to fatten poultry for the royal table, and broad beds producing 'great parcels of flowers'.[73] In place of George Louis's tigers were the giant tortoises presented to Caroline by the Doge of Venice, and a great many squirrels.

On completion, observers unfamiliar with the elaborate gardens of Herrenhausen or Göhrde identified in Caroline's vision at Kensington a metaphor for the Hanoverian regime: nature harnessed and celebrated rather than tortured into patterns and devices. A poem published in the *Gentleman's Magazine* contrasted Bridgeman's designs, 'all noble ... and all plain', with a French-style formality associated with absolutism: 'No costly Fountains, with proud Vigour rise,/Nor with their foaming Waters lash the Skies;/To such false Pride, be none but Louis prone/... Here nothing is profuse, nor nothing vain.' At her favourite palace, Caroline would create for her contemporaries a new Eden. The poet went further. She herself, he suggested, might have averted Eve's first sin: 'Had she [Eve] such Constancy of mind [as Caroline] possesst,/She had not fell, but we had still been blest.' It was a formidable claim for this fallible but mostly well-meaning woman. During the royal family's absences, the gardens were open to the public free of charge.

Within the palace, William Kent had replaced the costlier serjeant painter Sir James Thornhill as royal decorator, and

created for George Louis a handful of rooms that were the nearest the first Georges came to palace-building. The painted decoration of the King's Staircase depicted members of George
Louis's court, including Peter the wild boy and the Turkish servants Mohammed and Mustapha. Beyond the staircase Kent
designed a series of handsome if modestly scaled spaces that
provided a backdrop for court entertaining until Caroline's
death: the Presence Chamber, Privy Chamber, Cupola Room,
King's Drawing Room and King's Gallery. With painted ceilings
and wall paintings, extensive gilding and woven silk wall hang-
ings that acquired a velvety richness in the flickering illumination of silver candle sconces and giltwood chandeliers, Kent's
schemes conjured an aura of majesty every bit as impressive as
Caroline's borrowed coronation finery.

It was here and at St James's Palace that husband and wife
established their court. St James's was the official setting for the
winter season, beginning with George Augustus's birthday ball
in late October and closing with the parliamentary recess in
April. At Kensington, which both regarded in a more domestic
light, George Augustus occupied apartments on the first floor
overlooking the gardens. Caroline was less picturesquely settled
in rooms without views on the floor above, at a distance from
the state apartments. With them came their respective
households.

Testament to the desirability of court appointments, as well
as Caroline's virtues as mistress, her own household as queen
included many of those who had previously served her as
Princess of Wales. Ladies Bristol, Hertford, Pomfret and
Albemarle, and Sarah, Duchess of Richmond, remained as ladies
of the bedchamber, while Elizabeth, Duchess of Dorset's place
as groom of the stole was formalised on 16 July. In line with her
status as consort, Caroline appointed two extra ladies of the
bedchamber, the Countesses of Pembroke and Burlington – the
latter, according to Lord Hervey, in her manner like 'a cringing

House-Maid'; three gentlemen ushers of the privy chamber, four equerries and three pages of honour.[74] A fortnight after the coronation, she also nominated an additional chaplaincy – John Harris, who had served George Augustus as dean of the chapel, as her clerk of the closet. He remained with her until his promotion to the bishopric of Llandaff two years later, when he was replaced by Isaac Maddox, afterwards Bishop of St Asaph. Harris and Maddox were two of more than twenty royal chaplains to receive bishoprics during George Augustus's reign.[75] In both cases, Caroline's role in their promotion was key.

Caroline's decision to appoint a full roster of attendants is characteristic of her sense of rank. It also expresses the partnership between husband and wife that had been a feature of their marriage from the outset, with her own household balancing that of George Augustus. The opportunities for court employment offered by this sizeable household served to affiliate quantities of the social elite to George Augustus and Caroline's regime. By force of numbers, the court would occupy a significant place in London's social life. Sheer expense maintained its exclusivity. Lord Hervey suggested that only the wealthiest families could manage the 'necessary expenses incurred in dangling after a court'. The annual cost of clothes for the royal birthdays alone was estimated at £200 a year, equivalent to the entire salary of the lowest-paid court officials.[76] Few of these precious costumes could be worn twice.

As maids of honour the new queen retained Mary Meadows, Bridget Carteret, Penelope Dive, Mary Fitzwilliam, Anna Maria Mordaunt and Anne Vane. Spikily, Horace Walpole labelled Miss Vane 'a maid of honour who was willing to cease to be so – at the first opportunity', as events would shortly prove; John Perceval called her 'a fat ill-shaped dwarf'.[77] Miss Mordaunt, like Caroline, had the big 'breasts of an overgrown wet nurse'.[78] Like Mary Bellenden before her she attracted, but resisted, George Augustus's blunt advances. Though they disliked one another heartily, Charlotte Clayton and Henrietta Howard stayed on as two of Caroline's six women of the bedchamber. Henrietta's feelings were mixed; Charlotte Clayton's absorption in Caroline was wholehearted. At some point she stumbled on the secret of Caroline's umbilical rupture. The discovery further cemented the bond between mistress and attendant, albeit Caroline would have preferred to avoid such a disclosure, even to Mrs Clayton.

Henrietta remained in harness as George Augustus's mistress, though neither partner evidenced obvious pleasure in their arrangement. So bitter was George Augustus's upbraiding of Henrietta one evening after his accession that she wrote to him, 'with the utmost respect ... from your Majesty's behaviour to me, it is impossible not to think my removal from your presence must be most agreeable to your inclinations'.[79] In that instance the king's foot-stamping ill humour dispersed. For monarch and mistress, theirs would remain an uneven coupling. 'The sun has not darted one beam on you a great while,' Lady Hervey wrote to Henrietta in July 1729. 'You may freeze in the dog-days, for all the warmth you will find from our *Sol*.'[80] Henrietta might have frozen in her Kensington apartments too: despite five fireplaces, her basement rooms were damp enough to produce 'a constant crop of mushrooms'.[81] And thanks to Caroline, she found herself intermittently alone there. Lord Chesterfield, who disliked Caroline, claimed that in her jealousy she suspected Henrietta of acting as a magnet for dissidents, especially Walpole's political opponents. 'Representing [Henrietta's apartments] as the seat of a political faction', she prevented George Augustus from visiting his mistress for three or four days at a stretch, and so sought to contain her rival's influence.[82]

Dismissals balanced appointments. On 26 September the *Whitehall Evening Post* announced that the king had dispensed with the hated Lady Portland as royal governess. It was a symbolic rejection by George Augustus and Caroline of the

Caroline in her coronation
robes by Charles Jervas,
glittering with jewels,
many of them borrowed
for the occasion.

Venetian portraitist Jacopo Amigoni painted Caroline in 1735 as queen and mother, a cornucopia of royal offspring at her feet.

Martin Maingaud's portrait of Caroline's three eldest daughters – Anne, Amelia and Caroline – from whom Caroline was separated for much of their childhood.

Caroline and the son she loved best, William Augustus, Duke of Cumberland.

The son Caroline grew to hate, Frederick, Prince of Wales. George II described him unfairly as half-witted.

John, Lord Hervey, Caroline's vice chamberlain from 1730, her (almost wholeheartedly) devoted admirer, whose memoirs offer a sparkling if misleading portrait of court life.

A deliciously flattering portrait of Caroline as queen by Enoch Seeman. The artist deftly avoids any suggestion that Caroline, as one observer noted, had 'grown too stout'.

To Her most Excellent Majesty
QUEEN CAROLINE
This View of the HERMITAGE
in the Royal Garden at Richmond,
And of the Heads of Hon.ble Rob.t Boyle Esq.r Jn.o Locke Esq.r
S.r Isaac Newton Will.m Wollaston Esq.r & of y.e Rev.d Dr Sam.l Clarke
Done after the Marble Busto's placed therein
is most Humbly
Dedicated.

Publish'd according to Act of Parliament October 1735. And Sold by Tho. Bowles in S.t Pauls Church Yard, and by John Bowles at the Black Horse in Cornhill.

Caroline was an enthusiastic gardener and builder of garden follies, like the Hermitage in her garden at Richmond Lodge.

The seven surviving children of Caroline and George II, including Frederick, Prince of Wales (standing centre) and his brother and rival, William Augustus.

William Hogarth's oil sketch of the family of George II, a study in divisions. Caroline's attention is wholly consumed by William Augustus, far left.

A middle-aged Caroline, painted from memory in 1735 by Joseph Highmore, imposing in her statuesque magnificence.

John Vanderbank the Younger painted Caroline the year before her death, dignified and purposeful in full regal fig.

Caroline on her deathbed, by one of her female attendants, Dorothy, Countess of Burlington.

Rysbrack's marble bust of Caroline, completed after her death, captures both her shrewdness and her firmness of purpose.

decade-long family split. Amelia's continuing correspondence with her former governess suggests the feelings of parents and daughters were at variance. The elderly countess nevertheless took to heart her new sovereigns' antipathy. Lady Mary Wortley Montagu described her at the coronation as 'fall'n away since her dismission from Court'. Her funereal appearance 'represented very finely an Egyptian Mummy embroider'd over with Hieroglyphics'.[83] Her place was taken by Mary, Countess of Deloraine, until her marriage Caroline's maid of honour Mary Howard, a woman of nugatory intellect – Horace Walpole castigated her as 'a pretty idiot, with most of the vices of her own sex, and the additional one of ours, drinking'.[84] She attracted George Augustus sexually, developed a handful of shared interests with Caroline, and apparently treated her royal charges kindly. A painting by William Hogarth of 1732 shows her with Mary, Louisa, William Augustus and her own daughters, Georgiana and Henrietta, watching a children's performance of Dryden's *The Indian Emperor* at the house in Great George Street of Isaac Newton's nephew by marriage John Conduitt. In the audience are members of Caroline's household, Sarah, Duchess of Richmond and the Earl of Pomfret. Recalling court theatricals at Lützenburg, it was an activity of the sort Caroline approved, performed to an audience of whom she also approved.[85]

George Augustus dismissed the bulk of his father's court servants. These included George Louis's German staff – in Swift's 'Lilliputian Verse', 'Strange pack/sent back'.[86] This may have arisen after discussion with Caroline as part of the couple's policy of public 'Britishness', although the decision was made easier by the family rift, which meant that George Augustus was unfamiliar with many of the old king's servants; a number would be re-employed by Frederick on his arrival in London. On the other hand, redundancies among royal clergy apparently arose by accident. George Augustus meant to retain both his own and George Louis's court chaplains. An account by

Mary Dering, dresser extraordinary to Princesses Anne, Amelia and Caroline, suggests his decision was reversed by his lord chamberlain, the Duke of Grafton, either deliberately or as a result of a misunderstanding, probably without George Augustus's immediate knowledge.[87]

As in 1714, Caroline's household choices were made from among members of the traditional landowning and political elites. In some cases she employed more than one member of the same family, like her appointment of Thomas Fermor, Earl of Pomfret to the lucrative post of master of the horse. At the request of his wife Henrietta, one of Caroline's ladies of the bedchamber, Pomfret owed his preferment to the intervention of Charlotte Clayton – though he would prove his worth in the summer of 1729, when he 'discharged one of the Queen's chairmen, upon his being strongly suspected of having too good an understanding with some highwaymen'.[88] The earl's suitability notwithstanding, his wife rewarded Mrs Clayton for her pains with the gift of a pair of diamond earrings worth the considerable sum of £1,400.

Mrs Clayton's recommendation, at the request of the Dowager Lady Granville, also lay behind Bridget Carteret's place as maid of honour. Bridget's fellow maid Penelope Dive was a third Clayton appointment, a member of the bedchamber woman's own family. The extent of Charlotte Clayton's influence in the composition of Caroline's household is proof of the esteem in which Caroline held her, and of the key role played by personal recommendation in the process of obtaining positions at court. The paucity of Caroline's connections among the British aristocracy as a German princess inevitably increased Mrs Clayton's room to manoeuvre. Caroline's contemporaries focused on the queen's influence over her husband. It is clear that she in turn was influenced by others.

Not everyone shared in the good fortunes of the Clayton protégés. Among those thwarted in their ambitions were Mary

Pendarves, the future Mrs Delany, whose long period of place-seeking at Caroline's court ended only with her remarriage in 1743. Her failure recalled the fruitless twelve-year vigil of John Gay. Since 1714, Gay had followed Caroline from Hanover to St James's, Leicester House and Richmond Lodge. Calculatedly lavish in his verse effusions, at the end of 1726 he prepared for publication 'a collection of Fables entirely of my own invention to be dedicated to [the five-year-old] Prince William [Augustus]'.[89] With inadvertent irony he wrote, 'Princes, like beauties, from their youth/Are strangers to the voice of truth;/Learn to contemn all praise betimes;/For flattery's the nurse of crimes.'[90]

The reward he anticipated for such dainty compliments was anything but their being 'contemned'. It never materialised. Instead that year Caroline offered him an honorary position in the household of her youngest daughter, two-year-old Princess Louisa. Gay dismissed the sinecure as unfitting. His mood plummeted. 'My Melancholy increases, and every Hour threatens me with some Return of my Distemper,' he told Pope.[91] Disappointed to embitterment, he withdrew from court. 'I was appointed Gentleman-usher to the Princess Louisa, the youngest princess,' he wrote the following October. 'Upon account that I am so far advanc'd in life, I have declin'd accepting; and have endeavoured in the best manner I could, to make my excuses by a letter to her Majesty. So now all my expectations are vanish'd; and I have no prospect, but in depending wholly upon my self, and my own conduct ... As I can have no more hopes, I can no more be disappointed.'[92] With the Fables published, and encouraged by friends including Pope, Gay returned his attention to the stage. Like moonshine his admiration for Caroline vanished overnight. Henrietta Howard commiserated, but her friendship with Gay is one explanation for what may have been a deliberate snub on Caroline's part.

In part due to Caroline's support, in 1724 *The Captives* had earned Gay £1,000. His *Beggar's Opera* of 1727, produced by

John Rich the following year with tunes by John Christopher Pepusch, gained him £800 and a place in the theatrical canon. Famously it made Gay rich and Rich gay, Gay's earnings equivalent to four years' salary as gentleman usher to the infant princess. Among early audiences were Caroline and George Augustus. Sniffily Mary Pendarves wrote, 'the taste of the town is so depraved, that nothing will be approved of but the burlesque'.[93] Time would show that it was a taste George Augustus and his family were well able to satisfy.

Henceforth Gay's self-appointed role as poet-apologist would be seized by lesser practitioners Stephen Duck and 'the Volunteer Laureat' Richard Savage. Yet to experience Gay's disillusionment, Savage acclaimed Caroline as 'Supreamly Lovely, and Serenely Great!/Majestick Mother of a kneeling State!' Not for the last time in the history of royal women, he hailed her as 'Queen of a People's Hearts'.[94]

From Archbishop Wake, George Augustus had received a copy of his father's will at the first privy council meeting of the reign. Contrary to customary practice, he declined to open it, and did not publicise its contents. Instead, he devoted considerable energies to reclaiming two other copies of the document.

Of the three copies made of his will, George Louis had placed one in safekeeping at Lambeth Palace. A second he entrusted to the court of his cousins, the Dukes of Brunswick-Wolfenbüttel, and the third, as an elector of the Empire, to the imperial court in Vienna. Although it would take him a decade and significant expenditure of British government funds, George Augustus received, retrieved and suppressed all.

Included in his father's will were plans for the future inheritance of the British throne and the Hanoverian electorate. Despite discussion between father and son, it was an issue on which George Augustus had again found grounds for disagreement. Again Caroline had supported him in his opposition.

Almost a decade before George Louis's death, husband and wife had conceived a radical revision of his proposals, an inversion of the hereditary principle. It was proof of their detachment from the son they had not seen since 1714: Frederick.

On 31 January 1730, the future Earl of Egmont reported a telling incident. 'I was told today that the King, jesting with the Duke his son [William Augustus], and asking him which he would rather be, a king or a queen, he replied: "Sir, I never yet tried; let me be one of them a month, and I'll tell you."'[95]

Given his position as second son, William had no hereditary expectation of a crown. Discussions begun in 1716, five years before his birth, for a time encouraged his parents to think otherwise.

Quick-witted and lively, from infancy William was a favourite child with both prince and princess: George Augustus later described himself to him as 'a father that esteems and loves you dearly'.[96] William shared his father's military enthusiasms. According to a biography published in 1766, at the age of five he 'raised a company of young boys, much about his own age, whom he marshalled and trained up according to the method which at that time appeared to him most convenient'.[97] His tutor described him as 'not only diligent but diligence itself', and courtiers like Egmont noted 'very early marks of quickness and parts'.[98] His birth had provoked a tepid rapprochement between his parents and the king. With Frederick in Hanover until 1728, William spent his first seven years as an only son, praised for his intelligence and predilections certain to find favour with 'Young Hanover brave'. He would resent the return to the family fold of his 'German brother'.[99] This petulant response suggests that his parents had failed to make clear to him the gulf between Frederick's constitutional position and his own. Subsequent events – and testimony like Egmont's – indicate reluctance on the part of mother and father to confront this unalterable disparity.

George Louis's response to the Jacobite uprising of 1715 had been to consider means of denying his opponents grounds for dismissing the new regime as 'foreign'. His solution was a separation of Britain and Hanover. He outlined this first in a will made in February 1716. Four years later, he added a codicil. In the event of two male heirs in the same generation, he stated his wish that the elder inherit the British throne while the younger succeed to 'His Majesty's Dominions in Germany', namely the electorate.[100] Since both George Louis and George Augustus then had only a single son, his plans envisaged a future family of Frederick's. George Louis discussed his proposal with his grandson during his visit to Hanover in 1720.

He also revealed this aspect of his will to George Augustus, who inevitably discussed it with Caroline. The stillbirth of a baby boy in the autumn of 1716, and the early death of George William two years later, had seemed to restrict the king's plans, as he intended, to the next generation. Everything changed, however, with the birth of a healthy baby boy in 1721. At a stroke the hypothetical became concrete: robust William Augustus in the nursery at Leicester House enabled the implementing of George Louis's scheme a generation sooner than anticipated.

Exactly when George Augustus and Caroline first decided this, or when they chose to point it out to George Louis, is not clear, although discussion was probably prompted by Frederick's eighteenth birthday in 1725, when William was three. Crucially, the couple's suggestion reversed the order of George Louis's codicil. As the lord chancellor noted in his diary, 'The Prince of Wales and his wife were for excluding Prince Frederick from the throne of England, but that after the king and prince, he should be Elector of Hanover, and Prince William his brother King of Great Britain.'[101] On George Louis's orders Frederick had spent his whole life in Hanover, a focus for loyalty in the king-elector's absence and the centre of court ceremonial, familiar with the electorate's physical, cultural and political landscapes. By contrast, William's upbringing would be as exclusively British as his German parents could make it. Despite the coolness in their relations and his fondness for his eldest grandchild, the king appears to have received his son and daughter-in-law's scheme favourably. He made a single stipulation. He 'said it was unjust to do it without Prince Frederick's consent, who was now of an age to judge for himself, and so this matter now stood'.[102]

No record survives of George Augustus or Caroline consulting Frederick, and George Louis made no further amendments to his will or to the codicil of 1720. Since 1716, when he was granted a British peerage as Duke of Gloucester, Frederick had received English lessons from a tutor called Jean Hanet, who introduced him to Joseph Addison's satirical journal the *Spectator*. He also received lessons in 'artillerie'; he learned the genealogies of the leading princely families of the Empire. Such preoccupations ought to have commended him to his father.[103] He was in regular receipt of official reports from Parliament, like the 'Parcell of Speeches and Replies' that diplomat George Tilson reported him receiving on 6 August 1723.[104]

Whatever his parents' misapprehensions, time would show that Frederick's interest in his British prospects, cultivated long-distance from childhood and enlarged during George Louis's biennial visits, was considerable. In July 1726 George Louis conferred on his grandson a second award of titles, including the dukedom of Edinburgh. At the same time he made a secondary grant to William, who became 'Baron of the Isle of Alderney, Viscount of Trematon in the County of Cornwall, Earl of Kinnington in the County of Surrey, Marquis of Berkhamsted in the County of Hertford, and Duke of the County of Cumberland'.[105] 'Though Prince Frederick wants no addition to make him more valued & beloved,' Tilson wrote to Frederick, overlooking William's similar elevation, 'yet this new mark of the King's affection, with Titles known among us, will endear your Highness more to the Nation.'[106] More realistic in their assessment of likely outcomes than the boys' parents, British officials took pains to promote Frederick's loyalty and to assure him of their own, like secretary of state Lord Townshend's description of himself in a letter to Frederick as the prince's '*très humble, très obligant, & très fidelle Serviteur*'.[107]

Strangers to the eldest son whom they had not seen for more than a decade, George Augustus and Caroline clung to their alternative plan with characteristic obduracy. Certainly their decision to leave Frederick in Hanover after George Louis's death suggests that their own minds were made up: for his parents, Frederick's destiny lay with the electorate. With disastrous consequences, they failed to relinquish pipedreams conceived in the Leicester House nursery, even after their own accession to the throne. Witnesses of Caroline's unhappiness following her parting from Frederick in 1714 surely expected his recall soon after George Louis's death. Yet more than a year passed with no invitation from parents to child.

Frederick arrived at St James's Palace without fanfare soon after seven o'clock on a dark December evening in 1728. Lord Hervey described his return to the bosom of his family as forced upon the king and queen by an impatient Parliament and 'the voice of a whole nation'; he described George Augustus as giving in to this pressure 'as children take physic, forc[ing] himself to swallow this bitter draught for fear of having it poured down his throat in case he did not take it quietly and voluntarily'.[108] Their reunion lacked tears or euphoria, lacked ceremony, lacked even warmth. The *Daily Post* recorded Frederick's arrival at St James's 'privately in a hackney coach'.[109] From the outset, forgetful Caroline and George Augustus resented Frederick's failure to fall in line with their plans for William Augustus.

*   *   *

Marriage plans had also played their part in prompting Frederick's crossing of the Channel.

Since the early 1720s, George Louis had pursued a scheme to perpetuate into a third generation a recent tradition of coupling Hanoverian daughters with Prussian sons. His sister Figuelotte and his daughter Sophia Dorothea had married in turn an elector and a king of Prussia. With Frederick, Anne and Amelia on the brink of marriageability, George Louis proposed two further unions: that of Anne to his Prussian grandson Frederick, born in 1712, and of Hanoverian Frederick to Sophia Dorothea's daughter Wilhelmine, who was two years his junior.

Ambitious, haughty and with the Hanoverian regard for dynasty, Sophia Dorothea agreed readily. Her capricious, psychopathic, unpredictable husband Frederick William, whose abuse of his wife and children was physical as well as verbal, wavered in his consent. For the most part, George Louis and Sophia Dorothea confined their plotting to George Louis's visits to Hanover, when Sophia Dorothea joined him. Having taken pains in 1718 to legitimise his right to 'the Care and Approbation of [his grandchildren's] Marriages when grown up', George Louis did not initially disclose his wishes to George Augustus or Caroline, and Frederick almost certainly discovered his grandfather's plan before his parents. Death, however, prevented George Louis from clinching the long-drawn-out deal. George Augustus predictably disdained a scheme cherished by his father. Bluntly he dismissed it: 'Grafting my half-witted [son] upon a madwoman would not mend the breed.'[110]

Frederick's decision late in 1728 to send to Berlin a picturesquely named associate, Lieutenant Colonel August de la Motte, 'proved' to some that, in the absence of communication from his parents, he had decided to take matters into his own hands. De la Motte's purpose, it was rumoured, was to short-circuit diplomatic sloth, prosecute Frederick's suit for Wilhelmine's hand with Frederick William, and fulfil George Louis's purpose. This argument soon acquired specious credence. Apparently on George Augustus's orders, Frederick was all but kidnapped at a masquerade ball in Hanover. On a ship called the *Diligence*, inadequately attended by a single valet de chambre, he was secretly hurried to London and the cold indifference of his parents.[111]

In fact it was reports of another marriage plan that forced George Augustus's hand. Unlike her husband – and contrary to what Wilhelmine herself would later claim – Caroline the dynast favoured Frederick marrying his Prussian cousin. Her objections in December 1728 focused on her own family in Ansbach. The princess for whom, at Frederick's instigation, de la Motte negotiated with the King of Prussia was not Wilhelmine but her younger sister Frederica, the intended husband not Frederick but his maternal cousin, Caroline's nephew, Margrave Charles of Ansbach. Charles was the son of Caroline's brother William Frederick, who had died in 1723 at the young age of thirty-six. In his clandestine interference in the affairs of his mother's family, Frederick embarked on a perilous course. It was not de la Motte who betrayed him. That part most likely fell to spies at the court of Ansbach or Berlin.

And so anger played its part in Frederick's summons to London. It was an unfortunate prelude to family reunion, this busybody prince mischievously meddling in the alliances of his mother's family. Anger lay behind his hole-in-the-corner reception at St James's Palace, scuttling unceremoniously up the back stairs to his mother's apartments. Angrily the king and queen excused themselves from public brouhaha. It was necessary, they insisted, to restrict publicity to a minimum in order to protect the prince from besieging place-seekers. Their verbal shilly-shallying was as dishonest as Frederick's secrecy over Margrave Charles's marriage. After a separation of fourteen years, parents and child met in an atmosphere doused with mistrust. George Augustus was briefly distracted by novelty. 'The King was pleased with him as a new thing,' Hervey claimed, 'and soon after his arrival, said [to Robert Walpole] with an air of contempt and satisfaction: "I think this is not a son I need be much afraid of."'[112] For Caroline, who set store by her prerogatives and whose family pride was potent, Frederick's perfidy was a powerful antidote to maternal affection. Cleverer than her husband, she temporarily suspended judgement. Certainly she was unpersuaded by a poet's description of Frederick as one 'on whom every eye/With joy and admiration dwells'.[113]

The prince was short, slight, neat in appearance, graceful and lively in his movements. Mary Pendarves ascribed to him 'a great deal of spirit'; she recorded the undignified manner in which he winked at servants as he gobbled up jelly, which was then considered an aphrodisiac.[114] He shared his mother's fair hair and pink-and-white colouring; he shared her intelligence too, in Peter Wentworth's estimation – 'very quick at good inventions'.[115] From his father came the pale, bulging eyes that undermined claims to good looks.

As preserved in Croker's coronation medal and portrait miniatures of similar date by Christian Frederick Zincke, Caroline in her mid-forties was a stately presence, with full cheeks and a comfortably double chin.[116] Sculptor and miniaturist substituted solid majesty for youthful bloom. Strip away the layers of flattery and what is revealed is considerable weight gain, a woman 'grown too stout', as Saussure noted in coronation year.[117] A miscarriage as recently as 1725 proved Caroline's continuing attractiveness to George Augustus nonetheless. As the decade advanced, and much to her unhappiness, the corpulent Caroline would be forced to acknowledge the lessening of her sexual hold on her husband, a decisive development in the royal marriage. In the short term her worsening gout was more readily concealed from view than her mountainous silhouette.

To the son who scarcely remembered her, she presented an imposing figure, splendidly upholstered in the court dress known as a mantua: a fitted bodice extending into a bulky train draped to reveal a decorative petticoat stretched wide over whalebone hoops – or, as Lady Mary Wortley Montagu pictured her, 'Majesty with sweeping Train,/That does so many Yards contain,/Superior to her waiting Nymphs,/As Lobster to attendant Shrimps'.[118] As at her coronation, Caroline enhanced an impression of regal magnificence with jewellery, her 'stomacher ... prodigiously adorn'd with diamonds ... as broad as a shilling'.[119]

More altered than Caroline since their parting in 1714 was Frederick's nearest sister Anne, 'marked a good deal with the small pox'. Unrosily, Lord Hervey described 'the faults of her person' as 'that of being very ill-made and a great propensity to fat'.[120] She was a gifted musician. Like her sister Caroline, she enjoyed painting, though she confined her efforts to copying: the antiquarian George Vertue wrote that she 'never ... drew from the life at any time tho' she had drawn & Coppyd many several copies in oyl painting'.[121]

Hervey's bleak assessment of Amelia's faults, her sharp, brusque, witty tongue 'glad of any back to lash and the sorer it was the gladder she was to strike', is out of kilter with Lady Pomfret's account of the middle sister as 'one of the oddest princesses that ever was known; she has her ears shut to flattery and her heart open to honesty. She has honour, justice, good nature, sense, wit, resolution, and more good qualities than I have time to tell.'[122] There is truth in both appraisals – and in Horace Walpole's verdict that by 1728 Amelia's youthful bloom was rapidly vanishing.[123] Her letters to her former governess suggest she spent a certain amount of time longing to escape London and court life. Of a visit made by Lady Portland to Bath, Amelia wrote that she envied her 'the charming ball-nights and sweet mornings where everybody mett friendly and agreeably at the pumps. I can't hinder my heart being there sometimes.'[124]

Only Caroline Elizabeth, 'the loveliest and the best' of the three elder princesses, can have struck her brother as happily changed from the baby he had forgotten.[125] She 'had the finest complexion and the finest bright brown hair that could be seen ... She had affability without meanness, dignity without pride, cheerfulness without levity, and prudence without falsehood.'[126] Like Anne, she too had inherited her mother's girth. She suffered 'severe rheumatic pains' from an early age. Her family dismissed her complaints as hypochondria.

Palpable among all three sisters was the strain in their relationship with their father, in part a legacy of their upbringing at George Louis's court. On his accession George Augustus had created Anne princess royal. This accolade did not diminish her detachment from him, which included signs of contempt: 'She was glad of opportunities to point out his faults and wherever these were small enough to admit of it, she would magnify them and deepen the colours without caution.'[127] There was an uneasy, brittle quality to the exchanges between father and daughter, while Caroline's relationship with Anne as an adult appears to have lacked easy expressions of affection. All the sisters had also inherited their parents' hauteur. Nothing, Lady Pomfret wrote, made Amelia 'forget the King of England's daughter'. Lady Cowper had noted Anne's 'most ambitious temper' at the age of five. As an adult, Anne told Caroline that she would gladly die to be queen even for a single day; Hervey described her as 'the proudest of all her proud family'.[128] All three attached to points of ceremony an exaggerated concern inherited from their parents, although a letter written by John Arbuthnot in July 1728 suggests that Anne at least had acquired more positive qualities from Caroline: 'Her highness charms everybody by her affable and courteous behaviour.'[129]

Frederick's youngest siblings, William, Mary and the enchantingly pretty Louisa, whom he had never seen before, basked in their mother's approbation, childishly unaware of the currents and eddies. 'Grandissime comédienne' Caroline drew on all her resources to master conflicting emotions that December evening.

Frederick too needed his wits about him. Wisely he set out to charm.

In some quarters he succeeded. Lady Bristol rated him 'the most agreeable young man it is possible to imagine'. She noted 'a liveliness in his eyes that is indescribable, and the most oblig-ing address that can be conceived; but the crown of all his perfections is that just duty and regard he pays to the King and Queen, with such a mixture of affection as if obliging them were the greatest pleasure of his life'. She concluded that his parents received these good intentions 'with the utmost joy and satis-faction'; but evidence contradicts her.[130] Pettiness was George Augustus's watchword in his behaviour towards his eldest son; Caroline did not oppose him. She did not challenge his propos-als for Frederick's living arrangements at St James's Palace, without a separate establishment of his own, although she had recently acquired for his eldest sisters, in order to afford them a degree of independence when the court was at Richmond, a ninety-nine-year lease on the house today known as Kew Palace. She would shortly purchase from the widowed Lady Eyre a neighbouring house for William Augustus.[131] She did not query her husband's decision to restrict Frederick's allowance to £2,000 a month, supplemented by the £9,000 annual revenues of the Duchy of Cornwall, in contrast to the £100,000 a year he himself had enjoyed as heir to the throne. Although popular pressure played its part in Frederick's introduction to the House of Lords and George Augustus's bestowal on him of the title of Prince of Wales after his first 'British' birthday in January 1729, Caroline did not countermand the decision that his birth-day celebrations exclude the usual firing of guns in St James's Park. Signs are scant of any stirring of maternal softness towards Frederick.

Instead, visual sources indicate the resilience of Caroline's preference for her younger son. That year, Charles Jervas completed a new portrait of Caroline. Apparently unaged since

Kneller's official image of 1716, she wore the regal robes of state
of her coronation portrait. Between Caroline and her crown,
her hand on his shoulder, stood eight-year-old William
Augustus, Duke of Cumberland. Precocious in ermine and
velvet, in his hands a dagger and a coronet, he appears every
inch a king in waiting. The following year an unknown artist
completed a second version of this portrait, today in the collection of Orleans House, Twickenham. In this second image, a
stout and sturdy Caroline holds William by the right hand. With
her left hand she gestures towards the golden-haired boy beside
her, a smile playing about her heavy features. Above a thicken-
ing waist, her enormous bosom is scarcely contained by ermine-
trimmed velvet heavily loaded with jewels.

In 1729, Caroline finalised plans for the second stage of
William's education. Lessons in constitutional history and law,
military tactics, procedure, shipbuilding and architecture supplemented his varied timetable. It was schooling fit for a prince ...
schooling for kingship. No mention was made of Gay's Fables,
with their cautions against flattery and the deceits of a court.
And six years later, Caroline sat for a third similar portrait. A
Neapolitan artist called Jacopo Amigoni painted 'a large picture
of the Queen and the Duke standing by her; several attributes
of honour and sciences; the whole ... of fine glowing colours'.[132]
The painter was already known to Caroline. In 1732 he had
completed a picture begun by Kneller of the queen with her
three eldest daughters. Such 'family' images constructed a visible iconography of royal motherhood, a key facet of Caroline's
role as consort. But no double portrait survives of Caroline with
Frederick, and in Frederick's likeness by Amigoni the prince is
pictured alone.

At first, however, Frederick was easily absorbed into the
buoyant pattern of court life that Caroline had established on
George Augustus's accession. George Louis had held drawing
rooms on Sunday afternoons and weekday evenings. Beginning

at ten o'clock, the evening drawing room remained the focus of court entertaining in the new reign, at its best a glittering, lively scrimmage of the great, the good and the determinedly aspirant. Tracing the fate of that sumptuous silk and gold brocaded French cloth that Caroline had declined on grounds of cost in May 1727, César de Saussure wrote, 'the wife of a wealthy brewer, alderman of the City, ... purchased the cloth, had it made into a gown, and wore it at the next drawing-room or Court circle'.[133] So lavish a frock would certainly not have been out of place. An Italian visitor to St James's in 1731 wore two dozen large diamonds on his coat in place of buttons. And the royal drawing room was a ceremonial affair, albeit no invitations were issued and entry was open to anyone appropriately dressed. A procession heralded George Augustus and Caroline's entry: yeomen of the guard armed with polished halberds; the lord chamberlain and the master of the household with white wands of office; a pair of sergeants-at-arms; a favoured courtier carrying the jewel-encrusted sword of state. The royal children frequently accompanied their parents. At the family's entry, 'everyone [made] a profound reverence or bow as the King went by'.[134] The evening's social success rested mainly with Caroline. Her ready chatter balanced what Lord Chesterfield described as 'the sterility of [George Augustus's] conversation'.[135]

In 1728 the king and queen resumed the habit of weekly dining in public that once before, in that giddy summer of 1716, they had embraced with rebellious verve. It was as contrivedly theatrical a ritual as the drawing-room procession, and appealed alike to Caroline's conviction of rank. The royal table was 'plac'd in the midst of [the] hall, surrounded with benches to the very ceiling ... fill'd with an infinite number' of spectators.[136] With balletic precision – and at some effort – courtiers served king, queen, princes and princesses on bended knee, 'a very terrible fatigue to the Lady in waiting, who takes the covers off the dishes, carves for both their Majestys, the Prince and three

Princesses, besides giving the Queen drink and tasting upon the knee'.[137] An incident in July successfully punctured the formality of this stately tableau as well as proving its popularity. 'There was such a resort to Hampton Court last Sunday to see their Majesties dine that the rail surrounding the table broke, and causing some to fall, made a diverting scramble for hats and wigs, at which their Majesties laughed heartily.'[138]

Given the attachment of husband and wife to points of etiquette, these flashes of spontaneity were rare. A letter that summer from the Countess of Berkshire to Charlotte Clayton demonstrates that Caroline's reputation for affability was not enough to allay anxiety over how properly to treat her: '[I] desire you will … let me wait upon you to be informed in what manner I am to receive the Queen; for I should be extremely concerned to omit the smallest particular of showing that duty I ought to pay to her Majesty. And … I am sensible I am quite ignorant of the behaviour that is due to Majesty.'[139] A similarly 'anguished' Countess of Orkney, disappointed by her servants' treatment of Caroline in July 1729, praised 'the [great] goodness in the Queen to be so very easy' under the circumstances. Despite her own anxiety, Lady Orkney concluded that 'it was impossible to see [Caroline] and not love her'.[140]

George Augustus held daily levées. Around her own ritualised dressing Caroline constructed similar routines, holding mixed gatherings of courtiers, clergy and men of letters in her apartments. It was another instance of her behaviour mirroring her awareness of status, and in time Frederick would follow his mother's lead in copying the king.[141] In Caroline's case, prayers were read aloud in an adjoining room at the same time – Lord Hervey suggests with limited attention on Caroline's part. On one occasion the future Bishop of Worcester protested at reading prayers on a makeshift altar beneath a painting of a naked Venus.

The largeness of Caroline and George Augustus's family, with seven unmarried children, increased the number of formal celebrations, making for nine royal birthdays in addition to anniversaries, including that of the king's accession. The birthdays were occasions of particular note, with a large attendance at court and, at some expense to all involved, their best new finery for guests; Hervey suggests London's luxury goods trade suffered when birthdays were under-attended.[142] 'The Court is almost universally got into a French dress, which I am sorry for,' lady of the bedchamber Frances, Countess of Hertford, had lamented in 1724; elaborate French fashions extended to hair-dressing and fabric choices.[143] With Liselotte's death in 1722 ended her letters' sporadic commentary on French royal fashions. Instead, five years later, Caroline received from Lady Lansdowne in Paris a French fashion doll, 'a little young lady dressed in the court dress ... She was dressed by the person that dresses all the princesses here.'[144]

For their pains, well-dressed courtiers were singled out for royal note. Mary Pendarves was a skilled amateur botanical artist who designed embroidered stomacher panels and petticoats for her own and her friends' court dress. On her first visit to the new court in 1728, Caroline praised her skill: 'I dressed myself in all my best array, borrowed my Lady Sunderland's jewels, and made a tearing show. I went with my Lady Carteret and her two daughters. There was a vast Court, and my Lady Carteret got with some difficulty to the circle [the line-up of guests in place to catch a royal eye], and after she had made her curtsey made me stand before her. The Queen came up to her, and thanked her for bringing me forward, and she told me she was *obliged to me* for my pretty clothes, and admired my Lady Carteret's extremely; she told the Queen that they were my fancy and that I drew the pattern. Her Majesty said she had heard I could draw very well (I can't think who could tell her *such a story*).'[145] Her 'tearing show' – a dress of flower-patterned 'dark grass green' brocade, with pink and silver ribbons – had cost the widowed Mrs Pendarves £17.

After a lifetime of compliments given and received, Caroline may have been improvising in singling out the widow's draughtsmanship. Similar anecdotes, like her surprising Lord Egmont with her knowledge of his print collection, suggest she took trouble to apprise herself of details that indicated to those she encountered the extent of her interest, blandishments so 'very gracious that they confounded'.[146] Like George Augustus, Caroline understood the usefulness of court functions as a means of winning support for the regime through personal contact. In her much-publicised affability, her sense of humour and relish for risqué anecdotes, she enjoyed an advantage over her husband, whose 'want of conversation', according to Lady Hertford, showed less talent in that direction 'than anybody I ever knew who was to do the honors of a court'.[147] The story Caroline told to listeners in June 1732 of a Mr Spence, 'fond of frequent bathing', gives a flavour of her jockeying gossip. A visitor arrived while Spence was in his bath and swiftly made to withdraw. Punctilious in his courtesy, Spence 'leapt up, and naked as he was, waited on [his visitor] to the very street door'. 'Mr Spence,' commented Caroline to Lord Peterborough, 'was a man of extraordinary breeding to acknowledge the favour of a common visit in his birthday clothes.'[148]

Husband and wife understood too their opportunities as hosts for flattering or chastising members of the political classes admitted to the palace. At an early court of the reign, Caroline had taken the opportunity to inform Lord Orrery that he was 'much grown since She had seen me', a statement he recognised as a 'Reproof ... since it carries ... Reprimand for not having been at Court before in many years'.[149] Five years earlier, Orrery had been imprisoned in the Tower of London on suspicion of Jacobite plotting, charges that had failed to stick. Caroline may have hoped to effect his conversion through personal contact. Alternatively – a less kindly impulse – she may have expected visible proof of his loyalty in the form of court attendance. To

Lord Aberdour in January 1734, the Earl of Morton described the reception granted by the royal couple to a nobleman who had lately opposed Walpole and, in doing so, criticised Caroline: 'I believe you'll see in the prints that the Earl of Stair had waited on his Majesty and the Queen, but I am informed that neither the King nor Queen took notice of him, or spoke one word to him.'[150]

At other times, Caroline adopted a subtler approach. Hervey referred to her 'strok[ing] while she hated'.[151] The technique was surely learned from long exposure to the treacherous duplicity of courtly mores. King and queen were as capable of behaving with coolness as affability, each response deliberate and carefully calibrated. The warmth of Caroline's treatment of her closest attendants is proof that she at least did not merit Hervey's bitter claim that husband and wife 'looked upon humankind as so many commodities in a market, which, without favour or affection, they considered only in the degree they were useful'.[152] And Caroline was alert to George Augustus's social shortcomings. In February 1732, Anne wrote to Charlotte Clayton on Caroline's behalf about a measure she had conceived for smoothing ruffled feathers: 'Papa not having spoke to Lord Shaftesbury yesterday, Mama orders me to let you know, that she would be very glad if Lord Lymington would bring him to the levy to day, that that omission might be retrieved.'[153] It is an indication of Caroline's vigilance and the importance she attached to the role of court events in maintaining loyalty and affection for the crown.

Despite the absence of cannon fire, Frederick's birthday in 1729 was 'kept in a most splendid Manner … [with] a very numerous Appearance of Nobility and Persons of Distinction at St James's'.[154] It included a recital of birthday verses composed and delivered by the poet laureate Laurence Eusden. Court attendance was typically at its highest at birthday celebrations for senior royal figures, as Mary Pendarves's account of

Caroline's first birthday as queen indicates: 'At night sure nothing but the Coronation could exceed the squeezing and crowding that was there, the ballroom was so excessive full that I could not see one dance.' She likened attempting to cross the ballroom to 'attempt[ing] to swim across the sea in a storm'.[155] On these occasions the royal family set the tone for sumptuous dress. In his wife's honour, George Augustus chose 'blue velvet, with diamond buttons' and a hat 'buttoned up with prodigious fine diamonds'. Frederick appeared in 'mouse-coloured velvet turned up with scarlet and very richly embroidered with silver'. Caroline's own dress of black velvet was simple by comparison, *Applebee's Original Weekly Journal* explaining 'Kings and Queens [as] not dressing Grand on their own Birthdays'.[156] Simplicity notwithstanding, Caroline's inky velvet provided a dramatic foil for her pale complexion. Reporting on like occasions, the *Gentleman's Magazine* dwelt salivatingly on her 'pearls, diamonds, and other jewels'.[157] Unlike Hervey, the magazine resisted commenting that 'all the Birthdays are alike ... a great crowd, bad music, trite compliments upon new garments and old faces in the morning; feasting and drinking all day; and a ball with execrable dancers at night'.[158]

Formality oscillated with informality: family breakfasts of sour cream, fruit and hot chocolate away from the public gaze; afternoon theatricals performed by the younger children, like the 'comedy' described by Jenkin Thomas Philipps, in which Mary and Louisa as shepherdesses and William as 'a Racer' performed alongside a 'Lady cloathed in white as if she was a Priestess or a Ghost'; 'the Diversion of Hunting the Stag in Windsor Forest' reported in the *Craftsman*; evenings spent playing cards, walking in the palace gardens or, as the *Norwich Gazette* reported on 18 October 1729, at a private concert at Kensington, 'when the Harpsichord was played by Mr Handell'.[159] 'In bed both after dinner & after supper,' wrote Henrietta Howard, 'both [Caroline] & the King always read.'[160]

Lady Bristol recorded Caroline's pleasure in being read to aloud as she dressed.

In Lord Hervey's partisan account the felicity of all or any of these activities lay in George Augustus's hands, his testiness a pall that spared neither spouse nor attendants. 'His Majesty's brusqueries to everybody by turns, whoever came near him, his never bestowing anything from favour, and often even disobliging those on whom he conferred benefits, made him so disagreeable to all his servants, that people could not stand the ridicule even of affecting to love him for fear of being thought his dupes.'[161] Famously Hervey depicts a family breakfast soured by George Augustus's exactions. He 'snubbed the Queen who was drinking chocolate for being always stuffing, the Princess Emily [Amelia] for not hearing him, the Princess Caroline for having grown fat, the Duke [William Augustus] for standing awkwardly ... and then carried the Queen to walk and be resnubbed in the garden'.[162] Hervey's writing habitually subordinates truthfulness to dramatic effect or rhetorical flourish, but is supported in this instance by Mary Wortley Montagu's description of George Augustus in middle age as regarding 'all the men and women he saw as creatures he might kick or kiss for his diversion'.[163] Despite his affection for her, Caroline was frequently first in line for kicks as well as kisses: his irritation 'used always to discharge its hottest fire, on some pretence or other, on her'.[164] She had developed strategies for managing princely pique and her own equilibrium.

Letters written in the summer of 1729 by Peter Wentworth, one of Caroline's grooms of the chamber, testify to her passion for walking. That year she ordered the building of the Queen's Pavilion at Richmond Lodge, surrounded by trees, a woodland resting place during lengthy strolls, handsomely fitted out with an elaborate chimneypiece designed by William Kent. Sometimes musicians accompanied the royal perambulations. On 20 August, Wentworth reported, 'Her Majesty sent us word that she was going "to walk in the garden" … We walked till candlelight, being entertained with very fine French horns.'[165] Loyally Wentworth described his pleasure in a 'good long limping walk' with his mistress.[166] Caroline's taste for walking even shaped the routine of court days. Wentworth recorded 'go[ing] to dinner at three and start[ing] from table a little after five in order to walk with the Queen'.[167]

With vicious amusement, Sarah, Duchess of Marlborough recorded an unscripted encounter during one of Caroline's morning walks from Kensington Palace to St James's. 'Two or three days ago, Her Sacred Majesty was in great danger of being ravished. She was walking from Kensington to London early in the morning and, having a vast desire to appear more able in everything than other people, she walked so fast as to get before my Lord Chamberlain and the two princesses, quite out of sight … Lord Grantham meeting a country clown asked him if he had met any person and how far they were off? To which he answered he had met a jolly crummy woman with whom he had been fighting some time to kiss her. (I am surprised at the man's fancy!) And my Lord Grantham was so frightened that he screamed out and said it was the Queen. Upon which the country fellow was out of his wits, fell upon his knees, cried and earnestly begged of my Lord Grantham to speak for him, for he was sure he should be hanged for what he had done. But he did not explain further what it was. And Her Majesty does not own more than that he struggled with her, but that she got the better of him.'[168]

Peter Wentworth's letters dwell on less vexed diversions: an early-morning carriage ride from Kensington to Richmond so that Caroline and her daughters could breakfast on cherries they had picked themselves; a 'very pritty entertainment' at Richmond Lodge, in the form of an outdoor play arranged by Frederick for his mother and sisters. In the latter case, a specially written prologue explained an indisposition on Caroline's part as caused by sadness at her separation from her husband. Given George Augustus's irascibility, it was a barbed pleasantry.

On 14 May 1729 George Augustus had departed for Hanover. His absence lasted four months. In Caroline's lifetime he would make four visits to the electorate, crossing the Channel again in 1732, 1735 and 1736. Each time he took with him neither wife nor mistress. Instead he vested full powers of regency in Caroline and set out for Germany in the combined roles of conscientious *Landesvater*, bellicose prince of the Empire and footloose, lusty lothario. Only the previous year Caroline had been commended by John Conduitt for her 'steady attachment to true Religion … Liberality, Beneficence, and all those amiable Virtues, which increase and heighten the Felicities of a Throne, at the same time that they bless All around it'.[169] Her vain, exacting, irritable, goatish husband esteemed as well as loved her.

His decision to appoint her regent in his absence was expected. At least one coronation effusion had recognised Caroline's intelligence: 'If thy outward Form can thus surprize,/ Oh what a noble Pleasure would they [the people] find,/Could they but view the Picture of thy Mind!'[170] Since 1705 the partnership of husband and wife had been unusually close. On repeated occasions, most spectacularly at their coronation, they had indicated that theirs was a shared vision, a joint approach to eminence, and for twenty-one years since Oudenaarde they had scarcely been apart. George Augustus's opening speech to Parliament, at the end of June 1727, was delivered to a House of Lords swollen by the presence – unprecedented on such an occasion – of peers' wives. The new king was accompanied by his three eldest daughters and by Caroline, a symbolic assertion that the 'wifeless' George Louis had been replaced by a king *and* a queen, the former a man who was also husband and father.[171] There were recent precedents for a queen regent too. In the early 1690s Mary II had stood as regent no fewer than six times for her husband William III. The Regency Act of 1690 had granted her power in his absence to act in both monarchs' names. Critically, it permitted William authority to override her decisions; it stipulated the reversion of regal power to him on his return.[172] Eager as he was to deny uxoriousness, in 1729 George Augustus made a far more wholehearted statement of confidence in Caroline than William had in Mary. At his instigation, decisions on policy made during his absence were entrusted 'entirely to the Queen with the advice of the Lords of the Council'.[173]

Caroline repaid the trust he placed in her. She was careful in her exercise of powers she greatly coveted, with the result that his confidence in her grew. A letter dating from her third regency, written by the Earl of Harrington, secretary of state for the Northern Department (forerunner of the home office), expresses the extent of George Augustus's regard for her good sense and her ability to seek out sound advice. With British ships poised to resist a Spanish naval attack, Harrington informed his colleague, 'as Her Majesty will be able to have at all times the opinion of those versed in sea affairs, His Majesty orders me to acquaint you that he leaves it entirely to the Queen to send such orders as Her Majesty shall find necessary'.[174] There can be little doubt of Caroline's pleasure in such an endorsement, nor for this ambitious princess in the realisation that she had exceeded Mary's remit.

Like his father before him, George Augustus preferred to bypass his heir. Saccharine addresses at the time of the coronation had informed Frederick, 'Some Day shall see the Royal Sceptre thine;/... Glad be that day, but late before it shine.'[175] For all his disdain for poetry, George Augustus was in full agreement. The king's promotion of his wife over his son would contribute little to long-term family harmony. In the short term, courtiers – and Frederick – noted Caroline's relaxation in George Augustus's absence.

For the time being fissures in the relationship of mother and son remained unacknowledged, and at his father's removal, family tensions diminished. At Kensington Palace, at her first council meeting after George Augustus's departure, it was Frederick who first kissed Caroline's hand in token of his loyalty. Caroline took advantage of George Augustus's absence to undertake a number of visits – to the Earl and Countess of Orkney at Cliveden; to Claremont to dine with the Duke of Newcastle, prominent but not again to be trusted after events in 1717; to Walpole at his house in Chelsea, where with her children she 'breakfasted; after which [she] took Water at the Stairs adjoining to his Garden, and came down the River to Somerset House, and viewed the Royal Apartments there, and return'd to Sir Robert Walpole's'.[176] There were sojourns at Richmond Lodge and Windsor Castle.

On each occasion Frederick accompanied his mother, apparently content in her company. Together, he and Caroline invited themselves to the Duke of Grafton's hunting box at Richmond, much against the duke's will. Of dinner at Claremont, Peter Wentworth wrote on 21 August, 'The Prince of Wales came to us as soon as his, and our, dinner was over, and drank a bumper of rack-punch to the Queen's health, which you may be sure I devotedly pledged, and he was going on with another, but her Majesty sent us word that she was going to walk in the garden, so that broke up the company.'[177] With Anne, William, Mary and Louisa, Frederick hunted in Windsor Forest, dressed like them in a special 'hunting suit of ... blue, trimmed with gold, and faced and lined with red', in which all the royal children 'looked charming pretty'.[178] Caroline followed in a chaise. In company with his sisters Anne and Amelia, he danced country dances. He shared with Caroline and his sister Anne jokes at the expense of the doggedly solicitous Wentworth. In Wentworth's epistolary hagiography, nothing ruffled the even tenor of family life.

Caroline applied herself with diligence to the limited political concerns of her first solitary summer. A full regency council existed for her guidance: its members included the Archbishop of Canterbury. In practice a smaller 'sub-council', the 'Select Lords', met more often, at Kensington Palace, usually on days when post arrived from Hanover. The lord chancellor Peter King, lord privy seal Lord Trevor, the Duke of Grafton as lord chamberlain and master of the horse the Earl of Scarborough, both senior court appointments, joined Walpole among the 'Select Lords'.[179] Until the king's return their role was not to formulate policy but to assess unfolding events in line with existing policy. Foreign affairs formed the government's principal concern in the summer of Caroline's first regency. That a number of foreign ambassadors accredited to George's court followed him to Hanover for the duration of his stay lessened her workload and the extent of her responsibilities.

Husband and wife had been separated only once before. As from the Flemish battlefield, George Augustus often wrote to Caroline daily. He addressed her twice over, as temporary co-ruler and as husband, with the emphasis, Walpole claimed, on the second role. Diligently George Augustus refamiliarised himself with his homeland. There were diversions too along the way, as Lord Chesterfield reported to Henrietta Howard, and his letters to Caroline dwelt 'particularly [on] his amours, what women he admired and used'. In Chesterfield's account, Caroline's response was cynically self-serving: 'The Queen, to continue him in a disposition to do what she desired, returned as long letters, and approved even of his amours, and of the women he used.'[180] Her letters could as easily be interpreted as pragmatic, and there is no reason to discount hurt or anxiety on the part of this pursy but ambitious middle-aged woman whose vanishing hold on her difficult husband had always been grounded in cupidity. It is hard to imagine how else she could have reacted, or why she would have responded with any aim but to please. For a decade she had humoured George Augustus's liaison with Henrietta Howard. In doing so, she had won from him an unspoken gratitude and concessions she valued more highly than straightforward fidelity. In the summer of 1729 she did not concern herself unduly with what she dismissed as his fleeting *'guenipes'* (loose women).

The 'Select Lords' spent the quiet months finalising terms of the Treaty of Seville, which concluded recent Anglo–Spanish hostilities and tactfully omitted mention of ownership of Gibraltar. In June, Caroline intervened with the Portuguese ambassador following his country's embargo on a British ship in the River Tagus. In this period of febrile chauvinism, it was the sort of skirmish of high words and braggadocio that might easily have escalated. Caroline's intervention overturned the embargo. 'Destruction from her presence flies', the author of 'An Ode for Two Voices, for the Birth-Day of Her Royal Highness the Princess of Wales' had claimed, and so, in this instance, it proved.[181] From Hanover Townshend reported that 'the King likes extremely what Her Majesty said to the Portuguese envoy'.[182] The following month she offered Louis XV a homely diplomatic compliment in the form of 'a present of a dozen hogsheads of perry and cider'.[183] Predictably, it failed to stem the tide of worsening Anglo–French relations. For her part, Caroline found herself the recipient of an unusual gift from Britain's American colonies. 'I presume to present you with a young beaver alive, which I have not heard has yet been seen in England,' wrote the governor of New England, William Burnet, on 7 July. 'As this is a famous animal for its industry and policy, and, I think, peculiar to America, I hope it will not be unworthy of your acceptance.'[184] Caroline's response has been lost.

All summer long Caroline behaved with circumspection. As regent her conduct carefully denied George Augustus grounds for irritation. She established her court at Kensington to reassure him of the modesty of her ambitions, in contrast to the couple's flaunting grandeur of 1716 when, at Hampton Court, they had deliberately set out to eclipse George Louis's dull record. A quartet of quadrille tables, with fine leather covers and gold-laced edging, was delivered to the palace for evening card games – the game was a particular favourite of Caroline's, but not of George Augustus. In June, at a packed court at St James's Palace, she celebrated his accession day with appropriate fanfare. Letters ensured George Augustus's knowledge; his replies expressed his approval. In the warmth of his approbation, Hervey claimed, he resisted suggestions by Townshend that Caroline's powers be curtailed. Understanding of George Augustus's character – his vanity and self-importance – shaped Caroline's behaviour: her success laid foundations for her future regencies.

Townshend's interjection served only to consolidate Caroline's dislike. As early as 1716 she had labelled him one 'who ever strove to put on a Mask, which is no better than an Ass's Face'.[185] All too soon, forced to resign from office in 1730 on account of apparently irreconcilable differences with Walpole, the minister would identify a role for Caroline in his political downfall. Accompanying George Augustus to Hanover, 'Townshend [had] attempted to make a separate interest with the King ... independent of the Queen. It is unnecessary to say that her Majesty on the return of the King overthrew the whole fabric.'[186] Townshend wrote that 'it was my fate to be often in a very different way of thinking from her Majesty's, which was ye chief reason that induced me to retire'.[187] His resignation served only to increase Walpole's hegemony.

In her response to news of George Augustus's arrival in London in September, Caroline demonstrated her genius for public gestures and the sureness of her wife's touch. On foot she set off from Kensington with her children. Through the palace gardens, across the park, along Piccadilly to St James's they walked. They met George Augustus in his carriage. He alighted.

In view of the waiting crowds husband and wife embraced. For Peter Wentworth, this skilfully improvised scene of comfortable domesticity shed all its lustre on Caroline: 'I find virtue no more retires to cottages and cells, but secure of public triumph and applause, she makes the British Court her imperial residence.'[188]

It was the very role identified for Caroline on her arrival on British shores in October 1714.

Her decade as queen offered Caroline unprecedented opportunities for self-fulfilment. Hitherto there had been so many hindrances. She had put behind her the aimlessness of her early married years in Hanover, lived in Sophia's shadow; the focus on her childbearing that lifted only in her mid-forties; George Louis's repressive proscriptions; the emotional strain of family divisions; even financial anxieties. In the last ten years of her life, she discovered opportunities to spread her wings.

Regencies granted her legitimate access to the political arena. Through her jointure of 1727 she acquired property in her own right, including Richmond Lodge. She had learned enough to exercise patronage with discernment, although the deaths of Leibniz and Newton, her rejection by Pope and Swift and her alienation of John Gay meant that a number of those associated with Caroline as queen were undoubtedly lesser practitioners. That this is particularly true of men of letters arose from Caroline's faulty command of English and her close association with Walpole. Every leading poet of the period opposed the 'gros homme', nicknamed 'Bob the poet's foe'; gamekeeper's reports from Houghton, they sneered, were all he read with pleasure. Lord Tyrconnel's view that 'the best judges of poetry ... are the Queen and Mr Pope' won few adherents, least of all – in its claims for Caroline – Pope himself.[189] He castigated literary mediocrity in *The Dunciad*, published in 1728. Its chief sponsor in Pope's poem is the Goddess of Dulness, an unflattering image

of Caroline: 'Laborious, heavy, busy, bold and blind,/She ruled
… the mind.'

In gardening and architecture Caroline remained loyal to
Bridgeman and Kent. In the summer of 1727 the *Daily Journal*
reported her plans for a new royal library. A decade would pass
before construction of Kent's handsome neo-Palladian design
adjoining St James's Palace.[190] Kent also carried out artistic
commissions for Caroline, including decoration of the Queen's
Staircase at Hampton Court; his scheme included *trompe l'oeil*
architectural details and a scene of Britannia's coronation by
Neptune. He painted a trio of scenes from the life of Henry V,
proof that Caroline's enthusiasm for Britain's royal history was
not confined to the Tudors. *The Battle of Agincourt*, *The Meeting
between Henry V and the Queen of France* and *The Marriage of Henry
V*, delivered to Caroline in 1730 and 1731, contributed colourful
notes of cod-medieval romance to her dressing room at St
James's Palace. She commissioned portraits of herself and her
children from Jervas, Amigoni and Kneller's pupil John
Vanderbank, the son of a Huguenot tapestry weaver. She was
probably responsible for Amigoni's introduction to Charlotte
Clayton, whose portrait he also painted. She obtained portraits
of Newton and, following his death in 1729, Samuel Clarke,
which she hung at Kensington Palace. In 1726 Saussure wrote
that Caroline had embarked on further improving the setting of
Richmond Lodge: 'the princess takes a great interest in the
gardens, which are spacious and she has greatly embellished
them'.[191] Dismissed by George Augustus and others as 'childish
silly stuff', her 'embellishments' would continue through the
mid-1730s, and served by extension to associate Caroline with
a broader interest in natural history, especially botany. At an
audience in 1729 she received from naturalist Mark Catesby the
first twenty plates in his *Natural History of Carolina, Florida and
the Bahama Islands*, then British colonies.[192] Two years later,
Catesby dedicated the first of its two volumes to her. And she

continued to support Handel, whose fortunes fluctuated. In
1733 the word book to his grandiose oratorio *Deborah* was dedicated to her by its author Samuel Humphreys.

Caroline's decision soon after the accession to install in two
rooms at Kensington Palace, previously used as a library by
George Louis, her cabinet of curiosities – a collection she had
begun as Princess of Wales – showed the continuing influence
of her upbringing in German courts. As a child in Dresden she
may have seen renowned collections of naturalia and objets
d'art belonging to the Saxon electors. She was present when, in
1703, Frederick III oversaw the relocation of his collections of
antiquities and natural curiosities to rooms specially fitted up in
the town palace in Berlin.[193] In Hanover she had admired the
collections assembled by Sophia. She had revelled in the joys of
acquisition in letters to and from Liselotte: in both women's
cases their collections extended into traditionally masculine
areas, including coins and medals, of which Caroline eventually
amassed nearly a thousand. Her collection also included the two
'eggs of tortoise' given to her by Liselotte in 1717. There were
narwhal tusks, called 'unicorn horns', reputedly magical in their
properties. Like Sophia, Caroline owned hardstone and enamel
jewels and elaborate bibelots made from coral, agate and onyx.
She acquired paintings, especially portraits. A series of cameo
portraits of Tudor sovereigns – Henry VIII, Edward VI, Elizabeth
I, her cousin Mary, Queen of Scots – combined the excitement
of recondite craftsmanship with Caroline's particular interest in
the earlier dynasty and her desire to create a visual record of
Britain's monarchy culminating in George Augustus.

Horace Walpole would claim of Caroline as collector that she
took 'great pleasure in collecting and preserving the dispersed
remains of the collection belonging to the crown', a derivative
sort of husbandry.[194] His assessment reveals the importance
Caroline attached to royal provenance. Budgetary constraints
restricted the scope of her collecting, so, too, her purpose.

Voltaire described her, in *Letters Concerning the English Nation*, as 'born to encourage the whole Circle of Arts'.[195] In truth her focus was narrower. In Hanover she had promoted her interest in all things British as a means of indicating through the appropriately female medium of culture her fitness to share the British throne with George Augustus. As queen, her artistic energies were directed at emphasising the legitimacy of the Hanoverian succession, rooted in the family's descent from James I via Elizabeth of Bohemia. At Hampton Court, Windsor Castle and, especially, Kensington Palace, she redisplayed paintings, especially royal portraits and portrait miniatures. As in the collections she had known in Germany, she arranged images chronologically into the equivalent of a visual line of descent; she told Lord Egmont that this was the best way.[196] Her intention was to place George Augustus's family within a continuum of British monarchs. The undertaking appealed to her absorption in genealogy, bolstered the sense of belonging of this poor-relation princess. Caroline's arrangements of portraits depicted the Hanoverians as current occupants of an ancient throne, tied to their predecessors by consanguinity and religion. Each picture hang represented the same propagandist impulse. Inevitably their reach was restricted by the location of these displays within royal residences, visible only to the tiniest elite audience.

A chance discovery stimulated her zeal. In the early 1730s, George Vertue described the treasure trove Caroline happed upon in the first year of George Augustus's reign: 'Of late (about a year or two) the present Queen met with in the library at Kinsinton many pictures, drawings (in a book) from the life done by Hans Holbein. The pictures of persons living in the time and courts of Henry VIII and Edward VI. These pieces have long been buried in oblivion.'[197] In the same haul she also came across engravings by Wenceslaus Hollar, which inspired less excitement: she loaned them to her bedchamber lady, Lady

Burlington. Vertue located the discovery 'in a bureau'. He further identified the portrait sketches as 'one book of heads said to be King Henry VIII his Queens and Court etc, some with names, some without'.[198] There were sixty-three drawings in total, dating from two separate visits to London on Holbein's part.

To Caroline, who had demonstrated her enthusiasm for Tudor England as early as 1716, admiring the collection of Sir John Germaine, Holbein's preparatory drawings offered a window on to the country's first Protestant courts. It was a period regularly recalled on the London stage, with its staple diet of more or less rewritten plays by Shakespeare, bulked out by new 'Tudor' drama like Rowe's *Tragedy of Lady Jane Gray*; it was the period in which seeds of the Act of Settlement were first sown, with Henry VIII's break from Rome and England's Reformation. And by association, Holbein's drawings recalled aspects of the world of Elizabeth I, to whom Caroline had more than once been compared. Caroline ordered the drawings to be individually framed. Then she removed them to Richmond Lodge, the house that was her personal getaway, and displayed them there to chosen courtiers. Later she transferred all sixty-three images to Kensington Palace. In a new picture closet which she created in a room close to the State Drawing Room, they formed part of a scheme of sixteenth-century likenesses, alongside an extensive group of miniatures of the Dukes of Brunswick, forebears of George Augustus. She would acquire in addition a handful of Holbein's finished portraits.

'English men and women are very clean: not a day passes without their washing their hands, arms, faces, necks and throats in cold water, and that in winter as well as summer,' wrote César de Saussure in 1727.[199] It was a habit Caroline shared with her adopted countrymen. 'I cannot forebear doing Justice to the Queen my Mistress, and Glumdalclitch my Nurse, whose

Persons were as sweet as those of any Lady in England,' insists
Gulliver of the Queen of Brobdingnag, discussing the hygiene of
the gigantic courtiers in *Gulliver's Travels*.[200] It was equally true
of Caroline, whose ablutions extended beyond washing in cold
water. She was an early advocate of bathing, and encouraged it
in every member of her family. Over a ten-year period, beginning in 1727, more than twenty new wooden bathtubs were
ordered for the royal family from makers Thomas Ayliffe and
William Grindall, including the big new tub 'with large brass
strong handle, [and] large strong castors' delivered at the end of
1734. Caroline's household accounts also include regular orders
of a cosmetic preparation used for washing the face and hands,
William Lowman's 'Maydew' water.[201]

Caroline bathed regularly in a wooden 'body bath', a round
or oval tub bound with brass hoops. Some were fitted with
castors for easy moving into position in front of a fire, standing
on a painted floorcloth that protected wooden boards. Unlike
modern baths, the tubs were lined with linen; in each was a
wooden stool on which the bather sat. Bathers of the period
wore fine linen shifts like voluminous bathing costumes, one
reason Caroline was able to preserve for so long the secret of her
umbilical hernia. The necessary woman Mrs Susanna Ireland
was instructed to look after Caroline's baths. She received additional payments for filling tubs, carrying 'hot water and other
necessaries towards Their Majesties' bathing'.[202]

Caroline's unusual fondness for bathing may have been motivated by more than a desire for cleanliness. In the birthday
poem he addressed to her in 1732, Richard Savage toyed
heavy-handedly with an idea of the queen as arbiter of spring;
he presented her birthday on 1 March as heralding a new beginning, nature's rebirth: 'Cold, wintry sorrows fly;/... Cheerful the
vegetative world aspire,/Put forth unfolding blooms .../So gives
her birth, (like yon approaching spring)/The land to flourish.'[203]
Caroline understood Savage's metaphor as a pretty piece of

optimism and rewarded him with an annual pension of £50. In truth, as she recognised, her springtime had begun its descent towards autumn. Her worsening health was a debit to set against credits. An attack of gout had followed the exertions of the coronation. As the 1720s gave way to the 1730s, similar irruptions increased in frequency. The pain in her legs and feet made walking difficult: she resorted to occasional use of a wheelchair – a present from Augustus II of Saxony, brother of her step-father John George IV – as early as 1728.[204] Unable to take even gentle exercise, she continued to put on weight. She was gradually becoming obese, which further hindered her mobility. With good reason her detractors referred to her as George Augustus's 'great fat-arsed wife'.[205]

A handful of reported conversations indicate her concern about her health. Since the birth of Princess Louisa in 1724 she had suffered abdominal pains as a result of her 'rupture' or umbilical hernia, damage to the abdominal wall in the form of an opening, caused by the strain of multiple pregnancies. Her chief concern, however, appears not to have been her physical discomfort. Umbilical hernias may cause the navel to bulge outwards, and Caroline's principal anxiety was her shame at the unsightliness of this visible evidence of her condition, which she took pains to conceal. Given the infrequency with which she was naked, even when bathing, her fears were mostly exaggerated. The real source of her concern was almost certainly George Augustus's likely reaction, and her fear that discovery on his part would cause physical revulsion, with an inevitable lessening of the hold she exercised over him through sexual attraction.

Horace Walpole reported her strategies for diverting speculation: 'To prevent all suspicion her Majesty would frequently stand for some minutes in her shift talking to her Ladies, tho labouring with so dangerous a complaint.'[206] For the most part her confidence trickery succeeded. Either her vigilance once slipped or Charlotte Clayton was unusually beady-eyed. How the bedchamber woman stumbled upon her secret Caroline did not discover; it was not a welcome revelation. Nor did it lessen her preoccupation with her condition. To Robert Walpole, following his wife's death, Caroline addressed a series of questions unrelated to conventional condolence. Minutely she quizzed him about Lady Walpole's decline. Again and again, he noticed, she 'reverted to a rupture'.[207] Her fixity, he concluded, permitted a single explanation.

In the event a combination of causes hastened Caroline's physical decline. Painful gout deterred her from the lengthy brisk walks that had been her habit since the summers at Herrenhausen with Sophia. A regime of little exercise and an abundance of rich food, especially red meat, exacted its toll. With obesity and a consequent decline in muscle strength, pressure on the hernia increased, causing the opening in the abdominal wall to expand and thus increasing the possibility of the small intestine pushing out through the hole, with life-threatening consequences. Ill-defined and muddle-headed, Caroline's anxiety was nevertheless well-placed. Through fear of repelling George Augustus and a conviction of physical impairment as unbecomingly undignified she said nothing. Just as she concealed smallpox scars with patches, so she chose to hide an affliction that was altogether more serious. Her determined neglect inevitably hastened the fulfilment of her fears.

Meanwhile, Caroline made concessions to her growing physical discomfort. She abandoned whenever possible the stiff corsets that were an essential feature of court dress, creating the distinctive mantua silhouette of triangular bodice above a heavy train and skirts stretched wide over whalebone hoops; she ordered only a single set of stiff stays between 1730 and 1734.[208] In their place she adopted the soft corsetry, with silver hooks, more often worn during pregnancy, that exerted gentler pressure on her stomach and the painful hernia. Instances recorded by

Hervey, Wentworth and others of Caroline's indisposition during formal court entertainments suggest that it was only on these occasions that she continued to wear a full set of boned stays.

In Hervey's account, Caroline's martyrdom is exacerbated by the attitude of the royal family towards illness. Of robust constitution like his grandmother Sophia, George Augustus showed little tolerance of illness among his close relations. As a result his family affected an illusion of permanent good health that none but the hypochondriac younger Caroline ever punctured. Lady Pomfret reported Amelia's behaviour, though 'very much out of order', in April 1728: 'The occasion was this: she had a Drawing-room on Thursday, where it was extremely hot, and she (to oblige people) stayed above two hours; and, I believe, would not have gone then, (though far from well,) if I had not ventured to whisper what was o'clock.'[209] 'There is a strange affectation of an incapacity of being sick that ran through the whole Royal Family,' Hervey wrote. 'They carried [it] so far that no one of them was more willing to own any other of the family ill than to acknowledge themselves to be so. I have known the King to get out of bed, choking with a sore throat, and with a high fever, only to dress and have a levée, and in five minutes undress and return to his bed till the same ridiculous farce of health was to be presented the next day at the same hour.'[210]

Refusing to make allowances for his own physical weakness, George Augustus withheld similar concessions from Caroline or his children. At a drawing room in 1734 he permitted her – 'near swooning' and 'unable to stand any longer' – to withdraw early. 'Nothwithstanding [her condition],' Hervey recorded, 'at night he brought her into a still greater crowd at the ball, and there kept her till eleven o'clock.'[211] He '[did] not love that any about him should complain of being ill'.[212]

Towards those outside the royal family, his indulgence was kindlier. In a letter of January 1731 describing his recent collapse at court, Hervey acknowledged, 'the King assisted with more goodness than his general good-breeding alone would have exacted, and has sent here [i.e. to enquire about Hervey's health] perpetually'.[213] For the time being such consideration outstripped that extended towards Caroline. Her pride would not have wished it otherwise. Ahead of the brisk morning walks on which George Augustus continued to demand her company, she plunged her feet and ankles in painfully cold water to reduce their gouty swelling. To Anne in 1733 she confessed, 'I took the trouble to get my feet into a fit state for walking ... and could not sleep all night for pain.'[214]

In 1730, a courtier and a poet contributed materially to Caroline's happiness. The first was John, Lord Hervey. He took up his position as vice chamberlain in June, and embarked on the career as Caroline's *cavalier servente* that he chronicled in his memoirs with astringent relish. The second boasted none of Hervey's advantages of noble birth, familiarity with courts or close acquaintance with Robert Walpole. He did not, like Hervey, observe Caroline at close quarters in unguarded moments. He was not on terms of intimacy with leading politicians. He was not present when the drawing room emptied and the card tables were cleared; when, with her needlework, Caroline, 'a little angry, and a little peevish, and a little tired', steeled herself to endure George Augustus's nightly litany of grievances; when the King 'poured out an unintelligible torrent of German, to which the Queen made not one word of reply, but knotted on till she tangled her thread, then snuffed the candles that stood on the table before her', an entire marriage's frustrations in that tangled thread, humiliation concealed behind extinguished flames.[215] Yet he conceived in similar measure lasting affection for the woman who changed the course of his life. His name was Stephen Duck.

Hervey's appointment marked his return to court after a period in the House of Commons as MP for Bury St Edmunds and, following illness, a lengthy recuperative visit to Italy in company with the man who was almost certainly his lover, Stephen Fox, in place of his wife, Caroline's former maid of honour Molly Lepell. With his dazzling, willowy, girlish good looks, dandified clothes, clumsy make-up, brittle wit and talent for barbed repartee, Hervey had played the part of court butterfly from early in George Louis's reign. His marriage produced eight children; his attitude to his beautiful, serious-minded wife was neglectful and dismissive. Hervey indulged in numerous affairs. Soon after his return to court in 1730 he embarked on what historians have described as a 'homoerotically charged' friendship with Frederick, Prince of Wales that soured into lasting enmity.[216] Among objects of his contempt were George Augustus and Alexander Pope. 'When God created Thee,' he addressed Pope, 'one would believe,/He said the same as to the Snake of Eve;/To human Race Antipathy declare.'[217]

At times his urbanity was the thinnest of veneers. To his own surprise, this jaded cynic succumbed to an affection and admiration for Caroline that was wholehearted and unreserved. If the portraits of his memoirs are unreliable, that of Caroline at least offers an accurate measure of the powerful feelings she inspired in those closest to her: not only Hervey but Peter Wentworth, Charlotte Clayton, Frances Hertford and Henrietta Pomfret. Hervey claimed he looked upon her goodness daily 'like heav'n with fear and love'.[218] For her part, Caroline's fondness for him was such that she joked onlookers would suspect impropriety in their relationship were it not for the disparity in their ages. She gave him 'a ring … with her head upon it', which he kept until his death and afterwards bequeathed to her daughter Caroline; she gave him 'a gold snuff-box … with Arts and Sciences engraved upon it', and the 'prettiest and agreeablest' horse, which he rode alongside her chaise when she followed George Augustus hunting.[219] She overlooked accusations of bisexuality that involved Hervey in fighting a duel, and Pope's vicious characterisation of him as an 'amphibious thing': 'Now trips a lady, and now struts a Lord'.[220]

Dangerously, she allowed Hervey to usurp Frederick's place in her affections. In his role as an MP she relied on him as an alternative source of parliamentary gossip and information. His light, accomplished conversation balanced George Augustus's chafing, which Hervey decried as 'abominably and perpetually so harsh and rough', his temper 'seldom put in a sheath'.[221] When Caroline's talents as *grandissime comédienne* faltered and tears of frustration or humiliation succeeded her husband's criticisms and contradictions, Hervey agreed with her that the catch in her throat that she suppressed had been laughter, not sobs. 'You are one of the greatest pleasures of my life,' she told him.[222] He repaid her trust by acting as Walpole's agent, his political outlook closely aligned to that of the king's first minister. Insofar as he was able he returned Caroline's intense platonic affection.

There were no approaches to intimacy in Caroline's relationship with Stephen Duck. On 23 September 1730 the *Daily Post* reported that 'several ingenious poetical Compositions' had earned their author a royal pension and, at Caroline's gift, 'a little house in Richmond Park to live in'.[223] Duck, the author in question, was a farm worker from Wiltshire. Chief among his 'poetical Compositions' was *The Thresher's Labour*, his depiction of the annual cycle of 'endless Toils' of the labouring life in the country.

Duck came to Caroline's notice with lofty recommendations. The Earl of Tankerville sent copies of his poems to court; George Augustus's chaplain in ordinary Dr Alured Clarke passed on the view of 'some people of taste' that Duck 'must be the best poet of the age ... [and], with all his defects, a superior genius to Mr Pope'; Clarke employed Charlotte Clayton as his go-between with Caroline.[224] To her considerable enjoyment, *The Thresher's Labour* was read aloud to Caroline by Lord Macclesfield at Windsor Castle.

Afterwards she summoned Duck to Windsor. At their meeting on 2 October he presented her with two poems, 'Royal Benevolence' and 'On Providence'. Overwhelmed by the honour of royal patronage, he wrote clumsily: 'Your ROYAL MAJESTY a Muck-worm took/From Labour, pleas'd with his mean trifling Book/... Your Royal Bounty sets my Soul on fire;/ And what I lov'd before, I now admire.'[225] Duck's own benefits at Caroline's hands become, in 'Royal Benevolence', proof of the benignity of the regime: 'This contriving and performing Good,/Runs in each Vein of Hanoverian Blood.' For his loyalty, if not his artistry, Caroline rewarded him financially. She offered him a house and occupation in the gardens at Richmond; she made him keeper of Duck Island in St James's Park. In 1733 she appointed him a yeoman of the guard. At a stroke she severed his connection with the land. And thanks to her attention, broadcast in the journals of the day, Duck found himself a literary celebrity.

A pirated volume of his work, *Poems on Several Occasions*, published at the end of September, ran through seven editions within eleven days.[226] The following March no less a figure than the Oxford professor of poetry, Joseph Spence, turned a series of conversations with Duck into an early equivalent of celebrity biography, *A Full and Authentick Account of Stephen Duck the Wiltshire Poet*. Either misguidedly or mischievously, Caroline dispatched copies of Duck's verse to Alexander Pope. His response was predictably derisive. At Duck's expense Swift committed harsh invective to rhyme: 'From threshing corn he turns to thresh his brains/For which her Majesty allows him grains.'[227] Those 'grains' would continue until Caroline's death and beyond. Duck never again wrote verse with the easy facility or sincerity of *The Thresher's Labour*, but thanks to Caroline, nor was he ever again forced to earn his living threshing. Instead, in the words of the playwright and novelist Catharine Cockburn, Caroline 'seated him at ease near her lov'd Hermitage'.[228] In the gardens of Richmond Lodge she accorded him a principal role in the bucolic masquerade she created there, part escapist fantasy, part visual political allegory. In transplanting him from his native soil she consulted the views of Tankerville, Clarke and Charlotte Clayton. None consulted Duck himself.

The Hermitage referred to by Cockburn was first planned late in 1730. William Kent's commission, sited beyond a sweep of lawn in a thicket of pine trees in the garden's northernmost wooded enclave, was for a rustic building of picturesque desuetude. The picturesque note continued inside: vaulted ceilings artfully dripped stalactites.[229] One room was furnished as a library. In the main central space Caroline commissioned from Giovanni Battista Guelphi portrait busts of 'the brightest Stars in Learning's Hemisphere', a gallery of Whiggish Enlightenment thinkers: Isaac Newton and Samuel Clarke, known to her from Leicester House days, Clarke's disciple William Wollaston, author of the influential *Religion of Nature Delineated*, which Caroline reputedly read three times, the philosopher John Locke and philosopher-scientist Robert Boyle. Works by Clarke, Locke and Wollaston found their way on to the library's shelves.[230]

It was a folly at the cutting edge of garden design, with obvious affinities to the Tory Lord Cobham's Temple of British Worthies at Stowe. Stephen Duck was moved to verse. 'On the Queen's Grotto, in RICHMOND Gardens', published in the *Daily Post-Boy* on 11 December 1732, praised both Kent's design and Caroline: 'See how the Walls, in humble Form, advance,/With careless Pride, and simple Elegance:/... How small the Mansion, and the Guest how Great!'[231] Royal gardening became a metaphor for the civilising impulse, the replacement of 'Weeds and Thistles' by 'harmonious Lustre' a heroic image of progress: 'So, once, confus'd, the barb'rous Nations stood;/Unpolish'd were their Minds, their Manners rude;/Till Rome her conqu'ring Eagles wide display'd,/And bid the World reform.'[232] Others acclaimed 'Carolina, sapient queen', unaware of the Hermitage's enormous price tag, which eventually exceeded £3,000.[233] 'Every man and every boy is writing verses on the royal hermitage,' commented Pope sourly.[234] Despite criticism in the opposition journal the *Craftsman* – 'a heap of stones thrown into a very artful disorder, and curiously embellished with moss and shrubs, to represent rude Nature' – Caroline's Hermitage won widespread acclaim. The queen was praised for her patriotic choice of British worthies; she was praised for the outlook her choices represented, an attachment to philosophical debate and scientific enquiry and 'Your Esteem and Friendship for all Defenders of Truth, while they are living, [and] the Regard You pay to their Memories when dead'.[235] 'When her Majesty consecrated these dead heroes,' the *London Journal* offered, 'she built herself a temple in the hearts of the People of Britain who will by this instance of her love of liberty and public virtue, think their interests safe in the hands of the Government as their own.'[236] The absence of any representation of Leibniz was noted with approval.

To a markedly different reception, Caroline afterwards ventured a further sortie into garden-building. Kent's final folly at Richmond Lodge was dismissed by the *Craftsman* as 'an old Haystack thatch'd over'.[237] Caroline called it Merlin's Cave. A short distance from the Hermitage, it stood beyond a dancing lawn and a man-made pond in an enclosure of trees reached by winding woodland paths. In an engraving of 1736, ducks clog the pond. The 'cave' itself appears an eccentric structure of three simple Gothic bays topped by towering beehive-shaped thatched roofs like coconut shells. In a rare poetic commendation, William Mason, writing after the structure's demolition a generation later, called it a 'sweet design', its setting 'Fairy land'.[238] Other poets wavered in their views.

In the Hermitage Caroline had showcased a handful of her intellectual heroes, aligning herself, and by implication George

Augustus's regime, with developments in science, religion and rationalism. The message of Merlin's Cave, built during George Augustus's absence in Hanover in the summer of 1735, was less clear, especially after Caroline employed Duck's wife, an uneducated woman called Sarah Big, as visitor guide. Duck himself became hermit-interpreter.[239]

At the centre of the 'cave', a triptych of Gothic niches contained six life-size wax figures sculpted by a precursor to Madame Tussaud, Mary Salmon. One was identified as Merlin, another as Henry VII's wife Elizabeth of York, a third as Elizabeth I. A fourth figure represented Merlin's secretary. The remaining waxworks may have been intended as Minerva, goddess of learning and the arts, with whom Caroline herself had been associated in earlier imagery, and the well-known sorceress Mother Shipton; they were also identified as Britomart and Britomart's nurse, characters from Edmund Spenser's Elizabethan poem *The Faerie Queene*. Visiting in droves, Caroline's contemporaries were baffled. In Britain, unlike on the Continent, waxworks enjoyed a lowly status, as vulgar as fairground attractions. Horace Walpole dismissed the whole as 'an unintelligible puppet show'.[240] With Merlin as the key figure, Caroline may have intended to make a point about prophecy and the inevitability of the Hanoverian succession. Or perhaps she intended this combination of history and legend as an alternative narrative of Britishness, again with the Hanoverians as the culmination. 'I do not read romances but they say it is taken out of Spencer's *Fairy Queen*,' wrote Sarah Marlborough with pointed lack of interest.[241]

Fair-booth kitsch and a confusing message won Caroline few plaudits. *Fog's Weekly Journal* sprang to her defence. For all its ardour, the paper's apologia made matters no clearer: 'When we consider where and by whom this singular Edifice is erected, and these extraordinary Figures placed, we cannot imagine the Whole to be a mere useless Ornament; nor reflect without some

Indignation, on the Indecency of those who treat it as no better than an idle Whim, a Painter's Fancy, a Gardiner's Gugaw ... a Puppet-Shew ... Pretty-Shew, etc. On the contrary, we doubt not but that ... it is wholly Hieorglyphical [sic], Emblematical, Typical and Symbolical, conveying artful Lessons of Policy to Princes and Ministers of State.'[242] The substance of those lessons the paper failed to impart.

Like the Hermitage, Merlin's Cave was entrusted to Stephen Duck's care: to his literary bent Caroline tailored the position of librarian. The trouble she took equipping its library suggests that, despite adverse comment, it satisfied her as a diversion. Among her choice of titles were works by Samuel Clarke: her 'education' of Duck included inculcation in her own latitudinarian principles. Later Duck committed suicide. Commentators have traced the origins of his unhappiness to his removal by Caroline from his natural sphere, but Caroline had been dead many years by the time Duck killed himself in 1755. It may be that, in the 1730s, he was as much a toy for his royal mistress as any other of her servants. If so, her exploitation was inadvertent and her admiration for his talents – however misguided – apparently genuine. Duck described himself uncomplainingly to Caroline as 'a Tree, which You have transplanted out of a barren Soil into a fertile and beautiful Garden'.[243]

A sketch begun by William Hogarth in 1732, the same year he painted William Augustus, Mary and Louisa in the audience of *A Performance of 'The Indian Emperor or The Conquest of Mexico by the Spaniards'*, points to stark divisions within the royal family. A preliminary study for a commission that failed to materialise, *The Family of George II* depicts George Augustus and Caroline surrounded by their seven children. In front of the Tuscan temple designed by Kent for the southern end of the riverside terrace at Richmond Lodge, sovereign and consort sit in elaborately carved chairs. In the centre foreground, Mary and Louisa play with a spaniel. Their older sisters stand behind them, beside a table. On the farther side of the table, Frederick gestures to Amelia and the younger Caroline. They glance towards him, as do Mary and Louisa. Anne appears to be talking over her shoulder to her father. And Caroline, ignoring all else, gazes at William Augustus, a diminutive princely figure closer than any of his siblings to his parents' ersatz thrones.

Even in its unfinished state, it is an image of separations. Frederick is remote from his parents, an object of curiosity to his younger sisters. Anne pays him no attention at all, resentful of his higher status, likewise William Augustus, whom he had displaced on his arrival from Hanover. Amelia and Caroline are attentive to their brother, who fails to engage his parents. There is physical ease in Caroline and George Augustus's proximity, but no communication between them.

Hogarth appears to have intended the painting as the first in a series of royal commissions that would enhance his reputation and his practice. He did not mean it to expose the fragmented nature of the country's first family, but his disparate composition achieved precisely that. *The Family of George II* accurately reflects fissures within George Augustus's house.

Separately, Frederick and Anne were bent on escape. A decade before Hogarth's preparatory sketch, George Louis had discussed with Frederick his plans for the Prussian marriages. Frederick's summons to London in December 1728 had been motivated in part by George Augustus's determination that his elder son be prevented from interfering in the diplomatic wranglings of such a scheme. Recalled to the chilly bosom of his family, housed like his youngest siblings in apartments in St James's Palace on a fraction of the allowance his father had enjoyed as heir to the throne, Frederick found his ardour for marriage increased rather than otherwise. Marriage offered him the promise of an independent establishment, more money and a degree of status within his own home.

Although she swiftly came to nurture an overwhelming dislike of her elder brother, Anne's aspirations were similar. This imperious, accomplished princess craved the distinction of a throne, achievable only through marriage. From the polite diversions of life at court she drew limited fulfilment: music lessons with Handel, visits to the opera, gambling at cards, needlework. Stephen Duck's 'On a Screen, work'd in Flowers by Her Royal Highness Anne, Princess of Orange', published after her marriage, expresses the elegant futility of her existence: 'Each Flow'r does with such Lustre shine,/Such beauties crown the gay Design;/That Nature fix'd in Wonder stands,/To see she's rival'd by your Hands.'[244] Her sisters – and, to a lesser extent, Caroline too – were similarly constrained. Hervey presents life at Hampton Court as grinding, unvaried routine: 'no mill-horse ever went in a more constant track, or a more unchanging circle ... Walking, chaises, levees, and audiences fill the morning; at night the King plays at commerce and backgammon, and the Queen at quadrille.'[245] 'All our actions,' wrote Lady Pomfret, 'are as mechanical as the clock which directs them.'[246] Anne longed to escape the ossified roundelay. She longed to escape her father's pettifogging exactions. And the longer she lived alongside Frederick, the more she dreaded the prospect of her father's death and spinsterhood at the court of a brother she despised.

George Augustus felt little of his father's enthusiasm for the Prussian marriages. Ultimately the old king's plan foundered on vigorous mutual antipathy on the parts of brothers-in-law George Augustus and Prussia's King Frederick William, a contempt 'as great as one man can have for another'.[247] In both instances, husbands acted against the wishes of their wives. Left to Caroline and Sophia Dorothea, one or both marriages would have come about. As Caroline knew of old, hers was seldom the casting vote. There is no evidence to support the view of Frederick William's daughter Wilhelmine that Caroline herself

opposed Wilhelmine's marriage to Frederick because she 'strenuously desired to have him united to a female of no very prominent talent' instead of 'a princess of a great house'.[248] In
Wilhelmine's misleading account, Caroline's decision was made
in consultation with Melusine von der Schulenburg and Sophia
Charlotte von Kielmansegg, 'that they themselves might
continue to govern', despite Sophia Charlotte's death in 1725
and Melusine's withdrawal from court two years later on the
death of George Louis.

For an anxious interlude George Augustus and Frederick
William toyed with marital alliance as a means of point-scoring
one against the other. A letter written by a British diplomat in
December 1729 suggested that Frederick William had 'forced'
Sophia Dorothea 'to write an insolent letter of his dictating to
our Queen [Caroline], insisting upon her speedy performance
of the hopes she has given her of marrying Prince Frederick to
her eldest daughter [Anne], and this before February next, and
unconditionally, or else that she cannot hinder her husband
from disposing of her to someone else'.[249] In George Augustus,
to whom Caroline was bound to show such a letter, such
high-handedness inspired a predictable response. To-ing and
fro-ing between the courts continued nevertheless for another
two years, until Frederick William married Wilhelmine to the
Margrave of Bayreuth in 1731. The collapse of George Louis's
plans was part of a larger fracturing of relations between Britain
and Prussia. But failed engagements to their cousins did not
diminish Frederick or Anne's enthusiasm for marriage itself.

For Anne salvation would appear in an unexpected guise.
Few boasts could be made for William IV of Orange. He was a
prince without a throne, his sovereign power acknowledged in
Friesland, Groningen and Gelderland but not in the United
Provinces' key territories of Zeeland and Holland. He was a
bridegroom without romantic attractions. Hunchbacked, physically misshapen, 'his body as bad as possible' and teeth decayed

to the point at which his breath was 'more offensive than it is possible for those who have not been offended by it to imagine', he appeared a poor match for the eldest daughter of Europe's proudest Protestant king.[250] With a choice 'whether she would go to bed with this piece of deformity in Holland, or die an ancient maid immured in her royal convent at St James's', Anne 'resolved … she would marry him'.[251]

No one was more aware than Caroline and George Augustus of William's shortcomings. The couple's offer to their daughter of this cut-price princeling contained no element of coercion. 'I never said the least word to encourage her to this marriage or to dissuade her from it,' Caroline explained, remembering events in 1704, when Figuelotte had allowed her to make up her own mind about Archduke Charles. 'The King left her, too, absolutely at liberty to accept or reject it.'[252] Hervey describes father and daughter 'walking in the garden at Richmond tête à tête … a considerable time, her hand constantly in his, he speaking with great earnestness and seeming affection, and she listening with great emotion and attention, the tears falling so fast all the while that her other hand went every moment to her cheek to wipe them away'.[253] Their conversation evidently decided Anne. 'The ambitious girl replied, that she "would marry him if he were a baboon". "Well, then," replied the King, "there is baboon enough for you."'[254] Anne was rising twenty-four, scarred by smallpox, running to fat. For a decade she had been separated from both of her parents. For her father she felt impatience, for her brother loathing she was powerless to conceal. She knew the paucity of opportunities for escape. If she quailed at reports of William's deformity, she mastered her misgivings.

Her marriage took place on 14 March 1734 in the French Chapel at St James's Palace, against a backdrop of lavish decorations designed by Caroline's favourite, William Kent. Handel had composed a new anthem, *This is the Day that the Lord has made*, a setting of words from psalms 45 and 118 compiled by Anne herself. 'The Royal Maid consents with decent Pride/And crowns her Triumphs with the name of Bride,' offered one poet blandly; popular feeling, however, was strongly in support of the match.[255] Plans made by the royal household in advance stipulated each detail of the brief service, including Anne's entry: 'The Bride in Virgin habit with a Coronet conducted by the Lord Chamberlain and Vice Chamberlain, and supported by the Prince of Wales and Duke [William Augustus], both Bachelors.'[256] Her eight bridesmaids included Lady Hertford's daughter, Lady Betty Seymour. On 7 March Caroline asked the girl's father for his formal consent; she instructed him that 'all [bridesmaids] were to be dressed in white satin or damask, a stiff-bodied gown, the petticoat to be round and trimmed with a silver net, long locks, and jewels in her hair and upon her breast'.[257]

A dress of 'stiff blue French silk, embroidered with silver thread and lavishly trimmed with ruffles of the finest lace and loops of diamonds' struggled to flatter Anne's portly figure. At Caroline's insistence, the remainder of her trousseau – placed on display at Hampton Court – was of English manufacture.[258] William gave her jewellery valued at £30,000, including a diamond necklace whose stones were so large that twenty-two were enough to circle the thickness of her neck. In Hervey's account, her father offered her 'a thousand kisses and a shower of tears but not one guinea'. He resisted pressure to celebrate the marriage in St Paul's Cathedral in the interest of public visibility.[259] Parliament voted the princess a generous dowry of £80,000.

Given the success of her own sex life, Caroline undoubtedly felt compunction on Anne's behalf. Reflecting on her daughter's wedding night, she asked Lord Hervey, '*N'aviez-vous pas bien pitié de la pauvre Anne?*' ('Did you not pity poor Anne?')[260] She wrote to her daughter on the day of her departure, 'my sadness is indescribable. I never had any sorrows over you, Anne, this is the first, a cruel one. Caroline behaves so well, but our conversations always finish on the same sad note. The King, who sends you affectionate greetings, is worse than us all ... Love me always as tenderly as the most affectionate mother flatters herself that you do.'[261] Caroline addressed her daughter as 'dear heart'. From her own experience she knew the unlikelihood of ever seeing Anne again. Instead, bar a single visit, the relationship of mother and daughter was confined henceforth to their letters, full of advice on Caroline's part, larded with complaints on Anne's. Caroline's tone was consistently affectionate: characteristically she did not allow emotion to cloud political considerations. When Anne suggested returning to London during a pregnancy, her mother rebuffed her: 'You are now William's wife, God has given you skill and judgement, you are no longer a child.'[262] Hervey's statement that Caroline 'never ceased crying for three days' after Anne's departure, but forgot her within three weeks, is more effective rhetorically than as a record of fact.[263]

Adroitly, those with a grievance against Walpole or George Augustus encouraged Frederick's irritation at his sister's marriage ahead of his own. 'So very uneasy' had he become, after six years under his parents' roof, 'that to everybody his looks told he was so, and to many his words'.[264] 'One of his wise quarrels with the Princess Royal was her "daring to be married before him", and consenting to take a portion from the Parliament, and an establishment from her father, before those honours and favours were conferred upon him.'[265] But two years would pass before Frederick's engagement.

The popular rejoicing inspired by Anne's marriage was timely. A year earlier, a diplomat from Genoa had reported the threat of 'una generale rivoluzione' in London.[266] The cause of the unhappiness was a proposal by Walpole to impose a duty on wine and tobacco.

Walpole's Tobacco Excise Bill was intended to compensate for a loss in government revenue following his decision in 1732 to reduce the Land Tax paid by many among the political classes. It was also meant to discourage smuggling. In outlining the measure's potential for increasing civil list revenues, Walpole won George Augustus and Caroline's approval. Caroline further approved the scheme as likely to broaden support for the regime to include that of Tory landowners. Neither monarchs nor minister anticipated widespread opposition.

But Walpole had miscalculated badly. Within and outside Parliament, his political opponents moved swiftly. The Bill, they suggested, was a preliminary to escalating government intervention on several fronts. Darkly they hinted that tobacco and wine were only the first goods to attract indirect taxation; Walpole had been heard to let slip the words 'general excise'. Anxiously king and queen watched the Bill's uncertain progress. They demanded from Lord Hervey updates on key Commons debates. In answer to a request for information about the popular mood from the master of the horse, the Earl of Scarborough, Caroline was told, 'Madam, I will answer for my regiment against the Pretender [the Jacobite claimant to George Augustus's throne, James Francis Edward Stuart], but not against the excise.'[267] Caroline gave audience to the Earl of Stair, who berated her at length on the measure's folly. He told her that Walpole was the most hated man in the country, and that she shared in his unpopularity; he told her that the power Walpole exercised over her was universally acknowledged. With studied calmness, Caroline upbraided the blustering Scotsman for lack of principle; she made clear her contempt for his motives. He mistook her calmness for acquiescence. Her support for scheme and minister did not waver, nor that of George Augustus. Convinced of the connection between excise and the civil list, the king dismissed opposition as anti-monarchical, encouraged in this view by Walpole and Caroline.[268] Tension at court became palpable.

The decision to drop the Bill was Walpole's, on 11 April, in the face of overwhelming opposition and escalating threats of popular unrest. Excise had proved the strength of his royal support; it had exposed lack of support even within his own party. At court in its aftermath retribution for opposition peers who held household appointments was rapid. Lords of the bedchamber Lords Clinton and Burlington lost their places; after eighteen years' service Lord Chesterfield, whose mockery of Caroline was well known, forfeited the lord stewardship. The fall from grace of the Earl of Stair was inevitable. Chesterfield's revenge took the form of toadying to Frederick, Prince of Wales.

After dark, bonfires raged through London; the city erupted in celebration. At Charing Cross two figures were burnt in effigy. One represented Robert Walpole. The other was crudely shaped into the semblance of a fat woman, Caroline herself. From the dizzy heights of coronation day, Caroline's popularity had plummeted. Against a backdrop of howls and jeers, flames consumed the rough-hewn likeness. The emptiness of poets' florid claims lay vividly exposed, hollow the acclamations that likened her to classical deities, personifications of wisdom, prudence, charity, arbitress of springtime. For a moment in April 1733, in her self-appointed role as populariser of the Hanoverian regime, Caroline had failed. Opposition pamphlets trumpeted examples from history of 'an *Unpopular Queen* who supported a *detested first minister*'.[269]

Habitually 'mistress of her passions', a shaken Caroline gave vent to indignation. Angrily she protested 'against assertors of the people's rights ... call[ed] the King ... the humble servant of the Parliament, the pensioner of his people and a puppet of sovereignty, that was forced to go to them for every shilling he wanted, that was obliged to court those who were always abusing him, and could do nothing of himself. And once [she] added, that a good deal of that liberty that made them so insolent, if she could do it, should be much abridged'.[270] It was a statement of what Hervey characterised as her 'German' outlook, her inclination to authoritarianism, her aversion to contradiction, her conviction of royal prerogative. In a fictional exchange between Caroline and Walpole, imagined by Hervey, an exasperated queen tells the minister, 'There is your fine English liberty! The *canaille* may come and pull one by the nose, and unless one can prove which finger touched one's nose, one has but to put a plaster to one's nose, and wait to punish them till they pull it again; and then, may be, they shall pull one's eyes out of one's head too.'[271] It was a viewpoint George Augustus shared with his wife. As the failure of excise proved, they would struggle to impose it outside their family.

Like all else at court, the slow unravelling of the relationship between George Augustus and his mistress Henrietta Howard took place in public. By the late 1720s, observers agreed that they appeared 'so ill together that, when he did not neglect her, the notice he took of her was still a stronger mark of his dislike than his taking none'.[272] In her apartments at Richmond Lodge next to Henrietta's, Lady Bristol listened through adjoining walls to George Augustus's harsh rebukes and peremptory dismissals. It had become a relationship of perfunctory coitus and mutual irritation, but the king was a man of habit and routine, his life 'as uniform as that of a monastery ... [and] never the least change'.[273]

Henrietta's correspondence suggests that her position was not enviable. 'Forced to live in the constant subjection of a wife with all the reproach of a mistress', she was also plagued by a hearing impairment.[274] Through her forties her state of health worsened. A letter from Lady Hervey indicates that she had never been physically robust: 'All extremes are, I believe, equally detrimental to the health of a human body, and especially to yours, whose strength, like Sampson's, lies chiefly in your head.'[275] Against the vicissitudes of George Augustus's character and the petty revenge taken by Caroline in insisting on full observance, even during illnesses, of Henrietta's duties as her bedchamber woman ought to be set concrete advantages. From a position at court, Henrietta had hoped for financial security, and this she had attained. Afterwards she had craved protection from her abusive husband Charles Howard, and this too had been granted her. On more than one occasion Caroline had come to her assistance, notably the night Charles broke into the queen's apartments at St James's Palace and threatened Caroline with physically abducting his wife. With a greater show of courage than she felt, Caroline had challenged him to 'do it if he dare'. Afterwards she admitted, 'I was horribly afraid of him ... all the while I was thus playing the bully ... I knew him to be so brutal, as well as a little mad ... so I did not think it impossible that he might throw me out of the window.'[276] By such increments she won Henrietta's reluctant gratitude and bound her husband's mistress more tightly to her, but nothing in either woman's surviving papers points to real approaches to intimacy or sympathy.

Admittedly Henrietta's position lacked influence: both Caroline and George Augustus had always been determined it should be so. Nonetheless it afforded her meetings with prominent men and women, including politicians, poets and garden-makers, whose interests she shared. And George Augustus's beneficence, derisory in comparison with his father's enriching of Madame Schulenburg, had at least enabled her to buy land and build the house that compensated her for court drudgery: Marble Hill, in Twickenham.

Prior to 1728, even the idea of escape was impossible given her fear of returning to her husband. It was in that year, however, that Charles and Henrietta Howard signed a formal deed of separation. In addition, George Augustus agreed to pay Charles an annual pension of £1,200 for his wife's continuing presence at court.

Charles Howard was the heir to his childless brother Edward, Earl of Suffolk. Separation notwithstanding, a clause within the deed enabled Henrietta to become Countess of Suffolk in the event that Edward died and Charles succeeded to the earldom. This happened in June 1731. Henrietta's good fortune was twofold. Under her brother-in-law's will she received money he withheld from Charles; and her new status as countess disqualified her from serving any longer as Caroline's woman of the bedchamber. But Caroline was not ready yet to dispense with Henrietta's usefulness. Henrietta as George Augustus's mistress was a manageable challenge; another mistress might prove less so. Caroline offered her promotion to the rank of lady of the bedchamber. Within a week of Edward's death, with a degree of holding out on Henrietta's part, she had accepted the senior position of groom of the stole, resigned in her favour by an obliging Duchess of Dorset. 'Mrs Howard's friends say she was offered to be Lady of the Bedchamber, which she declined and wished for any other employment,' wrote Lady Pembroke to Charlotte Clayton.[277]

Henrietta's lighter duties enabled her to divide her attention between court and Marble Hill. She described her time as at last her own. With a degree of punctilio, setting aside personal feelings, she applied herself to the task of Caroline's wardrobe. Her purchases on Caroline's behalf included sumptuous gold fabric obtained at Henrietta's request by the Earl of Essex from Sardinia.[278]

Yet the challenge of successfully dressing Caroline's swollen figure could not outweigh Henrietta's aversion to the life she had once pursued so avidly. She was described coming 'in the Queen's train to the drawing-room ... with the most melancholy face that was possible'.[279] She had never loved George Augustus; her feelings for Caroline were equally bleak. Among her friends were so many opponents of the regime: Pope, Swift, Chesterfield, Walpole's particular enemy Henry St John,

Viscount Bolingbroke ... and, from 1730, a Whig MP called George Berkeley with whom she shortly fell in love. To Henrietta's relief, on 28 September 1733 Charles Howard died. In mid-September 1734 she requested from Caroline a six-week absence from court to recover her health in Bath, prompted by disaffection of long standing and her determination finally to experience life beyond Caroline's curt manipulations and George Augustus's 'contempt, neglect, snubs, and ill-humour'.[280]

Caroline granted Henrietta's request. She understood from previous conversations the younger woman's subtext. Her own health faltered that summer, she had awaited Walpole's victory in the recent general election with considerable anxiety, and it is possible that she temporarily lacked appetite for conflict. Walpole had lately lectured her on her health. His motives may have been selfish, concerned with his own political survival, but his anxiety was evidently real. Their conversation did not prompt Caroline to action: she did not consult her physicians beyond submitting to the routine futility of being blooded, or admit to George Augustus the oppression she laboured under. 'Your life is of such consequence to your husband, to your children, to this country, and indeed to many other countries, that any neglect of your health is really the greatest immorality you can be guilty of,' Walpole told her. 'Your Majesty knows that this country is entirely in your hands, that the fondness the King has for you, the opinion he has of your affection, and the regard he has for your judgement, are the only reins by which it is possible to restrain the natural violences of his temper, or to guide him through any part where he is wanted to go. Should any accident happen to Your Majesty, who can tell into what hands he should fall, who can tell what would become of him, of your children, and of us all?'[281] Caroline denied his flattery. Hervey described her 'coughing incessantly ... her head aching and heavy, her eyes half shut, her cheeks flushed, her pulse quick, her flesh hot, her spirits low, her breathing oppressed, and in short, all the symptoms upon her of a violent and universal disorder'.[282]

Henrietta made her excuses and, to the astonishment of court gossips, withdrew to Bath until George Augustus's birthday on 30 October. There she entertained friends including political opponents of Walpole. In Bath at the same time, Princess Amelia reported to her mother each incriminating encounter. At a stroke, George Augustus's indifference to his mistress of two decades coalesced into angry dislike.

His furious silence on her return lay behind an interview, lasting an hour and a half, between wife and mistress. For every argument in favour of Henrietta leaving court for good, Caroline offered complacent rebuttals. But Henrietta's mind was made up. She was no longer the frightened adventuress who, feigning admiration for Leibniz, had cast in her lot with the Electress Sophia's grandson and his wife. Taunt by taunt she refuted Caroline's smiling bullying. Long disillusionment, her sojourn in Bath and the confidence she drew from her growing intimacy with Berkeley had convinced her, as Lord Bathurst wrote to her within the month, 'that the sun shines, even ... above one hundred miles from London; and that there are men and women walking upon two legs, just as they do about St James's, only they seem to stand steadier upon them ... A great king, who happened to be a philosopher, could find out nothing more to be desired in human life, than these four things – old wood to burn, old wine to drink, old friends to converse with, and old books to read; you may be sure of enjoying all these, and the third of them ... in a more perfect degree than *his majesty or his queen*.'[283] Caroline saved face by insisting Henrietta take a further week to reconsider. Nastily she demanded she promise 'not to read any romances in that time'.[284] George Augustus protested, 'What the devil did you mean by trying to make an old, dull, deaf, peevish beast stay and plague me when I had so good an opportunity for getting rid of her?'[285]

Henrietta departed court at the week's end, inspiring 'a great deal of discourse' among those she left behind.[286] To Caroline's lot fell 'the ennui of seeing [George Augustus] for ever in her room'.[287] On 26 June 1735, Henrietta married George Berkeley. Casting happily about for her replacement, the king's eye alighted briefly on his youngest daughters' governess, the pretty, ambitious widow Mary, Countess of Deloraine.

William Augustus's twelfth birthday in 1733 inspired Stephen Duck to verse. He endowed his sturdy subject with godlike attributes: 'warlike Strength and Courage' from Mars; 'Venus's graceful Look'; 'Hermes's Eloquence' and 'superior Sense'.[288]

In its inventory of 'princely' qualities Duck's was a portrait of an idealised George Augustus, which Caroline approved whole-heartedly. Her younger son remained her favourite. Five years had not diminished her misgivings about Frederick nor her resentment of his place in the succession; George Augustus dismissed his myopic, insincere but charming heir as a 'Wechselbalg', or changeling. Mother and eldest son shared common interests but pursued their enthusiasms separately. Like George Augustus, Caroline was unmoved by Lord Egmont's assessment of Frederick's duty 'to his parents, who do not return it in love, and seem to neglect him'.[289] A neglected Frederick sought gratification in indiscriminate dalliances and extrava-gance. In 1732 he had commissioned from William Kent a splendid royal barge complete with gilded oars; the following year he purchased Carlton House, near St James's Palace, and at some expense invited Kent to re-landscape its gardens using native and exotic trees, including specimens imported from the New World: a 'Pennsylvanian Blew Bramble', black walnut trees and flowering maples from Virginia.[290] Kent designed an Octagonal Temple; Frederick commissioned from John Michael Rysbrack busts of King Alfred and an earlier Prince of Wales, the Black Prince, whose bust Caroline would also commission. He began acquiring paintings and appointed as his library keeper Philip Mercier, the German artist of Huguenot descent who taught painting to his three eldest sisters. According to Sir Lambert Blackwell, Frederick 'lov'd the Muse: For Pope reliev'd his hours,/And with melodious magic sweetly charm'd;/And Thomson [author of *The Seasons*], Nature's painter, spread his flow'rs/With more than Titian's glowing colours warm'd'.[291] From 1733 he championed a new opera company, the Opera of the Nobility. Despite overlaps in their cultural patronage, since Caroline's first regency in the summer of 1729 neither mother nor son had acknowledged any affinity.

Hervey suggests that by 1734 Caroline no longer desired amicable relations with Frederick, while Frederick could not forgive his mother for her closeness to Hervey, his own former intimate, whom she called 'child, her pupil and her charge'.[292] In an audience with George Augustus that summer, Frederick asked that a marriage be arranged for him and that his father explain his coldness of manner towards him. George Augustus 'told him that his behaviour in general was very childish and silly, but that his particular disregard to his mother and his undutiful conduct towards her was what offended him more than anything else, and that till he behaved better there he would never find it possible to please him'.[293] Hervey's Frederick retreats from his father to Caroline's apartments, only to find that she has deliberately absented herself, 'resolving not to see her son, till she had seen the King'. Mother and son meet a day later and Caroline upbraids Frederick for allowing himself to be influenced by people 'who think of nothing but distressing the King'. She resists itemising a catalogue of sexual indiscretions on Frederick's part that included fathering a child by her maid of honour Anne Vane and an affair with Miss Vane's chambermaid, and she overlooks Frederick's promotion of the Opera of the Nobility, currently operating in direct competition with Handel's company whose chief patron was George Augustus; Hervey labelled king and queen 'both Handelists'.

On 14 August, in a letter to Caroline, Frederick restated his desire to be married: 'Although the King did not receive my request as favourably as I had reason to expect, nevertheless I was consoled a little by the promise your Majesty gave me subsequently to do all in your power to help. I hope that your Majesty will be persuaded that it is not because of a lack of confidence in your promise, and in your kindness, that I am bothering you again; but that you will pardon a little impatience in a man of 28 years, who has never yet in his life demanded anything from your Majesty and who believes that his first request was based, not only on a sound and just reason from his own point of view, but also on the advantage to your Majesties and the public ... I beg you to be not only my mother but also my friend.'[294]

His plea fell on deaf ears: Caroline proved incapable of playing the part of Frederick's friend. As at every key moment during her marriage she acted in tandem with George Augustus. Six years after Frederick's arrival in London, forgetful of their own unhappiness at George Louis's intractability, neither husband nor wife acknowledged his grounds for protest at the absence of appropriate income and spouse. From their children they demanded the same unquestioning obedience they expected of the country at large: Caroline referred to Frederick's 'just sense of his duty to his Father'.[295] She understood it as precluding opposition.

Meanwhile George Augustus employed a Hanoverian agent, von Schrader, to report to him in secret on marriageable Protestant princesses in the Empire – in Wolfenbüttel, Holstein-Glucksburg and Saxe-Gotha.[296] He met his preferred candidate, plain, inelegant, fair-haired, unlettered fifteen-year-old Augusta of Saxe-Gotha, during his visit to Hanover in 1735. The following February he offered Frederick Augusta as his bride. With

Frederick's agreement, preparations began at once for a royal wedding on 27 April. Caroline oversaw appointments to Augusta's household.

Augusta spoke neither English nor French; she brought with her from the modest country house of her widowed mother her governess and her favourite doll. Her simplicity and apparent naïvety endeared her to Caroline. The profound obeisance the ungainly princess made to Caroline and George Augustus on first meeting, prostrating herself in front of them, endeared her to both. For the wedding ceremony at St James's Palace the king wore a suit of gold brocade, Caroline 'plain yellow silk, robed and faced with pearls, diamonds and other jewels of immense value'.[297] She translated the service for Augusta and prompted her responses: as she wrote to Anne, 'I told her to look at me and I would make a sign when she ought to kneel.'[298] Afterwards, the king increased his son's allowance to £50,000, exactly half the sum he himself had enjoyed as Prince of Wales. King and queen noted the new couple's boycott of the spectacular production of Handel's *Atalanta* staged in their honour.[299]

Like Caroline before her, Augusta won popular approval for her family's Protestantism. Unlike George Augustus, credit for the success of the marriage would extend to Frederick as well as Augusta. As Lord Stormont offered, 'From his example/Shall Hymen trim his torch, domestic praise/Be countenanc'd, and virtue fairer shew.'[300]

For Caroline the wedding day ended in mirth at the tallness of Frederick's nightcap, worn over a cloth-of-silver nightshirt. She had convinced herself her son was impotent. She prayed there would be no issue of the union, even consulting Hervey about Frederick's fertility, and took heart from Augusta's rested appearance the morning after. To Hervey she made clear that nothing had altered her determination that her 'dear William' succeed his father.[301]

* * *

On Caroline's part no surprise had greeted George Augustus's statement, on his return from Hanover in 1735, that the women of the electorate were patterns of 'beauty, wit and entertainment'.[302] As she had every reason to know, her husband had recently conceived an infatuation.

Husband and wife had lately been painted from memory by portraitist Joseph Highmore, praised by contemporaries for his 'happy pencil'.[303] Of the pair of images, only that of Caroline survives. At fifty-two she has a statuesque magnificence. A loose gown of ermine-lined velvet swathes her considerable bosom; in her hair are a Roman-inspired diadem and twists of pearls. Her cheeks are rosy pink, her throat and chest as pale as the silvery grey of her hair and her eyebrows. Her eyes are bright, firm the set of her jaw. Sarah Marlborough's 'Madam Ansbach' is no longer 'a little German princess', but every inch a queen. But youth has vanished, and with it the enticements of the flesh.

It was not to be hoped that her goatish husband would refrain from looking elsewhere for those pleasures he no longer found in Caroline's bed. He 'talked bawdy' with Lady Deloraine, he admired others among Caroline's ladies, but it was a Hanoverian noblewoman of unabashed physicality who would prove more than a passing fancy.

In the best-known likeness of Amalie von Walmoden – a portrait by Peter van Hoogh engraved by de Köning – she entices the viewer with all the subtlety of a talent-show contestant. Globular breasts are scarcely contained by an ermine-trimmed shift of plunging neckline; a come-hither expression in her bright, black eyes combines challenge, seduction and a suggestion of mirth at the folly of it all. A posthumous assessment claimed it was 'impossible for any man of taste and sensibility' not to love her.[304] Generous with her favours, Madame von Walmoden succumbed to several. In her tendency to weight gain, she resembled Caroline. The resemblance extended to strength of will and an eye to her own best interests. From Hanover in the summer of 1735, in a torrent of letters of forensic detail, George Augustus shared with Caroline the progress of his nascent affair with this 'young married woman of the first fashion'.[305] He praised Amalie's face while denying her beauty or wit. 'Had the Queen been a painter,' Hervey commented, 'she might have drawn her rival's picture at six hundred miles distance.'[306] To his wife of three decades, his thraldom was clear.

On his return in the autumn, Caroline greeted George Augustus effusively. She affected good humour, good health, good spirits.[307] He returned none of her careful unconcern, his behaviour towards her instead sharp and impatient. As he recounted afresh stories of his new mistress his irritation lifted, and he hung on the walls of Caroline's dressing room recent pictures of court life in Hanover. To Lord Hervey 'he was often so gracious ... when he was with their Majesties in this dressing room for an hour or two in the evening, to take a candle in his own royal hand, and tell him the stories of these pictures, running through the names and characters of all the persons represented in them, and what they had said and done'.[308] An increasingly disgruntled Caroline oscillated between 'lassitude ... [and] mirth', but the king appeared unaware of her reactions.

To courtiers less privileged than Hervey – as well as to Caroline – George Augustus offered unremitting boorishness. Forgotten was the illusion of anglophilia once cultivated at George Louis's expense. Now no English cook, confectioner, actor, coachman or jockey knew his business, 'nor were there any English horses fit to be ridden', or men or women capable of conversation, style, wit, or even 'any diversions in England, public or private'.[309] Only Hanover, rosy through the prism of his randiness, met with his approval. There 'plenty reigned, magnificence resided, arts flourished, diversions abounded, riches flowed, and everything was in the utmost perfection that contributes to make a prince great or a people blessed'.[310] For Caroline, his *volte face* represented a wholesale rejection of her life's work. George Augustus's attitude made it clear that, for the moment, he included her in his comprehensive disparagement.

Hervey believed the king's bullying overwhelmed Caroline in the winter of 1735. He criticised her eating habits, her habit of visiting the houses of her friends, her choice of paintings for the royal apartments. Tactlessly but accurately, Walpole traced the source of George Augustus's testiness, indicating to Caroline the demise of her physical allure. He suggested she find a home-grown replacement for Henrietta Howard to divert the king's attention from Madame von Walmoden: 'If the King would have somebody else, it would be better to have that somebody chosen by her than by him.'[311] Walpole's own choice fell on Camilla, Countess of Tankerville, foolish but beautiful wife of one of Frederick's gentlemen of the bedchamber.[312] Caroline ignored his advice. A description of her tending George Augustus at his bedside for a week in February in 'the most careful and affectionate manner' by Viscountess Irwin, afterwards lady of the bedchamber to Caroline's daughter-in-law, suggests self-control, patience and stamina alongside her customary determination that appearances be maintained.[313]

To Hanover, and the open arms of Amalie von Walmoden, the king returned soon after Frederick's marriage. Caroline decamped to Kensington, for the fourth time her husband's regent, Frederick again overlooked. A waggish notice was affixed to the gates of St James's Palace: 'Lost or strayed out of this house, a man who has left a wife and six children on the parish; whoever will give any tidings of him to the churchwardens of St James's Parish, so as he may be got again, shall receive four shillings and sixpence reward. NB – This reward will not be increased, nobody judging him to be worth a Crown.'[314] Flippancy could not disguise a darkening popular mood.

George Augustus's thoughts, however, were of the newborn son Amalie assured him was his own. Again his letters to Caroline enlarged on his newfound happiness. Not content with itemising Amalie's charms, the curmudgeonly swain had determined to bring her back to London. Caroline jibbed at such overwhelming proof of her loss of sexual sway. Uxorious even in his faithlessness, George Augustus besieged her with letters that flattered as they wounded. 'You know my weaknesses,' he wrote, 'there is nothing hidden from you in my heart, and please God that you will be able to correct my faults as easily as you can see into my soul. Please God that I could imitate you as well as I admire you and that I could learn from you all the virtues that you teach me to see, feel & love.'[315] On Caroline's lips the taste of these pieties was ashes, for all she claimed that 'she minded [George Augustus's dalliances] no more than his going to the close stool'.[316]

To Caroline's lot fell problems of government beyond her understanding. Three years earlier she had railed at the part played by popular pressure in the collapse of the Excise Bill. In the summer of 1736 she showed herself similarly at odds with the public mood. The regency government granted a six-week reprieve to Captain John Porteous, commander of the Edinburgh City Guard, after he was found guilty of murder following a riot in the Scottish capital in April. Its intervention, sanctioned by Caroline, provoked public resentment of such magnitude that a mob of several thousand people took the law into their own hands, and on 7 September dragged Porteous from his prison cell and killed him. Caroline responded to this insurrection with affrontedness, Walpole with shock; both intended harsh reprisals. 'Sooner than submit to such another insult I will turn Scotland into a hunting-field,' a bellicose Caroline told the Duke of Argyll.[317] Further discussion with the Scottish nobleman tempered her indignation.

It was an unhappy autumn nevertheless. With difficulty Walpole persuaded Caroline of the need to write to George

Augustus suggesting he bring Madame von Walmoden back
with him to court. Charlotte Clayton opposed the idea, seconded
by Lady Pomfret. Caroline gave in. At St James's Palace she
emptied rooms of books to make space for apartments for her
latest rival; the rooms in question adjoined Henrietta's old apartment.[318] The king's thanks were heartfelt, but Amalie would
remain in Hanover during Caroline's lifetime, sensibly wary of
face-to-face confrontation with her lover's formidable spouse.

The effort of reorganising her books nudged Caroline towards
advancing plans for the new library that the *Daily Journal* had
announced as long ago as the summer of 1727. As well as
accommodating three thousand volumes, it would provide a
setting for the 'Busto's in Marble of all the Kings of England
from William the Conqueror' that she had lately commissioned
from Rysbrack, initially as bookcase ornaments for the library at
Merlin's Cave.[319]

In George Augustus's continuing absence, Caroline remained
at Kensington Palace. St James's stood empty, inviting criticism
of the king's absenteeism. In some quarters this rebounded on
Caroline in the form of praise of her long suffering. Up to a
point sympathy for Caroline helped restore her public standing
from its nadir of the excise crisis, though an appearance at the
opera was greeted by hisses in place of cheering, and her support
of the Gin Act in September proved predictably unpopular. For
the first time since his accession George Augustus missed celebrations of his birthday.

In December weather thwarted George Augustus's journey
home: his ship was forced to return to port. Rumours of the ship
having been wrecked in ferocious storms caused panic for
Caroline and Walpole. Frederick's reaction, by contrast, Caroline
categorised as one of sang-froid, and wrote as much to George
Augustus. For her own part, her emotions were a compound of
love and fear for the future. Walpole claimed that on his accession Frederick 'would tear the flesh off [her] bones with hot

irons'; he dreaded her 'falling into the hands of a son who hates her'.[320] He feared for himself too, and inevitable loss of office. But George Augustus survived the storm's anger. Relief inspired magnanimity and he wrote a letter to Caroline thirty pages long, full of loving kindness and impatient longing. He called her his 'perfect Venus', and she preened herself to the extent of show-ing his letter to Walpole.[321] After a five-week enforced delay on the Dutch coast, George Augustus arrived at St James's on 15 January 1737. With chameleon unpredictability he greeted Caroline delightedly, and quickly succumbed to excruciating piles.

George Augustus's pleasure in being reunited with the wife he had harried, humiliated and abandoned for eight months did not extend to his eldest son. In January 1734 he had cancelled Frederick's birthday ball, citing as excuse Caroline's gout. The truth, Lord Egmont recalled, lay in a 'misunderstanding' between father and son that would not be resolved in Caroline's lifetime.

Money proved the catalyst. Before his departure for Hanover, George Augustus had omitted to make any provision for Augusta. For some time Frederick's spending had significantly exceeded his income. Pressed by creditors, he gave his backing to an opposition motion to lobby Parliament for the £100,000 allowance he considered his right. Walpole offered an out-of-house settlement: an additional annual payment to Augusta of £50,000. The message to the prince from the cabinet council on 21 February offered George Augustus's 'sudden going abroad' after the royal wedding and 'his late indisposition' as reasons 'retard[ing] the execution of [his] gracious intentions, from which short delay His Majesty did not apprehend any incon-veniences could arise'.[322] Politely Frederick indicated that the matter was no longer in his hands. The motion was defeated in both houses of Parliament, but not before public attention had focused firmly on divisions within the royal family that rekindled memories of 1717, to the benefit of neither parents nor son. For this sole reason George Augustus resisted banishing Frederick. Caroline contented herself with refusing to speak to him.

Frederick's decision to politicise personal grievances points to the extent of the breakdown between the two households. Caroline habitually resented disrespectful behaviour towards George Augustus. In Frederick's case, her emotions were highly wrought but unorthodox. She described her son as 'the most hardened of all liars'; she considered him weak, disputatious, faithless.[323] Famously, she caught sight of Frederick from her dressing-room window and exclaimed to Lord Hervey, 'Look, there he goes, that wretch! – that villain! – I wish the ground would open this moment and sink the monster to the lowest hole in hell.'[324] These were not conventional motherly responses, and her intimacy with Hervey did nothing to mitigate Caroline's furious loathing. His own failed, possibly homosexual relationship with Frederick made Hervey an unreliable sounding block.

Caroline's feelings went further. In clinging to her preference for William Augustus as George Augustus's heir, she was determined her elder son would prove infertile. With Hervey and in some detail she considered the possibility of Frederick substituting another man in his own place in Augusta's bed in order to guarantee his wife's conception. This unsavoury speculation became an *idée fixe*. In its wake Caroline entertained similarly improbable feats of gynaecological legerdemain. Mistrusting likely shenanigans, she resolved to be present at any lying-in of her daughter-in-law's. 'At her labour I positively will be, let her lie in where she will; for she cannot be brought to bed as quick as one can blow one's nose and I will be sure it is her child.'[325]

Evidently Frederick understood the direction of her thoughts. He was equally determined Augusta would give birth without his mother's presence. For six months after she conceived, assisted by the bulkiness of court fashions, husband and wife concealed her pregnancy. Augusta's waters broke at Hampton Court, in the evening of 31 July 1737, just twenty-six days after Frederick had written to his parents, 'Dr Hollings and Mrs Cannon have just told me that there is no longer any doubt of the Princess being with child.'[326] 'With an obstinacy equal to his folly, and a folly equal to his barbarity', Frederick insisted on an immediate departure for London, despite the princess's protests and warnings of the dangers to which he exposed her.

The royal coach was crowded. Augusta's mistress of the robes, two of her dressers, Frederick's equerry Bloodworth 'and two or three more' accompanied the flitting couple. With difficulty they prevented Augusta giving birth en route. They arrived at St James's Palace at ten o'clock, a sorry sight, Augusta howling with pain. Her clothes were stinking and sticky with 'filthy inundations', 'notwithstanding all the handkerchiefs that had been thrust one after another up Her Royal Highness's petticoats in the coach'.[327] In the dark, shuttered palace were neither clean sheets nor hot water. Lying on a tablecloth, Augusta was delivered of 'a little rat of a girl, about the bigness of a good large toothpick case'.[328] The Archbishop of Canterbury arrived fifteen minutes too late to witness her birth.

Informed of Frederick's perfidy by night messenger, Caroline saw the child in the early hours of the morning. She told Caroline and Amelia, the Duke of Grafton and Lord Hervey, 'if, instead of this poor, little, ugly she-mouse, there had been a brave, large, fat, jolly boy, I should not have been cured of my suspicions; nay, I believe ... that I should have been so confirmed in that opinion, that I should have gone about his [Frederick's] house like a madwoman, played the devil, and insisted on knowing what chairman's brat he had bought'.[329] Instead she treated Augusta with tepid kindness and cautioned Frederick against appearing too soon in front of his father. While George Augustus raged, she made a number of further visits to her first granddaughter over the coming days. She identified her motives cynically as *'une bonne grimace pour le publique'* (a good show for the public).

Caroline did not oppose George Augustus's decision in September to expel Frederick and Augusta from the royal palaces, as they themselves had once been expelled. To Augusta she wrote, 'I hope Time & due consideration will bring my Son to a just sense of his duty to his Father; which will be the only means of procuring that happy change, which you cannot more sincerely wish than I do.'[330] As it happened, it was her final act of loyalty to the husband who, in public, she had acknowledged as her lodestar for more than three decades.

In several accounts of her death, Caroline achieved the Protestant apotheosis forecast for her from the moment British writers learned of her rejection of the future Charles VI. These versions of the royal deathbed conjure a seamless transition from palace to afterlife. 'She never ... showed the least fear of the pain she endured, or of the closing scene,' wrote Lady Hertford, describing an unlikely coincidence of agony and tranquillity. Poet Mary Jones pictured the ailing Caroline magnified in her virtues: 'those noble Sentiments, which always warm'd her Breast ... exert[ed] themselves with greater vigour, the nearer they were being extinguished'.[331] A monody by Joseph Smith imagined Caroline in Heaven, in the poet's estimate her reward for earthly piety: 'Oft have I seen her, with submissive ear,/The oracles of God unfolded hear./Oft have I seen her, with seraphic love,/Her prayers preferring to the throne above:/ Where now the praises to the King of Kings,/Triumphant, with angelic notes, she sings.'[332] Lady Hertford made much of the attendance at Caroline's bedside of the Archbishop of Canterbury, John Potter. He 'told me he never saw a behaviour equally glorious and Christian to hers, and that all she said to him deserved to be printed'.[333] She claimed Caroline's earthly thoughts were of George Augustus, whose feelings she spared by sending away the candles that illuminated her final moments.

The truth was less orderly than the countess's smooth narrative or Smith's undeviating couplets. For twelve days Caroline faced the imminence of death, unable any longer to escape the consequences of the umbilical hernia she had concealed for so long. Hervey's eyewitness account denies elegance. Princess Caroline, plagued by nosebleeds and rheumatism, attends her mother ineptly. A conniving Frederick sends messages, instructs his courtiers to infiltrate the forbidden palace. Caroline herself is testy and fractious at key moments; her hatred of Frederick shows no abatement. Predictable in George Augustus's behaviour is every impulse from tenderness to boasting. Sporadically the sickroom stinks. Caroline is perversely angry at discovery of the cause of her affliction. The royal doctors are incompetent, the patent medicines Hervey foists upon his mistress useless quackery that help her not at all. Only Caroline's hard-won eleventh-hour dignity redeems his lengthy record.

The problem, which manifested itself as 'racking pains … in her belly', was caused by a section of Caroline's small intestine that had begun to poke through her ruptured stomach wall – predictably, given her obesity. By working the protuberance back where it came from, disaster might have been averted. Instead Dr John Ranby and an octogenarian assistant called Dr Bussier cut it away. In removing a section of Caroline's bowels in this way, they eliminated the possibility of her recovery.

Caroline's suffering began in the morning of Wednesday, 9 November. She had visited the library that Kent had completed for her only a month earlier, its long views out across St James's Park. By the early hours of Sunday morning, the wound had begun to fester. For another week Caroline loitered somewhere between life and death, offering last words to her unmarried daughters and William Augustus, whom she loved so much more than his older brother. She had made her will already, a straightforward document that bequeathed everything to her husband. To him she entrusted the ruby ring first given her at her coronation. From her sickbed she spoke to him with loving humility; she begged him, as she had done before, to marry again once she was dead. He wept and stammered over his reply and told her, with distinctive crass banality, that he would only have mistresses. And her sense of humour was restored, and she reminded him, as she knew so well, that this was scarcely an impediment to marriage.

Some days the surgeons cut away at the wound they ought never to have made. As the second week of Caroline's ordeal limped blackly onwards, her stomach erupted. 'In the afternoon one of the guts burst in such a manner that all her excrement came out of a wound in her belly,' drenching the bedclothes, spilling from the bed on to the floor.[334] Despite unimaginable pain, Caroline neither complained nor cried. Only once did she request opium for pain relief.

She died on 20 November 'at 11 o'clock this Night ... of a Mortification of ye Bowels ... aged 54 Years, 8 Months, and 20 Days', according to the *Gentleman's Magazine*. In some accounts George Augustus held her hand for her final moments, in others Amelia read aloud from a prayerbook. Dorothy, Countess of Burlington sketched the deathbed scene, complete with one of the large lace headdresses Caroline had so often worn, and at some expense her body was embalmed. For her funeral at Westminster Abbey, as at her coronation, Handel composed a new anthem, 'The Ways of Zion do Mourn', 'as good a piece as ever he made'.[335] More simply, George Augustus told courtiers, 'I never yet saw the woman worthy to buckle her shoe.'

The *London Gazette* published instructions for mourning: 'black bombazines, plain Cambrick Linnen, Crape Hoods, Shamoy Shoes and Gloves, and crape Fans' for women, for men 'black cloth without Buttons on the Sleeves or Pockets, plain Cambrick Cravats and Weepers, Shamoy shoes and gloves,

Crape Hatbands and black Sword and Bucklers'.[336] Carriages were also to be black. Persiflage posted on the Royal Exchange – 'Oh death, where is thy sting?/To take the Queen and leave the King?' – points to mourning for Caroline among all classes.

True to his word, within a year George Augustus had installed Amalie von Walmoden at St James's Palace. She was naturalised as a British citizen in February 1738 and created Countess of Yarmouth the following month. She survived George Augustus by a year, dying of breast cancer in 1761. Nothing suggests that George Augustus loved her, despite the unhappiness she had caused Caroline.

To his sister Sophia Dorothea he had written on 30 November that Caroline's memory would never be effaced; he described her as a princess of great and rare virtues.[337] In the aftermath of her death George Augustus paid her servants and the pensions she had granted; he continued to employ a librarian for Kent's new library; he maintained her gardens at Richmond, including the upkeep of the Hermitage and Merlin's Cave. Even twenty years after her death – a foreshadowing of later royal approaches to mourning – he 'ha[d] never suffered the Queen's room to be touched since She died'.[338]

George Augustus was mistaken about Caroline's memory, which the passage of time has indeed erased. Accurately he estimated her rare virtues.

Afterword

Oxford High Street is seldom quiet in daylight hours. Open-topped tourist buses and coaches to and from London plough its broad stretch. In front of the screen wall of The Queen's College, designed by Nicholas Hawksmoor in 1709, a sign for a bus stop has been fixed. Like the bicycles that lean against the foot of the wall in a ribbon of broken teeth, it stands alongside the grandeur of Hawksmoor's golden classicism as a reminder of human smallness.

Above the college entrance, high above the bus stop and the hurly burly of the thoroughfare, is a statue of Caroline of Ansbach for which sculptor Henry Cheere, a competitor of Rysbrack's, received payment from the college of £130.5s. It stands beneath a cupola, a generic image of classicised womanhood, and Caroline is unrecognisable from her portraits, draped in the long woollen garment Romans knew as a *stola*, a symbol in Augustus's empire of female rectitude.

Caroline is also commemorated at Queen's by an inscription: 'Carolina Regina, Nov. 12, 1733'. It marks the laying of the foundation stone of the screen wall visible from the high street, after Caroline's payment at the beginning of the month of the first instalment of a donation to the college of £1,000. Later she promised another £1,000, but died before payment could be made. She had responded to a petition from the college provost, Dr Joseph Smith. Smith had circulated two hundred copies of *The Present State of the New Buildings of Queen's College in Oxford*, as part of an appeal to complete the replacement of medieval buildings begun in 1352, after Edward III granted a charter for the college to his wife's chaplain, Robert of Englesfield. Like previous consorts, including Edward's own wife Philippa, Caroline was the college's royal patroness.

Few of those who travel along Oxford High Street are aware of the figure of Caroline, part-shielded by her splendid cupola. Nor would they recognise her name, or the story of this orphan princess who lacked formal education. But I like to think she would take pleasure that one of her few surviving images stands in the heart of this great university city. That she is visible only to those who raise their eyes heavenwards, craning their necks, risking being dazzled by the sun, would surely redouble her enjoyment.

Acknowledgements

Documents from the Royal Archives are quoted by kind permission of Her Majesty Queen Elizabeth II. I am grateful to Her Majesty for access to the Royal Archives and to the Registrar of the Royal Archives Allison Derrett and her staff for assistance during and after my visits.

I acknowledge with great gratitude the contributions of the following to the research and writing of this book: Dr Wolfgang F. Reddig, Leiter des Margrafensmuseums und Stadtarchivs, Ansbach; Jonathan Marsden, Director the Royal Collection Trust and Surveyor of the Queen's Works of Art; Jane Roberts; Deirdre Murphy, Historic Royal Palaces; Clarissa Campbell Orr; Dr Emrys Jones, King's College London; Rhys Kiminski-Jones for help with the history of the Society of Antient Britons; Dr Wolf Burchard; Dr Karin Shrader; Dr Mark Chambers, University of Durham; Timothy Morgan-Owen; Dr Lyn Williams, Honorary Secretary, The Honourable Society of Cymmrodorion; Patricia Plagemann, Landesarchiv – Standort Hannover; Dr Susan Frane, Department of Culture and Education, Embassy of the Federal Republic of Germany; Selina Schoelles for her reading at Shropshire Archives; Aidan Haley, The Devonshire Collection, Chatsworth; Mrs Clare Brown, archivist, Lambeth Palace

Library; Christopher Hunwick, archivist, Northumberland Estates.

I am grateful indeed for the contributions of my editor Arabella Pike, Robert Lacey and Jordan Mulligan at William Collins and, as always, my exceptional agent, Georgina Capel.

And heartfelt thanks, as ever, are due to my parents and, above all, my miraculous wife, Gráinne, rightly this book's dedicatee. As George Augustus told Caroline, 'The peace of my life depends upon ... the conviction of your continued affection for me.'

Matthew Dennison
Montgomeryshire
Feast of St Cuthbert, 2017

Notes

Introduction

1. Worsley, Lucy, *Courtiers: The Secret History of Kensington Palace* (Faber & Faber, London, 2010), p.102
2. Sedgwick, Romney, ed., *Some materials towards memoirs of the reign of George II*, by John, Lord Hervey, 3 vols (London, 1931), Vol. 1, p.69
3. See Royal Collection, RCIN 31317, Caroline, Consort of George II, by John Michael Rysbrack, c. 1739
4. Rosenthal, Norman, ed., *The Misfortunate Margravine: The Early Memoirs of Wilhelmina, Margravine of Bayreuth* (Macmillan, London, 1970), p.160
5. See Voltaire, François-Marie Arouet, *Letters on the English* (London, 1733), Letter XI
6. Rosenthal, op. cit., p.84; Thomson, Mrs, ed., *Memoirs of Viscountess Sundon* (Henry Colburn, London, 1847), Vol. 2, p.52
7. See Jones, Huw, ed., *Diddanwch Teuluaidd* (London, 1763), pp.261–5
8. Prescott, Sarah, *Eighteenth-Century Writing from Wales: Bards and Britons* (University of Wales Press, Cardiff, 2008), pp.42–3
9. Sophie Charlotte of Prussia to Hans Caspar von Bothmer, 9 September 1704, see Doebner, Richard, ed., *Briefe der Königin Sophie Charlotte von Preussen und der Kurfürstin Sophie von Hannover an hannoversche Diplomaten* (G. Hirzel, Leipzig, 1905), p.57
10. Sedgwick, op. cit. (Hervey), Vol. 1, p.179
11. *The Spectator*, 11 January 1902
12. West, Richard, *A Monody on the Death of Queen Caroline*, in *A Collection of Poems in Six Volumes by Several Hands*, ed. Robert Dodsley (London, 1765), Vol. 2, pp.331–7
13. Harris, Frances, *A Passion for Government: The Life of Sarah, Duchess of Marlborough* (Oxford University Press, Oxford, 1991), p.204
14. See Stephen Duck, 'Royal Benevolence', 2 October 1730 (W. Harris, London, 1730)

15. Clarke, Alured, *An Essay towards the Character of Her late Majesty Caroline, Queen-Consort of Great Britain* (London, 1738), p.3

16. Thomson, Mrs, ed., op. cit. (*Memoirs of Viscountess Sundon*), Vol. 1, p.386

17. Lady Mary Wortley Montagu to Henrietta Louisa, Countess of Pomfret, 26 July 1738, see Halsband, Robert, ed., *The Complete Letters of Lady Mary Wortley Montagu*, 3 vols (Oxford University Press, Oxford, 1965), Vol. 2, p.119

18. See Black, Jeremy, *George II* (University of Exeter Press, Exeter, 2007); Thompson, Andrew C., *George II* (Yale University Press, New Haven & London, 2011)

19. Rosenthal, op. cit., p.84

20. Clarke, Alured, op. cit., pp.44–5

Prologue

1. Smollett, Tobias, *Humphrey Clinker*, p.117

2. Fielding, Sarah, *The Adventures of David Simple*, p.77

3. Swift, Jonathan, 'A Description of a City Shower'

4. Anonymous, 'An Excellent New Ballad', Bodleian Library broadsheet ballads collection, MS. Rawl. poet. 207 (136, 137)

5. Walpole, Horace, *Reminiscences, written in 1788, for the amusement of Miss Mary and Miss Agnes B***y* (Oxford, 1924), p.60; see Borman, Tracy, *King's Mistress, Queen's Servant: The Life and Times of Henrietta Howard* (Pimlico paperback, London, 2008), p.99; Sedgwick, op. cit. (Hervey), Vol. 1, p.41

6. See Black, Jeremy, *A Subject for Taste: Culture in Eighteenth-Century*

England (Hambledon & London, London, 2005), p.26

7. 'The Happy Marriage and The Unhappy Marriage', print, published by John King, c. 1690, see British Museum, collection number 1906,0823.4

8. Anonymous, 'An Elegy upon the Young Prince', Bodleian Library broadsheet ballads collection, MS. Rawl. poet. 207 (151–153)

9. Anonymous, 'An Excellent New Ballad', Bodleian Library broadsheet ballads collection, MS. Rawl. poet. 207 (136, 137)

10. Lord Hervey to Henry Fox, 1 September 1734, see Ilchester, Earl of, ed., *Lord Hervey and his Friends* (John Murray, London, 1950), p.205

11. White, Jerry, *London in the Eighteenth Century: A Great and Monstrous Thing* (Vintage, London, 2012), p.10

12. Worsley, op. cit., p.358, note 42

13. Sheppard, Edgar, *Memorial of St James's Palace* (Longmans, Green & Co., London, 1894), p.48

14. Elisabeth Charlotte, Duchess of Orléans, to Raugravine Luise von Degenfeld, 23 December 1717, see Kroll, Maria, *Letters from Liselotte* (McCall Publishing, New York, 1971), p.191

15. Thomson, Mrs, ed., op. cit. (*Memoirs of Viscountess Sundon*), p.29

16. Quennell, Peter, *Caroline of England* (Collins, London, 1939), p.72

17. Worsley, op. cit., pp.38–9

18. See Ilchester, Earl of, ed., op. cit., p.ix

19. Anonymous, 'An Elegy upon the Young Prince', Bodleian Library broadsheet ballads collection, MS. Rawl. poet. 207 (151–153)

20. Melville, Lewis, *Maids of Honour* (Hutchinson & Co., London, 1927), p.26

21. George Augustus, Prince of Wales to George I, undated, Royal Archives RA GEO/MAIN/54046

22. Elisabeth Charlotte, Duchess of Orléans, to Raugravine Luise von Degenfeld, 23 December 1717, see Kroll, op. cit., p.191

23. Arkell, R.L., *Caroline of Ansbach: George the Second's Queen* (Oxford University Press, Oxford, 1939), p.103

PART ONE: GERMANY
Chapter I: Princess of Ansbach

1. See British Museum, Wenceslaus Hollar, Ansbach, from the Town Atlases, etching c. 1630s, collection number 1852,0612.136

2. See British Museum: Cooper, collection number 1888,0515.51; Bowles, collection number 1902,1011.1274

3. For information about Ansbach's ruling family and court life, I am grateful to Dr Wolfgang F. Reddig, Leiter des Margrafensmuseums und Stadtarchivs, Ansbach

4. See Yorke-Long, Alan, George II and Handel, *History Today*, 10 October 1951

5. Sharp, Tony, *Pleasures and Ambition: The Life, Loves and Wars of Augustus the Strong* (I.B. Tauris, London, 2001), p.22

6. Blesendorff, see Royal Collection, RCIN607275; Wissing, see National Portrait Gallery, NPG/D20409

7. Gufer, see Royal Collection, RCIN607270 and RCIN607271&2

8. Worsley, op. cit., p.355, note 7

9. Hatton, Ragnhild, *George I* (Thames & Hudson, London, 1978), p.15

10. Clarke, Alured, op. cit., p.5

11. Sharp, op. cit., p.22

12. Adamson, John, *The Princely Courts of Europe 1500–1750* (Weidenfeld & Nicolson, London, 1999), p.190

13. Elisabeth Charlotte, Duchess of Orléans, to Raugravine Luise von Degenfeld, 27 August 1719, see Kroll, op. cit., p.214

14. 'like a cat', RA GEO/ADD/28/52, Caroline to Charlotte Clayton, 1 March 1719; 'Lady Bomfrit', RA GEO/ADD/28/61, Caroline to Charlotte Clayton, 18 October 1725; 'Claiton' and 'Klethen' also occur in letters from Caroline to Charlotte Clayton, RA GEO/ADD/28/74 and RA GEO/ADD/28/76 respectively

15. George Smalridge, Bishop of Bristol; quoted by Leibniz in a letter to Caroline, Princess of Wales, 4 March 1715, G.W. Leibniz Bibliothek, Hanover, shelfmark LH 4, 4, 1 Bl.7–8

16. Marschner, Joanna, *Queen Caroline: Cultural Politics at the Early Eighteenth-Century Court* (Yale University Press, New Haven & London, 2014), pp.3–4

17. Sharp, op. cit., p.22

18. See National Archives, SP105/85/44, elegy by George Stepney, dedicated to the Electress of Saxony, 1694, and SP105/82/48, James Vernon to George Stepney, June 1692

19. Sharp, op. cit., p.22

20. Ibid., p.23

21. Ibid., p.21

22. See National Archives, SP 105/58/91v, George Stepney to William Blathwayt, 28 March 1693

23. Marschner, op. cit., p.3

24. See National Archives, SP105/60/104v, George Stepney to William Blathwayt, 26 September 1693

25. Sharp, op. cit., p.22

26. See Rare Book and Manuscript Library, University of Pennsylvania, Ms. Codex 1221, doc 2

27. Sharp, op. cit., p.24

28. See Massie, Robert, *Peter the Great: His Life and World* (Head of Zeus, London, 2012); Marschner, op. cit., p.155

29. See National Archives, SP105/60/43v, George Stepney to John Trenchard, 31 October 1693

30. See National Archives, SP105/60/100, Philip Plantamour to Leibniz, 29 December 1693

31. Sharp, op. cit., p.49

32. See National Archives, SP105/60/173, George Stepney to James Cresset, January 1694

33. See National Archives, SP105/54/68, George Stepney to William Blathwayt, August 1694

34. See Rare Book and Manuscript Library, University of Pennsylvania, Ms. Codex 1221, doc 1

35. See Rare Book and Manuscript Library, University of Pennsylvania, Ms. Codex 1221, doc 6

36. See National Archives, SP105/58/91v, George Stepney to William Blathwayt, 28 March 1693

37. See National Archives, SP105/60/97v, George Stepney to William Blathwayt and James Vernon, 8 January 1694

38. Sharp, op. cit., pp.55–6

39. See National Archives, SP105/84/100, Sir William

Dutton Colt to George Stepney, 23 January 1693

40. Sharp, op. cit., p.73

41. See National Archives, SP105/60/247/2, George Stepney to Charles Talbot, Duke of Shrewsbury, undated 1694

42. See National Archives, SP105/60/100v, George Stepney to 'Mr Polier' [unidentified], 8 January 1694

43. Ibid.

44. See National Archives, SP105/60/136v, George Stepney to Caspar Florentin Consbruch, April 1694

45. See National Archives, SP105/85/38/2, Frederick Augustus of Saxony to William III, 28 April 1694

46. See Rare Book and Manuscript Library, University of Pennsylvania, Ms. Codex 1221, doc 8

47. See National Archives, SP105/85/37/1 and SP105/85/45/1, George Stepney papers, undated 1694

48. See National Archives, SP105/85/44, elegy by George Stepney, dedicated to the Electress of Saxony, 1694

49. See National Archives, SP105/54/68 ('revels and dances') and SP105/54/75v ('frolicks and debauches'), George Stepney to William Blathwayt, August 1694

50. See Staatsarchiv Preussischer Kulturbesitz, I. HA GR, Rep.41, Nr.1065

51. See National Archives, SP105/54/68, George Stepney to William Blathwayt, 24 August 1694

52. Sharp, op. cit., p.114

53. Ibid., p.278

54. Arkell, op. cit., (*Caroline of Ansbach*), p.7; note, p.307

55. Elisabeth Charlotte, Duchess of Orléans, to Raugravine Amalie Elisabeth von Degenfeld, 29 July 1706, see Kroll, op. cit., p.124; Adamson, op. cit., p.220

56. Zedler, Beatrice H., The Three Princesses, *Hypatia*, Vol. 4, no 1 (spring 1989), p.53

57. Wilkins, W.H., *Caroline the Illustrious*, 2 vols (Longmans, Green & Co., London, 1901), Vol. 1, p.16

58. Look, Brandon C., ed., *Bloomsbury Companion to Leibniz* (Bloomsbury, London, 2014), p.11

59. Brown, Michael, *A Political Biography of John Toland* (Routledge, London, 2016), p.73

60. Arkell, op. cit., p.64

61. See Scharmann, Rudolf G., *Charlottenburg Palace: Royal Prussia in Berlin* (Prestel, Munich, 2007), p.10

62. See ibid., p.4

63. Caroline to Leibniz, 28 December 1704, see Wilkins, op. cit., Vol. 1, p.31

64. Marschner, op. cit., p25; Kroll, Maria, *Sophie, Electress of Hanover: A Personal Portrait* (Victor Gollancz, London, 1973), p.207

65. Theatricals, see, Doebner, Richard, ed., op. cit., p.32, Sophie Charlotte to Hans Caspar von Bothmer, 19 June 1703

66. Elisabeth Charlotte, Duchess of Orléans, to Sophie of Hanover, 24 July 1699, Kroll, op. cit., p.88

67. See National Archives, SP90/1/257, Philip Plantamour to Sir Charles Hedges, 30 September 1702

68. Brown, Michael, op. cit., p.74

69. See National Archives, SP90/1/37, George Stepney to James Vernon, 2 August 1698

70. Roinila, Markku, Leibniz and the Amour Pur Controversy, *Journal of Early Modern Studies*, Vol. 2 (fall 2013), p.46; Zedler, op. cit., p.57; Brown, Gregory, Leibniz's Endgame and the Ladies of the Courts, *Journal of the History of Ideas*, Vol. 65, no 1 (2004), p.80

71. Brown, Michael, op. cit., p.79

72. Kroll, op. cit. (*Sophie*), p.191; Look, ed., op. cit., p.11

73. Ibid., p.11

74. See Thornton, Peter, *Authentic Decor: The Domestic Interior 1620–1920* (Weidenfeld & Nicolson paperback, London, 1993), p.68

75. Jay, Emma, Queen Caroline's Library and its European Contents, *Book History*, Vol. 9 (2006), p.33

76. Marschner, op. cit, p.93

77. Adamson, op. cit., p.223

78. Walpole, Horace, *Memoirs of the Last Ten Years of the Reign of George II* (London, 1822), pp.158–9

79. See Smith, Hannah, *Georgian Monarchy: Politics and Culture, 1714–1760* (Cambridge University Press, Cambridge, 2006), p.45

80. Adamson, op. cit. p.219

81. Smith, op. cit., p.87; Brown, op. cit., p.63

82. Elisabeth Charlotte, Duchess of Orléans, to Sophie of Hanover, 30 July 1705, Kroll, op. cit., p.120

83. See National Archives, SP105/85/58/2, Gottfried Wilhelm Leibniz to Aurora von Königsmark, undated 1695

84. Kemble, John Mitchell, ed., *State papers and correspondence illustrative of the social and political*

state of Europe from the revolution to the accession of the House of Hanover (J.W. Parker, London, 1857), p.322

85. Arkell, op. cit., p.8
86. Ibid., p.10; Somerset, Anne, Queen Anne: The Politics of Passion (HarperPress, London, 2012), p.166
87. Somerset, op. cit., p.263
88. Leibniz, see Wilkins, op. cit, Vol. 1, p.27
89. Arkell, op. cit, p.10
90. Sophie Charlotte to Hans Caspar von Bothmer, 1 October 1703, see Doebner, Richard, ed., op. cit., p.37
91. See National Archives, SP89/18/42, Paul Methuen to Sir Charles Hedges, 12 March 1704
92. Gerhard Wolter Molanus, Abbé of Loccum, to Leibniz, 4 June 1700, in Strickland, Lloyd, The Philosophy of Sophie, Electress of Hanover, Hypatia, Vol. 24 no 2 (spring 2009), p.195
93. Wilkins, op. cit., Vol. 1, p.34
94. Arkell, op. cit., p.11
95. Ibid., p.12
96. Ibid.
97. Ibid.
98. See National Archives, SP105/85/42v, Frederick III of Brandenburg to Thomas Ernest von Danckelmann, 6 December 1692
99. Arkell, op. cit., pp.11–12
100. Ibid., p.13 and p.307, note
101. Ibid., p.13
102. Ibid., pp.29–30
103. Wilkins, op. cit., Vol. 1, p.31
104. Ibid., p.27
105. Arkell, op. cit., p.29
106. Brown, Gregory, op. cit., p.83
107. Arkell, op. cit., p.29
108. Sophie Charlotte to Hans Caspar von Bothmer, 1 November 1704,

see Doebner, Richard, ed., op. cit., p.59

109. A Character of her Highness the Princess ***, attempted by Richard Hollings, MD, in Private Correspondence of Sarah, Duchess of Marlborough, 2 vols (Henry Colburn, London, 1838), Vol. 2, p.207
110. See National Archives, SP105/60/9/2, George Stepney to James Vernon, 12 August 1693
111. Sophie Charlotte of Prussia to Hans Caspar von Bothmer, 21 June and 11 October 1704, see Doebner, Richard, ed., op. cit., p.50 and p.57
112. Ibid., Sophie Charlotte of Prussia to Hans Caspar von Bothmer, 9 September 1704, p.57
113. Hanham, Andrew, 'Caroline of Brandenburg-Ansbach and the "Anglicisation" of the House of Hanover', in Campbell Orr, Clarissa, ed., Queenship in Europe 1660–1815: The Role of the Consort (Cambridge University Press, Cambridge, 2004)
114. Wilkins, op. cit., p.29
115. See Marschner, op. cit., p.188, note 11
116. See National Archives, SP90/3/90, Thomas Wentworth, Lord Raby to Robert Harley, 4 November 1704
117. See National Archives, SP90/3/99, Thomas Wentworth, Lord Raby to Robert Harley, 11 November 1704
118. Sophie Charlotte to Hans Caspar von Bothmer, 2 December 1704, see Doebner, Richard, ed., op. cit., p.61
119. Brown, Gregory, op. cit., p.84
120. Wilkins, op. cit., p.30
121. Sophie of Hanover to Hans Caspar von Bothmer, 14

November 1704, see Doebner, Richard, ed., op. cit., p.231

122. Thompson, op. cit., p.29

123. Brown, Gregory, op. cit., p.84

124. Wilkins, op. cit., p.31

125. Sophie Charlotte to Hans Caspar von Bothmer, 6 November 1703, see Doebner, Richard, ed., op. cit., p.38

126. Ibid., Sophie of Hanover to Baron von Schütz, 28 June 1705, p.196

127. Rosenthal, op. cit., p.32

128. See National Archives, SP90/3/242, Thomas Wentworth, Lord Raby to Robert Harley, 14 March 1705, and SP90/3/280, Thomas Wentworth, Lord Raby to Robert Harley, 14 April 1705

129. Wilkins, op. cit., p.50

130. See National Archives, SP90/3/202, Thomas Wentworth, Lord Raby to Robert Harley, 14 February 1705

131. Ingrao, Charles W., and Thomas, Andrew L., 'Imperial Consorts, Piety and Power', in Campbell Orr, ed., op. cit. (*Queenship in Europe*), p.113

132. Ibid., p.112

133. See Lambeth Palace Library, Miscellaneous Papers, MS 935, no 20

134. Lady Mary Wortley Montagu to Lady Rich, 1 December 1716, see Halsband, Robert, ed., op. cit., Vol. 1, p.288

135. Clarke, Alured, op. cit., p.14

136. Smith, Hannah, op. cit., p.34

137. Jones, Thomas, *The Rise and Progress of the Most Honourable and Loyal Society of Antient Britons* (W. Wilkins, London, 1717), p.61

138. Cowper, Hon C.S., ed., *Diary of Mary, Countess Cowper, Lady of the Bedchamber to the Princess of Wales,* *1714–1720* (John Murray, London, 1864), p.41

139. Addison, Joseph, 'To Her Royal Highness the Princess of Wales, With the Tragedy of Cato. Nov. 1714'

140. Bertoloni Meli, Domenico, Caroline, Leibniz and Clarke, *Journal of the History of Ideas*, Vol. 60, no 3 (1999), p.473

Chapter II: Electoral Princess

1. Van der Kiste, John, *King George II and Queen Caroline* (Sutton Publishing, Stroud, 1997), p.9

2. See Black, Jeremy, op. cit. (*George II*), p.72; Chenevix Trench, Charles, *George II* (Allen Lane, London, 1973), p.7

3. Sophie Charlotte to Hans Caspar von Bothmer, 9 December 1702, see Doebner, Richard, ed., op. cit., p.28

4. Lady Mary Wortley Montagu to Lady Rich, 1 December 1716, see Halsband, Robert, ed., op. cit., Vol. 1, p.288

5. See National Archives, SP90/3/242, Thomas Wentworth, Lord Raby, to Robert Harley, 14 March 1705

6. Wilkins, op. cit., p.42

7. Ibid.

8. Clarke, Alured, op. cit., p.5

9. Arkell, op. cit., p.19

10. Clarke, Alured, op. cit., p.5; Plumb, J.H., *England in the Eighteenth Century* (Pelican, London, 1960), p.42

11. Arkell, op. cit., p.23

12. Wilkins, op. cit., pp.47–8

13. See Shropshire Archives, MI5444/18, Thomas Wentworth, Lord Raby, to George Stepney, 7 July 1705

14. Worsley, op. cit., p.10

15. Wilkins, op. cit., p.52
16. See Arkell, op. cit., p.22; copy of Caroline's will, Devonshire Collections, Chatsworth House
17. Thompson, op. cit., p.30
18. See National Archives, SP90/3/352 and SP90/3/358, Thomas Wentworth, Lord Raby to Robert Harley, 25 July 1705 and 1 August 1705
19. Wilkins, op. cit., Vol. 1, p.30 and p.56
20. Kroll, op. cit. (*Sophie*), p.215
21. Elisabeth Charlotte, Duchess of Orléans, to Raugravine Amalie Elisabeth von Degenfeld, 20 August 1705, see Kroll, op. cit. (*Liselotte*), p.121
22. Van der Kiste, op. cit., p.35
23. Clarke, Alured, op. cit., p.17
24. Somerset, Anne, op. cit., p.163
25. Kroll, op. cit. (*Sophie*), p.203
26. Ibid., p.217
27. See Glowienka, Edward W., review of *Leibniz and the Two Sophies: The Philosophical Correspondence*, ed. Lloyd Strickland, *Journal of the History of Philosophy*, Vol. 50, no 4, October 2012, pp.617–18
28. Brown, Gregory, op. cit., p.77
29. Hatton, op. cit., p.47
30. See Lambeth Palace Library, Miscellaneous Papers, MS 930/16
31. See Lambeth Palace Library, Miscellaneous Papers, MS 930/186–9
32. See Lambeth Palace Library, Miscellaneous Papers, MS 930/216
33. British Library, Stowe MS 222, Hanover Papers Vol. 1 (ff525)
34. Cowper, op. cit. (*Diary of Mary, Countess Cowper*), pp.149–50
35. Ibid., p.149
36. Brown, Gregory, op. cit., p.86
37. Wilkins, op. cit., Vol. 1, pp.49–50
38. Arkell, op. cit., p.24
39. See British Museum, collection number 1982,U.536
40. Elisabeth Charlotte, Duchess of Orléans, to Sophie of Hanover, 11 January 1711, see Kroll, op. cit. (*Liselotte*), p.145
41. Vivian, Frances, *A Life of Frederick, Prince of Wales, 1707–1751: A Connoisseur of the Arts* (The Edwin Mellen Press, Lewiston, 2006), p.61
42. Lady Mary Wortley Montagu to Lady Bristol, 25 November 1716, and Lady Mary Wortley Montagu to Lady Mar, 17 December 1716, see Halsband, Robert, ed., op. cit., Vol. 1, pp.286, 290
43. Lady Mary Wortley Montagu to Lady Mar, 17 December 1716, see Halsband, Robert, ed., op. cit., Vol. 1, p.290
44. Thompson, op. cit., p.20
45. See National Archives, SP105/84/23, J. Schweinfurt to George Stepney, 18 January 1692
46. Chenevix Trench, op. cit., p.5, and p.302, note 12; Borman, op. cit., p.41
47. Elisabeth Charlotte, Duchess of Orléans, to Sophie, Electress of Hanover, 21 April 1704, see Kroll, op. cit. (*Liselotte*), pp.114–15; Hatton, op. cit., p.98
48. Hatton, op. cit., p.97
49. Greenwood, Alice Drayton, *Lives of the Hanoverian Queens of England* (George Bell & Sons, London, 1909), p.154
50. Borman, op. cit., p.42
51. Wilkins, op. cit., Vol. 1, p.57
52. Hatton, op. cit., p.91
53. Kroll, op. cit. (*Sophie*), p.216; Cowper, op. cit. (*Diary of Mary, Countess Cowper*), p.65
54. Kroll, op. cit. (*Sophie*), p.216

55. Moore, Lucy, *Amphibious Thing: The Life of Lord Hervey* (Viking, London, 2000), p.163

56. Kroll, op. cit. (*Sophie*), p.187

57. See Hatton, op. cit., p.62

58. See Smith, Hannah, op. cit., p.6

59. Marlow, Joyce, *The Life and Times of George I* (Weidenfeld & Nicolson, London, 1973), p.21

60. Van der Kiste, John, *The Georgian Princesses* (Sutton Publishing, Stroud, 2000)

61. Black, Jeremy, *The Hanoverians: The History of a Dynasty* (Hambledon & London, London, 2004), p.57

62. Somerset, Anne, op. cit., pp.36–7

63. Ibid.

64. Hatton, op. cit., p.41

65. Coxe, William, *Memoirs of the Life and Administration of Sir Robert Walpole, Earl of Orford*, 4 vols (London, 1816), Vol. 1, p.151

66. Kroll, op. cit. (*Sophie*), p.87

67. Thackeray, William Makepeace, *The Four Georges* (London, 1860), p.45; Sinclair-Stevenson, Christopher, *Blood Royal: The Illustrious House of Hanover* (Jonathan Cape, London, 1979), p.25

68. See National Archives, SP105/84/24, J. Schweinfurt to George Stepney, 3 February 1692

69. Van der Kiste, op. cit. (*Georgian Princesses*)

70. Sinclair-Stevenson, op. cit., p.25

71. See National Archives, SP105/54/40v, George Stepney to William Blathwayt, 20 July 1694

72. Gold, Claudia, *The King's Mistress: The True and Scandalous Story of the Woman who Stole the Heart of George I* (Quercus, London, 2012), p.60

73. See National Archives, SP105/54/52, George Stepney to William Blathwayt, 3 August 1694

74. See National Archives, SP105/54/28v, George Stepney to Thomas Wentworth, 19 June 1694

75. Greenwood, op. cit., p.115

76. Ibid., p.117

77. Ibid.

78. Van der Kiste, op. cit. (*Georgian Princesses*)

79. Hatton, op. cit., p.333, note 14

80. Greenwood, op. cit., p.122

81. Van der Kiste, op. cit. (*Georgian Princesses*), p.34

82. Hatton, op. cit., p.69

83. See National Archives, SP105/54/40v, George Stepney to William Blathwayt, 20 July 1694

84. Greenwood, op. cit., p.101

85. Gold, op. cit., p.61

86. Clarke, Alured, op. cit., p.9

87. Wilkins, op. cit., Vol. 1, pp.65–6

88. Greenwood, op. cit., p.150

89. Gold, op. cit., p.77

90. Vivian, op. cit., p.14

91. Worsley, op. cit., p.135; Philip Dormer Stanhope, Earl of Chesterfield, to his son, 11 February 1751, in Mahon, Lord, *The Letters of Philip Dormer Stanhope, Earl of Chesterfield*, 4 vols (Richard Bentley, London, 1845), Vol. 2, p.98

92. See National Archives, SP87/3/5, John, Duke of Marlborough to Henry Boyle, 27 April 1708

93. Hibbert, Christopher, *The Marlboroughs: John and Sarah Churchill 1650–1744* (Viking, London, 2001), p.160 and p.183

94. See National Archives, SP81/161/434, Edmund Poley papers, undated

95. Arkell, op. cit., p.44
96. Ibid., p.34
97. Thompson, op. cit., p.22
98. Greenwood, op. cit., p.151
99. Royal Collection RCIN 406073, Sir Godfrey Kneller, George II when Prince of Wales, 1716
100. Rosenthal, op. cit., p.40
101. Arkell, op. cit., p.46
102. Greenwood, op. cit., p.166
103. Thompson, op. cit., p.22
104. Sophie of Hanover to Baron von Schütz, 30 October 1705, see Doebner, Richard, ed., op. cit., p.199
105. Robbins Landon, H.C., Handel and his World (Weidenfeld & Nicolson, London, 1984), p.83
106. Yorke-Long, op. cit.
107. Sophie of Hanover to Baron von Schütz, 8 December 1705, see Doebner, Richard, ed., op. cit., p.200
108. Arkell, op. cit., p.31
109. 'distemper', see Wilkins, op. cit., Vol. 1, p.89; Arkell, op. cit., p.33
110. Lady Mary Wortley Montagu to Lady Bristol, 25 November 1716, see Halsband, Robert, ed., op. cit., Vol. 1, p.286
111. Sophie of Hanover to Hans Caspar von Bothmer, 5 April 1707, see Doebner, Richard, ed., op. cit., p.246
112. Wilkins, op. cit., Vol. 1, p.90
113. Somerset, Anne, op. cit., p.210
114. Murray, General the Right Hon Sir George, Letters and Dispatches of John Churchill, First Duke of Marlborough, from 1702 to 1712 (John Murray, London, 1845), Vol. 3, p.309
115. Somerset, Anne, op. cit., p.293
116. Van der Kiste, op. cit. (George II and Queen Caroline), p.21
117. Addison, Joseph, op. cit.
118. Batey, Mavis, The Pleasures of the Imagination: Joseph Addison's Influences on Early Landscape Gardens, Garden History, Vol. 33, no 2 (2005), p.205
119. Sophie of Hanover to Hans Caspar von Bothmer, 11 January 1707, see Doebner, Richard, ed., op. cit., p.242
120. Seward, Desmond, Renishaw Hall: The Story of the Sitwells (Elliott & Thompson, London, 2015), p.21
121. Conduitt, John, 'To The Queen', in The Chronology of Ancient Kingdoms Amended, Isaac Newton (London, 1728), p.x
122. See Sundt Urstad, Tone, Sir Robert Walpole's Poets: The Use of Literature as Pro-Government Propaganda, 1721–1742 (Associated University Presses, London & Newark, 1999), pp.164–5
123. Leibniz to John Toland, 6 October 1707, Gottfried Wilhelm Leibniz Bibliothek, Hanover, LBr933Bl.12r
124. Cowper, op. cit. (Diary of Mary, Countess Cowper), p.14; Clarke, Alured, op. cit., p.9
125. Thomson, Mrs, ed., op. cit. (Memoirs of Viscountess Sundon), Vol. 2, p.287
126. See letter, George Augustus to Caroline, undated, qu Arkell, op. cit., p.46
127. Vivian, op. cit., pp.15–16
128. Clarke, Alured, op. cit., pp.21–2
129. Kroll, op. cit. (Sophie), p.233
130. Arkell, op. cit., p.46
131. Ibid.
132. Sophie of Hanover to Hans Caspar von Bothmer, 9 November 1709, see Doebner, Richard, ed., op. cit., p.288
133. Arkell, op. cit., p.46; Baker-Smith, Veronica, A Life of Anne of

Hanover, Princess Royal (Brill, 1995), p.6

134. Van der Kiste, op. cit. (*Georgian Princesses*), p.36

135. Thompson, op. cit., p.26

136. Somerset, Anne, op. cit., p.293

137. Elisabeth Charlotte, Duchess of Orléans, to Sophie of Hanover, 14 April 1712, see Kroll, op. cit. (*Liselotte*), p.158

138. Brooks, William, Nostalgia in the letters of Elisabeth Charlotte, the second Madame, *Cahiers du 17e siècle*, 10 (2006), p.7; Elisabeth Charlotte, Duchess of Orléans, to Raugravine Luise von Degenfeld, 16 September 1714, see Kroll, op. cit. (*Liselotte*), p.167

139. Mademoiselle Schutz to Mary, Countess Cowper, 11 September 1710, Hertfordshire Records Collection, DE/P/F204

140. Thompson, op. cit., p.41

141. Worsley, op. cit., p.10; Sophie of Hanover to Hans Caspar von Bothmer, 29 April 1712, see Doebner, Richard, ed., op. cit., p.320

142. Clarke, Alured, op. cit., p.5

143. Hatton, op. cit., p.132, note 66

144. John Gay to Charles Ford, 7 August 1714, in Burgess, C.F., ed., *The Letters of John Gay* (Oxford University Press, Oxford, 1966), p.12

145. Wilkins, op. cit., Vol. 1, pp.83–4

146. Murray, ed., op. cit., Vol. 5, p.415

147. Borman, op. cit., p.39

148. Black, op. cit. (*Hanoverians*), p.39

149. Borman, op. cit., p.30; Sedgwick, Romney, ed., *Lord Hervey's Memoirs* (William Kimber, London, 1952), p.75

150. Worsley, op. cit., p.10

151. See Royal Collection RCIN420182

152. Quennell, op. cit., p.37; Thomson, Mrs, ed., op. cit. (*Memoirs of Viscountess Sundon*), Vol. 2, p.52

153. Sedgwick, Romney, ed., op. cit. (Kimber edition), p.74

154. *The Flying Post*, 12 October 1714

155. 'low cunning', Grundy, Isobel, *Lady Mary Wortley Montagu, Comet of the Enlightenment* (Oxford University Press, Oxford, 1999); Clarke, Alured, op. cit., p.8

156. Borman, op. cit., p.38

157. Arkell, op. cit., p.65

158. *The Flying Post*, 12 October 1714

159. Campbell Orr, ed., op. cit. (*Queenship in Europe*), p.284

160. Borman, op. cit., p.102

161. Melville, op. cit., p.64

162. Ibid., p.61

163. Worsley, op. cit., p.370, note 20

164. Ibid., p.139; Bryant, Julius, *Mrs Howard: A Woman of Reason (1688–1767)* (English Heritage, London, 1988), p.7

165. Melville, op. cit., p.61

166. Wilkins, op. cit., Vol. 1, p.97

167. Elisabeth Charlotte, Duchess of Orléans, to Caroline, Princess of Wales, 19 March 1716, see Kroll, op. cit. (*Liselotte*), p.182

168. See Wilkins, op. cit., Vol. 1, p.102

169. Ibid.

170. Ibid., Vol. 1, pp.103–4

171. Ibid.

172. Marlow, op. cit., p.63

173. Anderson Winn, James, *Queen Anne: Patroness of Arts* (Oxford University Press, Oxford, 2014), p.631

174. Van der Kiste, op. cit. (*King George II and Queen Caroline*), p.23

175. Somerset, Anne, op. cit., p.505

176. Wilkins, op. cit., Vol. 1, p.109

177. See British Library, Stowe MS 242, Vol. II, ff218.12

178. Arkell, op. cit., p.56

179. Ibid.
180. Kroll, op. cit. (*Sophie*), p.246
181. John Arbuthnot to Jonathan Swift, 12 August 1714, in *Dean Swift's Works*, 19 vols (London, 1801), Vol. 11
182. Lady Mary Wortley Montagu to Edward Wortley Montagu, 3 August 1714, see Halsband, Robert, ed., op. cit., Vol. 1, p.213
183. Elisabeth Charlotte, Duchess of Orléans, to Herr von Harling, 5 April 1716, see Kroll, op. cit. (*Liselotte*), p.183
184. See William Adolphus Ward, *Dictionary of National Biography*, entry Caroline of Ansbach
185. Wilkins, op. cit., Vol. 1, p.258
186. 'A Ceremonial for the Reception of His Most Sacred Majesty, George, By the Grace of God, King of Great Britain, etc, Upon His Arrival from Holland to his Kingdom of Great Britain', 6 September 1714, Royal Archives RA GEO/ADD/1/17
187. Beattie, John M., *The English Court in the Reign of George I* (Cambridge University Press, Cambridge, 1967), pp.258–9; Tillyard, Stella, *A Royal Affair: George III and his Troublesome Siblings* (Chatto & Windus, London, 2006), p.12
188. Wilkins, op. cit., Vol. 1, p.196
189. Elisabeth Charlotte, Duchess of Orléans, to Sophie of Hanover, 7 January 1714, see Kroll, op. cit. (*Liselotte*), p.162
190. Sackville-West, V., *Knole and the Sackvilles* (Ernest Benn, London, 1922), p.151
191. Cowper, op. cit. (*Diary of Mary, Countess Cowper*), pp.23–4
192. Ibid., p.2
193. Ibid.
194. Campbell Orr, Clarissa, ed., *Queenship in Britain 1660–1837: Royal Patronage, Court Culture and Dynastic Politics* (Manchester University Press, Manchester, 2002), p.160

PART TWO: BRITAIN
Chapter I: Princess of Wales

1. Hatton, Edward, *A New View of London, 1708*, quoted in White, Jerry, *London in the Eighteenth Century: A Great and Monstrous Thing* (Vintage, London, 2012), p.1
2. *The Private Diary of William, First Earl Cowper* (E. Williams, Eton, 1833), 21 September 1714
3. Defoe, Daniel, see *The Review*, 25 June 1709
4. Addison, Joseph, op. cit.
5. Seward, op. cit., pp.21–2; Cowper, op. cit. (*Diary of Mary, Countess Cowper*), p.104
6. *The Daily Courant*, 12 October 1714
7. British Museum, collection number 1888,0515.51
8. 'Wilhelmina Charlotta, Princessin von Wallis', anonymous print, c. 1705–27, British Museum, collection number Bb,8.272
9. Gay, John, *Poems on Several Occasions* (London, 1752), pp.4–6
10. Worsley, Lucy and Souden, David, *Hampton Court Palace: The Official Illustrated History* (Merrell, London, 2005), p.82
11. Addison, Joseph, op. cit.
12. Campbell Orr, op. cit. (*Queenship in Europe*), p.285
13. Arkell, op. cit., p.80
14. Campbell Orr, op. cit. (*Queenship in Europe*), p.286
15. Jones, Thomas, *The Rise and Progress of the Most Honourable and*

Loyal Society of Antient Britons (W. Wilkins, London, 1717), p.56

16. Jones, Mary, *Miscellanies in Prose and Verse* (Oxford, 1750), pp.367–8

17. Thompson, op. cit., p.40

18. See British Museum, collection number 1877,1013.1178

19. Brett, Cécile, Revealing Thornhill's mythological scene at Hampton Court, *British Art Journal*, Vol. 13, no 3 (winter 2012/13), p.4

20. See Royal Collection RCIN603771 and National Portrait Gallery NPG/D33029

21. Jones, Thomas, op. cit., p.25

22. Wilkins, op. cit., Vol. 1, p.150

23. Cowper, op. cit. (*Diary of Mary, Countess Cowper*), p.38

24. Thomson, Mrs, ed., op. cit. (*Memoirs of Viscountess Sundon*), Vol. 1, p.287; Baker-Smith, op. cit., p.8

25. See Robbins Landon, op. cit., p.74

26. Defoe, Daniel, *A Tour Thro the Whole Island of Great Britain*, 3 vols (London, 1724–27), Vol. 1, p.12

27. The British Museum owns a set of Pierce Tempest's edition of 1688 of Laroon's *The Cryes of the City of London Drawne after the Life*, including, for example, 'Buy a fine singing Bird', collection number 1972,U.370.10

28. Van Muyden, Madame, trans. and ed., *A Foreign View of England in the Reigns of George I and George II: The Letters of Monsieur César de Saussure to his Family* (John Murray, London, 1902), p.177

29. Dobrée, Bonamy, *The Early Eighteenth Century 1700–1740: Swift, Defoe, and Pope* (Clarendon Press, Oxford, 1959), p.6

30. Black, Jeremy, *Politics and Foreign Policy in the Age of George I, 1714–27* (Ashgate, Farnham, 2014), p.43

31. Van Muyden, op. cit., p.193

32. Worsley, op. cit., p.20

33. Wilkins, op. cit., Vol. 1, p.151; Hughes, Helen, ed., *The Gentle Hertford: Her Life and Letters* (Macmillan, London, 1940), p.209

34. See Smith, Hannah, op. cit., p.118

35. Jones, Thomas, op. cit., p.24

36. Wright, Gillian, *Producing Women's Poetry, 1600–1730: Text and Paratext, Manuscript and Print* (Cambridge University Press, Cambridge, 2013), p.216

37. Gay, John, *Poems on Several Occasions*, op. cit., p.6

38. Thomson, Mrs, ed., op. cit. (*Memoirs of Viscountess Sundon*) Vol. 1, p.66

39. Smith, Hannah, op. cit., p.35

40. See White, Jerry, op. cit., p.139

41. Cowper, op. cit. (*Diary of Mary, Countess Cowper*), p.41

42. *The Daily Courant*, 31 January 1733, quoted in Wilkins, op. cit., Vol. 2, p.226

43. Black, Jeremy, op. cit. (*Hanoverians*), p.51

44. Field, Ophelia, *The Favourite: Sarah, Duchess of Marlborough* (Hodder & Stoughton, London, 2002), p.340

45. See Marschner, op. cit., p.12

46. Thomson, Mrs, ed., op. cit. (*Memoirs of Viscountess Sundon*), Vol. 1, p.104

47. Cowper, op. cit. (*Diary of Mary, Countess Cowper*), p.102

48. Peter Wentworth papers, p.431, quoted in Wilkins, op. cit., Vol. 2, p.69; Clarke, Alured, op. cit., p.14

49. Cowper, op. cit. (*Diary of Mary, Countess Cowper*), p.102

50. Black, Jeremy, op. cit. (*George II*), p.47

51. Wilkins, op. cit., Vol. 1, p.187; Smith, Hannah, op. cit., p.118

52. Marco Ricci, 'View of the Mall in St James's Park, after 1709–10', National Art Gallery, Washington, Ailsa Mellon Bruce Collection 1970.17.132: see Einberg, Elizabeth, et al., *Manners and Morals: Hogarth and British Painting 1700–1760* (Tate Gallery Publications, London, 1987), p.37; Hughes, Helen, ed., op. cit., p.65

53. John Gay to Charles Ford, 30 December 1714, in Burgess, C.F., ed., op. cit., p.16

54. Marschner, Joanna, and Bindman, David, *Enlightened ....: Caroline, Augusta, Charlotte and the Shaping of the Modern World* (Yale University Press, New Haven & London, 2017), p.208

55. Marschner, op. cit. (*Queen Caroline*), p.189, note 13; Wilkins, op. cit., Vol. 1, p.162

56. Dudley Ryder, quoted in Worsley, op. cit., p.169

57. Wilkins, op. cit., Vol. 1, p.201

58. Strong, Roy, *Coronation: A History of Kingship and the British Monarchy* (HarperCollins, London, 2005), p.372

59. Black, Jeremy, op. cit. (*A Subject for Taste*), p.29

60. Robbins Landon, op. cit., p78

61. Christian Friedrich Zincke, Caroline of Ansbach, c. 1716–20, Royal Collection RCIN 421942

62. Cowper, op. cit. (*Diary of Mary, Countess Cowper*), p.4

63. Marlow, op. cit., p.80

64. Monod, Paul Kleber, *Jacobitism and the English People, 1688–1788* (Cambridge University Press, Cambridge, 1993), p.175

65. Cowper, op. cit. (*Diary of Mary, Countess Cowper*), p.5; see National Archives, SP55/3/10, the Duke of Montrose to the Earl of Kinnoull, 9 October 1714

66. Campbell Orr, ed., op. cit. (*Queenship in Britain*), p.146

67. Hatton, op. cit., p.352, note 65

68. Gay, John, *Poems on Several Occasions*, op. cit., p.10

69. Bryant, op. cit., p.8

70. Marschner and Bindman, op. cit., p.204

71. Campbell Orr, ed., op. cit. (*Queenship in Britain*), p.168

72. Thompson, op. cit., p.40

73. Beattie, op. cit., p.264; Black, op. cit. (*A Subject for Taste*), p.32

74. A..... , op. cit., p.79

75. Sheppard, Edgar, *Memorial of St James's Palace*, 2 vols (Longmans, Green & Co., London, 1894), pp.8–10

76. See ibid., p.11

77. See ibid., p.10

78. Souden, David, *Royal Palaces of London* (Merrell, London, 2008), p.149

79. Beattie, op. cit., note, p.9; Thompson, op. cit., pp.45, 62

80. Hatton, op. cit., p.143

81. Cowper, op. cit. (*Diary of Mary, Countess Cowper*), pp.8–9; Beattie, op. cit., p.265

82. Lady Mary Wortley Montagu to Edward Wortley Montagu, 23 October 1714, see Halsband, Robert, ed., op. cit., Vol. 1, p.233

83. Ibid.

84. Quoted in Moore, op. cit., p.19

85. Cowper, op. cit. (*Diary of Mary, Countess Cowper*), p.14

86. 'worst sollicitor', Beattie, op. cit., p.162. See Lady Mary Wortley Montagu to Edward Wortley Montagu, 24 September 1714: 'I don't say 'tis impossible for an Impudent Man not to rise in the World, but a Moderate Merit with a large share of Impudence is more probable to be advanc'd than the greatest Qualifications without it.' In Halsband, Robert, ed., op. cit., Vol. 1, pp.226–7

87. Cowper, op. cit. (*Diary of Mary, Countess Cowper*), p.26

88. Clarke, Alured, op. cit., p.6

89. Gold, op. cit., p.166

90. Somerset, Anne, *Ladies in Waiting: From the Tudors to the Present Day* (Weidenfeld & Nicolson, London, 1984), p.201

91. Cowper, op. cit. (*Diary of Mary, Countess Cowper*), p.7

92. Caroline to Charlotte Clayton, 1718, Royal Archives RA GEO/ADD/28/40

93. Cowper, op. cit. (*Diary of Mary, Countess Cowper*), p.10

94. see Harris, Frances, *A Passion for Government: The Life of Sarah, Duchess of Marlborough* (Oxford University Press, Oxford, 1991), pp.204–5; Caroline to Charlotte Clayton, 8 December 1719, Royal Archives RA GEO/ADD/28/56

95. Smith, Hannah, The Court in England, 1714–1760: A Declining Political Institution?, *History*, Vol. 90, no 1 (January 2005), p.37

96. Grundy, Isobel, Lady Mary Wortley Montagu and the Theatrical Eclogue, *Lumen*, 17 (1998), note 14

97. Sedgwick, Romney, ed., op. cit. (Kimber edition), p.66

98. Greenwood, op. cit., p.189

99. Worsley, Lucy and Souden, David, op. cit., p.81

100. Beattie, op. cit., p.262

101. Quoted in Melville, op. cit., p.50

102. Burchard, Wolf, St James's Palace: George II's and Queen Caroline's Principal London Residence, *Court Historian*, 2011, p.182

103. Smith, Hannah, op. cit. (*Georgian Monarchy*), p.206

104. Philip Dormer Stanhope, Earl of Chesterfield to G. Bubb Dodington, 20 August 1716, in Mahon, Lord, *The Letters of Philip Dormer Stanhope, Earl of Chesterfield*, 4 vols (Richard Bentley, London, 1845), Vol. 1, p.12

105. Quoted in Greenwood, op. cit., p.184

106. See Liselotte's letter to Caroline of 15 December 1719: 'When the *princesses du sang* or other ladies ate with the King, they were not served by *gentilhommes servants* but by officers of the King's household, who used to wait from behind the chairs like pages.' See Kroll, op. cit. (*Liselotte*), p.218

107. Princess Anne, daughter of George II and Caroline, on Caroline's behalf, to Charlotte Clayton, undated [1730?], Royal Archives RA GEO/ADD/28/69

108. Caroline to Charlotte Clayton, both undated, Royal Archives RA GEO/ADD/28/29 and RA GEO/ADD/28/26

109. 'Merry pranks', see Worsley, op. cit., p.105

110. Campbell Orr, ed., op. cit. (*Queenship in Britain*), p.147; Jones, Mary, op. cit., p.361

111. Caroline to Charlotte Clayton, undated [March?] 1719, Royal Archives RA GEO/ADD/28/50

112. Marschner, op. cit., p.12

113. Thomson, Mrs, ed., op. cit. (*Memoirs of Viscountess Sundon*), Vol. 1, p.122

114. Quoted in Melville, op. cit., pp.102–3

115. Cowper, op. cit. (*Diary of Mary, Countess Cowper*), p.19

116. Cumming, Valerie, *Royal Dress: The Image and the Reality 1580 to the Present Day* (Batsford, London, 1989), p.48; Hatton, op. cit., p.143

117. Worsley, op. cit., p.363, note 91; Marschner, op. cit. (*Queen Caroline*), p.12

118. Marschner, op. cit. (*Queen Caroline*), pp.152–3

119. Elisabeth Charlotte, Duchess of Orléans, to Raugravine Luise von Degenfeld, 10 May 1715, see Kroll, op. cit. (*Liselotte*), pp.172–3

120. Cowper, op. cit. (*Diary of Mary, Countess Cowper*), p.79

121. Ibid., p.21, p.89

122. Brett, Cécile, op. cit., p.8, note 6

123. Sinclair-Stevenson, op. cit., p.60

124. Elisabeth Charlotte, Duchess of Orléans, to Raugravine Luise von Degenfeld, 23 April 1715, see Kroll, op. cit. (*Liselotte*), p.171

125. Chenevix Trench, op. cit., p.39

126. Pricy Council, see Black, Jeremy, op. cit. (*George II*), p.43; Civil List, see Hatton, op. cit., pp.144–5; Thompson, op. cit., p.63

127. See Cowper, op. cit. (*Diary of Mary, Countess Cowper*), p.104

128. Quoted in Smith, Hannah, op. cit. (*Georgian Monarchy*), p.207

129. Unsigned memorandum, 22 November 1722, Royal Archives RA GEO/MAIN/52715–6

130. Lady Mary Wortley Montagu to Edward Wortley Montagu, 3 August 1714, see Halsband, Robert, ed., op. cit., Vol. 1, p.213

131. Anonymous, 'A Sacred Ode to King George', Bodleian Library broadsheet ballads collection, BOD20209, Roud number V7971

132. Anonymous, 'An Excellent New Ballad', Bodleian Library broadsheet ballads collection, MS. Rawl. poet. 207 (136, 137)

133. Elisabeth Charlotte, Duchess of Orléans, to Raugravine Luise von Degenfeld, 23 April 1715, see Kroll, op. cit. (*Liselotte*), p.172

134. Dickson, Patricia, *Red John of the Battles* (Sidgwick & Jackson, London, 1973), p.179

135. Ibid., p.188

136. Ibid., p.189

137. Quoted in Smith, Hannah, op. cit. (*Georgian Monarchy*), p.215; 'A Poem on Her Majesty's Birthday, 1731–2', in *The Poetical Works of Richard Savage*, 2 vols (Apollo Press, Edinburgh, 1780)

138. Baker-Smith, Veronica, *Royal Discord: The Family of George II* (Athena Press, London, 2008), p.26

139. Quoted in Beattie, op. cit., p.262

140. Clarke, Alured, op. cit., p.9

141. Dobrée, op. cit., p.381

142. Marschner, op. cit., p.102

143. See Cowper, op. cit. (*Diary of Mary, Countess Cowper*), p.72

144. Marsden, Jean I, Sex, Politics, and She-Tragedy: Reconfiguring Lady Jane Grey, *Studies in English Literature, 1500–1900*, Vol. 42, no 3 (2002), p.502, p.514

145. John Gay and Alexander Pope to John Caryll, April 1715, in Burgess, C.F., ed., op. cit., p.23

146. Cowper, op. cit. (*Diary of Mary, Countess Cowper*), p.99

147. Ibid.

148. Campbell Orr, op. cit. (*Queenship in Britain*), p.147

149. Van Muyden, Madame, op. cit., p.177

150. Prescott, Sarah, op. cit., p.2

151. Jones, Thomas, op. cit., p.28

152. Ibid., p.55

153. Quoted in Smith, Hannah, op. cit. (*Georgian Monarchy*), p.199

154. Morgan-Guy, John, and Gibson, William, *Religion and Society in the Diocese of St Davids 1485–2011* (Routledge, 2015), p.126

155. Jones, Thomas, op. cit., p.44

156. *The Musical Times*, 1878 volume, p.484

157. Jones, Thomas, op. cit., p.45

158. Walpole, Horace, *Reminiscences, written in 1788, for the amusement of Miss Mary and Miss Agnes B***y* (London, 1818), p.27

159. Wilkins, op. cit., Vol. 1, p.284

160. Quoted in Worsley, op. cit., p.102

161. Cowper, op. cit. (*Diary of Mary, Countess Cowper*), p.28

162. Ibid., p.79

163. Hatton, op. cit., p.196

164. Black, Jeremy, op. cit. (*George II*), p.45

165. Cowper, op. cit. (*Diary of Mary, Countess Cowper*), p.109

166. Ibid., p.115

167. Royal Collection RCIN/405313

168. Cowper, op. cit. (*Diary of Mary, Countess Cowper*), p.105

169. Arkell, op. cit., p.93

170. Baker-Smith, op. cit. (*Anne*), p.12

171. Royal Collection RCIN404986

172. Quoted in Worsley, op. cit., p.195

173. Lady Mary Wortley Montagu to Lady Bristol, 25 November 1716, see Halsband, Robert, ed., op. cit., Vol. 1, p.286

174. Campbell Orr, op. cit. (*Queenship in Britain*), p.147; Mahaffey, Kathleen, Pope's 'Artemisia' and 'Phryne' as Personal Satire, *The Review of English Studies*, Vol. 21, no 84 (1970), p.466; Rosenthal,

ed., op. cit., p.85; Impey, Edward, *Kensington Palace: The Official Illustrated History* (Merrell, London, 2003), p.70

175. Elisabeth Charlotte, Duchess of Orléans, to Raugravine Luise von Degenfeld, 4 January 1715, see Kroll, op. cit. (*Liselotte*), p.169

176. Thomas Tickell, 'Kensington Gardens', 1722

177. 'A proportion of table linen to serve Their Royall Highnesses the Prince and Princess of Wales and Family for Fourteen days as ye service was at Hampton Court', 15 October 1715, Royal Archives RA GEO/ADD/1/28

178. Cowper, op. cit. (*Diary of Mary, Countess Cowper*), p.121; Borman, op. cit., p.75

179. Cowper, op. cit. (*Diary of Mary, Countess Cowper*), p.125; Greenwood, op. cit., p.208; Smith, Hannah, op. cit. (*Georgian Monarchy*), p.101

180. Cowper, op. cit. (*Diary of Mary, Countess Cowper*), p.117

181. Quoted in Chenevix Trench, op. cit., p.67

182. Cowper, op. cit. (*Diary of Mary, Countess Cowper*), p.125

183. Ibid., pp.93–5

184. Clarke, Alured, op. cit., p.19

185. Thomson, Mrs, ed., op. cit. (*Memoirs of Viscountess Sundon*), Vol. 1, p.334

186. Matthews, William, ed., *The Diary of Dudley Ryder 1715–1716* (Methuen & Co., London, 1939), p.298

187. Campbell Orr, ed., op. cit., p.148

188. Borman, op. cit., p.71

189. Cowper, op. cit. (*Diary of Mary, Countess Cowper*), p.121

190. Borman, op. cit., p.75

191. Cowper, op. cit. (*Diary of Mary, Countess Cowper*), p.114

192. Ibid., p.123
193. Ibid.
194. Ibid., pp.123–4
195. Scott, Walter, *The Heart of Midlothian* (Archibald Constable & Co., Edinburgh, 1818), see Chapter 36
196. Thomson, Mrs, ed., op. cit. (*Memoirs of Viscountess Sundon*), Vol. 1, p.334
197. See Thompson, op. cit., p.47
198. Cowper, op. cit. (*Diary of Mary, Countess Cowper*), p.117
199. Hatton, op. cit., p.199
200. Baroness von Gemmingen, to Mary, Countess Cowper, 9 October 1716, Hertfordshire Record Office, DE/P/F203
201. Elisabeth Charlotte, Duchess of Orléans, to Raugravine Luise von Degenfeld, 19 November 1716, see Kroll, op. cit. (*Liselotte*), p.185
202. Quoted in Worsley, op. cit., p.233
203. Dr White Kennett to Mr Blackwell, in Ellis, Henry, ed., *Original Letters Illustrative of English History*, 4 vols (Harding and Lepard, London, 1827), Vol. 4, p.299
204. Cowper, op. cit. (*Diary of Mary, Countess Cowper*), p.126
205. Ibid., p.127
206. Ibid.; Ellis, Henry, ed., op. cit., Vol. 4, p.299
207. Smith, Hannah, op. cit. (*Georgian Monarchy*), p.233
208. Ibid., p.208
209. Quoted in Worsley, op. cit., p.31
210. Quoted in Wilkins, op. cit., Vol. 1, p.275
211. Anonymous, 'An Elegy upon the Young Prince', Bodleian Library broadsheet ballads collection, MS. Rawl. poet. 207 (151–153)
212. Quoted in Chenevix Trench, op. cit., p.117
213. Black, Jeremy, op. cit. (*George II*), p.46
214. Borman, op. cit., p.79
215. Melville, op. cit., p.25
216. Elisabeth Charlotte, Duchess of Orléans, to Raugravine Luise von Degenfeld, 9 December 1717, see Kroll, op. cit. (*Liselotte*), p.191
217. Hatton, op. cit., p.200
218. Worsley, op. cit., p.35
219. Robbins Landon, op. cit., p.91
220. Sinclair-Stevenson, op. cit., p.60
221. Hatton, op. cit., p.215, note
222. Wilkins, op. cit., Vol. 1, p.284
223. 'Message from the late King to Prince of Wales, with the Answers', undated, Royal Archives RA GEO/MAIN/54046
224. Ibid.
225. Clarke, Alured, p.22
226. Wilkins, op. cit., Vol. 1, p.284

Chapter II: Leicester House

1. Cowie, Leonard W, Leicester House, *History Today*, Vol. 23 (1973)
2. British Museum, collection number BM1880,1113.2999
3. Elisabeth Charlotte, Duchess of Orléans, to Raugravine Luise von Degenfeld, 27 August 1719, see Kroll, op. cit. (*Liselotte*), pp.213–14
4. Thompson, op. cit., p.63; Connor, T.P., Colen Campbell as Architect to the Prince of Wales, *Architectural History*, Vol. 22 (1979), p.70, note 6
5. Baker-Smith, op. cit. (*Royal Discord*), p.30
6. Tillyard, op. cit., p.21
7. See White, Christopher, *The Dutch Pictures in the Collection of Her Majesty the Queen* (Cambridge University Press, Cambridge, 1982)

8. See van der Kiste, op. cit. (*King George II and Queen Caroline*), p.67

9. Anonymous, 'An Elegy upon the Young Prince', Bodleian Library broadsheet ballads collection, MS. Rawl. poet. 207 (151–153)

10. Campbell Orr, ed., op. cit. (*Queenship in Britain*), p.151

11. Elisabeth Charlotte, Duchess of Orléans, to Raugravine Luise von Degenfeld, 24 February 1718, see Kroll, op. cit. (*Liselotte*), pp.192–3

12. See Borman, op. cit., p.85

13. See Stephen Taylor, *Oxford Dictionary of National Biography*, entry William Wake

14. Hatton, op. cit., pp.353–4, note; Somerset, Anne, op. cit. (*Ladies in Waiting*), p.212

15. To Lady Cowper, undated, Hertfordshire Record Office, DE/P/D203

16. Somerset, Anne, op. cit. (*Ladies in Waiting*), p.214

17. Thomson, Mrs, ed., op. cit. (*Memoirs of Viscountess Sundon*), Vol. 1, p.332

18. Caroline to Charlotte Clayton, 30 July 1719, Royal Archives RA GEO/ADD/28/53

19. Caroline to Charlotte Clayton, 8 May 1716, Royal Archives GEO/ADD/28/36

20. Caroline to Charlotte Clayton, undated [late 1717 to early 1718], Royal Archives GEO/ADD/28/38

21. Caroline to Charlotte Clayton, 1 March 1719, Royal Archives GEO/ADD/28/52

22. Caroline to Charlotte Clayton, undated [after January 1718], Royal Archives GEO/ADD/28/46

23. Baroness von Gemmingen to Mary, Countess Cowper, 12 July 1718, Hertfordshire Record Office, DE/P/203

24. Clarke, Alured, op. cit., p.13

25. See Melville, op. cit., pp.180–1

26. Greenwood, op. cit., p.243

27. Cowie, op. cit.

28. Greenwood, op. cit. p.244

29. British Library, BL Add MS.22627, fol.13

30. Melville, op. cit., p.202

31. Quoted in Borman, op. cit., p.111

32. Arkell, op. cit., p.132

33. Melville, op. cit., p.239; Bryant, op. cit., p.9

34. See Connor, T.P., op. cit., p.68

35. Melville, op. cit., p.202

36. Walpole, Horace, op. cit. (*Memoirs of the Last Ten Years*), p.512

37. Sedgwick, Romney, ed., op. cit. (Hervey), Vol. 1, p.41

38. Elisabeth Charlotte, Duchess of Orléans, to Caroline, Princess of Wales, 11 June 1717, see Kroll, op. cit. (*Liselotte*), pp.187–8

39. Arkell, op. cit., p.132

40. Hughes, ed., op. cit., p.45

41. Beattie, op. cit., p.274

42. Ibid., p.275

43. Thomson, Mrs, ed., op. cit. (*Memoirs of Viscountess Sundon*), Vol. 1, p.78

44. Tite, Catherine, 'The Choice of Paris': Representing Frederick, Prince of Wales: a brief reconsideration, *British Art Journal*, Vol. 9, no 2 (2008), p.26

45. Lord Chancellor Cowper to Lord Chief Justice Parker, 20 January 1718, Royal Archives GEO/ADD/53017

46. Cowper, op. cit. (*Diary of Mary, Countess Cowper*), p.131

47. Hatton, op. cit., pp.213–14

48. See Caroline to Charlotte Clayton, Royal Archives GEO/ADD/28/14, GEO/ADD/28/7 and GEO/ADD/28/20, all undated (textual evidence suggests 1726–7 for RA GEO/ADD/28/7)

49. Wilkins, op. cit., Vol. 1, p.317
50. Quoted in Baker-Smith, op. cit. (*Anne*), p.14
51. Princess Anne to Caroline, undated, Royal Archives GEO/MAIN/52700
52. Arkell, op. cit., p.314, note 49
53. Ibid., p.110
54. Sedgwick, Romney, ed., *Some materials towards memoirs of the reign of George II*, op. cit., Vol. 2, p.406
55. Groom, Susanne, and Prosser, Lee, *Kew Palace: The Official Illustrated History* (Merrell, London, 2006), pp.29–30
56. Ibid., p.27
57. Anderson Winn, James, *A Window in the Bosom: The Letters of Alexander Pope* (Archon Books, Connecticut, 1977), p.70
58. Quoted in Groom and Prosser, op. cit., pp.30–1
59. Wilkins, op. cit., Vol. 1, p.313
60. Groom and Prosser, op. cit., p.29
61. Marschner, Joanna, Baths and Bathing at the Early Georgian Court, *Furniture History Society*, Vol. 31 (1995), p.24
62. 'some sort of pleasure': Lady Mary Wortley Montagu to Lady Mar, June 1723, see Halsband, Robert, ed., op. cit., Vol. 2, p.25
63. Batey, op. cit., p.205
64. Marschner, op. cit. (*Queen Caroline*), p.34
65. Groom and Prosser, op. cit., p.30
66. Wilkins, op. cit., Vol. 1, p.312
67. Quoted in Chenevix Trench, op. cit., p.124
68. Invoice for household expenses, undated, Royal Archives GEO/ADD/1/41
69. Wilkins, op. cit., Vol. 1, p.319
70. Ibid., p.326
71. Elisabeth Charlotte, Duchess of Orléans, to Raugravine Luise von Degenfeld, 31 March 1718, see Kroll, op. cit. (*Liselotte*), p.194
72. Quoted in Borman, op. cit., p.120
73. Black, Jeremy, op. cit. (*Hanoverians*), p.68
74. Wilkins, op. cit., Vol. 1, pp.292–3
75. Gold, op. cit., p.204
76. Instructions to the Dowager Countess of Portland as royal governess, 4 May 1719, Royal Archives GEO/MAIN/53038
77. Caroline to Charlotte Clayton, undated 1719, Royal Archives GEO/ADD/28/51a
78. Clarke, Alured, op. cit., pp.5–6
79. Worsley, op. cit., p.47
80. Wilkins, op. cit., Vol. 2, pp.162–3
81. Arkell, op. cit., p.137
82. Jonathan Swift, in Johnson, Samuel, *The Works of the Poets of Great Britain and Ireland; with Prefaces Biographical and Critical* (Andrew Miller, London, 1800), Vol. 5, p.421
83. Jonathan Swift, 'On Poetry, A Rapsody [sic]'
84. Wilkins, op. cit., Vol. 1, p.291
85. See Alexander Pope, *Sober Advice from Horace, to the Young Gentleman about Town* (London, 1735)
86. Marschner, op. cit. (*Queen Caroline*), p.139
87. Ibid., p.128
88. Wilkins, op. cit., Vol. 2, p.158
89. John Conduitt, 'To The Queen', in Newton, Isaac, op. cit., p.xi
90. Quoted in Worsley, op. cit., p.37
91. Smith, Hannah, op. cit. (*Georgian Monarchy*), p.201
92. Schaich, Michael, ed., *Monarchy and Religion: The Transformation of Royal Culture in Eighteenth-Century Europe* (Oxford University Press, Oxford, 2007), p.148
93. Cowper, op. cit. (*Diary of Mary, Countess Cowper*), p.13

94. Ibid., p.14
95. See John Gascoigne, *Oxford Dictionary of National Biography*, entry Samuel Clarke
96. Cowper, op. cit. (*Diary of Mary, Countess Cowper*), p.17
97. Quoted in Smith, Hannah, op. cit. (*Georgian Monarchy*), p.91; Cowper, op. cit. (*Diary of Mary, Countess Cowper*), p.74
98. Cowper, op. cit. (*Diary of Mary, Countess Cowper*), pp.90–2
99. Greenwood, op. cit., p.284
100. Jay, Emma, op. cit., p.35
101. Caroline to Charlotte Clayton, date 1718, Royal Archives GEO/ADD/28/27
102. Campbell Orr, ed., op. cit. (*Queenship in Britain*), p.162
103. 'Detached Anecdotes', *Belfast Monthly Magazine*, 31 March 1809
104. Marschner, op. cit. (*Queen Caroline*), p.150
105. Sedgwick, Romney, ed., op. cit. (Kimber edition), p.75
106. See Taylor, Stephen, 'Queen Caroline and the Church of England', in Taylor, Stephen, Connors, Richard, and Jones, Clyve, eds, *Hanoverian Britain and Empire: Essays in Memory of Philip Lawson* (The Boydell Press, Woodbridge, 1987)
107. Quoted in Marschner, op. cit. (*Queen Caroline*), p.145; Lord Hervey to Stephen Fox, 30 December 1731, in Ilchester, op. cit., p.131
108. See Marschner, op. cit. (*Queen Caroline*), p.18; Taylor, Stephen, op. cit.
109. Ibid. (Marschner), p.122
110. Cowper, op. cit. (*Diary of Mary, Countess Cowper*), p.137
111. Quoted in Wilkins, op. cit., Vol. 1, p.319
112. Ibid., p.320

113. Ibid., p.322
114. Cowper, op. cit. (*Diary of Mary, Countess Cowper*), p.134
115. See Black, Jeremy, op. cit. (*George II*), pp.50–1
116. Caroline to Charlotte Clayton, ? March 1719, Royal Archives GEO/ADD/28/51
117. Cowper, op. cit. (*Diary of Mary, Countess Cowper*), p.134
118. Ibid., p.135
119. Caroline to Charlotte Clayton, 1 March 1719, Royal Archives GEO/ADD/28/52
120. Caroline to Charlotte Clayton, undated, Royal Archives GEO/ADD/28/55
121. Caroline to Charlotte Clayton, 8 December 1719, Royal Archives GEO/ADD/28/17/56
122. Lady Mary Wortley Montagu to Lady Mar, March 1725, see Halsband, Robert, ed., op. cit., Vol. 2, p.50
123. Cowper, op. cit. (*Diary of Mary, Countess Cowper*), p.128
124. Ibid., p.131
125. Ibid.
126. Ibid.
127. Ibid., p.132
128. Ibid.
129. Ibid., pp.136, 142
130. Ibid., p.164
131. Caroline to Charlotte Clayton, 22 April 1720, Royal Archives GEO/ADD/28/59
132. Van der Kiste, op. cit. (*King George II and Queen Caroline*), p.73
133. Sloane, Hans, and Birch, Thomas, An Account of Inoculation by Sir Hans Sloane, Bart. Given to Mr Ranby, to be Published, Anno 1736. Communicated by Thomas Birch, DD, Secret RS, *Philosophical Transactions* (1683–1775), Vol. 49, published by the Royal Society, p.517

134. Cowper, op. cit. (*Diary of Mary, Countess Cowper*), p.140
135. Ibid., p.141
136. Ibid., p.150
137. Ibid.
138. Ibid., p.163
139. Arkell, R.L., George I's Letters to His Daughter, *The English Historical Review*, Vol. 52, no 207 (July 1937), p.497
140. Thompson, op. cit., p.58
141. Robbins Landon, op. cit., pp.99–100
142. Cowper, op. cit. (*Diary of Mary, Countess Cowper*), pp.151–2
143. Arkell, op. cit. (George I's Letters), p.497
144. Moore, op. cit., p.163
145. Caroline to Charlotte Clayton, 2 July 1720, Royal Archives GEO/ADD/28/60
146. Thomson, Mrs, ed., op. cit. (*Memoirs of Viscountess Sundon*), Vol. 1, p.341
147. Ibid., p.333
148. Arkell, op. cit. (George I's Letters), p.497
149. Quoted in Worsley, op. cit., p.47
150. Marschner, op. cit. (*Queen Caroline*), p.15
151. Baker-Smith, op. cit. (*Royal Discord*), p.33
152. Thomson, Mrs, ed., op. cit. (*Memoirs of Viscountess Sundon*), Vol. 1, p.123
153. Arkell, op. cit. (George I's Letters), p.499
154. Ibid., p.127
155. Vivian, op. cit., p.64
156. See Worsley, op. cit., p.123
157. Campbell Orr, op. cit. (*Queenship in Britain*), p.151
158. Jenkin Thomas Philipps (letters in Latin, translated by Prince William Augustus and Princess Mary), Royal Archives GEO/ADD/1/9, letter 34
159. Sloane, Hans, op. cit., p.518
160. Conduitt, John, 'To The Queen', in Newton, Isaac, op. cit., p.v
161. Wilkins, op. cit., Vol. 2, p.152
162. Quoted in Chenevix Trench, op. cit., p.126
163. Waller, Maureen, *1700: Scenes from London Life* (Hodder & Stoughton, London, 2000), p.64
164. Marschner, op. cit. (*Queen Caroline*), p.189, note 32
165. Martin Maingaud, Princesses Anne, Amelia and Caroline, 1721, Royal Collection, RCIN 404985
166. Arkell, op. cit., p.110
167. Borman, op. cit., p.130
168. Princess Mary, Royal Archives GEO/ADD/1/9, letter 49
169. Princess Mary, Royal Archives GEO/ADD/1/9, letter 26
170. Princess Mary, Royal Archives GEO/ADD/1/9, letter 37
171. Princess Mary, Royal Archives GEO/ADD/1/9, letter 9
172. Princess Mary, Royal Archives GEO/ADD/1/9, letter 8
173. Grundy, op. cit., p.209; Sloane, op. cit., p.518
174. Grundy, op. cit., p.210
175. Ibid., p.211
176. Ibid., p.213
177. Smith, Hannah, op. cit. (*Georgian Monarchy*), p.93
178. Quoted in Arkell, op. cit., pp.134–5
179. Lady Mary Wortley Montagu to Lady Mar, June 1723, see Halsband, Robert, ed., op. cit., Vol. 2, p.26
180. Elisabeth Charlotte, Duchess of Orléans, to Raugravine Luise von Degenfeld, 11 June 1722, see Kroll, op. cit., pp.240–1
181. Black, op. cit. (*Hanoverians*), p.79
182. Elisabeth Charlotte, Duchess of Orléans, to Raugravine Luise von

Degenfeld, 11 June 1722, see Kroll, op. cit., p.241

183. Voltaire, François-Marie Arouet, *Letters on the English* (London, 1733), letter XI

184. Smith, Hannah, op. cit. (*Georgian Monarchy*), p.94

185. Cowper, op. cit. (*Diary of Mary, Countess Cowper*), pp.161, 174

186. Ibid., p.175

187. Quoted in Smith, Hannah, op. cit. (*Georgian Monarchy*), p.222

188. Quoted in Borman, op. cit., p.123

189. Cowper, op. cit. (*Diary of Mary, Countess Cowper*), p.158

190. Caroline to Charlotte Clayton, end 1719, Royal Archives GEO/ADD/28/57

191. Hervey, MD, p.34

192. Quoted in Curteis, Captain Henry, *A Forgotten Prince of Wales* (Everett & Co., London, 1912), p.63

193. 'Account of George I's South Sea stock, by Sir Charles Vernon', Royal Archives GEO/MAIN/52847

194. Lady Mary Wortley Montagu to Lady Mar, August 1725, see Halsband, Robert, ed., op. cit., Vol. 2, p.54

195. Groom and Prosser, op. cit., p.31

196. Thomson, Mrs, ed., op. cit. (*Memoirs of Viscountess Sundon*), Vol. 1, p.121

197. Quoted in Curteis, op. cit., p.61

198. Hughes, op. cit., p.86

199. Ibid., p.65

200. Lady Mary Wortley Montagu to Lady Mar, 31 October 1723, see Halsband, Robert, ed., op. cit., Vol. 2, p.31

201. Wilkins, op. cit., Vol. 1, p.370

202. Ibid.

203. Yorke-Long, op. cit.

204. Ibid.

205. Robbins Landon, op. cit., p.108

206. Quoted in Worsley, op. cit., p.88

207. Ibid., p.110

208. Ibid., p.10

209. Caroline to Charlotte Clayton, 18 October 1725, Royal Archives GEO/ADD/28/61

210. Cowper, op. cit. (*Diary of Mary, Countess Cowper*), p.21

211. Somerset, Anne, op. cit. (*Ladies in Waiting*), p.215

212. Cowper, op. cit. (*Diary of Mary, Countess Cowper*), p.168

213. Hughes, op. cit., p.127

214. Caroline to Charlotte Clayton, 13 July 1726, Royal Archives GEO/ADD/28/62

215. Borman, op. cit., p.127

216. Sedgwick, Romney, ed., op. cit. (Hervey), Vol. 1, p.278; Baker-Smith, op. cit. (*Anne*), p.21

217. Walpole, Horace, op. cit., p.447

218. Borman, op. cit., p.129

219. Lane Furdell, Elizabeth, *James Welwood: Physician to the Glorious Revolution* (Combined Publishing, Pennsylvania, 1998), p.221

220. Ibid.

221. Sedgwick, Romney, ed., op. cit. (Hervey), Vol. 2, p.474

222. Quoted in Worsley, op. cit., p.173

223. Furdell, op. cit., p.261, note 31

224. Philip Dormer Stanhope, Earl of Chesterfield to Henrietta Howard, 21 October 1728, in Mahon, Lord, ed., op. cit., Vol. 1, p.356

225. Ibid.

226. Quoted in Marschner, op. cit. (*Queen Caroline*), p.133

227. Quoted in Hammond, Eugene, *Jonathan Swift: Irish Blow-in* (University of Delaware Press, 2016), p.387

228. Ibid., p.393

229. Ibid.

230. Van der Kiste, op. cit. (*Georgian Princesses*), p.94

231. Marlow, op. cit., p.212
232. Sedgwick, Romney, ed., op. cit. (Hervey), Vol. 1, p.28
233. Quoted in Black, Jeremy, op. cit. (*George II*), p.55

Chapter III: Queen

1. See Smith, Hannah, op. cit. (*Georgian Monarchy*), p.118
2. Hibbert, Christopher, *The Marlboroughs: John and Sarah Churchill 1650–1744* (Viking, London, 2001), p.334
3. Robbins Landon, op. cit., p.115
4. Wilkins, op. cit., Vol. 2, p.34
5. *Verses on the Coronation of their late Majesties King George II and Queen Caroline, October 11, MDCCXXVII* (W. Bowyer, London, 1761), p.xv
6. Sedgwick, Romney, ed., op. cit. (Hervey), Vol. 1, p.66
7. Quoted in Moore, op. cit., pp.31–2
8. Van Muyden, op. cit., p.205
9. 'To the Queen', in *Verses on the Coronation*, op. cit., p.xv
10. Campbell Orr, ed., op. cit. (*Queenship in Europe*), p.292
11. Ibid.
12. Strong, op. cit., p.372; Thompson, op. cit., p.73
13. *Verses on the Coronation*, op. cit., p.xxv
14. Quennell, op. cit., p.124
15. Greenwood, op. cit., p.298
16. Swift, Jonathan, *Gulliver's Travels* (Penguin Classics reprint, London, 2003), pp.31–2
17. Quoted in Smith, Hannah, op. cit. (*Georgian Monarchy*), p.100
18. Caroline to Charlotte Clayton, May 1719, Royal Archives GEO/ADD/28/53
19. Quoted in Hammond, op. cit., p.551
20. Sophie of Hanover to Hans Caspar von Bothmer, 29 September 1708, see Doebner, Richard, ed., op. cit., p.265
21. Hughes, op. cit., p.268
22. Sedgwick, Romney, ed., op. cit. (Kimber edition), p.88
23. Arkell, op. cit., p.242
24. Queen Caroline's jointure, 10 August 1727, Royal Archives GEO/MAIN 52760-6
25. See Urstad, op. cit., p.262, note 19
26. Prescott, op. cit., p.42; Poem XLIII, in *Verses on the Coronation*, op. cit., p.21
27. Royal Collection RCIN443222
28. Conduitt, John, 'To The Queen', in Newton, Isaac, op. cit., p.xii
29. See Wilkins, op. cit., Vol. 2, p.151
30. See Yorke-Long, op. cit.
31. Sedgwick, Romney, ed., op. cit. (Kimber edition), pp.44–5
32. See Taylor, Stephen, 'Queen Caroline and the Church of England', in Taylor, Stephen, Connors, Richard, and Jones, Clyve, eds, op. cit.
33. British Museum, collection number Cc,3.173
34. Caroline to Charlotte Clayton, undated, Royal Archives GEO/ADD/28/18
35. Black, op. cit. (*George II*), p.89; Richard Savage, *The Bastard* (1728)
36. Arkell, op. cit., p.153; Black, op. cit. (*George II*), p.93
37. 'To the Queen', in *Verses on the Coronation*, op. cit., p.xvi
38. Black, Jeremy, *Walpole in Power* (Sutton Publishing, Stroud, 2001), p.30
39. Ibid.
40. Van Muyden, op. cit., p.227
41. Black, op. cit. (*Walpole in Power*), p.31
42. Wilkins, op. cit., Vol. 2, p.44

43. Sedgwick, Romney, ed., op. cit. (Kimber edition), p.44

44. Ibid., p.39

45. Quoted in Arkell, op. cit., p.207

46. Black, op. cit. (*George II*), p.81

47. Sedgwick, Romney, ed., op. cit. (Kimber edition), p.39

48. Black, op. cit. (*George II*), p.87

49. Sedgwick, Romney, ed., op. cit. (Kimber edition), p.61

50. Ibid., p.103

51. Ibid., p.106

52. Black, op. cit. (*Walpole in Power*), p.62

53. Worsley, op. cit., p.150; Wilkins, op. cit., Vol. 2, p.42

54. Walpole, Horace, *Reminiscences, written in 1788, for the amusement of Miss Mary and Miss Agnes B***y* (London, 1818), p.71

55. Ibid., pp.253–4

56. Vivian, op. cit., p.86

57. Ibid., p.87

58. *Verses on the Coronation*, op. cit., p.xvi

59. Arkell, op. cit., p.158

60. Poem VXLIX, in *Verses on the Coronation*, op. cit., p.24

61. Jay, Emma, op. cit., p.35

62. Baker-Smith, op. cit. (*Anne*), p.20; van der Kiste, op. cit. (*King George II and Queen Caroline*), p.109

63. Lady Mary Wortley Montagu to Lady Mar, October 1727, see Halsband, Robert, ed., op. cit., Vol. 2, p.85

64. Quoted in Smith, Hannah, op. cit. (*Georgian Monarchy*), p.206

65. Impey, op. cit., p.56

66. Quoted in Greenwood, op. cit., p.347

67. 'epidemical distempers', see Marschner, op. cit. (*Queen Caroline*), p.45

68. Thomas Tickell, 'Kensington Gardens', 1722

69. White, Christopher, op. cit., 68

70. *HMC Manuscripts of the Earl of Egmont*, 3 vols (London, 1920–23), Vol. 2, p.445, Vol. 2, p.138

71. See Marschner, op. cit. (*Queen Caroline*), pp.37–40

72. 'On the Queen's Mount at Kensington', anonymous, *St James' Evening Post*, 29 March 1733

73. Worsley, op. cit., p.157

74. Lord Hervey to Lady Mary Wortley Montagu, 7 November 1727, see Halsband, Robert, ed., op. cit., Vol. 2, p.87

75. Schaich, op. cit., p.148

76. Moore, op. cit., p.83

77. Borman, op. cit., p.177; Sinclair-Stevenson, op. cit., p.65

78. Worsley, op. cit., p.270

79. Quoted in Borman, op. cit., p.164

80. Quoted in Worsley, op. cit., p.152

81. Ibid., p.153

82. Borman, op. cit., p.163

83. Lady Mary Wortley Montagu to Lady Mar, October 1727, see Halsband, Robert, ed., op. cit., Vol. 2, p.86

84. Walpole, Horace, op. cit., p.514

85. See Einberg, Elizabeth, et al., op. cit., pp.88–91

86. Jonathan Swift, *A Poem to His Majesty King George II on the present state of affairs in England: with remarks on the alterations expected at court, after the rise of Parliament* (Dublin, 1727)

87. Black, op. cit. (*George II*), pp.118–19

88. Thomson, Mrs, ed., op. cit. (*Memoirs of Viscountess Sundon*), Vol. 2, pp.39–40

89. John Gay to Brigadier James Dormer, 22 November 1726, in Burgess, C.F., ed., op. cit., p.63

90. John Gay, *Fables*, Vol. 1 (1727), Fable 1

91. John Gay to Alexander Pope, October 1727, in Burgess, C.F., ed., op. cit., p.65

92. John Gay and Alexander Pope to Jonathan Swift, 22 October 1727, ibid., pp.68–9

93. Quoted in Robbins Landon, op. cit., p.109

94. Richard Savage, *The Bastard*

95. *HMC Manuscripts of the Earl of Egmont*, op. cit., Vol. 1, p.16

96. George II to William Augustus, Duke of Cumberland, 9 August 1757, Royal Archives GEO/MAIN 52970

97. Oates, Jonathan, *Sweet William or The Butcher? The Duke of Cumberland and the '45* (Pen & Sword, 2008), p.33

98. Jenkin Thomas Philipps to Prince William Augustus, December 1727, Royal Archives GEO/ADD/1/9, letter 7; quoted in Oates, op. cit., p.33

99. Arkell, op. cit., p.165

100. See Royal Archives GEO/MAIN/53040 (undated)

101. Quoted in Sinclair-Stevenson, op. cit., p.62

102. Ibid.

103. Tillyard, op. cit., pp.12–13

104. Vivian, op. cit., p.64

105. See Royal Archives GEO/ADD/1/6

106. George Tilson to Prince Frederick, 15 July 1726, Royal Archives GEO/ADD/1/5

107. Townshend to Prince Frederick, 16 August 1726, Royal Archives GEO/ADD/1/8

108. Quoted in Sinclair-Stevenson, op. cit., p.62

109. *The Daily Post*, 8 December 1728

110. Sedgwick, Romney, ed., op. cit. (Hervey), Vol. 3, p.814; Baker-Smith, op. cit. (*Anne*), p.29

111. Vivian, op. cit., p.94

112. Quoted in Sinclair-Stevenson, op. cit., p.63

113. Wilkins, op. cit., Vol. 2, p.92

114. Greenwood, op. cit., p.304

115. Wilkins, op. cit., Vol. 2, p.128

116. See Royal Collection RCIN421802

117. Quoted in Moore, op. cit., p.162

118. Lady Mary Wortley Montagu to Lord Hervey, 30 October 1734, see Halsband, Robert, ed., op. cit., Vol. 2, p.99

119. Worsley, op. cit., p.163

120. Quoted in Moore, op. cit., p.174

121. Campbell Orr, ed., op. cit., p.169

122. Baker-Smith, op. cit. (*Anne*), p.23; van der Kiste, op. cit. (*Georgian Princesses*), p.65

123. Bushell, T.L., Princess Amelia and the Politics of Georgian England, *The Centennial Review*, Vol. 17, no 4 (1973), p.360, note 10

124. Quoted in Greenwood, op. cit., p.368

125. Thomson, Mrs, ed., op. cit. (*Memoirs of Viscountess Sundon*), Vol. 2, p.288

126. Sedgwick, ed., op. cit. (Kimber edition), p.82

127. Sedgwick, Romney, ed., op. cit. (Hervey), Vol. 1, p.277

128. Ibid., Vol. 1, p.26

129. Campbell Orr, ed., op. cit. (*Queenship in Britain*), p.166

130. Vivian, op. cit., p.116

131. Groom and Prosser, op. cit., p.33

132. Woodward, John, Amigoni as Portrait Painter in England, *The Burlington Magazine*, Vol. 99, no 646 (1957), p.22

133. Van Muyden, op. cit., p.205

134. Quoted in Moore, op. cit., p.81

135. Campbell Orr, ed., op. cit. (*Queenship in Europe*), p.294

136. Quoted in Worsley, op. cit., p.160

137. Smith, Hannah, op. cit., p.101

138. Wilkins, op. cit., Vol. 2, p.64

139. Thomson, Mrs, ed., op. cit. (*Memoirs of Viscountess Sundon*), Vol. 1, pp.167–8

140. Quoted in Wilkins, op. cit., Vol. 2, p.120

141. See Smith, Hannah, op. cit., p.201

142. Sedgwick, Romney, ed., op. cit. (Hervey), Vol. 2, p.609

143. Hughes, ed., op. cit., p.86

144. Lady Lansdowne to Henrietta Howard, 20 August 1727, in *Letters to and from Henrietta, Countess of Suffolk, and her second husband, the Hon George Berkeley; from 1712 to 1767* (John Murray, London, 1824), Vol. 1, p.269

145. Quoted in Greenwood, op. cit., p.303

146. Quoted in Worsley, op. cit., p.133

147. Hughes, ed., op. cit., p.209

148. Egmont diaries, quoted in Marschner, Joanna, op. cit. (*Baths and Bathing*), p.27

149. Quoted in Smith, Hannah, op. cit. (*Georgian Monarchy*), p.220

150. See Black, Jeremy, 'George II and All That Stuff': On the Value of the Neglected, *Albion: A Quarterly Journal Concerned with British Studies*, Vol. 36, no 4 (2004), p.605

151. Sedgwick, Romney, ed., op. cit. (Hervey), Vol. 2, p.495

152. Quoted in Moore, op. cit., p.86

153. Smith, Hannah, op. cit. (*Georgian Monarchy*), p.208

154. Vivian, op. cit., p.101

155. Greenwood, op. cit., p.303

156. Vivian, op. cit., p.115

157. *Gentleman's Magazine*, April 1736

158. Lord Hervey to Stephen Fox, 30 May 1727, in Ilchester, Earl of, ed., op. cit., pp.16–17

159. Jenkin Thomas Philipps to Princess Mary, Royal Archives GEO/ADD/1/9, letter 153; *Craftsman*, 16 August 1727; quoted in Robbins Landon, op. cit., p.134

160. Jay, Emma, op. cit., p.37

161. Sedgwick, Romney, ed., op. cit. (Hervey), Vol. 3, p.751

162. Ibid., Vol. 1, p.102

163. Worsley, op. cit., p.166

164. Ibid., p.240

165. Quoted in Curteis, op. cit., pp.65–6

166. Worsley, op. cit., p.154

167. Ibid., p.155

168. Thomson, Mrs A.T., *Memoirs of Sarah Duchess of Marlborough and of the Court of Queen Anne*, 2 vols (Henry Colburn, London, 1839), Vol. 1, p.279

169. 'To the Queen', in *Verses on the Coronation*, op. cit., p.xii

170. *Verses on the Coronation*, op. cit., Verse XXIV, p.17

171. Campbell Orr, ed., op. cit. (*Queenship in Europe*), p.292

172. Schwoerer, Lois G., Images of Queen Mary II, 1689–95, *Renaissance Quarterly*, Vol. 42, no 4 (1989), pp.735–6

173. Arkell, op. cit., p.168

174. Black, Jeremy, op. cit. ('George II and All That Stuff'), p.599

175. *Verses on the Coronation*, op. cit., Verse XLIX, p.24

176. *St James's Evening Post*, 6 September 1729

177. Wilkins, op. cit., Vol. 2, p.125

178. Ibid., p.124

179. Thompson, op. cit., p.90

180. Ibid., p.92

181. Jones, Thomas, op. cit., p.45

182. Van der Kiste, op. cit. (*King George II and Queen Caroline*), p.119

183. Wilkins, op. cit., Vol. 2, p.115

184. Thomson, Mrs, ed., op. cit. (*Memoirs of Viscountess Sundon*), Vol. 1, p.173

185. Cowper, op. cit. (*Diary of Mary, Countess Cowper*), p.114

186. Black, Jeremy, op. cit. (*George II*), p.103

187. Townshend letter, 28 November 1737, BM.Add.Mss.28058, fo.152, see Hanson, L.W., Townshend on the Death of Queen Caroline, *The English Historical Review*, Vol. 46, no 184 (1931)

188. Wilkins, op. cit., Vol. 2, pp.134–5

189. Thomson, Mrs, ed., op. cit. (*Memoirs of Viscountess Sundon*), Vol. 2, p.241

190. Jay, Emma, op. cit., p.37

191. Marschner and Bindman, op. cit., p.333

192. Colton, Judith, Merlin's Cave and Queen Caroline: Garden Art as Political Propaganda, *Eighteenth-Century Studies*, Vol. 10, no 1 (1976), p.3

193. Marschner, op. cit. (*Queen Caroline*), p.154

194. Paget Toynbee, Mrs, ed., *The Letters of Horace Walpole, Fourth Earl of Orford*, 16 vols (Clarendon Press, Oxford, 1903–05), Vol. 16, p.322

195. Voltaire, François-Marie Arouet, op. cit., Letter XI

196. *HMC Manuscripts of the Earl of Egmont*, op. cit., Vol. 1, p.311

197. Marschner, op. cit. (*Queen Caroline*), p.196, note 3

198. Ibid., p.94

199. Van Muyden, op. cit., p.205

200. Swift, Jonathan, *Gulliver's Travels* (Penguin Classics reprint, London, 2003), p.110

201. Marschner, op. cit. (*Baths and Bathing*), pp.25–6

202. Ibid., pp.24–6

203. *The Poetical Works of Richard Savage*, 2 vols (Apollo Press, Edinburgh, 1780), Vol. 2, p.180

204. Arkell, op. cit., p.229

205. Sedgwick, Romney, ed., op. cit. (Hervey), Vol. 1, p.107

206. Quoted in Borman, op. cit., p.101

207. Walpole, op. cit. (*Reminiscences*), (London, 1818), p.89

208. Worsley, op. cit., p.236

209. Thomson, Mrs, ed., op. cit. (*Memoirs of Viscountess Sundon*), Vol. 1, p.147

210. Quoted in Rushton, Alan R., *Royal Maladies: Inherited Diseases in the Ruling Houses of Europe* (Trafford Publishing, 2008), p.51

211. Hervey, MD, p.110

212. Quoted in Arkell, op. cit., p.223

213. Thompson, op. cit., p.100

214. Arkell, op. cit., p.230

215. Worsley, op. cit., p.211; Sedgwick, ed., op. cit. (Kimber edition), p.164

216. See Taylor, Stephen and Smith, Hannah, Hephaestion and Alexander: Lord Hervey, Frederick, Prince of Wales, and the Royal Favourite in England in the 1730s, *The English Historical Review*, Vol. 124, no 507 (2009); Thompson, op. cit., p.99

217. *Verses Addressed to the Imitator of the 1st Satire on the 2nd Book of Horace*. Lady Mary Wortley Montagu's verse may have been co-written by Hervey

218. Worsley, op. cit., p.252

219. Hughes, op. cit., p.288; Sedgwick, ed., op. cit. (Kimber edition), p.80; Moore, op. cit., p.175

220. Alexander Pope, 'Epistle to Dr Arbuthnot'

221. Sedgwick, Romney, ed., op. cit. (Hervey), Vol. 2, p.496; Worsley, op. cit., pp.168, 196

222. Moore, op. cit., p.239

223. See Batt, Jennifer, From the Field to the Coffeehouse: Changing Representations of Stephen

Duck, *Criticism*, Vol. 47 no 4 (2005), pp.451–2

224. Thomson, Mrs, ed., op. cit. (*Memoirs of Viscountess Sundon*), Vol. 1, p.187

225. Stephen Duck, 'Royal Benevolence' (W. Harris, London, 1730)

226. Batt, op. cit., p.460; Christmas, William J., *The Lab'ring Muses: Work, Writing and the Social Order in English Plebeian Poetry, 1730–1830* (University of Delaware Press, Newark, 2001), p.187

227. Wilkins, op. cit., Vol. 2, p.182

228. Batt, op. cit., p.459

229. Marschner, op. cit. (*Queen Caroline*), p.59

230. Ibid., p.136

231. Duck, Stephen, *Poems on Several Occasions* (John Osborn, London, 1738), p.166

232. Ibid., p.58

233. Colton, op. cit., p.190

234. Groom and Prosser, op. cit., p.35

235. Stephen Duck, dedication to *Poems on Several Occasions*, p.vii

236. Marschner, op. cit. (*Queen Caroline*), p.76

237. Groom and Prosser, op. cit., p.37

238. William Mason, 'An Heroic Epistle to Sir William Chambers', 1773

239. Marschner, op. cit. (*Queen Caroline*), p.84

240. Marschner, Joanna, and Bindman, David, op. cit., p.334

241. Marschner, op. cit. (*Queen Caroline*), p.79

242. Quoted in Colton, op. cit., p.11

243. Stephen Duck, dedication to *Poems on Several Occasions*, p.vi

244. Duck, *Poems on Several Occasions*, p.96

245. Wilkins, op. cit., Vol. 2, p.221

246. Ibid., p.222

247. Black, Jeremy, op. cit. (*George II*), p.99

248. Rosenthal, ed., op. cit., p.85

249. Black, Jeremy, op. cit. (*George II*), p.98

250. Sedgwick, Romney, ed., op. cit. (Hervey), Vol. 1, p.194

251. Quoted in Moore, op. cit., p.174; Wakefield, Geoffrey, *The Princesses Royal* (Robert Hale, London, 1973), p.85

252. Wakefield, op. cit., p.85

253. Sedgwick, ed., op. cit. (Kimber edition), p.59

254. Thomson, Mrs, ed., op. cit. (*Memoirs of Viscountess Sundon*), Vol. 2, p.288

255. Baker-Smith, op. cit. (*Anne*), p.44

256. Document detailing ceremonial for Princess Anne's marriage, 14 March 1734, Royal Archives GEO/MAIN 52790

257. Hughes, op. cit., p.110

258. Baker-Smith, op. cit. (*Anne*), pp.46–7; Arkell, op. cit., p.238

259. Baker-Smith, op. cit. (*Anne*), p.47

260. Sedgwick, ed., op. cit. (Kimber edition), p.77

261. Quoted in Arkell, op. cit., p.212

262. Baker-Smith, op. cit. (*Anne*), p.59

263. Sedgwick, ed., op. cit. (Kimber edition), p.84

264. Ibid., p.60

265. Ibid., p.78

266. Black, op. cit. (*Walpole in Power*), p.38

267. Quoted in Arkell, op. cit., p.203

268. Thompson, op. cit., p.102

269. Quoted in Greenwood, op. cit., p.329

270. Sedgwick, ed., op. cit., pp.150–1

271. See Hervey, 'The Death of Lord Hervey; or, a morning at court, a drama'

272. Borman, op. cit., p.180

273. Ibid., p.182

274. Sedgwick, Romney, ed., op. cit. (Hervey), Vol. 1, p.43

275. Lady Hervey to Henrietta Howard, 30 August 1729, in *Letters to and from Henrietta, Countess of Suffolk, and her second husband, the Hon George Berkeley; from 1712 to 1767*, op. cit., Vol. 1, p.360

276. Quoted in Borman, op. cit., p.166

277. Thomson, Mrs, ed., op. cit. (*Memoirs of Viscountess Sundon*), Vol. 1, p.243

278. Borman, op. cit., p.187

279. Thomson, Mrs, ed., op. cit. (*Memoirs of Viscountess Sundon*), Vol. 1, p.243

280. Sedgwick, ed., op. cit. (Kimber edition), p.115

281. Ibid., pp.110–11

282. Ibid., p.113

283. Lord Bathurst to Henrietta Howard, 26 November 1734, in *Letters to and from Henrietta, Countess of Suffolk, and her second husband, the Hon George Berkeley; from 1712 to 1767*, op. cit., Vol. 2, pp.122–6

284. Sedgwick, ed., op. cit. (Kimber edition), p.135

285. Worsley, op. cit., p.178

286. Thomson, Mrs, ed., op. cit. (*Memoirs of Viscountess Sundon*), Vol. 1, p.248

287. Arkell, op. cit., p.227

288. Stephen Duck, 'To His Royal Highness The Duke of Cumberland, on his Birth-Day', *Poems on Several Occasions*, p.97

289. Tillyard, op. cit., p.15

290. Vivian, op. cit., p.145

291. Sir Lambert Blackwell, 'To the Princess of Wales', in *The English Poems Collected from the Oxford and Cambridge Verses on the Death of His Royal Highness Frederick Prince of Wales* (Hamilton Bruce, Edinburgh, 1751), p.18

292. See Moore, op. cit., p.181

293. Sedgwick, ed., op. cit. (Kimber edition), p.90

294. Quoted in Vivian, op. cit., p.200

295. Caroline to Augusta, Princess of Wales, undated [1737], Royal Archives GEO/MAIN 52823

296. Tillyard, op. cit., p.16

297. *Gentleman's Magazine*, April 1736

298. Arkell, op. cit., p.270

299. Campbell Orr, ed., op. cit. (*Queenship in Britain*), p.153

300. 'By the Right Honourable David Lord Viscount Stormont, B. A. Student of Ch. Ch', in *The English Poems*, op. cit., p.6

301. See Moore, op. cit., p.236

302. Van der Kiste, op. cit. (*King George II and Queen Caroline*), p.142

303. Paulson, Ronald, *Hogarth: High Art and Low, 1732–50* (James Clarke & Co., 1992), p.155

304. Worsley, op. cit., p.261

305. Sedgwick, Romney, ed., op. cit. (Hervey), Vol. 2, p.457

306. Somerset, Anne, op. cit. (*Ladies in Waiting*), p.221

307. Moore, op. cit., p.214

308. Sedgwick, Romney, ed., op. cit. (Hervey), Vol. 1, p.528

309. Van der Kiste, op. cit. (*King George II and Queen Caroline*), p.142

310. Ibid.

311. Sedgwick, Romney, ed., op. cit. (Hervey), Vol. 1, p.491

312. See National Archives SP36/20/321, to Lord Tankerville, 12 October 1730

313. Thompson, op. cit., p.116

314. Arkell, op. cit., p.260

315. Moore, op. cit., p.237

316. *HMC Manuscripts of the Earl of Egmont*, op. cit., Vol. 2, p.445

317. Jesse, John Heneage, *Memoirs of the Court of England During the Reign of the Stuarts*, 3 vols (Henry G. Bohn, London, 1857), p.100

318. Jay, Emma, op. cit., p.38

319. Marschner, op. cit. (*Queen Caroline*), p.85

320. Van der Kiste, op. cit. (*King George II and Queen Caroline*), p.151

321. Wilkins, op. cit., Vol. 2, p.323

322. Black, op. cit. (*George II*), p.159

323. Sedgwick, Romney, ed., op. cit. (Kimber edition), p.257

324. Sedgwick, Romney, ed., op. cit. (Hervey), Vol. 3, p.681

325. Ibid., Vol. 3, p.757

326. Frederick, Prince of Wales to King George II and Queen Caroline, 5 July 1737, Royal Archives GEO/MAIN 52809

327. Sedgwick, Romney, ed., op. cit. (Kimber edition), p.275

328. Ibid.

329. Ibid., p.280

330. Caroline to Augusta, Princess of Wales, undated [1737], Royal Archives GEO/MAIN 52823

331. Jones, Mary, op. cit., p.362

332. Dr Joseph Smith, 'Monody', in Jesse, John Heneage, op. cit., p.84

333. Hughes, ed., op. cit., p.111

334. Sedgwick, ed., op. cit. (Hervey), Vol. 3, p.905

335. Van der Kiste, op. cit. (*King George II and Queen Caroline*), p.165

336. Bland, Olivia, *The Royal Way of Death* (Constable, London, 1986), p.95

337. George II to Sophia Dorothea, Queen of Prussia, 30 November 1737, Royal Archives RA GEO/MAIN/52697

338. Quoted in Smith, Hannah, op. cit. (*Georgian Monarchy*), p.101

Bibliography

Primary Sources (Unpublished)
Bodleian Library, Oxford (broadside ballads collection)
Chatsworth House, Derbyshire
Gottfried Wilhelm Leibniz Bibliothek, Hanover
Hertfordshire Archives (Mary, Countess Cowper papers)
Historic Royal Palaces (Master cook William Daniel,
    Kensington Palace menu book 1736–7)
Lambeth Palace Library
The National Archives (State Paper Office, including papers of
    the Secretaries of State up to 1782)
Rare Book & Manuscript Library, University of Pennsylvania
    (Neitschütz papers)
Preussisches Staatsarchiv, Hanover
The Royal Archives (GEO/MAIN/52697–53087, GEO/
    MAIN/54037, 54040, 54041, GEO/ADD/01/1–17, 25–55,
    GEO/ADD/28/1–27, 29–40, 43–68, 70–141, 143)
Shropshire Record Office

Secondary Sources
Adamson, John, *The Princely Courts of Europe 1500–1750*
    (Weidenfeld & Nicolson, London, 1999)

Anderson Winn, James, *Queen Anne: Patroness of Arts* (Oxford University Press, Oxford, 2014)

Arkell, R.L., *Caroline of Ansbach: George the Second's Queen* (Oxford University Press, Oxford, 1939)

Ashdown, Dulcie, *Ladies-in-Waiting* (Arthur Barker, London, 1976)

Baily, F.E., *Sophia of Hanover* (Hutchinson & Co., London, 1936)

Baird, Rosemary, *Mistress of the House: Great Ladies and Grand Houses 1670–1830* (Weidenfeld & Nicolson, London, 2003)

Baker-Smith, Veronica, *A Life of Anne of Hanover, Princess Royal* (Brill, 1995)

– *Royal Discord: The Family of George II* (Athena Press, London, 2008)

Barlo Jr, Nik, Komachi, Hanae, and Queren, Henning, *Herrenhausen Gardens* (Hinstorff, Rostock, 2008)

Beattie, John M., *The English Court in the Reign of George I* (Cambridge University Press, Cambridge, 1967)

Black, Jeremy, *Walpole in Power* (Sutton Publishing, Stroud, 2001)

– *The Hanoverians: The History of a Dynasty* (Hambledon & London, London, 2004)

– *A Subject for Taste: Culture in Eighteenth-Century England* (Hambledon & London, London, 2005)

– *George II* (University of Exeter Press, Exeter, 2007)

– *Politics and Foreign Policy in the Age of George I, 1714–27* (Ashgate, Farnham, 2014)

Black, Jeremy, ed., *Britain in the Age of Walpole* (Macmillan Education, Basingstoke, 1984)

Bland, Olivia, *The Royal Way of Death* (Constable, London, 1986)

Borman, Tracy, *King's Mistress, Queen's Servant: The Life and Times of Henrietta Howard* (Pimlico paperback, London, 2008)

Brown, Jane, *My Darling Heriott: Henrietta Luxborough, Poetic Gardener and Irrepressible Exile* (HarperPress, London, 2006)

Brown, Michael, *A Political Biography of John Toland* (Routledge, London, 2016)

Bryant, Julius, *Marble Hill House Twickenham* (English Heritage, London, 1988)

– *Mrs Howard: A Woman of Reason* (1688–1767) (English Heritage, London, 1988)

Burns, William E., *An Age of Wonders: Prodigies, Politics and Providence in England 1657–1727* (Manchester University Press, Manchester, 2002)

Campbell Orr, Clarissa, ed., *Queenship in Britain 1660–1837: Royal Patronage, Court Culture and Dynastic Politics* (Manchester University Press, Manchester, 2002)

– *Queenship in Europe 1660–1815: The Role of the Consort* (Cambridge University Press, Cambridge, 2004)

Chenevix Trench, Charles, *George II* (Allen Lane, London, 1973)

Christmas, William J., *The Lab'ring Muses: Work, Writing and the Social Order in English Plebeian Poetry, 1730–1830* (University of Delaware Press, Newark, 2001)

Coxe, William, *Memoirs of the Life and Administration of Sir Robert Walpole, Earl of Orford*, 4 vols (London, 1816)

Cumming, Valerie, *Royal Dress: The Image and the Reality 1580 to the Present Day* (Batsford, London, 1989)

Curteis, Captain Henry, *A Forgotten Prince of Wales* (Everett & Co., London)

Dickens, A.G., ed., *The Courts of Europe: Politics, Patronage and Royalty 1400–1800* (Outlet, 1985)

Dickson, Patricia, *Red John of the Battles* (Sidgwick & Jackson, London, 1973)

Dillon, Patrick, *The Much-Lamented Death of Madam Geneva* (Review, London, 2002)

Dobrée, Bonamy, *The Early Eighteenth Century 1700–1740: Swift, Defoe, and Pope* (Clarendon Press, Oxford, 1959)

Doderer-Winkler, Melanie, *Magnificent Entertainments: Temporary Architecture for Georgian Festivals* (Yale University Press, New Haven & London, 2013)

Dodson, Aidan, *The Royal Tombs of Great Britain* (Gerald Duckworth & Co., London, 2004)

Drayton Greenwood, Alice, *Lives of the Hanoverian Queens of England* (George Bell & Sons, London, 1909)

Duggan, J.N., *Sophia of Hanover: From Winter Princess to Heiress of Great Britain, 1630–1714* (Peter Owen, London, 2009)

Edwards, Averyl, *Frederick Louis Prince of Wales 1707–1751* (Staples Press, London, 1947)

Einberg, Elizabeth, et al., *Manners and Morals: Hogarth and British Painting 1700–1760* (Tate Gallery Publications, London, 1987)

Erskine-Hill, Howard, ed., *Alexander Pope: World and Word* (Proceedings of the British Academy, Oxford University Press, Oxford, 1998)

Fara, Patricia, *Pandora's Breeches: Women, Science and Power in the Enlightenment* (Pimlico, London, 2004)

Field, Ophelia, *The Favourite: Sarah, Duchess of Marlborough* (Hodder & Stoughton, London, 2002)

– *The Kit-Cat Club: Friends Who Imagined a Nation* (HarperPress, London, 2008)

Gattrell, Vic, *City of Laughter: Sex and Satire in Eighteenth-Century London* (Atlantic, London, 2006)

Glendinning, Victoria, *Jonathan Swift* (Hutchinson, London, 2008)

Gold, Claudia, *The King's Mistress: The True and Scandalous Story of the Woman who Stole the Heart of George I* (Quercus, London, 2012)

Grant, Douglas, *The Fortunate Slave* (Oxford University Press, Oxford, 1968)

Groom, Susanne, and Prosser, Lee, *Kew Palace: The Official Illustrated History* (Merrell, London, 2006)

Grundy, Isobel, *Lady Mary Wortley Montagu, Comet of the Enlightenment* (Oxford University Press, Oxford, 1999)

Halsband, Robert, *Lord Hervey: Eighteenth Century Courtier* (Clarendon Press, Oxford, 1973)

Hammond, Eugene, *Jonathan Swift: Our Dean* (University of Delaware Press, 2016)

– *Jonathan Swift: Irish Blow-in* (University of Delaware Press, 2016)

Hancox, Joy, *The Queen's Chameleon: The Life of John Byrom. A Study of Conflicting Loyalties* (Jonathan Cape, London, 1994)

Harris, Frances, *A Passion for Government: The Life of Sarah, Duchess of Marlborough* (Oxford University Press, Oxford, 1991)

Hatton, Ragnhild, *George I* (Thames & Hudson, London, 1978)

Haywood, Trevor, *Flesh and Bone: The Lives, Deaths and Funerals of British Monarchs* (El Corvo Publishing, 2007)

Hibbert, Christopher, *The Marlboroughs: John and Sarah Churchill 1650–1744* (Viking, London, 2001)

Hilton, Lisa, *Mistress Peachum's Pleasure: The Life of Lavinia, Duchess of Bolton* (Weidenfeld & Nicolson, London, 2005)

Impey, Edward, *Kensington Palace: The Official Illustrated History* (Merrell, London, 2003)

Jesse, John Heneage, *Memoirs of the Court of England During the Reign of the Stuarts*, 3 vols (Henry G. Bohn, London, 1857)

Jones, J.R., *Country and Court: England 1658–1714* (Edward Arnold, London, 1978)

Kroll, Maria, *Letters from Liselotte* (McCall Publishing, New York, 1971)

– *Sophie, Electress of Hanover: A Personal Portrait* (Victor Gollancz, London, 1973)

Laird, Mark, and Weisberg-Roberts, Alicia, *Mrs Delany and Her Circle* (Yale University Press, New Haven & London, 2009)

Lane Furdell, Elizabeth, *James Welwood: Physician to the Glorious Revolution* (Combined Publishing, Pennsylvania, 1998)

Livingstone, Natalie, *The Mistresses of Cliveden: Three Centuries of Scandal, Power and Intrigue in an English Stately Home* (Hutchinson, London, 2015)

Lock, F.P., *The Politics of Gulliver's Travels* (Clarendon Press, Oxford, 1980)

Look, Brandon C., ed., *Bloomsbury Companion to Leibniz* (Bloomsbury, London, 2014)

Mangan, J.J., *The King's Favour: Three Eighteenth-Century Monarchs and the Favourites who Ruled Them* (Sutton Publishing, Stroud, 1991)

Marlow, Joyce, *The Life and Times of George I* (Weidenfeld & Nicolson, London, 1973)

Marschner, Joanna, *Queen Caroline: Cultural Politics at the Early Eighteenth-Century Court* (Yale University Press, New Haven & London, 2014)

– 'Michael Rysbrack's Sculpture Series for Queen Caroline's Library at St James's Palace', in Dethloff, Diana, Murdoch, Tessa, Sloan, Kim, and Elam, Caroline, eds, *Burning Bright: Essays in Honour of David Bindman* (UCL Press, London, 2015)

Marschner, Joanna, and Bindman, David, *Enlightened Princesses: Caroline, Augusta, Charlotte and the Shaping of the Modern World* (Yale University Press, New Haven & London, 2017)

Massey, Victoria, *The First Lady Diana: Lady Diana Spencer, 1710–1735* (Allison & Busby, London, 1999)

Massie, Robert, *Peter the Great: His Life and World* (Head of Zeus, London, 2012)

Melville, Lewis, *Maids of Honour* (Hutchinson, London, 1927)

Molesworth, H.D., *The Princes* (Weidenfeld & Nicolson, London, 1969)

Monod, Paul Kleber, *Jacobitism and the English People, 1688–1788* (Cambridge University Press, Cambridge, 1993)

Moore, Lucy, *Amphibious Thing: The Life of Lord Hervey* (Viking, London, 2000)

Morgan-Guy, John, and Gibson, William, *Religion and Society in the Diocese of St Davids 1485–2011* (Routledge, 2015)

Mowl, Timothy, *William Kent: Architect, Designer, Opportunist* (Jonathan Cape, London, 2006)

Oates, Jonathan, *Sweet William or The Butcher? The Duke of Cumberland and the '45* (Pen & Sword, 2008)

Paulson, Ronald, *Hogarth: High Art and Low, 1732–50* (James Clarke & Co., 1992)

Plumb, J.H., *The First Four Georges* (Batsford, London, 1956)

– *Sir Robert Walpole*, 2 vols (Cresset Press, London, 1956 and 1960)

– *England in the Eighteenth Century* (Pelican, London, 1960)

Porter, Roy, *Enlightenment: Britain and the Creation of the Modern World* (Allen Lane, London, 2000)

Prescott, Sarah, *Eighteenth-Century Writing from Wales: Bards and Britons* (University of Wales Press, Cardiff, 2008)

Quennell, Peter, *Caroline of England* (Collins, London, 1939)

Riding, Jacqueline, *Jacobites: A New History of the '45 Rebellion* (Bloomsbury, London, 2016)

Robbins Landon, H.C., *Handel and his World* (Weidenfeld & Nicolson, London, 1984)

Rogers, Nicholas, *Crowds, Culture, and Politics in Georgian Britain* (Clarendon Press, Oxford, 1998)

Sackville-West, V., *Knole and the Sackvilles* (Ernest Benn, London, 1922)

Schaich, Michael, ed., *Monarchy and Religion: The Transformation of Royal Culture in Eighteenth-Century Europe* (Oxford University Press, Oxford, 2007)

Scharmann, Rudolf G., *Charlottenburg Palace: Royal Prussia in Berlin* (Prestel, Munich, 2007)

Scott, Jennifer, *The Royal Portrait: Image and Impact* (Royal Collection Publications, London, 2010)

Seward, Desmond, *Renishaw Hall: The Story of the Sitwells* (Elliott & Thompson, London, 2015)

Sharp, Tony, *Pleasures and Ambition: The Life, Loves and Wars of Augustus the Strong* (I.B. Tauris, London, 2001)

Shawe-Taylor, Desmond, *The Conversation Piece: Scenes of Fashionable Life* (Royal Collection Publications, London, 2009)

Shawe-Taylor, Desmond, and Burchard, Wolf, *The First Georgians: Art and Monarchy 1714–1760* (Royal Collections Trust, London, 2014)

Sheppard, Edgar, *Memorial of St James's Palace*, 2 vols (Longmans, Green & Co., London, 1894)

Sinclair-Stevenson, Christopher, *Blood Royal: The Illustrious House of Hanover* (Jonathan Cape, London, 1979)

Smith, Hannah, *Georgian Monarchy: Politics and Culture, 1714–1760* (Cambridge University Press, Cambridge, 2006)

Somerset, Anne, *Ladies in Waiting: From the Tudors to the Present Day* (Weidenfeld & Nicolson, London, 1984)

– *Queen Anne: The Politics of Passion* (HarperPress, London, 2012)

Souden, David, *Royal Palaces of London* (Merrell, London, 2008)

Strong, Roy, *The Artist and the Garden* (Yale University Press, New Haven & London, 2000)

– *Coronation: A History of Kingship and the British Monarchy* (HarperCollins, London, 2005)

Stuart, D.M., *Molly Lepell, Lady Hervey* (London, 1936)

Sundt Urstad, Tone, *Sir Robert Walpole's Poets: The Use of Literature as Pro-Government Propaganda, 1721–1742* (Associated University Presses, London & Newark, 1999)

Taylor, Stephen, 'Queen Caroline and the Church of England', in Taylor, Stephen, Connors, Richard, and Jones, Clyve, eds, *Hanoverian Britain and Empire: Essays in Memory of Philip Lawson* (The Boydell Press, Woodbridge, 1987)

Tennant, C.M., *Peter the Wild Boy* (James Clarke & Co., London, 1938)

Thompson, Andrew C., *George II* (Yale University Press, New Haven & London, 2011)

Thornton, Peter, *Authentic Decor: The Domestic Interior 1620–1920* (Weidenfeld & Nicolson paperback, London, 1993)

Tillyard, Stella, *A Royal Affair: George III and his Troublesome Siblings* (Chatto & Windus, London, 2006)

van der Kiste, John, *King George II and Queen Caroline* (Sutton Publishing, Stroud, 1997)

– *The Georgian Princesses* (Sutton Publishing, Stroud, 2000)

Vivian, Frances, *A Life of Frederick, Prince of Wales, 1707–1751: A Connoisseur of the Arts* (The Edwin Mellen Press, Lewiston, 2006)

Wakefield, Geoffrey, *The Princesses Royal* (Robert Hale, London, 1973)

Walker, Richard, *The Monarchy in Portrait Miniatures from Elizabeth I to Queen Victoria* (D.S. Lavender Antiques, London, 1993)

Waller, Maureen, *1700: Scenes from London Life* (Hodder & Stoughton, London, 2000)

Weber, Susan, *William Kent: Designing Georgian Britain* (Yale University Press, New Haven & London, 2013)

Wheatcroft, Andrew, *The Habsburgs: Embodying Empire* (Viking, London, 1995)

White, Christopher, *The Dutch Pictures in the Collection of Her Majesty the Queen* (Cambridge University Press, Cambridge, 1982)

White, Jerry, *London in the Eighteenth Century: A Great and Monstrous Thing* (Vintage, London, 2012)

Whitworth, Rex, *William Augustus Duke of Cumberland* (Leo Cooper, London, 1992)

Wilkins, W.H., *Caroline the Illustrious*, 2 vols (Longmans, Green & Co., London, 1901)

Williams, Glyn, and Ramsden, John, *Ruling Britannia: A Political History of Britain 1688–1988* (Longman, London, 1990)

Willis, Peter, *Charles Bridgeman and the English Landscape Garden* (Elysium Press revised edition, 2002)

Worsley, Lucy, *Courtiers: The Secret History of Kensington Palace* (Faber & Faber, London, 2010)

Worsley, Lucy, and Souden, David, *Hampton Court Palace: The Official Illustrated History* (Merrell, London, 2005)

Wright, Gillian, *Producing Women's Poetry, 1600–1730: Text and Paratext, Manuscript and Print* (Cambridge University Press, Cambridge, 2013)

Published Primary Sources

Anderson Winn, James, *A Window in the Bosom: The Letters of Alexander Pope* (Archon Books, Connecticut, 1977)

Burgess, C.F., ed., *The Letters of John Gay* (Oxford University Press, Oxford, 1966)

Clarke, Alured, *An Essay Towards the Character of Her late Majesty Caroline, Queen-Consort of Great Britain* (London, 1738)

Cowper, Hon C.S., ed., *Diary of Mary, Countess Cowper, Lady of the Bedchamber to the Princess of Wales, 1714–1720* (John Murray, London, 1864)

The Private Diary of William, First Earl Cowper (E. Williams, Eton, 1833)

Curll, Edmund, *The Rareties of Richmond: Being Exact Descriptions of the Royal Hermitage and Merlin's Cave, with his Life and Prophesies* (London, 1736)

Doebner, Richard, ed., *Briefe der Königin Sophie Charlotte von Preussen und der Kurfürstin Sophie von Hannover an hannoversche Diplomaten* (G. Hirzel, Leipzig, 1905)

The English Poems Collected from the Oxford and Cambridge Verses on the Death of His Royal Highness Frederick Prince of Wales (Hamilton Bruce, Edinburgh, 1751)

Halsband, Robert, ed., *The Complete Letters of Lady Mary Wortley Montagu*, 3 vols (Oxford University Press, Oxford, 1965)

A Character of her Highness the Princess ***, attempted by Richard Hollings, MD, in Private Correspondence of Sarah, Duchess of Marlborough, 2 vols (Henry Colburn, London, 1838)

Hughes, Helen, ed., *The Gentle Hertford: Her Life and Letters* (Macmillan, London, 1940)

Ilchester, Earl of, ed., *Lord Hervey and his Friends* (John Murray, London, 1950)

Jones, Mary, *Miscellanies in Prose and Verse* (Oxford, 1750)

Jones, Thomas, *The Rise and Progress of the Most Honourable and Loyal Society of Antient Britons* (W. Wilkins, London, 1717)

Kemble, John Mitchell, ed., *State papers and correspondence illustrative of the social and political state of Europe from the revolution to the accession of the House of Hanover* (J.W. Parker, London, 1857)

Llanover, Lady, ed., *The Autobiography and Correspondence of Mary Granville, Mrs Delany*, 3 vols (London, 1861)

Mahon, Lord, *The Letters of Philip Dormer Stanhope, Earl of Chesterfield*, 4 vols (Richard Bentley, London, 1845)

Matthews, William, ed., *The Diary of Dudley Ryder 1715–1716* (Methuen & Co., London, 1939)

Murray, General the Right Hon Sir George, ed., *Letters and Dispatches of John Churchill, First Duke of Marlborough, from 1702 to 1712* (John Murray, London, 1845), 5 vols

Newton, Sir Isaac, *The Chronology of Ancient Kingdoms Amended* (London, 1728)

Paget Toynbee, Mrs, ed., *The Letters of Horace Walpole, Fourth Earl of Orford*, 16 vols (Clarendon Press, Oxford, 1903–1905)

Pollnitz, Karl Ludwig von, *The Amorous Adventures of Augustus of Saxony* (George Allen & Unwin, London, 1929)

Quarrell, W.H., and Mare, Margaret, eds, *London in 1710: From the Travels of Zacharias Conrad von Uffenbach* (Faber & Faber, London, 1934)

Roberts, David, ed., *Lord Chesterfield's Letters* (Oxford University Press, Oxford, 2008)

Rosenthal, Norman, ed., *The Misfortunate Margravine: The Early Memoirs of Wilhelmina, Margravine of Bayreuth* (Macmillan, London, 1970)

Sedgwick, Romney, ed., *Some materials towards memoirs of the reign of George II*, by John, Lord Hervey, 3 vols (London, 1931)

Sloane, Hans, and Birch, Thomas, *An Account of Inoculation by Sir Hans Sloane, Bart. Given to Mr Ranby, to be Published, Anno 1736. Communicated by Thomas Birch, D.D., Secret RS, Philosophical Transactions (1683–1775)*, Vol. 49, published by the Royal Society

Stevenson, Gertrude Scott, ed., *The Letters of Madame: The Correspondence of Elisabeth Charlotte of Bavaria*, 2 vols (Arrowsmith, London)

Thomson, Mrs, ed., *Memoirs of Viscountess Sundon* (Henry Colburn, London, 1847)

Toland, John, *An Account of the courts of Prussia and Hanover: sent to a Minister of State in Holland* (London, 1705)

van Muyden, Madame, trans. and ed., *A Foreign View of England in the Reigns of George I and George II: The Letters of Monsieur César de Saussure to his Family* (John Murray, London, 1902)

Verses on the Coronation of their late Majesties King George II and Queen Caroline, October 11, MDCCXXVII (W. Bowyer, London, 1761)

Voltaire, François-Marie Arouet, *Letters on the English* (London, 1733)

Walpole, Horace, *Reminiscences, written in 1788, for the amusement of Miss Mary and Miss Agnes B***y* (London, 1818)

– *Memoirs of the Last Ten Years of the Reign of George II* (London, 1822)

Periodicals

Albertyn, Erik, The Hanover Orchestral Repertory, 1672–1714: Significant Source Discoveries, *Early Music*, Vol. 33, no 3 (2005)

Arkell, R.L., George I's Letters to His Daughter, *The English Historical Review*, Vol. 52, no 207 (July 1937)

Aspden, Suzanne, 'An Infinity of Factions': Opera in Eighteenth-Century Britain and the Undoing of Society, *Cambridge Opera Journal*, Vol. 9, no 1 (1997)

Batey, Mavis, The Pleasures of the Imagination: Joseph Addison's Influences on Early Landscape Gardens, *Garden History*, Vol. 33, no 2 (2005)

Bertoloni Meli, Domenico, Caroline, Leibniz and Clarke, *Journal of the History of Ideas*, Vol. 60, no 3 (1999)

Black, Jeremy, Additional Light on the Fall of Townshend, *The Yale University Gazette*, Vol. 63, no 3/4 (1989)

– Georges I & II: Limited Monarchs, *History Today*, Vol. 53, issue 2 (2003)

– 'George II and All That Stuff': On the Value of the Neglected, *Albion: A Quarterly Journal Concerned with British Studies*, Vol. 36, no 4 (2004)

Brett, Cécile, Revealing Thornhill's mythological scene at Hampton Court, *The British Art Journal*, Vol. 13, no 3 (winter 2012/13)

Brooks, William, Nostalgia in the letters of Elisabeth Charlotte, the second Madame, *Cahiers du 17e siècle*, 10 (2006)

Brown, Gregory, Leibniz's Endgame and the Ladies of the Courts, *Journal of the History of Ideas*, Vol. 65, no 1 (2004)

Burchard, Wolf, St James's Palace: George II's and Queen Caroline's Principal London Residence, *Court Historian*, 2011

Bushell, T.L., Princess Amelia and the Politics of Georgian England, *The Centennial Review*, Vol. 17, no 4 (1973)

Campbell Orr, Clarissa, Life and Culture at Court in England and Hanover. An Anglo-German Comparison, *Prince Albert Studies*, Vol. 32, Duncker & Humblot, Berlin, 2015

Carswell, John, George Bubb Dodington, 1691–1762, *History Today*, Vol. 4 (December 1954)

Cavendish, Richard, Death of Frederick, Prince of Wales, *History Today*, Vol. 51 (2001)

Cohen, Michael, Empowering the Sister: Female Rescue and Authorial Resistance in *The Heart of Midlothian*, *College Literature*, Vol. 20, no 2 (1993)

Colton, Judith, Merlin's Cave and Queen Caroline: Garden Art as Political Propaganda, *Eighteenth-Century Studies*, Vol. 10, no 1 (1976)

Connor, T.P., Colen Campbell as Architect to the Prince of Wales, *Architectural History*, Vol. 22 (1979)

Cornforth, John, Kensington Palace, London, *Country Life*, January 1995

Cowie, Leonard W., Leicester House, *History Today*, Vol. 23 (1973)

Dickson, Peter, The South Sea Bubble, 1720, *History Today*, Vol. 4 (1954)

Engel, Carl, The Literature of National Music, *The Musical Times and Singing Circular*, Vol. 19, no 427 (September 1878)

Erskine-Hill, Howard, Under Which Caesar? Pope in the Journal of Mrs Charles Caesar, 1724–1741, *The Review of English Studies*, Vol. 33, no 132 (1982)

Field, Ophelia, Queens and Their Gifts, *Times Literary Supplement*, 3 April 2015

Fritz, Paul S., The Trade in Death: The Royal Funerals in England, 1685–1830, *Eighteenth-Century Studies*, Vol. 15, no 3 (1982)

George, Dorothy, The Cartoon in the Eighteenth Century, *History Today*, Vol. 4 (September 1954)

Goldie, Mark, John Locke: Icon of Liberty, *History Today*, Vol. 54 (2004)

Grundy, Isobel, Lady Mary Wortley Montagu and the Theatrical Eclogue, *Lumen*, 17 (1998)

Halsband, Robert, A Prince, a Lord and a Maid of Honour, *History Today*

– Lady Mary Wortley Montagu: Her Place in the Eighteenth Century, *History Today*, Vol. 16 (February 1966)

Hanson, L.W., Townshend on the Death of Queen Caroline, *The English Historical Review*, Vol. 46, no 184 (1931)

Heckscher, Morrison, Eighteenth-century Rustic Furniture Designs, *Furniture History*, Vol. 11 (1975)

Hunter, David, Senesino Disobliges Caroline, Princess of Wales, and Princess Violante of Florence, *Early Music*, Vol. 30, no 2 (2002)

Jalobeanu, Dana, The Missing Part of a Definition: Clarke, 'Newton's Sect' and Another Way of Saving the Miracles in Seventeenth Century, *Arches* 7 (2004)

Jay, Emma, Queen Caroline's Library and its European Contents, *Book History*, Vol. 9 (2006)

Jones, Emrys D., Royal Ruptures: Caroline of Ansbach and the Politics of Illness in the 1730s, *Journal of Medical Ethics; Medical Humanities*, 37 (2011)

Kern, Jean B., The Fate of Thomson's Edward and Eleanora, *Modern Language Notes*, Vol. 52, no 7 (1937)

McCulloch, Derek, Royal Composers: The Composing Monarchs that Britain Nearly Had, *The Musical Times*, Vol. 122, no 1662 (August 1981)

Mahaffey, Kathleen, Pope's 'Artemisia' and 'Phryne' as Personal Satire, *The Review of English Studies*, Vol. 21, no 84 (1970)

Manfredi, Martina, Jacopo Amigoni: A Venetian Painter in Georgian London, *The Burlington Magazine*, Vol. 147, no 1231 (2005)

Marschner, Joanna, Baths and Bathing at the Early Georgian Court, *Furniture History Society*, Vol. 31 (1995)

Marsden, Jean I., Sex, Politics, and She-Tragedy: Reconfiguring Lady Jane Grey, *Studies in English Literature*, 1500–1900, Vol. 42, no 3 (2002)

Morris, Marilyn, Transgendered Perspectives on Premodern Sexualities, *Studies in English Literature, 1500–1900*, Vol. 46, no 3 (summer 2006)

Newman, A.N., The Political Patronage of Frederick Lewis,
    Prince of Wales, *The Historical Journal*, Vol. 1, no 1 (1958)
Nussbaum, Felicity A., 'Savage' Mothers: Narratives of
    Maternity in the Mid-Eighteenth Century, *Cultural Critique*,
    no 20 (1991–92)
Paffard, Michael, Stephen Duck: The Thresher Poet, *History
    Today*, Vol. 27 (1977)
Prescott, Sarah, The Cambrian Muse: Welsh Identity and
    Hanoverian Loyalty in the Poems of Jane Brereton (1685–
    1740), *Eighteenth-Century Studies*, Vol. 38, no 4 (2005)
Reese, T.R., A Red Indian Visit to 18th Century England,
    History Today, Vol. 4 (1954)
Roinila, Markku, Leibniz and the Amour Pur Controversy,
    Journal of Early Modern Studies, Vol. 2 (fall 2013)
Schonhorn, Manuel, The Audacious Contemporaneity of
    Pope's Epistle to Augustus, *Studies in English Literature*,
    1500–1900, Vol. 8, no 3 (1968)
Schwoerer, Lois G., Images of Queen Mary II, 1689–95,
    Renaissance Quarterly, Vol. 42, no 4 (1989)
Shipley, John B., A Note on the Authorship of The Whale, *The
    Review of English Studies*, Vol. 18, no 70 (1967)
Smith, Hannah, The Court in England, 1714–1760: A Declining
    Political Institution?, *History*, Vol. 90, no 1 (January 2005)
Strickland, Lloyd, The Philosophy of Sophie, Electress of
    Hanover, *Hypatia*, Vol. 24, no 2 (spring 2009)
Sykes, Norman, Queen Caroline and the Church, *New Series*,
    Vol. 11, no 44 (1927)
Taylor, Stephen, and Smith, Hannah, Hephaestion and
    Alexander: Lord Hervey, Frederick, Prince of Wales, and the
    Royal Favourite in England in the 1730s, *The English
    Historical Review*, Vol. 124, no 507 (2009)
Tite, Catherine, 'The Choice of Paris': Representing Frederick,
    Prince of Wales: a brief reconsideration, *The British Art
    Journal*, Vol. 9, no 2 (2008)

Turner, Edward Raymond, The Lords Justices of England, *The English Historical Review*, Vol. 29, no 115 (1914)

Weichel, Eric, 'Fixed by so much better a fire': Wigs and Masculinity in Early 18th-Century British Miniatures, *Shift, Queen's Journal of Visual & Material Culture*, issue 1 (2008)

Willoughby, Edwin Elliott, The Chronology of the Poems of Thomas Wharton, the Elder, *The Journal of English and Germanic Philology*, Vol. 30, no 1 (1931)

Woodward, John, Amigoni as Portrait Painter in England, *The Burlington Magazine*, Vol. 99, no 646 (1957)

Yorke-Long, Alan, George II and Handel, *History Today*, 10 October 1951

Zedler, Beatrice H, The Three Princesses, *Hypatia*, Vol. 4, no 1 (spring 1989)

Index